THE MODERN STUDENT'S LIBRARY

BACON
Selections

BACON
SELECTIONS

EDITED BY

MATTHEW THOMPSON McCLURE

PROFESSOR OF PHILOSOPHY, UNIVERSITY OF ILLINOIS

CHARLES SCRIBNER'S SONS

NEW YORK CHICAGO BOSTON

Printed in the United States of America

INTRODUCTION

I

"Francis Bacon, the glory of his age and nation, the adorner and ornament of learning, was born in York House, or York Place, in the Strand, on the two and twentieth day of January, in the year of our Lord 1560 (old style). His father was that famous counsellor to Queen Elizabeth, the second prop of the kingdom in his time, Sir Nicholas Bacon, knight, lordkeeper of the great seal of England; a lord of known prudence, sufficiency, moderation, and integrity. His mother Anne, one of the daughters of Sir Anthony Cook; unto whom the erudition of King Edward the Sixth had been committed, a choice lady, and eminent for piety, virtue, and learning, being exquisitely skilled, for a woman, in the Greek and Latin tongues. These being the parents, you may easily imagine what the issue was like to be; having had whatsoever nature and breeding could put into him." [1]

Very little is known of Bacon's early life. At the age of thirteen he was sent to Trinity College, Cambridge. His three years at the University ended in disappointment. He was oppressed with the barrenness of the current intellectual atmosphere. Just such a feeling of disappointment with university education was a little later to be expressed by Descartes, whose in-

[1] Dr. Rawley's Life of Bacon, published 1657; reprinted by Spedding, Ellis, and Heath, *Bacon's Works*, vol. I; this reference, vol. I, p. 3.

tellectual reactions to the learning of his time and whose efforts toward intellectual reconstruction have many points of similarity with Bacon's program for building the sciences anew. The tendency of thought to be revolutionary was characteristic of the founders of modern philosophy. With Descartes, however, judgment was long suspended, and his thought took constructive form only after a prolonged period of doubt. Bacon on the other hand never floundered. The central purpose of his life, about which he was never in doubt, and from which he never departed, was clearly formed before he left the University. "While he was commorant in the university, about sixteen years of age (as his lordship hath been pleased to impart to myself), he first fell into the dislike of the philosophy of Aristotle; not for the worthlessness of the author, to whom he would ever ascribe all high attributes, but for the unfruitfulness of the way; being a philosophy (as his lordship used to say) only strong for disputations and contentions, but barren of the production of works for the benefit of the life of man; in which mind he continued to his dying day."[1] Coincident with the realization of the futility and barrenness of the Aristotelian philosophy, came the determination to seek a new method of scientific investigation. This resolution, formed while a mere boy in college, is regarded by Spedding "as the most important event of his life." "From that moment he had a vocation which employed and stimulated all the energies of his mind, gave a value to every vacant interval of time, an interest and significance to every random thought and casual accession of knowledge; an object to live for as wide as humanity, as immortal as the human race; an idea to live in vast and lofty enough to fill the soul forever with religious and

[1] Dr. Rawley's Life of Bacon, vol. I, p. 4.

heroic aspirations. From that moment, though still subject to interruptions, disappointments, errors and regrets, he would never be without either work or hope or consolation."[1]

Spedding's judgment of the singleness of purpose which animated Bacon is corroborated by the following instructive passage taken from *De Interpretatione Naturae Prooemium,* written probably about 1603.

"Whereas, I believed myself born for the service of mankind, and reckoned the care of the common weal to be among those duties that are of public right, open to all alike, even as the waters and the air, I therefore asked myself what could most advantage mankind, and for the performance of what tasks I seemed to be shaped by nature. But when I searched, I found no work so meritorious as the discovery and development of the arts and inventions that tend to civilize the life of man. . . . Above all, if any man could succeed—not merely in bringing to light some one particular invention, however useful—but in kindling in nature a luminary which would, at its first rising, shed some light on the present limits and borders of human discoveries, and which afterwards, as it rose still higher, would reveal and bring into clear view every nook and cranny of darkness, it seemed to me that such a discoverer would deserve to be called the true Extender of the Kingdom of Man over the universe, the Champion of human liberty, and the Exterminator of the necessities that now keep men in bondage. Moreover, I found in my own nature a special adaptation for the contemplation of truth. For I had a mind at once versatile enough for that most important object—I mean the recognition of similitudes—and at the same time sufficiently steady

[1] James Spedding, *The Letters and the Life of Francis Bacon,* vol. I, p. 4.

and concentrated for the observation of subtle shades of difference. I possessed a passion for research, a power of suspending judgment with patience, of meditation with pleasure, of assenting with caution, of correcting false impressions with readiness, and of arranging my thoughts with scrupulous pains. I had no hankering after novelty, no blind admiration for antiquity. Imposture in every shape I utterly detested. For all these reasons I considered that my nature and disposition had, as it were, a kind of kinship and connection with truth.

"But my birth, my rearing, and education, had all pointed, not toward philosophy, but toward politics: I had been, as it were, imbued in politics from childhood. And as is not unfrequently the case with young men, I was sometimes shaken in my mind by opinions. I also thought that my duty towards my country had special claims upon me, such as could not be urged by other duties of life. Lastly, I conceived the hope that, if I held some honourable office in the state, I might secure helps and supports to aid my labours, with a view to the accomplishment of my desired task. With these motives I applied myself to politics."[1]

Bacon's entrance to politics, therefore, was undertaken in order to provide the necessary means for the realization of his life purpose. The means came near destroying the end. It is doubtful whether, but for his public disgrace, he would ever have retired from political life in order to devote himself to philosophy. His political career began under Queen Elizabeth and continued through the reign of King James the first. His fortunes are thus described by Dr. Rawley:

"His birth and other capacities qualified him above

[1] Quoted by W. Durant, *The Story of Philosophy*, from Abbott, *Francis Bacon*, London, 1885, p. 37.

others of his profession to have ordinary success at court, and to come frequently into the queen's eye, who would often grace him with private and free communication, not only about matters of his profession or business in law, but also about the arduous affairs of estate; from whom she received from time to time great satisfaction. Nevertheless, though she cheered him much with the bounty of her countenance, yet she never cheered him with the bounty of her hand; having never conferred upon him any ordinary place or means of honour or profit, save only one dry reversion of the Register's Office in the Star Chamber, worth about 1600 *l. per annum,* for which he waited in expectation either fully or near twenty years; . . . which might be imputed, not so much to Her Majesty's averseness and disaffection towards him, as to the arts and policy of a great statesman then, who laboured by all industrious and secret means to suppress and keep him down; lest, if he had risen, he might have obscured his glory.

"But though he stood long at a stay in the days of his mistress, Queen Elizabeth, yet after the change, and coming in of his new master King James, he made a great progress; by whom he was much comforted in places of trust, honour, and revenue. I have seen a letter of his lordship's to King James, wherein he makes acknowledgment, *That he was that master to him, that had raised and advanced him nine times; thrice in dignity, and six times in office.* His offices (as I conceive) were Counsel Learned Extraordinary to His Majesty, as he had been to Queen Elizabeth; King's Solicitor-General; His Majesty's Attorney-General; Counsellor of Estate, being yet but Attorney; Lord-Keeper of the Great Seal of England; lastly, Lord Chancellor; which two last places, though they be the same in authority and power, yet they differ in patent, height, and favour of the prince; since whose time none of his successors, until this present honourable lord, did ever bear the title of Lord Chancellor. His dignities were first Knight, then Baron of Verulam; lastly, Viscount St. Alban; besides other good gifts and bounties of the hand which His Majesty gave him, both out of the Broad Seal and out of the Alienation Office, to the value in both of eighteen hundred pounds per annum; which, with his manor of Corhambury, and other lands and possessions near thereunto adjoining, amounting to a third part more, he retained to his dying day."[1]

The following letter, addressed to his powerful uncle, Lord Burghley, expresses the duality of Bacon's political and philosophical interests:

"I ever bear in mind (in some middle place that I could discharge) to serve Her Majesty, not as a man born under Sol, that loveth honour; not under Jupiter, that loveth business (for the contemplative planet carrieth me away wholly); but as a man born under an excellent Sovereign, that deserveth the dedication of all men's abilities. . . . Again, the meanness of my estate doth somewhat move me; for though I cannot accuse myself that I am either prodigal or slothful, yet my health is not to spend, nor my course to get. Lastly, I confess that I have as vast contemplative ends, as I have moderate civil ends; for I have taken all knowledge to be my province; and if I could purge it of two sorts of rovers, whereof the one with frivolous disputations, confutations, and verbosities, the other with blind experiments and auricular traditions and impostures, hath committed so many spoils, I hope I should bring in industrious observations, grounded conclusions, and profit-

[1] Dr. Rawley's Life of Bacon. See Spedding, Ellis, and Heath, *Bacon's Works*, vol. I, pp. 6–8.

able inventions and discoveries; the best state of that province. This, whether it be curiosity, or vain glory, or nature, or (if one take it favourably) *philanthropia*, is so fixed in my mind as it cannot be removed."[1]

Into the details of Bacon's political career it is unnecessary to go. His fall was as sudden as his rise had been gradual. In 1621, while Lord Chancellor, he was brought to trial on the charge of having accepted bribes. He admitted his guilt, was condemned, divested of all political honours, made the subject of an enormous fine, and assigned to life imprisonment. The fine was never paid and the life sentence was never executed. The last five years of his life were spent in retirement and obscurity. These years were devoted to the composition of philosophical and literary works, the chief of which were the *De Augmentis Scientiarum* and a *History of Henry VII*. He regretted that he had not earlier devoted his life to philosophy. His death occurred the ninth of April, 1626. While driving from Highgate to London he conceived the idea that dead flesh might be preserved longer if kept very cold. With Bacon to conceive was to execute. He alighted from his carriage, procured a chicken from a nearby house, killed it, and packed it in snow. The weather was very cold, and due to the exposure to which he was subjected, he caught a severe cold which swiftly led to his death. Thus by a peculiar irony of fate the founder of the experimental method was hurried to his death by conducting an experiment, the only one on record which he himself ever performed.

Volumes have been written on the moral character of Bacon. That he was a profound admirer of Machiavelli is evident from his writings, considering the many times he is quoted with approval. That Machiavellian

[1] J. Spedding, *Life and Letters*, vol. I, pp. 108–109.

principles of statecraft were in operation in the court life of Elizabethan England is known to all historians of the period. That Bacon himself, in that part of *The Advancement of Learning* dealing with the science of rising in life, expressed many precepts relating to the exercise of intelligence in the interest of material advancement is a matter of record. It is a faint excuse to say that he was no worse than his times. His public disgrace, though brought about in part by his enemies, was the culmination of his private morals. The truth of the matter is probably best expressed in his own words: "I was the justest judge that was in England these fifty years, but it was the justest judgment that was in Parliament these two hundred years."

II

The philosophy of Bacon is at once a reaction, a reformation, and a prophecy. As a reaction it is set in contrast to much that we have come to call ancient and medieval. As a reformation and a prophecy, it is the embodiment and prevision of what we now term modern. The spirit that breathes through the writings of Bacon is the spirit of modernity. Foremost among the ideas that enter into the definition of modern is the idea of progress. And it is just this conception that is of central interest in the intellectual outlook of Bacon. It is with the "advancement of learning" that he is chiefly concerned. Intellectual history had come to a standstill. Philosophy was coming down in the form of "master and scholar," but not in the form of "inventor and improver." Bacon points to the mechanical arts which daily were showing advance and improvement, while the intellectual sciences were "like statutes, celebrated and adorned, but never advanced."

Let us briefly characterize the intellectual situation at the beginning and at the end of the middle ages, for only in this way can we understand the significance of Bacon's reaction. History represents a series of reactions to concrete situations. On the one side, in the form of stimulus, we have the "classical heritage" and the theology of the Church Fathers. On the other, as agents, we have the younger races of the north, different from the ancients in race, in character, and in training. In a situation like this, what is man's intellectual task? It is not to create nor to invent; it is to learn and to understand. Add to this the further consideration that the past came under the constraint of authority; the antique culture was acquired with a characteristic deference for antiquity, and Christianity was accepted under the notion that it was necessary for salvation. This deference of a younger race for the traditions of an older race was an inevitable part of the situation. It was the controlling factor in setting the intellectual task of the middle ages. Man's task was not to create nor to alter, enough for him that he understand and admire. This felt humility in the presence of a superior past tended toward the subordination of free intellectual inquiry.

Let us now shift our point of view to the end of the middle ages. After centuries of learning man had accomplished his task. He had learned his lesson. Surely there had been progress and advance. But how about *further* progress? The situation was such that with the given subject-matter no further progress was possible. With the given material all had been done that could be done. Its subject-matter had been worked through with a thoroughness that left nothing more to be accomplished. The given stock of premises had been squeezed dry. Unproductiveness had become congenital.

In his reaction to this situation Bacon does not condemn the past. His attitude is not one of fault finding. His philosophy is not a renovation, but an innovation. When advance is no longer possible in a given direction the obvious thing to do is to change the direction. "Let there be," he says, "one method of cultivating the sciences, and another for discovering them." Cultivation is all right, but it is not discovery, and progress is to be sought in discovery. There is no need to refute the past. The need is to widen man's intellectual outlook, to extend knowledge beyond its already too narrow limits. It is with the extension of knowledge into new fields that Bacon is concerned. Advance involves a new point of departure, a new interest, a new subject-matter, and a new method. It is important that one believe in the possibility of progress, for the absence of such a belief commits one either to an arrogant dogmatism, a complacent satisfaction with things as they are, or to a hopeless skepticism, the dangerous doubt that things can be improved. On this subject Bacon writes: "But by far the greatest obstacle to the progress of science and to the undertaking of new tasks and provinces therein, is found in this—that men despair and think things impossible."[1] It is this firm faith in the possibility of progress that forms the basis of Bacon's scientific optimism.

Closely connected with the idea of progress are the cognate ideas of control, utility, and responsibility. It is for emphasis on these ideas that Bacon is held up as the exponent of the modern spirit. They form the basis of his scientific optimism, and it is for this

[1] *Novum Organum*, Bk. I, Aph. XCII. Ed. by Spedding, Ellis and Heath, London, 1857, vol. IV, p. 90. It is to this edition that all future references will be made.

optimism that his writing will continue to be of lasting value.[1]

1. *The Advancement of Learning* [2]

The Advancement of Learning is an essay on the intellectual life of England at the opening of the seventeenth century. It consists of two books. Book One contains a penetrating analysis of the intellectual temper of the age and an eloquent eulogy of the dignity and value of learning. Book Two contains a comprehensive and critical survey of the entire body of extant knowledge, noting wherein learning is defective and deficient, and outlining a program for its improvement and propagation. The analysis and survey are undertaken in order to pave the way for a complete reorganization of all branches of scientific knowledge.

It was necessary at the outset to deliver learning from the disgraces into which it had fallen due to the zeal of the theologians, the arrogancy of the politicians, and the shortcomings of the learned themselves. Theologians had discouraged free intellectual inquiry on the ground that too much learning was subversive of religion. Bacon's reply to this charge is found in the classic statement "that a little or superficial knowledge of philosophy may incline the mind to atheism, but a further proceeding therein brings the mind back again to religion." [3] According to the politicians, learning

[1] The foregoing paragraphs have been taken from the writer's essay on *Francis Bacon and the Modern Spirit*, Journal of Philosophy, vol. XIV, no. 19: September 13, 1917.

[2] *The Advancement of Learning*, published in 1605, is selected for re-publication rather than the *De Augmentis Scientiarum* chiefly because it is written in Bacon's own English, whereas the *De Augmentis*, though a later and more elaborate composition, was written in Latin and is available for English readers only in translation.

[3] *Advancement of Learning*, vol. III, p. 267.

unfits a man for participation in practical affairs and brings about a separation between the contemplative and the active life. This charge is met by an appeal to the verdict of history. "The evidence of time doth clear this assertion, considering that the most barbarous, rude, and unlearned times have been the most subject to tumults, seditions, and changes."[1] By far the greatest discredit has been brought upon learning by the learned themselves, partly from their poverty, their obscurity, and their pedantry, partly from the 'queerness' of their manners, but mostly from the nature of their studies. Touching the last point Bacon condemns the learning of his time as too fantastic, as seen in the visions of astrology and magic, as too contentious, as seen in the idle disputations of the scholastics, and as too delicate, as seen in the literary effects of humanism.

The foregoing constitute the major criticism, or as Bacon terms them, the "distempers" of learning. There follows a series of minor criticisms termed by him the "peccant humours." These "humours," eleven in all, constitute a vivid description of the intellectual habits and dispositions of the age. The first and last of the criticisms are of special interest. "We are the ancients" is Bacon's reply to those who are surcharged with reverential deference for antiquity. "And to speak truly, *Antiquitas saeculi juventus mundi*. These times are the ancient times, when the world is ancient, and not those which we account ancient *ordine retrogrado*, by a computation backward from ourselves."[2] The last criticism touches what Bacon conceives to be the true end of knowledge: "But the greatest error of all the rest is the mistaking or misplacing of the last or furthest end of knowledge. For men have entered into

[1] *Advancement of Learning*, vol. III, p. 273.

[2] *Ibid.*, vol. III, p. 291.

a desire of learning and knowledge, sometimes upon a natural curiosity and inquisitive appetite; sometimes to entertain their minds with variety and delight; sometimes for ornament and reputation; and sometimes to enable them to victory of wit and contradiction; and most times for lucre and profession; and seldom sincerely to give a true account of their reason, to the benefit and use of men; . . ."[1]

In as much as the fixing of the legitimate goal or true end of knowledge is one of the outstanding features of the Baconian philosophy, I append other quotations which bear on the subject: "Lastly, I would address one general admonition to all; that they consider what are the true ends of knowledge, and that they seek it not either for pleasure of the mind, or for contention, or for superiority to others, or for profit, or fame, or power, or any of these inferior things; but for the benefit and use of life; and that they perfect and govern it in charity."[2] "Now the true and lawful goal of the sciences is none other than this: that human life be endowed with new discoveries and powers."[3] "The end of our foundation is the knowledge of causes, and the secret motions of things; and the enlarging of the bounds of Human Empire, to the effecting of all things possible."[4] It is not to be thought, however, that Bacon sets up a purely utilitarian end of knowledge. In the above quotation it is stated that knowledge is to be perfected and governed in the spirit of charity. And in the second place, Bacon thought that ultimately truth and utility were the same. "Now these two directions, the one active, the other contemplative, are one and the

[1] *Advancement of Learning*, vol. III, p. 294.
[2] Preface to *The Great Instauration*, vol. IV, pp. 20–21.
[3] *Novum Organum*, Bk. I, Aph. LXXXI, vol. IV, p. 79.
[4] *The New Atlantis*, vol. III, p. 156.

same things; and what in operation is most useful, that in knowledge is most true."[1]

In the second part of Book One there is adduced in the praise of learning both divine testimonies and human proofs. Power and wisdom are the attributes of God as exemplified in the history of creation. Love, wisdom, and power characterize the order of the spirits as set forth in the celestial hierarchy of Pseudo Dionysius. The primacy of light (wisdom) is emphasized in the formation of the sensible world. The contemplative function of intelligence is characteristic of man both before and after the fall. The dignity of learning is further testified to by the citation of examples from the Scriptures, from the Church Fathers, from the Reformation, and from the rise of the Jesuit Order, all bearing witness to the value of learning for faith and religion.

First among the human proofs to be noted is the superiority of scientific invention over practical statesmanship among the ancients. On this point Bacon is certainly right. Thales, for example, was accounted one of the Seven Wise Men on account of his scientific knowledge rather than for his political competence. The influence of learning on political and military virtue is then recounted and the book closes with a veritable prose poem in praise of wisdom in relation to private virtue.

Book Two contains the statement and the elaboration of Bacon's famous classification of the sciences. The value of this classification "was attested in the middle of the eighteenth century, when the great French *Encyclopaedia* was projected by Diderot and D'Alembert. The former, its chief editor and contributor, wrote in the Prospectus: 'If we come out successful from this vast

[1] *Novum Organum*, Bk. II, Aph. IV, vol. IV, p. 122.

undertaking, we shall owe it mainly to Chancellor Bacon, who sketched the plan of a universal dictionary of sciences and arts at a time when there were not, so to speak, either arts or sciences. This extraordinary genius, when it was impossible to write a history of what men knew, wrote one of what they had to learn.'"[1] The classification is based on the faculties of the human mind. "The parts of human learning have reference to the three parts of Man's Understanding, which is the seat of learning: History to his Memory, Poesy to his Imagination, and Philosophy to his Reason."[2] The subdivisions of these major headings will appear as we proceed.

Natural history is the first subdivision of the general subject of history. This study has a most important place in Bacon's general scheme. It is to be remembered that the survey of the intellectual globe is not undertaken as an end in itself, but as a preliminary exploration with a view to the ultimate regeneration of the sciences. The ultimate goal of natural science, as we shall see, is the discovery of "forms," or as we should probably say of "causes." Now it is most important that scientific knowledge should rest on an inductive inquiry into natural phenomena, and not on an *a priori* analysis. "For I am building in the human understanding a true model of the world, such as it is in fact, not such as a man's own reason would have it to be; a thing which cannot be done without a very diligent dissection and anatomy of the world. But I say that those foolish and apish images of worlds which the fancies of men have created in philosophical systems, must be utterly scattered to the winds."[3] All scientific knowledge, there-

[1] W. Libby, *History of Science*, p. 58.
[2] *Advancement of Learning*, vol. III, p. 329.
[3] *Novum Organum*, Bk. I, Aph. CXXIV, vol. IV, p. 110.

fore, must rest on the facts of observation. It is the business of Natural History to gather these facts, and thus to afford a factual point of departure for the more advanced forms of scientific knowledge. "But if my judgment be of any weight, the use of History Mechanical (a branch of natural history) is of all others the most radical and fundamental towards natural philosophy; such natural philosophy as shall not vanish in the fume of subtile, sublime, or delectable speculation, but such as shall be operative to the endowment and benefit of man's life."[1]

In Bacon's treatment of Civil History there is a division of time into ancient, middle, and modern. So far as I know this is the first use of a three-fold division of history. The division, however, does not correspond to our ancient, medieval, and modern, but to pre-classical, classical, and post classical. Bacon's view that it is the function of Poetry to re-create in the imagination a world more in accordance with the desires and pleasures of men than the one discovered and described by science seems an unduly narrow conception of the nature of Poetry. It would certainly exclude such a poem as Lucretius' *De Rerum Natura*.

Philosophia Prima is the first subject treated under the general division of Philosophy. It is a general or summary inquiry whose function is to treat of the universal axioms and categories common to all the special sciences. It is a mistake, according to Bacon, to limit such an inquiry to mere logic, because "the truth of being and the truth of knowing are one." That is to say, the distinctions and forms of thought are as much objects of reality as they are objects of thought. First Philosophy, therefore, is "*a receptacle for all such profitable observations and axioms as fall not within the compass*

[1] *Advancement of Learning*, vol. III, pp. 332–333.

of any of the special parts of philosophy or science, but are more common and of a higher stage."[1] Moreover, First Philosophy is the parent from which the other branches of philosophy are derived. These branches are Divine Philosophy, Natural Philosophy comprising Physics and Metaphysics, and Human Philosophy.

In this classification it will be seen that *Philosophia Prima,* Divine Philosophy, or Natural Theology (as opposed to Divinity, or Revealed Theology), and Metaphysics are treated as separate subjects of inquiry. Hitherto these three types of inquiry had not been separated into distinct fields. Thus writes Bacon: "For I find a certain rhapsody of Natural Theology, and of divers parts of Logic; and of that part of Natural Philosophy which concerneth the Principles, and of that other part of Natural Philosophy which concerneth the Soul or Spirit; all these strangely commixed and confused. . . ."[2] The confusion of which Bacon speaks goes eventually back to Aristotle. For a complete understanding of Bacon's classification and of the distinctions which he makes it is necessary to understand Aristotle's treatment of the subject. Aristotle's classification of the sciences is given in book Epsilon of the *Metaphysics.* Types of inquiry are divided into theoretical, practical, and productive, dealing respectively with science (in the sense of disinterested and universal knowledge), conduct (comprising politics and ethics), and art (comprising rhetoric and poetics). The theoretical sciences are physics, mathematics, and metaphysics, or as Aristotle terms it theology, or first philosophy. These three theoretical sciences are distinguished as follows: "For physics deals with things which are inseparable from matter but not immovable, and some parts of mathe-

[1] *Advancement of Learning,* vol. III, p. 347.
[2] *Ibid.,* vol. III, p. 347.

matics deal with things which are immovable, but probably not separable, but embodied in matter; while the first science deals with things which are both separable and immovable."[1]

Aristotle is not consistent in his views about metaphysics, the subject-matter of which is stated differently in different places. There seem to be three different descriptions of the subject-matter of metaphysics. (1) In books Alpha and Gamma of the *Metaphysics,* metaphysics is said to deal with the causes and first principles of existence as a whole. (2) In other places, notably in books Epsilon and Lambda, metaphysics is said to deal with only a part of existence, namely, that part which is highest and which is characterized as "capable of existing apart" and as "immovable." Theology is the name which Aristotle gives to this inquiry. (3) In book Beta, Aristotle says that it belongs to metaphysics to study the axioms and starting points of demonstration which are universal and common to all the sciences. Thus it is seen that metaphysics as conceived by Aristotle comprises three distinct types of inquiry. Considering the influence of Aristotle upon subsequent thought it is natural that this confusion should have persisted.

Bacon's separation of *Philosophia Prima,* Natural Theology, and Metaphysics into distinct sciences is an attempt to avoid the traditional confusion. *Philosophia Prima* corresponds more or less roughly to Aristotelian metaphysics in the third sense. Natural Theology corresponds to Aristotelian metaphysics in the second sense. Metaphysics corresponds *in certain respects* to Aristotelian metaphysics in the first sense. Bacon's distinction between physics and metaphysics is in part like that made by Aristotle and in part quite unlike it.

[1] *Metaphysics,* 1026^a, 14.

His view is expressed as follows: "It is therefore now a question, what is left remaining for Metaphysics; wherein I may without prejudice preserve thus much of the conceit of antiquity, that Physics should contemplate that which is inherent in matter and therefore transitory, and Metaphysics that which is abstracted and fixed. And again that Physics should handle that which supposeth in nature only a being and moving, and Metaphysics should handle that which supposeth further in nature a reason, understanding, and platform."[1] So far Bacon and Aristotle are in substantial agreement, as will be seen by re-reading the above quotation setting forth the Aristotelian distinction between physics and metaphysics. But Bacon departs widely from Aristotle in assigning to physics the investigation of material and efficient causes,[2] and to metaphysics the investigation of formal and final causes. In Aristotle all the four causes appear in the treatment both of physics and metaphysics.

So much for Bacon's classification in its relation to antiquity. Let us now return to the Baconian treatment of Natural Science and seek to determine the object and character of scientific knowledge in the spheres of physics and metaphysics. Both departments of natural science have to do with the discovery and investigation of causes. Bacon's philosophy of nature will be considered more fully in the introduction to the *Novum Organum*. We shall deal with it here merely

[1] *Advancement of Learning*, vol. III, pp. 353–354.

[2] Science, according to Aristotle, is knowledge of things through their 'causes.' 'Causes,' therefore, are the ultimate principles of scientific explanation. Aristotle thought that there were four such first principles, or explanatory concepts, which were termed by him the *formal* cause, the *material* cause, the *efficient* cause, and the *final* cause. The formal cause gives the essence, the material cause the substance, the efficient cause the source of change or movement, the final cause the end or purpose.

in outline. Natural knowledge passes through three stages. The first is Natural History, the purpose of which is to collect data. Knowledge at this stage is purely descriptive. In physics and metaphysics knowledge passes from description to explanation. Explanation is in terms of causes. Physics which treats of material and efficient causes is mid way between Natural History and Metaphysics, which treats of formal and final causes. The distinction is relative to degrees of explanation. Formal causes are more general, more constant, and higher in the scale of explanatory value than efficient causes which are variable and proximate. To quote Bacon: "For knowledges are as pyramids, whereof history is the basis; so of Natural Philosophy the basis is Natural History; the stage next the basis of Physics; the stage next the vertical point is Metaphysics. As for the vertical point, . . . the Summary Law of Nature, we know not whether man's inquiry can attain unto it."[1]

Two further points should be noted with respect to Bacon's treatment of metaphysics. In the first place, metaphysics is a branch of natural science. There is no "transcendental moonshine" about it. Knowledge of forms is the ultimate aim of metaphysical inquiry. This knowledge is not arrived at deductively, it is no construction of rational speculation. It is, on the contrary, the highest achievement of inductive discovery. The great systems of metaphysics which belong to the classical period of modern philosophy have all been logical constructions based on *a priori* deductions. A closer adherence to the Baconian conception would have saved philosophy from transcendentalism. For after all it is the business of the scientist to tell us what reality is. In the second place Bacon does not say that

[1] *Advancement of Learning,* vol. III, p. 356.

metaphysics is a knowledge of ultimate reality. It is a knowledge of "forms" and forms are many. Whether there is a higher type of synthetic reality unifying the forms is an inquiry at present lying beyond the range of scientific investigation.

Bacon makes a radical departure from the Aristotelian classification in his treatment of mathematics. For Aristotle mathematics was a branch of theoretical knowledge coordinate with physics and metaphysics. In the Baconian classification it is treated as a branch of metaphysics. The significance of mathematics in subsequent scientific method has shown Bacon to be a false prophet. His trust in the inductive method and his mistrust of rationalistic deduction led him to this undervaluation. Furthermore no excuse can be given for his failure to acquaint himself with the advances that were being made during his own time in the development of mathematics. On the other hand the over emphasis on the mathematical method by Descartes, Spinoza, and Leibniz led to metaphysical extravagances that were not corrected until Hume made it clear that we can have no *a priori* knowledge of matters of fact.

Natural science, dealing with the discovery of causes, is one branch of Natural philosophy; natural prudence, dealing with the production of effects is the other. We have here Bacon's most characteristic departure from the Greeks. Indeed, it is here, if anywhere, that his claim to scientific eminence rests. His doctrine of Natural Prudence is no less than a scientific revolution. For Aristotle prudence was an affair of art, never of nature. Art deals with that which is modifiable, nature with that which "can not be otherwise." Nature can only be contemplated, her forms classified, and her divisions reported. No knowledge of forms, however perfected, could effect a change in a natural body. Contemplative knowledge was always qualitatively superior to practical knowledge. Contemplation, therefore, was the end or final goal of all science. There scientific knowledge came to an end. The idea of using this knowledge with a view to changing nature was entirely foreign. Bacon's scientific revolution is summarized in the statement that "knowledge is power." Man's highest intellectual endeavor consists in the application of theoretical knowledge to the control and guidance of Nature. It was the aim of the Greeks to adjust man to nature; it is the aim of Bacon to adjust nature to man. For the Greeks nature was unalterable, her frame was solid and unyielding, her forms were fixed and unchanging. For Bacon nature is plastic and modifiable. The introduction of the idea of change, and with it the creation of the conditions of progress, is the thing that is new in the Baconian philosophy of science. "For whosoever knoweth any *form,* knoweth the utmost possibility of *superinducing that nature upon any variety of matter,* and so is less restrained in operation."[1] Natural Prudence, therefore, is the art of controlling nature and has as its aim the restoration of man to a position of command and sovereignty.

Human Philosophy has two main subdivisions: psychology, dealing with man as individual, and civil knowledge dealing with man in society. The treatment throughout is thoroughly naturalistic. "This knowledge, as it is the end and term of natural philosophy in the intention of man, so notwithstanding it is but a portion of natural philosophy in the continent of nature."[2] There is nothing of the dualism of Descartes. Man is not separated from nature, and the body is not separated from the mind. The close union and interrelation of the

[1] *Advancement of Learning,* vol. III, p. 357.
[2] *Ibid.,* vol. III, p. 366.

body and the mind is one of the most interesting features of Bacon's psychology.

Psychology treats of the substance of the mind and of the faculties of the mind. Questions pertaining to the former, namely, the origin of the soul, its exemption from matter, and its immortality are relegated to the sphere of religion. These were just the questions which were of major interest in scholastic metaphysics. Bacon's real interests were with the faculties of the mind. The distinction is made between the understanding and the reason, on the one hand, and the will, appetites, and affections, on the other. The imagination is an intermediate faculty being the agent for both reason and will. It should be recalled that a similar intermediary function is ascribed to the imagination by Kant.

Invention and judgment are the two most important faculties of the reason. Under these headings is to be found Bacon's criticism of the traditional logic with special reference to its total inadequacy to provide a method of rational discovery such as is needed in the regeneration of the sciences. This subject will receive fuller treatment in the Introduction to the *Novum Organum*.

In his treatment of the will Bacon proves himself to be a psychologist of the first order. His reputation has been connected almost exclusively with his philosophy of science. This is a narrow estimate of his genius. His psychological and ethical views deserve a great deal more attention than has usually been given to them. The element of control which dominated his treatment of natural prudence is carried over and applied to the philosophy of human nature. "In the handling of this science, those which have written seem to me to have done as if a man that professeth to teach to write did only exhibit fair copies of alphabets and letters joined, without giving any precepts or directions for the carriage of the hand and framing of the letters. So have they made good and fair exemplars and copies, carrying the draughts and portraitures of Good, Virtue, Duty, Felicity; . . . but how to attain these excellent marks, and how to frame and subdue the will of man to become true and conformable to these pursuits, they pass it over altogether or slightly and unprofitably."[1] The passages relating to the "Culture of the Mind" are among the most instructive to be found in the entire realm of ethical literature. The development of character must rest on the descriptive science of human nature. "The first article of this knowledge is to set down sound and true distributions of the several characters and tempers of men's natures and dispositions. . . ."[2] Here as elsewhere theoretical knowledge is not an end in itself but is a point of departure for the control and guidance of conduct. Moral progress is the end, moral knowledge is the means. The regeneration of the social and moral sciences is as much a part of the Baconian scheme of reform as the regeneration of the physical sciences. "It may also be asked (in the way of doubt rather than objection) whether I speak of natural philosophy only, or whether I mean that the other sciences, logic, ethics, and politics, should be carried on by this method. Now I certainly mean what I have said to be understood of them all; and as the common logic, which governs by the syllogism, extends not only to natural but to all sciences; so does mine also, which proceeds by induction, embrace everything."[3] The conception of the modifiability of human nature and of its development under scientific control

[1] *Advancement of Learning*, vol. III, p. 418.
[2] *Ibid.*, vol. III, p. 434.
[3] *Novum Organum*, Bk. I, Aph. CXXVII, vol. IV, p. 112.

is as revolutionary for the social sciences as the conception of natural prudence is for the physical sciences.

The practical aims of progress, control, and utility are further seen in Bacon's treatment of civil knowledge. In public affairs there is a lamentable divorcement between wisdom and learning. As we say, "knowledge comes, but wisdom lingers." This adage has no place in Bacon's characterization of the science of rising in life. Not even a Protagoras nor a Calicles, perhaps not even a Machiavelli could charge Bacon with failure to mobilize his intellectual resources in the interest of public eminence.

2. The *Novum Organum* [1]

The *Novum Organum* contains Bacon's philosophy of science. The treatment of this subject falls into two main divisions, one dealing with the subject-matter, the other dealing with the method of science. Inquiry concerning subject-matter is sub-divided into two entirely different types of investigation, the discovery of "Forms" and the production or transformation of "Forms." The first is termed natural science and the second natural prudence. Although Bacon is quite clear in his conception of the aim of science, he is neither clear nor consistent in his conception of the meaning of "Forms." One finds the term used in two distinct senses.

Before discussing the two meanings of "Form," let us note three general considerations. In the first place we may state Bacon's relation to Plato. Plato's doctrine of Ideas or Forms was rightly conceived in two respects, wrongly conceived in three respects, and left unclear in one respect. He was right in making "Forms"

[1] Published in 1620.

the true objects of scientific knowledge, and in treating them as the true causes of sense appearances. He was wrong in treating "Forms" as separate and distinct from material things. He was also wrong in conceiving them as universals. "In nature nothing really exists besides individual bodies."[1] And in the third place he was wrong in not resolving complex "Forms" into their simple natures. "In the same manner to enquire the Form of lion, of an oak, of gold, nay of water, of air, is a vain pursuit; but to enquire the Forms of sense, of voluntary motion, of vegetation of colours, of gravity and levity, of density, of tenuity, of heat, of cold, and all other natures and qualities, which like an alphabet are not many and of which the essences (upheld by matter) of all creatures do consist; to enquire I say the *true forms* of these, is that part of Metaphysics which we now define of."[2] And finally, Plato far from clear in his conception of the mode of causal relation between the "Forms" and the sensory appearances.

In as much as the meaning of "Form" is very unclear it will assist us if, in the second place, we make a comparison between Bacon and Hume. Bacon's conception of nature was just precisely that against which Hume directed his destructive critique. If we understand what it was that Hume denied we will know what it was that Bacon affirmed. For Hume all objects of scientific inquiry (termed by him "matters of fact") are resolved into impressions, or as we should now say, sense data. The mechanism by means of which sensory data are produced is entirely unknown and lies wholly beyond the range and power of scientific discovery. Neither the source from which sense qualities spring nor the

[1] *Novum Organum*, Bk. II, Aph. II, vol. IV, p. 120.
[2] *Advancement of Learning*, vol. III, pp. 355–356.

process by means of which they are produced is an object of scientific investigation. There is no reality behind the given impressions, or if there is, it can never be known. The impressions themselves constitute the only legitimate date of science.

Now what for Hume constituted no object of science at all was for Bacon the *central quest* of all scientific endeavor. Hume was a subjective idealist; he denied the existence of an objective order of nature. He thus laid the foundations for scientific positivism. Bacon, on the other hand, was a metaphysical realist. He believed in a real order of nature, independent of, objective to, and uncomplicated by the subjective processes of knowing. Things in nature are objects of existence before they are objects of knowledge. There is in Bacon no entanglement of metaphysics with theories of knowing. According to him there is an objective, though cryptic mechanism of nature, deftly concealed from the senses, and very subtile, by means of which that which is apparent to the senses is produced. Sense qualities (Humian impressions) are objects of perception only after they are completely formed. But every sense quality passes through a natural process of formation. The process, being latent, eludes the senses. It comes out into the open only when it is finished. The quality green, for example, when it is an object of perception, is the end term of a continuous natural process which starts in an objective body seated in the order of nature. The source from which it emanates and the process of its emanation are both concealed. But they are there behind the scenes. Nature is apparent only on the surface, but under the surface things are going on. It is the business of science to discover these sub-surface operations. "The subtlety of nature is greater many times over than the subtlety of the senses and understanding."[1] "Toward the effecting of works, all that man can do is to put together or put asunder natural bodies. The rest is done by nature *working within.*"[2]

In the third place, it should be noted that Bacon stands on the dividing line between scholasticism and the beginnings of modern empirical science. It is this transitional position that gives rise to the inconsistencies in his treatment of "Forms." He refers to "Forms" as "nature-engendering natures." Three different things are implied in this phrase: (1) the nature engendering; (2) the nature engendered; and (3) the process of engendering. Bacon uses the term "Form" to stand for both the first and the third of these meanings. The nature engendered is some sensible quality in a natural body; the nature engendering is the cause of that sensible quality; the process of engendering refers to the law descriptive of the process by means of which the sensible quality is produced.

(1) The nature engendering, "Form" in the sense of *cause.* With all of Bacon's repudiation of tradition he never succeeded in completely extricating himself from its influence, as indeed no man can. His treatment of "Form" as cause is one in which the scholastic doctrine of essence persists. There are beyond the reach of sense perceptions hidden essences, active creative natures, "the source of emanation" from which sense qualities spring. These essences are causes in a metaphysical sense. The conception of causality, however, is not that of the succession of events conceived in terms of antecedent and consequent; it is rather that involved in the scholastic doctrine of substance and attribute. The nature engendering is the substance, the nature

[1] *Novum Organum,* Bk. I, Aph. X, vol. IV, p. 48.

[2] *Ibid.,* Bk. I, Aph. IV, vol. IV, p. 47. The italics are mine.

engendered is the attribute. "For since the Form of a thing is the very thing itself, and the thing differs from the form no otherwise than as the apparent (attribute) differs from the real (substance) or the external from the internal, or the thing in reference to man from the thing in reference to the universe. . . ."[1] Although Bacon's conception of a cause is scholastic, his definition of a cause is extremely modern. It is stated in terms of the method of agreement, the method of difference, and the method of concomitant variations, as those methods were later formulated by Mill. "For the Form of a nature is such, that given the Form the nature infallibly follows. Therefore it is always present when the nature is present, and universally implies it, and is constantly inherent in it."[2] The phrase "constantly inherent in it" is further confirmation of the view that the conception of cause is that of substance and attribute. "Again, the Form is such, that if it be taken away, the nature infallibly vanishes. Therefore it is always absent when the nature is absent, and implies its absence, and inheres in nothing else."[3] And finally, "It necessarily follows that no nature can be taken as the true form, unless it always decreases when the nature in question decreases, and in like manner always increases when the nature in question increases."[4]

(2) The nature engendering, or "Form" in the sense of *law*. The discovery of "Form" in the sense of causal essence is the highest aim of science. "Of a given nature to discover the form, or true specific difference, or nature-engendering nature, or source of emanation . . . is the work and aim of Human Knowledge."[5] There fol-

[1] *Novum Organum*, Bk. II, Aph. XIII, vol. IV, p. 137.
[2] *Ibid.*, Bk. II, Aph. IV, vol. IV, p. 121.
[3] *Ibid.*, Bk. II, Aph. IV, vol. IV, p. 121.
[4] *Ibid.*, Bk. II, Aph. XIII, vol. IV, p. 137.
[5] *Ibid.*, Bk. II, Aph. I, vol. IV, p. 119.

lows directly the following passage: "Subordinate to these primary works are two others that are secondary and of inferior rank; to the former, the transformation of concrete bodies, so far as this is possible; to the later, the discovery, and in every case of generation and motion, of the *latent process* carried on from the manifest efficient and the manifest material to the form which is engendered."[1] This passage gives rise to the use of "Form" in the second sense, namely, the law descriptive of the latent process of engendering. Although Bacon says in the passage just quoted that this second aim of science is subordinate to the discovery of cause, still it is the meaning of "Form" that is given primary consideration. There are, as we have already seen, individual and non-sensible bodies (essences). And these bodies are active natures; they perform "pure individual acts according to fixed law."[2] And then he adds: "And it is this law, with its clauses, that I mean when I speak of Forms."[3] And again: "For forms are figments of the human mind, unless you will call those laws of action forms."[4] The "Form" therefore is *both* the essence of the thing *and* the law of its genesis. It is in this sense that Bacon's view of "Form" comes nearest to the modern conception of law.

We may now turn our attention to the method of science. Scientific method consists in two things, regulating the method of investigation and regulating the mind of the investigator. As applied to Bacon the former concerns his theory of induction, the latter his doctrine of Idols.

The elimination of preconceptions and the develop-

[1] *Novum Organum*, Bk. II, Aph. I, vol. IV, p. 119.
[2] *Ibid.*, Bk. II, Aph. II, vol. IV, p. 120.
[3] *Ibid.*, Bk. II, Aph. II, vol. IV, p. 120.
[4] *Ibid.*, Bk. I, Aph. LI, vol. IV, p. 58.

ment of an unprejudiced attitude of mind is an integral part of scientific method. "He who will investigate," say Joachim Rheticus, the pupil of Copernicus, "must possess a free mind." The significance of *animus liber* had been emphasized by the founders of modern empirical science, Copernicus, Kepler, and Galileo. But it had nowhere received such exhaustive and impressive treatment as in Bacon's exposition of the Idols. This exposition is one of Bacon's most brilliant achievements, and is, perhaps, that by which he is best known, or certainly that by which he is most popularly known. The part of the treatise dealing with the Idols is so clearly conceived and executed that there is no need for an introductory exposition. Suffice it to say that the doctrine of the Idols contains much that is of permanent value to scientific investigators of all ages. A first hand acquaintance with Bacon's Idols is necessary part of a liberal education.

Bacon considered his theory of induction to be his most original contribution. Its originality is indicated by the title, *Novum Organum.* While still a student at Cambridge, Bacon conceived the idea not only of regenerating the science, but also of refuting Aristotle. As every one knows, the logical writings of Aristotle had been collected and edited under the title of the *Organon.* Since science was conceived by Aristotle to be *proved* knowledge, the syllogism setting forth the method of deductive demonstration, was of prime importance. Since science was an *a priori* deduction from first principles, there was little need for a logic of induction. The *a priori* character of scientific knowledge had for the most part persisted in the elaborate schemes of scholastic metaphysics. The application of the deductive method had led men far astray from the true nature of things. Hence the need for a *New Organon,* or instrument of scientific procedure, one that would conduct inquiry nearer to the real constitution of nature.

The need for a new method of investigation is seen when we consider the nature of the subject-matter of science. The "Forms" whether conceived as causes or as laws, the discovery of which constitutes the true aim of science, are inaccessible to sense experience. The method of discovery must of necessity be indirect. Neither the method of extreme empiricism, nor the method of extreme rationalism is of any value. Simple enumeration is the method of empiricism. Since this method never carries one beyond the accumulation of sense data it can never reveal the character of non-sensible reality. The empiricist is like the ant which piles up material, but never succeeds in penetrating into the inner connections of things. The rationalist, on the other hand, is like the spider; he merely spins webs of fancy which express no more than the texture of his mind. "God forbid," says Bacon, "that I should give out a work of the imagination for a pattern of the universe." Rationalism is the belief that by agitating your mind you can discover something about the world. The following passage illustrates Bacon's distrust of excessive rationalism: "Another error hath proceeded from too great a reverence, and a kind of adoration of the mind and understanding of man; by means whereof men have withdrawn themselves too much from the contemplation of nature and the observation of experience, and have tumbled up and down in their own reason and conceits. Upon these intellectualists, which are not withstanding commonly taken for the most sublime and divine philosophers, Heraclitus gave a just censure, saying, *Men sought truth in their own little worlds, and not in the great and common world;* for they disdain to spell and so by degrees to read in the volume of God's works; and contrariwise by continual meditation and agitation of wit do urge and as it were invocate their own spirits to divine and give oracles unto them, whereby they are deservedly deluded." [1]

The true method consists in the use of what is valuable in each of the two extremes. Bacon's mid way position is prophetic of Kant, who more than two hundred fifty years later took it as his special work to adjudicate the rival claims of empiricism and rationalism. The empiricist is right, according to Bacon, in insisting on the appeal to facts. But natural history (empiricism) is description and not explanation. The rationalist is right in maintaining that the discovery of "Forms" is the work of the mind. But the understanding can accomplish nothing by the *mere* operation of thought. It requires the aid of instruments and helps. Induction is the instrument by the aid of which the understanding, which in itself is no match for nature, is equipped for the task of discovering the latent causes, laws, and configurations of non-sensible things. "Forms" are not given actualities of sense, they are not logical deductions of thought; they are inferences based on experimentation.

Bacon's method of induction is very much like the Socratic method of definition. The concept, which for Socrates was the object of definition, was analyzed out of a group of instances by abstracting the element that was common to them all. Experience was implied in the collecting of the instances, thought was implied in the higher process of abstracting the universal. The Socratic method was called by Aristotle the *inductive* method. Bacon himself referred to this method as the one most like his own. The method in general may be termed "Induction through Analysis." "But the induc-

[1] *Advancement of Learning*, vol. III, p. 292.

tion which is to be available for the discovery and demonstration of sciences and arts, must analyze nature by proper rejections and exclusions; and then, after a sufficient number of negatives, come to a conclusion on the affirmative instances."[1] The law, or cause, or "Form" is not a summation of instances, but is read out of the instances by subjecting the instances to analysis. The tabulation of selected instances, termed by Bacon "prerogative instances" is a preliminary step, but it is only a step. The "Form" is to be abstracted from the instances by further experimental technique. This experimental, as opposed to mere *observational* treatment of nature, must precede the final abstraction (an intellectual process) of the "Form." Nature does not reveal herself to the casual and listless observer, she must be tortured, hounded, given the third degree before she yields her secrets.

Two criticisms are usually urged against Bacon's account of induction. In the first place, it is said that his theory of induction provides no place for the 'working' hypothesis, a concept which is of central importance in modern scientific methodology. The criticism is in part justifiable and in part unjustifiable. The division of appraisal grows out of the wavering position taken by Bacon himself. The view one takes will depend on the selection of passages he chooses to emphasize. There are passages in which Bacon speaks as if the imagination should be held in leash during the entire period of inquiry, and as if the judgment were to be held in suspense until all the facts are in. "The understanding must not however be allowed to jump and fly from particulars to remote axioms and of almost the highest generality . . . and taking stand upon them as truths that cannot be shaken, proceed to prove and frame the

[1] *Novum Organum*, Bk. I, Aph. CV, vol. IV, p. 97.

middle axioms by reference to them; which has been the practice hitherto."[1] And again: "The understanding must not therefore be supplied with wings but rather hung with weights to keep it from leaping and flying."[2]

Now this, as we know, is not the method of scientific procedure. The mind dwells on facts for a period, and then by a lofty imaginative flight leaps forward (the so-called 'inductive' leap of thought) to a provisional or tentative hypothesis. The hypothesis is then used as a basis of prediction, theoretical implications are deduced from it, and these serve as guides to further discovery. Now Bacon was led to his extreme view out of a zeal to guard against what he called "anticipations of nature," those hypotheses which spring partly from an inveterate impatience of mind and partly from emotional preference and subjective bias. He was eager to avoid the mistake of forcing facts to fit the theory, a mistake all too common among the ancients and the scholastics. The Pythagoreans, for example, had postulated the existence of the counter-earth in order to bring the number of the planets up to the ideal number ten. Although Aristotle had criticised them for such high-handed deduction, he was himself the prince of sinners in this respect. His entire physics was a dialectical romance in which the number, and motion, and position of the heavenly bodies were deductions from pre-conceived theories.

And furthermore Bacon often speaks as if scientific investigation were solely a matter of experimental technique, the explanation or generalization coming automatically at the end of the process as a matter of course, thus assigning but little place to individual genius and the constructive power of the mind. "I, on the con-

[1] *Novum Organum,* Bk. I, Aph. CIV, vol. IV, p. 97.
[2] *Ibid.,* Bk I, Aph. CIV, vol. IV, p. 97.

trary, dwelling purely and constantly among the facts of nature, withdraw my intellect from them no further than may suffice to let the images and rays of natural objects meet in a point, as they do in the sense of vision; whence it follows that the strength and excellency of the wit has but little to do in the matter."[1]

There are, on the other hand, passages in which Bacon clearly recognizes the use of hypothesis, but such hypotheses only as "follow the lead of the subject-matter." He speaks of "the new light of axioms, which having been educed from those particulars by a certain method and rule, shall in their turn point out the way again to new particulars, . . . For our road does not lie on a level, but ascends and descends; first ascending to axioms, then descending to works."[2] And furthermore, under the caption "First Vintage," Bacon makes explicit reference to the value of hypothesis. "I think it expedient that the understanding should have permission, after the three Tables of First Presentation (such as I have exhibited) have been made and weighed, to make an essay of the Interpretation of Nature in the affirmative way; on the strength both of the instances given in the tables, and of any others it may meet with elsewhere. Which kind of essay I call the *Indulgence of the Understanding,* or the *Commencement of Interpretation,* or the *First Vintage.*"[3] An example of this is given in the formulation of the hypothesis that heat is motion. From this hypothesis Bacon proceeds to deduce implications which are open to experimental verification.

The second charge brought against Bacon's theory of induction is the under evaluation of deduction as an

[1] Preface to *The Great Instauration,* vol. IV, p. 19.
[2] *Novum Organum,* Bk. I, Aph. CIII, vol. IV, p. 96.
[3] *Ibid.,* Bk. II, Aph. XX, vol. IV, p. 149.

integral part of scientific method. The charge, it must be acknowledged, is for the most part just. This, together with the subordinate part assigned to mathematics, constitutes the most serious defect in the Baconian methodology of science. The two defects spring from the same source, namely, a deeply seated distrust of excessive rationalism, based on the examples of that excess seen in the science of the Greeks and the scholastics.

3. Outline of the *Advancement of Learning*

Book One: The demerits and merits of learning

- A. The discredits and disgraces of learning
  - I. The major criticisms: The Distempers
    - 1. From the zeal and jealousy of divines
    - 2. From the severity and arrogancy of politicians
    - 3. From the learned themselves
      - a. From their fortunes
        - (1). Scarcity of means (poverty)
        - (2). Privateness of life (obscurity)
        - (3). Meanness of employment (pedantry)
      - b. From their manners
      - c. From the nature of their studies
        - (1). Fantastical
        - (2). Contentious
        - (3). Delicate
  - II. The minor criticisms: The peccant humours
    - 1. Reverence for antiquity and enthusiasm for novelty
    - 2. Distrust of present possibilities
    - 3. Conceit
    - 4. Premature finality to science

5. Abandonment of universality
6. Excessive rationalism
7. Prejudice
8. Bias of impatience
9. Dogmatism
10. Personal vs. scientific detachment
11. Misconception of the true ends of knowledge

B. The dignity and value of learning
  I. Testimonies from the divine
    1. History of creation
      a. Attributes of God: power and wisdom
      b. Order of the spirits: love, wisdom, power
      c. The sensible world: primacy of light (wisdom)
    2. Contemplative function of intelligence
      a. Before the fall
      c. After the fall
    3. Examples from the Scriptures: Moses, Job, Solomon, Christ, The Holy Spirit, St. Paul
    4. The Church Fathers
    5. The Reformation and the Jesuit Order
    6. Value of learning for faith and religion

  II. Testimonies from the human
    1. Superiority of scientific invention over practical statesmanship
    2. Influence of learning on political virtue
    3. Influence of learning on military virtue
    4. Influence of learning on moral and private virtue

Book Two: Survey of the intellectual globe

Introduction

A. History

- I. Natural history
  - 1. History of creatures
  - 2. History of marvels
  - 3. History of arts
- II. Civil history
  - 1. Memorials
    - a. Commentaries
    - b. Registers
  - 2. Perfect histories
    - a. Times (chronicles)
    - b. Persons (lives)
    - c. Actions (narratives)
  - 3. Antiquities
- III. Ecclesiastical history
  - 1. History of the Church
  - 2. History of Prophecy
  - 3. History of Providence

B. Poetry

- I. Narrative
- II. Representative
- III. Allusive

C. Philosophy

Part One: Philosophy

Division One: *Prima Philosophia,* Summary Philosophy

Division Two: Divine Philosophy, or Natural Theology

Division Three: Natural Philosophy

- I. As to subject-matter
  - 1. Natural science: Discovery of causes
    - a. Physics: material and efficient causes
    - b. Metaphysics: formal and final causes
    - c. Mathematics: a branch of metaphysics
  - 2. Natural prudence: Production of effects
    - a. Experimental
    - b. Philosophical
    - c. Magical
- II. As to method of inquiry
  - 1. Calendar of doubts: the aporematic method
  - 2. Calendar of errors

Division Four: Human Philosophy

- I. Man as individual
  - 1. Close relation of body and mind
  - 2. Body
    - a. Medicine
    - b. Cosmetic
    - c. Athletic
    - d. Arts of pleasure sensual
  - 3. Mind
    - a. Substance of the mind
      - (1). Divination
      - (2). Fascination
    - b. Faculties of the mind

- (1). Understanding and reason: judicial Imagination and agent for both reason and will
    - (a). Invention
        - (a′). Of arts and science
        - (b′). Of speech and arguments
    - (b). Judgment
        - (a′). Judgment as invention
        - (b′). Judgment as syllogism
            - (a″). Analytics
            - (b″). Elenches: the idols
    - (c). Memory
    - (d). Tradition
- (2). Will, appetite, and affection: ministerial
    - (a). Nature of the good
        - (a′). Kings of good
        - (b′). Degrees of good
            - (a″). Private good
            - (b″). Social good
    - (b). Statement of the problem
    - (c). The method of application
    - (d). The method of alteration

II. Man in society: Civil knowledge
1. Conversation: Behavior
2. Negotiation: Business
3. Government: Statesmanship

* * * * * * *

Part Two: Divinity

The selections from the writings of Bacon which appear in this volume are taken from the edition of Bacon's *Works* by Spedding, Ellis, and Heath, London, 1858.

MATTHEW THOMPSON MCCLURE.

The following is a partial list of the Baconian writings, the arrangement being made on the basis of the division given by Spedding, Ellis and Heath:—

I. Works published, or designed for publication, as parts of the *Instauratio Magna*

Novum Organum, 1620. The second part of the Instauratio.

De Augmentis Scientiarum, 1623. Intended for the first part of the Instauratio.

Historia Naturalis et Experimentalis ad condendam philosophiam; sive Phaenomena Universi; quae est Instaurationis Magnae pars tertia. (Natural and experimental history for the foundation of philosophy; or phenomena of the universe: being the third part of the Instauratio Magna.) This volume, published in 1622, contains Historia Ventorum, and the titles of five other treatises which were left in fragmentary form.

Sylva Sylvarum; or Natural History. (Published after the author's death by William Rawley. 1627.) This treatise, written in English, "gives some account of Bacon's views touching the kind of natural history required as the foundation of the instauration of the sciences." (Ellis)

Scala Intellectua, sive Filum Labyrinthi. 1653. (A preface intended for the fourth part of the Instauratio.)

Prodromi, sive Anticipationes Philosophiae Secundae. 1653. (A preface intended for the fifth part of the Instauratio.)

II. Works on subjects connected with the Instauratio, but not meant to be included in it. In this division the most important is:

New Atlantis: a work unfinished. (First published by Dr. Rawley in 1627.)

III. Works originally designed for parts of the Instauratio Magna, but superseded or abandoned.

Cogitationes de Scientia Humana. (Fragmentary and of uncertain date.)

Valerius Terminus of the Interpretation of Nature; with annotations of Hermes Stella. 1734.

The Twoo Bookes of Francis Bacon on the Proficience and Advancement of Learning Divine and Humane. 1605.

(There appear in this division about twelve other titles of works less known and fragmentary in character.)

CONTENTS

THE
GREAT INSTAURATION

PROŒMIUM

FRANCIS OF VERULAM

REASONED THUS WITH HIMSELF,

AND JUDGED IT TO BE FOR THE INTEREST OF THE PRESENT AND FUTURE GENERATIONS THAT THEY SHOULD BE MADE ACQUAINTED WITH HIS THOUGHTS

Being convinced that the human intellect makes its own difficulties, not using the true helps which are at man's disposal soberly and judiciously; whence follows manifold ignorance of things, and by reason of that ignorance mischiefs innumerable; he thought all trial should be made, whether that commerce between the mind of man and the nature of things, which is more precious than anything on earth, or at least than anything that is of the earth, might by any means be restored to its perfect and original condition, or if that may not be, yet reduced to a better condition than that in which it now is. Now that the errors which have hitherto prevailed, and which will prevail for ever, should (if the mind be left to go its own way), either by the natural force of the understanding or by help of the aids and instruments of Logic, one by one correct themselves, was a thing not to be hoped for: because the primary notions of things which the mind readily and passively imbibes, stores up, and accumulates (and it is from them that all the rest flow) are false, confused, and overhastily abstracted from the facts; nor are the secondary and subsequent notions less arbitrary and inconstant; whence it follows that the entire fabric of human reason which we employ in the inquisition of nature, is badly put together and built up, and like some magnificent structure without any foundation. For while men are occupied in admiring and applauding the false powers of the mind, they pass by and throw away those true powers, which, if it be supplied with the proper aids and can itself be content to wait upon nature instead of vainly affecting to overrule her, are within its reach. There was but one course left, therefore,—to try the whole thing anew upon a better plan, and to commence a total reconstruction of sciences, arts, and all human knowledge, raised upon the proper foundations. And this, though in the project and undertaking it may seem a thing infinite and beyond the powers of man, yet when it comes to be dealt with it will be found sound and sober, more so than what has been done hitherto. For of this there is some issue; whereas in what is now done in the matter of science there is only a whirling round about, and perpetual agitation, ending where it began. And although he was well aware how solitary an enterprise it is, and how hard a thing to win faith and credit for, nevertheless he was resolved not to abandon either it or himself; nor to be deterred from trying and entering upon that one path which is alone open to the human mind. For better it is to make a beginning of that which may lead to something, than to engage in a perpetual struggle and pursuit in courses which have no exit. And certainly the two ways of contemplation are much like those two ways of action, so much celebrated, in this—that the one, arduous and difficult in the beginning, leads out at last into the open country; while the other, seeming at first sight easy and free from obstruction, leads to pathless and precipitous places.

Moreover, because he knew not how long it might be before these things would occur to any one else, judging especially from this, that he has found no man hitherto who has applied his mind to the like, he resolved to publish at once so much as he has been able to complete. The cause of which haste was not ambition for himself, but solicitude for the work; that in case of his death there might remain some outline and project of that which he had conceived, and some evidence likewise of his honest mind and inclination towards the benefit of the human race. Certain it is that all other ambition whatsoever seemed poor in his eyes compared with the work which he had in hand; seeing that the matter at issue is either nothing, or a thing so great that it may well be content with its own merit, without seeking other recompence.

THE GREAT INSTAURATION

PREFACE

That the state of knowledge is not prosperous nor greatly advancing; and that a way must be opened for the human understanding entirely different from any hitherto known, and other helps provided, in order that the mind may exercise over the nature of things the authority which properly belongs to it.

It seems to me that men do not rightly understand either their store or their strength, but overrate the one and underrate the other. Hence it follows, that either from an extravagant estimate of the value of the arts which they possess, they seek no further; or else from too mean an estimate of their own powers, they spend their strength in small matters and never put it fairly to the trial in those which go to the main. These are as the pillars of fate set in the path of knowledge; for men have neither desire nor hope to encourage them to penetrate further. And since opinion of store is one of the chief causes of want, and satisfaction with the present induces neglect of provision for the future, it becomes a thing not only useful, but absolutely necessary, that the excess of honour and admiration with which our existing stock of inventions is regarded be in the very entrance and threshold of the work, and that frankly and without circumlocution, stripped off, and men be duly warned not to exaggerate or make too much of them. For let a man look carefully into all that variety of books with which the arts and sciences abound, he will find everywhere endless repetitions of the same thing, varying in the method of treatment, but not new in substance, insomuch that the whole stock, numerous as it appears at first view, proves on examination to be but scanty. And for its value and utility it must be plainly avowed that that wisdom which we have derived principally from the Greeks is but like the boyhood of knowledge, and has the characteristic property of boys: it can talk, but it cannot generate; for it is fruitful of controversies but barren of works. So that the state of learning as it now is appears to be represented to the life in the old fable of Scylla, who had the head and face of a virgin, but her womb was hung round with barking monsters, from which she could not be delivered. For in like manner the sciences to which we are accustomed have certain general positions which are specious and flattering; but as soon as they come to particulars, which are as the parts of generation, when they should produce fruit and works, then arise contentions and barking disputations, which are the end of the matter and all the issue they can yield. Observe also, that if sciences of this kind had any life in them, that could never have come to pass which has been the case now for many ages—that they stand almost at a stay, without receiving any augmentations worthy of the human race; insomuch that many times not only what was asserted once is asserted still, but what was a question once is a question still, and instead of being resolved by discussion is only fixed and fed; and all the tradition and succession of schools is still a succession of masters and scholars, not of inventors and those who bring to further perfection the things invented. In the mechanical arts we do not find it so; they, on the contrary, as having in them some breath of life, are continually growing and becoming more perfect. As originally invented they are commonly rude, clumsy, and shapeless; afterwards they acquire new powers and more commodious arrangements and constructions; in so far that men shall sooner leave the study and pursuit of them and turn to something else, than they arrive at the ultimate perfection of which they are capable. Philosophy and the intellectual sciences, on the contrary, stand like statues, worshipped and celebrated, but not moved or advanced. Nay, they sometimes flourish most in the hands of the first author, and afterwards degenerate. For when men have once made over their judgments to others' keeping, and (like those senators whom they called *Pedarii*) have agreed to support some one person's opinion, from that time they make no enlargement of the sciences themselves, but fall to the servile office of embellishing certain individual authors and increasing their retinue. And let it not be said that the sciences have been growing gradually till they have at last reached their full stature, and so (their course being completed) have settled in the works of a few writers; and that there being now no room for the invention of better, all that remains is to embellish and cultivate those things which have been invented already. Would it were so! But the truth is that this appropriating of the sciences has its origin in nothing better than the confidence of a few persons and the sloth and indolence of the rest. For after the sciences had been in several parts perhaps cultivated and handled diligently, there has risen up some man of bold disposition, and famous for methods and short ways which people like, who has in appearance reduced them to an art, while he has in fact only spoiled all that the others had done. And yet this is what posterity like, because it makes the work short and easy, and saves further inquiry, of which they are weary and impatient. And if any one take this general acquiescence and consent for an argument of weight, as being the judgment of Time, let me tell him that the reasoning on which he relies is most fallacious and weak. For, first, we are far from knowing all that in the matter of sciences and arts has in various ages and places been brought to light and published; much less, all that has been by private persons secretly attempted and stirred; so neither the births nor the miscarriages of Time are entered in our records. Nor, secondly, is the consent itself and the time it has continued a consideration of much worth. For however various are the forms of civil polities, there is but one form of polity in the sciences; and that always has been and always will be popular. Now the doctrines which find most favour with the populace are those which are either contentious and pugnacious, or specious and empty; such, I say, as either entangle assent or tickle it. And therefore no doubt the greatest wits in each successive age have been forced out of their own course; men of capacity and intellect above the vulgar having been fain, for reputation's sake, to bow to the judgment of the time and the multitude; and thus if any contemplations of a higher order took light anywhere, they were presently blown out by the winds of vulgar opinions. So that Time is like a river, which has brought down to us things light and puffed up, while those which are weighty and solid have sunk. Nay, those very authors who have usurped a kind of dictatorship in the sciences and taken upon them to lay down the law with such confidence, yet when from time to time they come to themselves again, they fall to complaints of the subtlety of nature, the hiding-places of truth, the obscurity of things, the entanglement of causes, the weakness of the human mind; wherein nevertheless they show themselves never the more modest, seeing that they will rather lay the blame upon the common condition of men and nature than upon themselves. And then whatever any art fails to attain, they ever set it down upon the authority of that art itself as impossible of attainment; and how can art be found guilty when it is judge in its own cause? So it is but a device for exempting ignorance from ignominy. Now for those things which are delivered and received, this is their condition: barren of works, full of questions; in point of enlargement slow and languid; carrying a show of perfection in the whole, but in the parts ill filled up; in selection popular, and unsatisfactory even to those who propound them; and therefore fenced round and set forth with sundry artifices. And if there be any who have determined to make trial for themselves, and put their own strength to the work of advancing the boundaries of the sciences, yet have they not ventured to cast themselves completely loose from received opinions or to seek their knowledge at the fountain; but they think they have done some great thing if they do but add and introduce into the existing sum of science something of their own; prudently considering with themselves that by making the addition they can assert their liberty, while they retain the credit of modesty by assenting to the rest. But these mediocrities and middle ways so much praised, in deferring to opinions and customs, turn to the great detriment of the sciences. For it is hardly possible at once to admire an author and to go beyond him; knowledge being as water, which will not rise above the level from which it fell. Men of this kind, therefore, amend some things, but advance little; and improve the condition of knowledge, but do not extend its range. Some, indeed, there have been who have gone more boldly to work, and taking it all for an open matter and giving their genius full play, have made a passage for themselves and their own opinions by pulling down and demolishing former ones; and yet all their stir has but little advanced the matter; since their aim has been not to extend philosophy and the arts in substance and value, but only to change doctrines and transfer the kingdom of opinions to themselves; whereby little has indeed been gained, for though the error be the opposite of the other, the causes of erring are the same in both. And if there have been any who, not binding themselves either to other men's opinions or to their own, but loving liberty, have desired to engage others along with themselves in search, these, though honest in intention, have been weak in endeavour. For they have been content to follow probable reasons, and are carried round in a whirl of arguments, and in the promiscuous liberty of search have relaxed the severity of inquiry. There is none who has dwelt upon experience and the facts of nature as long as is necessary. Some there are indeed who have committed themselves to the waves of experience, and almost turned mechanics; yet these again have in their very experiments pursued a kind of wandering inquiry, without any regular system of operations. And besides they have mostly proposed to themselves certain petty tasks, taking it for a great matter to work out some single discovery;—a course of proceeding at once poor in aim and unskillful in design. For no man can rightly and successfully investigate the nature of anything in the thing itself; let him vary his experiments as laboriously as he will, he never comes to a resting-place, but still finds something to seek beyond. And there is another thing to be remembered; namely, that all industry in experimenting has begun with proposing to itself certain definite works to be accomplished, and has pursued them with premature and unseasonable eagerness; it has sought, I say, experiments of Fruit, not experiments of Light; not imitating the divine procedure, which in its first day's work created light only and assigned to it one entire day; on which day it produced no material work, but proceeded to that on the days following. As for those who have given the first place to Logic, supposing that the surest helps to the sciences were to be found in that, they have indeed most truly and excellently perceived that the human intellect left to its own course is not to be trusted; but then the remedy is altogether too weak for the disease; nor is it without evil in itself. For the Logic which is received, though it be very properly applied to civil business and to those arts which rest in discourse and opinion, is not nearly subtle enough to deal with nature; and in offering at what it cannot master, has done more to establish and perpetuate error than to open the way to truth.

Upon the whole therefore, it seems that men have not been happy hitherto either in the trust which they have placed in others or in their own industry with regard to the sciences; especially as neither the demonstrations nor the experiments as yet known are much to be relied upon. But the universe to the eye of the human understanding is framed like a labyrinth; presenting as it does on every side so many ambiguities of way, such deceitful resemblances of objects and signs, natures so irregular in their lines, and so knotted and entangled. And then the way is still to be made by the uncertain light of the sense, sometimes shining out, sometimes clouded over, through the woods of experience and particulars; while those who offer themselves for guides are (as was said) themselves also puzzled, and increase the number of errors and wanderers. In circumstances so difficult neither the natural force of man's judgment nor even any accidental felicity offers any chance of success. No excellence of wit, no repetition of chance experiments, can overcome such difficulties as these. Our steps must be guided by a clue, and the whole way from the very first perception of the senses must be laid out upon a sure plan. Not that I would be understood to mean that nothing whatever has been done in so many ages by so great labours. We have no reason to be ashamed of the discoveries which have been made, and no doubt the ancients proved themselves in everything that turns on wit and abstract meditation, wonderful men. But as in former ages when men sailed only by observation of the stars, they could indeed coast along the shores of the old continent or cross a few small and mediterranean seas; but before the ocean could be traversed and the new world discovered, the use of the mariner's needle, as a more faithful and certain guide, had to be found out; in like manner the discoveries which have been hitherto made in the arts and sciences are such as might be made by practice, meditation, observation, argumentation,—for they lay near to the senses, and immediately beneath common notions; but before we can reach the remoter and more hidden parts of nature, it is necessary that a more perfect use and application of the human mind and intellect be introduced.

For my own part at least, in obedience to the everlasting love of truth, I have committed myself to the uncertainties and difficulties and solitudes of the ways, and relying on the divine assistance have upheld my mind both against the shocks and embattled ranks of opinion, and against my own private and inward hesitations and scruples, and against the fogs and clouds of nature, and the phantoms flitting about on every side; in the hope of providing at last for the present and future generations guidance more faithful and secure. Wherein if I have made any progress, the way has been opened to me by no other means than the true and legitimate humiliation of the human spirit. For all those who before me have applied themselves to the invention of arts have but cast a glance or two upon facts and examples and experience, and straightway proceeded, as if invention were nothing more than an exercise of thought, to invoke their own spirits to give them oracles. I, on the contrary, dwelling purely and constantly among the facts of nature, withdraw my intellect from them no further than may suffice to let the images and rays of natural objects meet in a point, as they do in the sense of vision; whence it follows that the strength and excellency of the wit has but little to do in the matter. And the same humility which I use in inventing I employ likewise in teaching. For I do not endeavour either by triumphs of confutation, or pleadings of antiquity, or assumption of authority, or even by the veil of obscurity, to invest these inventions of mine with any majesty; which might easily be done by one who sought to give lustre to his own name rather than light to other men's minds. I have not sought (I say) nor do I seek either to force or ensnare men's judgments, but I lead them to things themselves and the concordances of things, that they may see for themselves what they have, what they can dispute, what they can add and contribute to the common stock. And for myself, if in anything I have been either too credulous or too little awake and attentive, or if I have fallen off by the way and left the inquiry incomplete, nevertheless I so present these things naked and open, that my errors can be marked and set aside before the mass of knowledge be further infected by them; and it will be easy also for others to continue and carry on my labours. And by these means I suppose that I have established for ever a true and lawful marriage between the empirical and the rational faculty, the unkind and ill-starred divorce and separation of which has thrown into confusion all the affairs of the human family.

Wherefore, seeing that these things do not depend upon myself, at the outset of the work I most humbly and fervently pray to God the Father, God the Son, and God the Holy Ghost, that remembering the sorrows of mankind and the pilgrimage of this our life wherein we wear out days few and evil, they will vouchsafe through my hands to endow the human family with new mercies. This likewise I humbly pray, that things human may not interfere with things divine, and that from the opening of the ways of sense and the increase of natural light there may arise in our minds no incredulity or darkness with regard to the divine mysteries; but rather that the understanding being thereby purified and purged of fancies and vanity, and yet not the less subject and entirely submissive to the divine oracles, may give to faith that which is faith's. Lastly, that knowledge being now discharged of that venom which the serpent infused into it, and which makes the mind of man to swell, we may not be wise above measure and sobriety, but cultivate truth in charity.

And now having said my prayers I turn to men; to whom I have certain salutary admonitions to offer and certain fair requests to make. My first admonition (which was also my prayer) is that men confine the sense within the limits of duty in respect of things divine: for the sense is like the sun, which reveals the face of earth, but seals and shuts up the face of heaven. My next, that in flying from this evil they fall not into the opposite error, which they will surely do if they think that the inquisition of nature is in any part interdicted or forbidden. For it was not that pure and uncorrupted natural knowledge whereby Adam gave names to the creatures according to their propriety, which gave occasion to the fall. It was the ambitious and proud desire of moral knowledge to judge of good and evil, to the end that man may revolt from God and give laws to himself, which was the form and manner of the temptation. Whereas of the sciences which regard nature, the divine philosopher declares that "it is the glory of God to conceal a thing, but it is the glory of the King to find a thing out." Even as though the divine nature took pleasure in the innocent and kindly sport of children playing a hide and seek, and vouchsafed of his kindness and goodness to admit the human spirit for his playfellow at that game. Lastly, I would address one general admonition to all; that they consider what are the true ends of knowledge, and that they seek it not either for pleasure of the mind, or for contention, or for superiority to others, or for profit, or fame, or power, or any of these inferior things; but for the benefit and use of life; and that they perfect and govern it in charity. For it was from lust of power that the angels fell, from lust of knowledge that man fell; but of charity there can be no excess, neither did angel or man ever come in danger by it.

The requests I have to make are these. Of myself I say nothing; but in behalf of the business which is in hand I entreat men to believe that it is not an opinion to be held, but a work to be done; and to be well assured that I am labouring to lay the foundation, not of any sect or doctrine, but of human utility and power. Next, I ask them to deal fairly by their own interests, and laying aside all emulations and prejudices in favour of this or that opinion, to join in consultation for the common good; and being now freed and guarded by the securities and helps which I offer from the errors and impediments of the way, to come forward themselves and take part in that which remains to be done. Moreover, to be of good hope, nor to imagine that this Instauration of mine is a thing infinite and beyond the power of man, when it is in fact the true end and termination of infinite error; and seeing also that it is by no means forgetful of the conditions of mortality and humanity, (for it does not suppose that the work can be altogether completed within one generation, but provides for its being taken up by another); and finally that it seeks for the sciences not arrogantly in the little cells of human wit, but with reverence in the greater world. But it is the empty things that are vast: things solid are most contracted and lie in little room. And now I have only one favour more to ask (else injustice to me may perhaps imperil the business itself)—that men will consider well how far, upon that which I must needs assert (if I am to be consistent with myself), they are entitled to judge and decide upon these doctrines of mine; inasmuch as all that premature human reasoning which anticipates inquiry, and is abstracted from the facts rashly and sooner than is fit, is by me rejected (so far as the inquisition of nature is concerned), as a thing uncertain, confused, and ill built up; and I cannot be fairly asked to abide by the decision of a tribunal which is itself on its trial.

THE PLAN OF THE WORK.

The work is in six Parts:—

1. *The Divisions of the Sciences.*
2. *The New Organon; or Directions concerning the Interpretation of Nature.*
3. *The Phenomena of the Universe; or a Natural and Experimental History for the foundation of Philosophy.*
4. *The Ladder of the Intellect.*
5. *The Forerunners; or Anticipations of the New Philosophy.*
6. *The New Philosophy; or Active Science.*

The Arguments of the several Parts.

It being part of my design to set everything forth, as far as may be, plainly and perspicuously (for nakedness of the mind is still, as nakedness of the body once was, the companion of innocence and simplicity), let me first explain the order and plan of the work. I distribute it into six parts.

The first part exhibits a summary or general description of the knowledge which the human race at present possesses. For I thought it good to make some pause upon that which is received; that thereby the old may be more easily made perfect and the new more easily approached. And I hold the improvement of that which we have to be as much an object as the acquisition of more. Besides which it will make me the better listened to; for "He that is ignorant (says the proverb) receives not the words of knowledge, unless thou first tell him that which is in his own heart." We will therefore make a coasting voyage along the shores of the arts and sciences received; not without importing into them some useful things by the way.

In laying out the divisions of the sciences however, I take into account not only things already invented and known, but likewise things omitted which ought to be there. For there are found in the intellectual as in the terrestrial globe waste regions as well as cultivated ones. It is no wonder therefore if I am sometimes obliged to depart from the ordinary divisions. For in adding to the total you necessarily alter the parts and sections; and the received divisions of the sciences are fitted only to the received sum of them as it stands now.

With regard to those things which I shall mark as omitted, I intend not merely to set down a simple title or a concise argument of that which is wanted. For as often as I have occasion to report anything as deficient, the nature of which is at all obscure, so that men may not perhaps easily understand what I mean or what the work is which I have in my head, I shall always (provided it be a matter of any worth) take care to subjoin either directions for the execution of such work, or else a portion of the work itself executed by myself as a sample of the whole: thus giving assistance in every case either by work or by counsel. For if it were for the sake of my own reputation only and other men's interests were not concerned in it, I would not have any man think that in such cases merely some light and vague notion has crossed my mind, and that the things which I desire and offer at are no better than wishes; when they are in fact things which men may certainly command if they will, and of which I have formed in my own mind a clear and detailed conception. For I do not propose merely to survey these regions in my mind, like an augur taking auspices, but to enter them like a general who means to take possession.—So much for the first part of the work.

Having thus coasted past the ancient arts, the next point is to equip the intellect for passing beyond. To the second part therefore belongs the doctrine concerning the better and more perfect use of human reason in the inquisition of things, and the true helps of the understanding: that thereby (as far as the condition of mortality and humanity allows) the intellect may be raised and exalted, and made capable of overcoming the difficulties and obscurities of nature. The art which I introduce with this view (which I call *Interpretation of Nature*) is a kind of logic; though the difference between it and the ordinary logic is great; indeed immense. For the ordinary logic professes to contrive and prepare helps and guards for the understanding, as mine does; and in this one point they agree. But mine differs from it in three points especially; viz. in the end aimed at; in the order of demonstration; and in the starting point of the inquiry.

For the end which this science of mine proposes is the invention not of arguments but of arts; not of things in accordance with principles, but of principles themselves; not of probable reasons, but of designations and directions for works. And as the intention is different, so accordingly is the effect; the effect of the one being to overcome an opponent in argument, of the other to command nature in action.

In accordance with this end is also the nature and order of the demonstrations. For in the ordinary logic almost all the work is spent about the syllogism. Of induction the logicians seem hardly to have taken any serious thought, but they pass it by with a slight notice, and hasten on to the formulæ of disputation. I on the contrary reject demonstration by syllogism, as acting too confusedly, and letting nature slip out of its hands. For although no one can doubt that things which agree in a middle term agree with one another (which is a proposition of mathematical certainty), yet it leaves an opening for deception; which is this. The syllogism consists of propositions; propositions of words; and words are the tokens and signs of notions. Now if the very notions of the mind (which are as the soul of words and the basis of the whole structure) be improperly and over-hastily abstracted from facts, vague, not sufficiently definite, faulty in short in many ways, the whole edifice tumbles. I therefore reject the syllogism; and that not only as regards principles (for to principles the logicians themselves do not apply it) but also as regards middle propositions; which, though obtainable no doubt by the syllogism, are, when so obtained, barren of works, remote from practice, and altogether unavailable for the active department of the sciences. Although therefore I leave to the syllogism and these famous and boasted modes of demonstration their jurisdiction over popular arts and such as are matter of opinion (in which department I leave all as it is), yet in dealing with the nature of things I use induction throughout, and that in the minor propositions as well as the major. For I consider induction to be that form of demonstration which upholds the sense, and closes with nature, and comes to the very brink of operation, if it does not actually deal with it.

Hence it follows that the order of demonstration is likewise inverted. For hitherto the proceeding has been to fly at once from the sense and particulars up to the most general propositions, as certain fixed poles for the argument to turn upon, and from these to derive the rest by middle terms: a short way, no doubt, but precipitate; and one which will never lead to nature, though it offers an easy and ready way to disputation. Now my plan is to proceed regularly and gradually from one axiom to another, so that the most general are not reached till the last: but then when you do come to them you find them to be not empty notions, but well defined, and such as nature would really recognise as her first principles, and such as lie at the heart and marrow of things.

But the greatest change I introduce is in the form itself of induction and the judgment made thereby. For the induction of which the logicians speak, which proceeds by simple enumeration, is a puerile thing; concludes at hazard; is always liable to be upset by contradictory instance; takes into account only what is known and ordinary; and leads to no result.

Now what the sciences stand in need of is a form of induction which shall analyse experience and take it to pieces, and by a due process of exclusion and rejection lead to an inevitable conclusion. And if that ordinary mode of judgment practised by the logicians was so laborious, and found exercise for such great wits, how much more labour must we be prepared to bestow upon this other, which is extracted not merely out of the depths of the mind, but out of the very bowels of nature.

Nor is this all. For I also sink the foundations of

the sciences deeper and firmer; and I begin the inquiry nearer the source than men have done heretofore; submitting to examination those things which the common logic takes on trust. For first, the logicians borrow the principles of each science from the science itself; secondly, they hold in reverence the first notions of the mind; and lastly, they receive as conclusive the immediate informations of the sense, when well disposed. Now upon the first point, I hold that true logic ought to enter the several provinces of science armed with a higher authority than belongs to the principles of those sciences themselves, and ought to call those putative principles to account until they are fully established. Then with regard to the first notions of the intellect; there is not one of the impressions taken by the intellect when left to go its own way, but I hold it for suspected, and no way established, until it has submitted to a new trial and a fresh judgment has been thereupon pronounced. And lastly, the information of the sense itself I sift and examine in many ways. For certain it is that the senses deceive; but then at the same time they supply the means of discovering their own errors; only the errors are here, the means of discovery are to seek.

The sense fails in two ways. Sometimes it gives no information, sometimes it gives false information. For first, there are very many things which escape the sense, even when best disposed and no way obstructed; by reason either of the subtlety of the whole body, or the minuteness of the parts, or distance of place, or slowness or else swiftness of motion, or familiarity of the object, or other causes. And again when the sense does apprehend a thing its apprehension is not much to be relied upon. For the testimony and information of the sense has reference always to man, not to the universe; and it is a great error to assert that the sense is the measure of things.

To meet these difficulties, I have sought on all sides diligently and faithfully to provide helps for the sense —substitutes to supply its failures, rectifications to correct its errors; and this I endeavour to accomplish not so much by instruments as by experiments. For the subtlety of experiments is far greater than that of the sense itself, even when assisted by exquisite instruments; such experiments, I mean, as are skilfully and artificially devised for the express purpose of determining the point in question. To the immediate and proper perception of the sense therefore I do not give much weight; but I contrive that the office of the sense shall be only to judge of the experiment, and that the experiment itself shall judge of the thing. And thus I conceive that I perform the office of a true priest of the sense (from which all knowledge in nature must be sought, unless men mean to go mad) and a not unskilful interpreter of its oracles; and that while others only profess to uphold and cultivate the sense, I do so in fact. Such then are the provisions I make for finding the genuine light of nature and kindling and bringing it to bear. And they would be sufficient of themselves, if the human intellect were even, and like a fair sheet of paper with no writing on it. But since the minds of men are strangely possessed and beset, so that there is no true and even surface left to reflect the genuine rays of things, it is necessary to seek a remedy for this also.

Now the idols, or phantoms, by which the mind is occupied are either adventitious or innate. The adventitious come into the mind from without; namely, either from the doctrines and sects of philosophers, or from perverse rules of demonstration. But the innate are inherent in the very nature of the intellect, which is far more prone to error than the sense is. For let men please themselves as they will in admiring and almost adoring the human mind, this is certain: that as an uneven mirror distorts the rays of objects according to its own figure and section, so the mind, when it receives impressions of objects through the sense, cannot be trusted to report them truly, but in forming its notions mixes up its own nature with the nature of things.

And as the first two kinds of idols are hard to eradicate, so idols of this last kind cannot be eradicated at all. All that can be done is to point them out, so that this insidious action of the mind may be marked and reproved (else as fast as old errors are destroyed new ones will spring up out of the ill complexion of the mind itself, and so we shall have but a change of errors, and not a clearance); and to lay it down once for all as a fixed and established maxim, that the intellect is not qualified to judge except by means of induction, and induction in its legitimate form. This doctrine then of the expurgation of the intellect to qualify it for dealing with truth, is comprised in three refutations: the refutation of the Philosophies; the refutation of the Demonstrations; and the refutation of the Natural Human Reason. The explanation of which things, and of the true relation between the nature of things and the nature of the mind, is as the strewing and decoration of the bridal chamber of the Mind and the Universe, the Divine Goodness assisting; out of which marriage let us hope (and be this the prayer of the bridal song) there may spring helps to man, and a line and race of inventions that may in some degree subdue and overcome the necessities and miseries of humanity. This is the second part of the work.

But I design not only to indicate and mark out the ways, but also to enter them. And therefore the third part of the work embraces the Phenomena of the Universe; that is to say, experience of every kind, and such a natural history as may serve for a foundation to build philosophy upon. For a good method of demonstration or form of interpreting nature may keep the mind from going astray or stumbling, but it is not any excellence of method that can supply it with the material of knowledge. Those however who aspire not to guess and divine, but to discover and know; who propose not to devise mimic and fabulous worlds of their own, but to examine and dissect the nature of this very world itself; must go to facts themselves for everything. Nor can the place of this labour and search and worldwide perambulation be supplied by any genius or meditation or argumentation; no, not if all men's wits could meet in one. This therefore we must have, or the business must be for ever abandoned. But up to this day such has been the condition of men in this matter, that it is no wonder if nature will not give herself into their hands.

For first, the information of the sense itself, sometimes failing, sometimes false; observation, careless, irregular, and led by chance; tradition, vain and fed on rumour; practice, slavishly bent upon its work; experiment, blind, stupid, vague, and prematurely broken off; lastly, natural history trivial and poor;—all these have contributed to supply the understanding with very bad materials for philosophy and the sciences.

Then an attempt is made to mend the matter by a preposterous subtlety and winnowing of argument. But this comes too late, the case being already past remedy; and is far from setting the business right or sifting away the errors. The only hope therefore of any greater increase or progress lies in a reconstruction of the sciences.

Of this reconstruction the foundation must be laid in natural history, and that of a new kind and gathered on a new principle. For it is in vain that you polish the mirror if there are no images to be reflected; and it is as necessary that the intellect should be supplied with fit matter to work upon, as with safeguards to guide its working. But my history differs from that in use (as my logic does) in many things,—in end and office, in mass and composition, in subtlety, in selection also and setting forth, with a view to the operations which are to follow.

For first, the object of the natural history which I propose is not so much to delight with variety of matter or to help with present use of experiments, as to give light to the discovery of causes and supply a suckling philosophy with its first food. For though it be true that I am principally in pursuit of works and the active department of the sciences, yet I wait for harvest-time, and do not attempt to mow the moss or to reap the green corn. For I well know that axioms once rightly discovered will carry whole troops of works along with them, and produce them, not here and there one, but in clusters. And that unseasonable and puerile hurry to snatch by way of earnest at the first works which come within reach, I utterly condemn and reject, as an Atalanta's apple that hinders the race. Such then is the office of this natural history of mine.

Next, with regard to the mass and composition of it: I mean it to be a history not only of nature free and at large (when she is left to her own course and does her work her own way),—such as that of the heavenly bodies, meteors, earth and sea, minerals, plants, animals,—but much more of nature under constraint and vexed; that is to say, when by art and the hand of man she is forced out of her natural state, and squeezed and moulded. Therefore I set down at length all experiments of the mechanical arts, of the operative part of the liberal arts, of the many crafts which have not yet grown into arts properly so called, so far as I have been able to examine them and as they conduce to the end in view. Nay (to say the plain truth) I do in fact (low and vulgar as men may think it) count more upon this part both for helps and safeguards than upon the other; seeing that the nature of things betrays itself more readily under the vexations of art than in its natural freedom.

Nor do I confine the history to Bodies; but I have thought it my duty besides to make a separate history of such Virtues as may be considered cardinal in nature. I mean those original passions or desires of matter which constitute the primary elements of nature; such as Dense and Rare, Hot and Cold, Solid and Fluid, Heavy and Light, and several others.

Then again, to speak of subtlety: I seek out and get together a kind of experiment much subtler and simpler than those which occur accidentally. For I drag into light many things which no one who was not proceeding by a regular and certain way to the discovery of causes would have thought of inquiring after; being indeed in themselves of no great use; which shows that they were not sought for on their own account; but having just the same relation to things and works which the letters of the alphabet have to speech and words—which, though in themselves useless, are the elements of which all discourse is made up.

Further, in the selection of the relation and experiments I conceive I have been a more cautious purveyor than those who have hitherto dealt with natural history.

For I admit nothing but on the faith of eyes, or at least of careful and severe examination; so that nothing is exaggerated for wonder's sake, but what I state is sound and without mixture of fables or vanity. All received or current falsehoods also (which by strange negligence have been allowed for many ages to prevail and become established) I proscribe and brand by name; that the sciences may be no more troubled with them. For it has been well observed that the fables and superstitions and follies which nurses instil into children do serious injury to their minds; and the same consideration makes me anxious, having the management of the childhood as it were of philosophy in its course of natural history, not to let it accustom itself in the beginning to any vanity. Moreover, whenever I come to a new experiment of any subtlety (though it be in my own opinion certain and approved), I nevertheless subjoin a clear account of the manner in which I made it; that men knowing exactly how each point was made out, may see whether there be any error connected with it, and may arouse themselves to devise proofs more trustworthy and exquisite, if such can be found; and finally, I interpose everywhere admonitions and scruples and cautions, with a religious care to eject, repress, and as it were exorcise every kind of phantasm.

Lastly, knowing how much the sight of man's mind is distracted by experience and history, and how hard it is at the first (especially for minds either tender or preoccupied) to become familiar with nature, I not unfrequently subjoin observations of my own, being as the first offers, inclinations, and as it were glances of history towards philosophy; both by way of an assurance to men that they will not be kept for ever tossing on the waves of experience, and also that when the time comes for the intellect to begin its work, it may find everything the more ready. By such a natural history then as I have described, I conceive that a safe and convenient approach may be made to nature, and matter supplied of good quality and well prepared for the understanding to work upon.

And now that we have surrounded the intellect with faithful helps and guards, and got together with most careful selection a regular army of divine works, it may seem that we have no more to do but to proceed to philosophy itself. And yet in a matter so difficult and doubtful there are still some things which it seems necessary to premise, partly for convenience of explanation, partly for present use.

Of these the first is to set forth examples of inquiry and invention according to my method, exhibited by anticipation in some particular subjects; choosing such subjects as are at once the most noble in themselves among those under inquiry, and most different one from another; that there may be an example in every kind. I do not speak of those examples which are joined to the several precepts and rules by way of illustration (for of these I have given plenty in the second part of the work); but I mean actual types and models, by which the entire process of the mind and the whole fabric and order of invention from the beginning to the end, in certain subjects, and those various and remarkable, should be set as it were before the eyes. For I remember that in the mathematics it is easy to follow the demonstration when you have a machine beside you; whereas without that help all appears involved and more subtle than it really is. To examples of this kind,—being in fact nothing more than an application of the second part in detail and at large,—the fourth part of the work is devoted.

The fifth part is for temporary use only, pending the completion of the rest; like interest payable from time to time until the principal be forthcoming. For I do not make so blindly for the end of my journey, as to neglect anything useful that may turn up by the way. And therefore I include in this fifth part such things as I have myself discovered, proved, or added,—not however according to the true rules and methods of interpretation, but by the ordinary use of the understanding in inquiring and discovering. For besides that I hope my speculations may in virtue of my continual conversancy with nature have a value beyond the pretensions of my wit, they will serve in the meantime for wayside inns, in which the mind may rest and refresh itself on its journey to more certain conclusions. Nevertheless I wish it to be understood in the meantime that they are conclusions by which (as not being discovered and proved by the true form of interpretation) I do not at all mean to bind myself. Nor need any one be alarmed at such suspension of judgment, in one who maintains not simply that nothing can be known, but only that nothing can be known except in a certain course and way; and yet establishes provisionally certain degrees of assurance, for use and relief until the mind shall arrive at a knowledge of causes in which it can rest. For even those schools of philosophy which held the absolute impossibility of knowing anything were not inferior to those which took upon them to pronounce. But then they did not provide helps for the sense and understanding, as I have done, but simply took away all their authority: which is quite a different thing—almost the reverse.

The sixth part of my work (to which the rest is subservient and ministrant) discloses and sets forth that philosophy which by the legitimate, chaste, and severe course of inquiry which I have explained and provided is at length developed and established. The completion however of this last part is a thing both above my strength and beyond my hopes. I have made a beginning of the work—a beginning, as I hope, not unimportant:—the fortune of the human race will give the issue;—such an issue, it may be, as in the present condition of things and men's minds cannot easily be conceived or imagined. For the matter in hand is no mere felicity of speculation, but the real business and fortunes of the human race, and all power of operation. For man is but the servant and interpreter of nature: what he does and what he knows is only what he has observed of nature's order in fact or in thought; beyond this he knows nothing and can do nothing. For the chain of causes cannot by any force be loosed or broken, nor can nature be commanded except by being obeyed. And so those twin objects, human Knowledge and human Power, do really meet in one; and it is from ignorance of causes that operation fails.

And all depends on keeping the eye steadily fixed upon the facts of nature and so receiving their images simply as they are. For God forbid that we should give out a dream of our own imagination for a pattern of the world; rather may he graciously grant to us to write an apocalypse or true vision of the footsteps of the Creator imprinted on his creatures.

Therefore do thou, O Father, who gavest the visible light as the first fruits of creation, and didst breathe into the face of man the intellectual light as the crown and consummation thereof, guard and protect this work, which coming from thy goodness returneth to thy glory. Thou when thou turnedst to look upon the works which thy hands had made, sawest that all was very good, and didst rest from thy labours. But man, when he turned to look upon the work which his hands had made, saw that all was vanity and vexation of spirit, and could find no rest therein. Wherefore if we labour in thy works with the sweat of our brows thou wilt make us partakers of thy vision and thy sabbath. Humbly we pray that this mind may be steadfast in us, and that through these our hands, and the hands of others to whom thou shalt give the same spirit, thou wilt vouchsafe to endow the human family with new mercies.

THE TWOO BOOKES OF FRANCIS BACON

OF THE PROFICIENCE AND ADVANCEMENT OF LEARNING DIVINE AND HUMANE.

TO THE KING.

AT LONDON:
Printed for Henrie Tomes, and are to be sold at his shop at Graies Inne Gate in Holborne.
1605.

THE

FIRST BOOK OF FRANCIS BACON

OF THE

PROFICIENCE AND ADVANCEMENT OF LEARNING

DIVINE AND HUMAN.

TO THE KING.

THERE were under the Law (excellent King) both daily sacrifices and freewill offerings; the one proceeding upon ordinary observance, the other upon a devout cheerfulness. In like manner there belongeth to kings from their servants both tribute of duty and presents of affection. In the former of these I hope I shall not live to be wanting, according to my most humble duty, and the good pleasure of your Majesty's employments: for the later, I thought it more respective to make choice of some oblation which might rather refer to the propriety and excellency of your individual person, than to the business of your crown and state.

Wherefore representing your Majesty many times unto my mind, and beholding you not with the inquisitive eye of presumption to discover that which the Scripture telleth me is inscrutable, but with the observant eye of duty and admiration; leaving aside the other parts of your virtue and fortune, I have been touched, yea and possessed with an extreme wonder at those your virtues and faculties which the philosophers call intellectual; the largeness of your capacity, the faithfulness of your memory, the swiftness of your apprehension, the penetration of your judgment, and the facility and order of your elocution: and I have often thought that of all the persons living that I have known, your Majesty were the best instance to make a man of Plato's opinion, that all knowledge is but remembrance, and that the mind of man by nature knoweth all things, and hath but her own native and original notions (which by the strangeness and darkness of this tabernacle of the body are sequestered) again revived and restored: such a light of nature I have observed in your Majesty, and such a readiness to take flame and blaze from the least occasion presented, or the least spark of another's knowledge delivered. And as the Scripture saith of the wisest king, *That his heart was as the sands of the sea;* which though it be one of the largest bodies yet it consisteth of the smallest and finest portions; so hath God given your Majesty a composition of understanding admirable, being able to compass and comprehend the greatest matters, and nevertheless to touch and apprehend the least; whereas it should seem an impossibility in nature for the same instrument to make itself fit for great and small works. And for your gift of speech, I call to mind what Cornelius Tacitus saith of Augustus Cæsar; *Augusto profluens, et quæ principem deceret, eloquentia fuit;* [that his style of speech was flowing and prince-like:[1]] for if we note it well, speech that is uttered

[1] Observe that the translations within brackets are not in the original, but inserted by myself. My reasons for adopting this plan, and the principle upon which I have proceeded in translating, are explained in the preface.

with labour and difficulty, or speech that savoureth of the affectation of art and precepts, or speech that is framed after the imitation of some pattern of eloquence, though never so excellent,—all this has somewhat servile, and holding of the subject. But your Majesty's manner of speech is indeed prince-like, flowing as from a fountain, and yet streaming and branching itself into nature's order, full of facility and felicity, imitating none, and inimitable by any. And as in your civil estate there appeareth to be an emulation and contention of your Majesty's virtue with your fortune; a virtuous disposition with a fortunate regiment; a virtuous expectation (when time was) of your greater fortune, with a prosperous possession thereof in the due time; a virtuous observation of the laws of marriage, with most blessed and happy fruit of marriage; a virtuous and most Christian desire of peace, with a fortunate inclination in your neighbour princes thereunto: so likewise in these intellectual matters, there seemeth to be no less contention between the excellency of your Majesty's gifts of nature and the universality and perfection of your learning. For I am well assured that this which I shall say is no amplification at all, but a positive and measured truth; which is, that there hath not been since Christ's time any king or temporal monarch which hath been so learned in all literature and erudition, divine and human. For let a man seriously and diligently revolve and peruse the succession of the emperors of Rome, of which Cæsar the dictator, who lived some years before Christ, and Marcus Antoninus were the best learned; and so descend to the emperors of Græcia, or of the West, and then to the lines of France, Spain, England, Scotland, and the rest; and he shall find this judgment is truly made. For it seemeth much in a king, if by the compendious extractions of other men's wits and labours he can take hold of any superficial ornaments and shews of learning, or if he countenance and prefer learning and learned men: but to drink indeed of the true fountains of learning, nay to have such a fountain of learning in himself, in a king, and in a king born, is almost a miracle. And the more, because there is met in your Majesty a rare conjunction as well of divine and sacred literature as of profane and human; so as your Majesty standeth invested of that triplicity which in great veneration was ascribed to the ancient Hermes; the power and fortune of a King, the knowledge and illumination of a Priest, and the learning and universality of a Philosopher. This propriety inherent and individual attribute in your Majesty deserveth to be expressed not only in the fame and admiration of the present time, nor in the history or tradition of the ages succeeding; but also in some solid work, fixed memorial, and immortal monument, bearing a character or signature both of the power of a king and the difference and perfection of such a king.

Therefore I did conclude with myself, that I could not make unto your Majesty a better oblation than of some treatise tending to that end; whereof the sum will consist of these two parts: the former concerning the excellency of learning and knowledge, and the excellency of the merit and true glory in the augmentation and propagation thereof; the later, what the particular acts and works are which have been embraced and undertaken for the advancement of learning, and again what defects and undervalues I find in such particular acts; to the end that though I cannot positively or affirmatively advise your Majesty, or propound unto you framed particulars, yet I may excite your princely cogitations to visit the excellent treasure of your own mind, and thence to extract particulars for this purpose agreeable to your magnanimity and wisdom.

In the entrance to the former of these,—to clear the way, and as it were to make silence to have the true testimonies concerning the dignity of learning to be better heard without the interruption of tacit objections,—I think good to deliver it from the discredits and disgraces which it hath received; all from ignorance; but ignorance severally disguised; appearing sometimes in the zeal and jealousy of divines, sometimes in the severity and arrogancy of politiques, and sometimes in the errors and imperfections of learned men themselves.

I hear the former sort say, that knowledge is of those things which are to be accepted of with great limitation and caution; that the aspiring to over-much knowledge was the original temptation and sin, whereupon ensued the fall of man; that knowledge hath in it somewhat of the serpent, and therefore where it entereth into a man it makes him swell,—*Scientia inflat,* [knowledge puffeth up;] that Salomon gives a censure, *That there is no end of making books, and that much reading is weariness of the flesh;* and again in another place, *That in spacious knowledge there is much contristation, and that he that increaseth knowledge increaseth anxiety;* that St. Paul gives a caveat, *That we be not spoiled through vain philosophy;* that experience demonstrates how learned men have been arch-heretics, how learned times have been inclined to atheism, and how the contemplation of second causes doth derogate from our dependence upon God, who is the first cause.

To discover then the ignorance and error of this opinion and the misunderstanding in the grounds thereof, it may well appear these men do not observe or consider that it was not the pure knowledge of nature and universality, a knowledge by the light whereof man did give names unto other creatures in Paradise, as they were brought before him, according unto their proprieties, which gave the occasion to the fall; but it was the proud knowledge of good and evil, with an intent in man to give law unto himself and to depend no more upon God's commandments, which was the form of the temptation. Neither is it any quantity of knowledge how great soever that can make the mind of man to swell; for nothing can fill, much less extend, the soul of man, but God and the contemplation of God; and therefore Salomon speaking of the two principal senses of inquisition, the eye and the ear, affirmeth that the eye is never satisfied with seeing, nor the ear with hearing; and if there be no fulness, then is the continent greater than the content: so of knowledge itself and the mind of man, whereto the senses are but reporters, he defineth likewise in these words, placed after that calendar or ephemerides which he maketh of the diversities of times and seasons for all actions and purposes; and concludeth thus: *God hath made all things beautiful, or decent, in the true return of their seasons: Also he hath placed the world in man's heart, yet cannot man find out the work which God worketh from the beginning to the end:* declaring not obscurely that God hath framed the mind of man as a mirror or glass capable of the image of the universal world, and joyful to receive the impression thereof, as the eye joyeth to receive light; and not only delighted in beholding the variety of things and vicissitude of times, but raised also to find out and discern the ordinances and decrees which throughout all those changes are infallibly observed. And although he doth insinuate that the supreme or summary law of nature, which he calleth *the work which God worketh from the beginning to the end,* is not possible to be found out by man; yet that doth not derogate from the capacity of the mind, but may be referred to the impediments, as of shortness of life, ill conjunction of labours, ill tradition of knowledge over from hand to hand, and many other inconveniences whereunto the condition of man is subject. For that nothing parcel of the world is denied to man's inquiry and invention he doth in another place rule over, when he saith, *The spirit of man is as the lamp of God, wherewith he searcheth the inwardness of all secrets.* If then such be the capacity and receit of the mind of man, it is manifest that there is no danger at all in the proportion or quantity of knowledge, how large soever, lest it should make it swell or out-compass itself; no, but it is merely the quality of knowledge, which be it in quantity more or less, if it be taken without the true corrective thereof, hath in it some nature of venom or malignity, and some effects of that venom, which is ventosity or swelling. This corrective spice, the mixture whereof maketh knowledge so sovereign, is Charity, which the apostle immediately addeth to the former clause; for so he saith, *knowledge bloweth up, but charity buildeth up;* not unlike unto that which he delivereth in another place: *If I spake* (saith he) *with the tongues of men and angels, and had not charity, it were but as a tinkling cymbal;* not but that it is an excellent thing to speak with the tongues of men and angels, but because if it be severed from charity, and not referred to the good of men and mankind, it hath rather a sounding and unworthy glory than a meriting and substantial virtue. And as for that censure of Salomon concerning the excess of writing and reading books and the anxiety of spirit which redoundeth from knowledge, and that admonition of St. Paul, *That we be not seduced by vain philosophy;* let those places be rightly understood, and they do indeed excellently set forth the true bounds and limitations whereby human knowledge is confined and circumscribed; and yet without any such contracting or coarctation, but that it may comprehend all the universal nature of things. For these limitations are three. The first, *that we do not so place our felicity in knowledge, as we forget our mortality.* The second, *that we make application of our knowledge to give ourselves repose and contentment, and not distaste or repining.* The third, *that we do not presume by the contemplation of nature to attain to the mysteries of God.* For as touching the first of these, Salomon doth excellently expound himself in another place of the same book, where he saith; *I saw well that knowledge recedeth as far from ignorance as light doth from darkness, and that the wise man's eyes keep watch in his head, whereas the fool roundeth about in darkness: but withal I learned that the same mortality involveth them both.* And for the second, certain it is, there is no vexation or anxiety of mind which resulteth from knowledge otherwise than merely by accident; for all knowledge and wonder (which is the seed of knowledge) is an impression of pleasure in itself: but when men fall to framing conclusions out of their knowledge, applying it to their particular, and ministering to themselves thereby weak fears or vast desires, there groweth that carefulness and trouble of mind which is spoken of: for then knowledge is no more *Lumen siccum* [a dry light], whereof Heraclitus the profound said, *Lumen siccum optima anima,* [the dry light is the best soul;] but it becometh *Lumen madidum* or *maceratum,* [a light charged with moisture,] being steeped and infused in the humours of the affections. And as for the third point, it deserveth to be a little stood upon and not to be lightly passed over: for if any man shall think by view and inquiry into these sensible and material things to attain that light whereby he may reveal unto himself the nature or will of God, then indeed is he spoiled by vain philosophy: for the contemplation of God's creatures and works produceth (having regard to the works and creatures themselves) knowledge; but having regard to God, no perfect knowledge, but wonder, which is broken knowledge. And therefore it was most aptly said by one of Plato's school, *That the sense of man carrieth a resemblance with the sun, which (as we see) openeth and revealeth all the terrestrial globe; but then again it obscureth and concealeth the stars and celestial globe: so doth the sense discover natural things, but it darkeneth and shutteth up divine.* And hence it is true that it hath proceeded that divers great learned men have been heretical, whilst they have sought to fly up to the secrets of the Deity by the waxen wings of the senses. And as for the conceit that too much knowledge should incline a man to atheism, and that the ignorance of second causes should make a more devout dependence upon God which is the first cause; first, it is good to ask the question which Job asked of his friends, *Will you lie for God, as one man will do for another, to gratify him?* For certain it is that God worketh nothing in nature but by second causes; and if they would have it otherwise believed, it is mere imposture, as it were in favour towards God; and nothing else but to offer to the author of truth the unclean sacrifice of a lie. But farther, it is an assured truth and a conclusion of experience, that a little or superficial knowledge of philosophy may incline the mind of man to atheism, but a farther proceeding therein doth bring the mind back again to religion; for in the entrance of philosophy, when the second causes, which are next unto the senses, do offer themselves to the mind of man, if it dwell and stay there, it may induce some oblivion of the highest cause; but when a man passeth on farther, and seeth the dependence of causes and the works of Providence; then, according to the allegory of the poets, he will easily believe that the highest link of nature's chain must needs be tied to the foot of Jupiter's chair. To conclude therefore, let no man, upon a weak conceit of sobriety or an ill-applied moderation, think or maintain that a man can search too far or be too well studied in the book of God's word or in the book of God's works; divinity or philosophy; but rather let men endeavour an endless progress or proficience in both; only let men beware that they apply both to charity, and not to swelling; to use, and not to ostentation; and again, that they do not unwisely mingle or confound these learnings together.

And as for the disgraces which learning receiveth from politiques, they be of this nature; that learning doth soften men's minds, and makes them more unapt for the honour and exercise of arms; that it doth mar and pervert men's dispositions for matter of government and policy, in making them too curious and irresolute by variety of reading, or too peremptory or positive by strictness of rules and axioms, or too immoderate and overweening by reason of the greatness of examples, or too incompatible and differing from the times by reason of the dissimilitude of examples; or at least that it doth divert men's travails from action and business, and bringeth them to a love of leisure and privateness; and that it doth bring into states a relaxation of discipline, whilst every man is more ready to argue than to obey and execute. Out of this conceit

Cato surnamed the Censor, one of the wisest men indeed that ever lived, when Carneades the philosopher came in embassage to Rome, and that the young men of Rome began to flock about him, being allured with the sweetness and majesty of his eloquence and learning, gave counsel in open senate that they should give him his dispatch with all speed, lest he should infect and inchant the minds and affections of the youth, and at unawares bring in an alteration of the manners and customs of the state. Out of the same conceit or humour did Virgil, turning his pen to the advantage of his country and the disadvantage of his own profession, make a kind of separation between policy and government and between arts and sciences, in the verses so much renowned, attributing and challenging the one to the Romans, and leaving and yielding the other to the Grecians; *Tu regere imperio populos, Romane, memento, Hæ tibi erunt artes*, &c.

[Be thine, O Rome,
With arts of government to rule the nations.]

So likewise we see that Anytus, the accuser of Socrates, laid it as an article of charge and accusation against him that he did with the variety and power of his discourses and disputations withdraw young men from due reverence to the laws and customs of their country; and that he did profess a dangerous and pernicious science, which was to make the worse matter seem the better, and to suppress truth by force of eloquence and speech.

But these and the like imputations have rather a countenance of gravity than any ground of justice; for experience doth warrant that both in persons and in times there hath been a meeting and concurrence in learning and arms, flourishing and excelling in the same men and the same ages. For as for men, there cannot be a better nor the like instance, as of that pair, Alexander the Great and Julius Cæsar the dictator; whereof the one was Aristotle's scholar in philosophy, and the other was Cicero's rival in eloquence; or if any man had rather call for scholars that were great generals than generals that were great scholars, let him take Epaminondas the Theban, or Xenophon the Athenian; whereof the one was the first that abated the power of Sparta, and the other was the first that made way to the overthrow of the monarchy of Persia. And this concurrence is yet more visible in times than in persons, by how much an age is greater object than a man. For both in Ægypt, Assyria, Persia, Græcia, and Rome, the same times that are most renowned for arms are likewise most admired for learning; so that the greatest authors and philosophers and the greatest captains and governors have lived in the same ages. Neither can it otherwise be: for as in man the ripeness of strength of the body and mind cometh much about an age, save that the strength of the body cometh somewhat the more early; so in states, arms and learning, whereof the one correspondeth to the body, the other to the soul of man, have a concurrence or near sequence in times.

And for matter of policy and government, that learning should rather hurt than enable thereunto, is a thing very improbable. We see it is accounted an error to commit a natural body to empiric physicians, which commonly have a few pleasing receits whereupon they are confident and adventurous, but know neither the causes of diseases, nor the complexions of patients, nor peril of accidents, nor the true method of cures. We see it is a like error to rely upon advocates or lawyers which are only men of practice and not grounded in their books, who are many times easily surprised when matter falleth out besides their experience, to the prejudice of the causes they handle. So by like reason it cannot be but a matter of doubtful consequence, if states be managed by empiric statesmen, not well mingled with men grounded in learning. But contrariwise, it is almost without instance contradictory, that ever any government was disastrous that was in the hands of learned governors. For howsoever it hath been ordinary with politic men to extenuate and disable learned men by the names of *Pedantes;* yet in the records of time it appeareth in many particulars, that the governments of princes in minority (notwithstanding the infinite disadvantage of that kind of state) have nevertheless excelled the government of princes of mature age, even for that reason which they seek to traduce, which is, that by that occasion the state hath been in the hands of *Pedantes:* for so was the state of Rome for the first five years, which are so much magnified, during the minority of Nero, in the hands of Seneca, a *Pedanti:* so it was again for ten years space or more, during the minority of Gordianus the younger, with great applause and contentation in the hands of Misitheus, a *Pedanti:* so was it before that, in the minority of Alexander Severus, in like happiness, in hands not much unlike, by reason of the rule of the women, who were aided by the teachers and preceptors. Nay let a man look into the government of the bishops of Rome, as by name into the government of Pius Quintus and Sextus Quintus in our times, who were both at their entrance esteemed but as pedantical friars, and he shall find that such popes do greater things, and proceed upon truer principles of estate, than those which have ascended to the papacy from an education and breeding in affairs of estate and courts of princes; for although men bred in learning are perhaps to seek in points of convenience and accommodating for the present, which the Italians call *ragioni di stato,* whereof the same Pius Quintus could not hear spoken with patience, terming them inventions against religion and the moral virtues; yet on the other side, to recompense that, they are perfect in those same plain grounds of religion, justice, honour, and moral virtue; which if they be well and watchfully pursued, there will be seldom use of those other, no more than of physic in a sound or well-dieted body. Neither can the experience of one man's life furnish examples and precedents for the events of one man's life: for as it happeneth sometimes that the grandchild or other descendant resembleth the ancestor more than the son; so many times occurrences of present times may sort better with ancient examples than with those of the later or immediate times: and lastly, the wit of one man can no more countervail learning than one man's means can hold way with a common purse.

And as for those particular seducements or indispositions of the mind for policy and government, which learning is pretended to insinuate; if it be granted that any such thing be, it must be remembered withal, that learning ministereth in every of them greater strength of medicine or remedy, than it offereth cause of indisposition or infirmity. For if by a secret operation it make men perplexed and irresolute, on the other side by plain precept it teacheth them when and upon what ground to resolve; yea, and how to carry things in suspense without prejudice till they resolve. If it make men positive and regular, it teacheth them what things are in their nature demonstrative, and what are conjectural; and as well the use of distinctions and exceptions, as the latitude of principles and rules. If it mislead by disproportion or dissimilitude of examples, it teacheth men the force of circumstances, the errors of comparisons, and all the cautions of application; so that in all these it doth rectify more effectually than it can pervert. And these medicines it conveyeth into men's minds much more forcibly by the quickness and penetration of examples. For let a man look into the errors of Clement the seventh, so lively described by Guicciardine, who served under him, or into the errors of Cicero painted out by his own pencil in his epistles to Atticus, and he will fly apace from being irresolute. Let him look into the errors of Phocion, and he will beware how he be obstinate or inflexible. Let him but read the fable of Ixion, and it will hold him from being vaporous or imaginative. Let him look into the errors of Cato the second, and he will never be one of the Antipodes, to tread opposite to the present world.

And for the conceit that learning should dispose men to leisure and privateness, and make men slothful; it were a strange thing if that which accustometh the mind to a perpetual motion and agitation should induce slothfulness; whereas contrariwise it may be truly affirmed that no kind of men love business for itself but those that are learned; for other persons love it for profit, as an hireling that loves the work for the wages; or for honour, as because it bareth them up in the eyes of men, and refresheth their reputation which otherwise would wear; or because it putteth them in mind of their fortune, and giveth them occasion to pleasure and displeasure; or because it exerciseth some faculty wherein they take pride, and so entertaineth them in good humour and pleasing conceits toward themselves; or because it advanceth any other their ends. So that as it is said of untrue valours that some men's valours are in the eyes of them that look on, so such men's industries are in the eyes of others, or at least in regard of their own designments; only learned men love business as an action according to nature, as agreeable to health of mind as exercise is to health of body, taking pleasure in the action itself, and not in the purchase: so that of all men they are the most indefatigable, if it be towards any business which can hold or detain their mind.

And if any man be laborious in reading and study and yet idle in business and action, it groweth from some weakness of body or softness of spirit, such as Seneca speaketh of; *Quidam tam sunt umbratiles, ut putent in turbido esse quicquid in luce est,* [there are some men so fond of the shade, that they think they are in trouble whenever they are in the light;] and not of learning. Well may it be that such a point of a man's nature may make him give himself to learning, but it is not learning that breedeth any such point in his nature.

And that learning should take up too much time or leisure; I answer, the most active or busy man that hath been or can be hath (no question) many vacant times of leisure, while he expecteth the tides and returns of business, (except he be either tedious and of no dispatch, or lightly and unworthily ambitious to meddle in things that may be better done by others;) and then the question is but how those spaces and times of leisure shall be filled and spent; whether in pleasures or in studies; as was well answered by Demosthenes to his adversary Æschines, that was a man given to pleasure, and told him *that his orations did smell of the lamp: Indeed* (said Demosthenes) *there is a great difference between the things that you and I do by lamp-light.* So as no man need doubt that learning will expulse business; but rather it will keep and defend the possession of the mind against idleness and pleasure, which otherwise at unawares may enter to the prejudice of both.

Again, for that other conceit that learning should undermine the reverence of laws and government, it is assuredly a mere depravation and calumny without all shadow of truth. For to say that a blind custom of obedience should be a surer obligation than duty taught and understood, it is to affirm that a blind man may tread surer by a guide than a seeing man can by a light. And it is without all controversy that learning doth make the minds of men gentle, generous, maniable, and pliant to government; whereas ignorance makes them churlish, thwart, and mutinous: and the evidence of time doth clear this assertion, considering that the most barbarous, rude, and unlearned times have been most subject to tumults, seditions, and changes.

And as to the judgment of Cato the Censor, he was well punished for his blasphemy against learning, in the same kind wherein he offended; for when he was past threescore years old, he was taken with an extreme desire to go to school again and to learn the Greek tongue, to the end to peruse the Greek authors; which doth well demonstrate, that his former censure of the Grecian learning was rather an affected gravity, than according to the inward sense of his own opinion. And as for Virgil's verses, though it pleased him to brave the world in taking to the Romans the art of empire, and leaving to others the arts of subjects; yet so much is manifest, that the Romans never ascended to that height of empire till the time they had ascended to the height of other arts; for in the time of the two first Cæsars, which had the art of government in greatest perfection, there lived the best poet, Virgilius Maro; the best historiographer, Titus Livius;

the best antiquary, Marcus Varro; and the best, or second orator, Marcus Cicero, that to the memory of man are known. As for the accusation of Socrates, the time must be remembered when it was prosecuted; which was under the thirty tyrants, the most base, bloody, and envious persons that have governed; which revolution of state was no sooner over, but Socrates, whom they had made a person criminal, was made a person heroical, and his memory accumulate with honours divine and human; and those discourses of his, which were then termed corrupting of manners, were after acknowledged for sovereign medicines of the mind and manners, and so have been received ever since till this day. Let this therefore serve for answer to politiques, which in their humorous severity or in their feigned gravity have presumed to throw imputations upon learning; which redargution nevertheless (save that we know not whether our labours may extend to other ages) were not needful for the present, in regard of the love and reverence towards learning which the example and countenance of two so learned princes, queen Elizabeth and your Majesty, being as Castor and Pollux, *lucida sidera,* stars of excellent light and most benign influence, hath wrought in all men of place and authority in our nation.

Now therefore we come to that third sort of discredit or diminution of credit, that groweth unto learning from learned men themselves, which commonly cleaveth fastest. It is either from their fortune, or from their manners, or from the nature of their studies. For the first, it is not in their power; and the second is accidental; the third only is proper to be handled. But because we are not in hand with true measure, but with popular estimation and conceit, it is not amiss to speak somewhat of the two former. The derogations therefore which grow to learning from the fortune or condition of learned men, are either in respect of scarcity of means, or in respect of privateness of life and meanness of employments.

Concerning want, and that it is the case of learned men usually to begin with little and not to grow rich so fast as other men, by reason they convert not their labours chiefly to lucre and increase; it were good to leave the common place in commendation of poverty to some friar to handle, to whom much was attributed by Machiavel in this point, when he said, *That the kingdom of the clergy had been long before at an end, if the reputation and reverence towards the poverty of friars had not borne out the scandal of the superfluities and excesses of bishops and prelates.* So a man might say that the felicity and delicacy of princes and great persons had long since turned to rudeness and barbarism, if the poverty of learning had not kept up civility and honour of life. But without any such advantages, it is worthy the observation what a reverend and honoured thing poverty of fortune was for some ages in the Roman state, which nevertheless was a state without paradoxes. For we see what Titus Livius saith in his introduction: *Cæterum aut me amor negotii suscepti fallit, aut nulla unquam respublica nec major, nec sanctior, nec bonis exemplis ditior fuit; nec in quam tam seræ avaritia luxuriaque immigraverint; nec ubi tantus ac tam diu paupertati ac parsimoniæ honos fuerit:* [that if affection for his subject did not deceive him, there was never any state in the world either greater or purer or richer in good examples; never any into which avarice and luxury made their way so late; never any in which poverty and frugality were for so long a time held in so great honour]. We see likewise, after that the state of Rome was not itself but did degenerate, how that person that took upon him to be counsellor to Julius Cæsar after his victory, where to begin his restoration of the state, maketh it of all points the most summary to take away the estimation of wealth: *Verum hæc et omnia mala pariter cum honore pecuniæ desinent; si neque magistratus, neque alia vulgo cupienda, venalia erunt:* [but these and all other evils (he says) will cease as soon as the worship of money ceases; which will come to pass when neither magistracies nor other things that are objects of desire to the vulgar shall be to be had for money]. To conclude this point, as it was truly said that *rubor est virtutis color,* [a blush is virtue's colour,] though sometime it come from vice; so it may be fitly said that *paupertas est virtutis fortuna,* [poverty is virtue's fortune,] though sometime it may proceed from misgovernment and accident. Surely Salomon hath pronounced it, both in censure, *Qui festinat ad divitias non erit insons,* [he that maketh haste to be rich shall not be innocent;] and in precept, *Buy the truth, and sell it not; and so of wisdom and knowledge;* judging that means were to be spent upon learning, and not learning to be applied to means. And as for the privateness or obscureness (as it may be in vulgar estimation accounted) of life of contemplative men; it is a theme so common to extol a private life, not taxed with sensuality and sloth, in comparison and to the disadvantage of a civil life, for safety, liberty, pleasure, and dignity, or at least freedom from indignity, as no man handleth it but handleth it well; such a consonancy it hath to men's conceits in the expressing and to men's consents in the allowing. This only I will add, that learned men forgotten in states, and not living in the eyes of men, are like the images of Cassius and Brutus in the funeral of Junia; of which not being represented, as many others were, Tacitus saith, *Eo ipso præfulgebant, quod non visebantur;* [they had the preëminence over all—in being left out].

And for meanness of employment, that which is most traduced to contempt is that the government of youth is commonly allotted to them; which age, because it is the age of least authority, it is transferred to the disesteeming of those employments wherein youth is conversant, and which are conversant about youth. But how unjust this traducement is (if you will reduce things from popularity of opinion to measure of reason) may appear in that we see men are more curious what they put into a new vessel than into a vessel seasoned, and what mould they lay about a young plant than about a plant corroborate; so as the weakest terms and times of all things use to have the best applications and helps. And will you hearken to the Hebrew Rabbins? *Your young men shall see visions, and your old men shall dream dreams;* say they youth is the worthier age, for that visions are nearer apparitions of God than dreams. And let it be noted, that howsoever the conditions of life of *Pedantes* have been scorned upon theatres, as the ape of tyranny; and that the modern looseness or negligence hath taken no due regard to the choice of school-masters and tutors; yet the ancient wisdom of the best times did always make a just complaint that states were too busy with their laws and too negligent in point of education: which excellent part of ancient discipline hath been in some sort revived of late times by the colleges of the Jesuits; of whom, although in regard of their superstition I may say, *quo meliores, eo deteriores,* [the better the worse;] yet in regard of this, and some other points concerning human learning and moral matters, I may say, as Agesilaus said to his enemy

Pharnabazus, *talis quum sis, utinam noster esses,* [they are so good that I wish they were on our side]. And thus much touching the discredits drawn from the fortunes of learned men.

As touching the manners of learned men, it is a thing personal and individual: and no doubt there be amongst them, as in other professions, of all temperatures: but yet so as it is not without truth which is said that *abeunt studia in mores,* studies have an influence and operation upon the manners of those that are conversant in them.

But upon an attentive and indifferent review, I for my part cannot find any disgrace to learning can proceed from the manners of learned men; not inherent to them as they are learned; except it be a fault (which was the supposed fault of Demosthenes, Cicero, Cato the second, Seneca, and many more) that because the times they read of are commonly better than the times they live in, and the duties taught better than the duties practised, they contend sometimes too far to bring things to perfection, and to reduce the corruption of manners to honesty of precepts or examples of too great height. And yet hereof they have caveats enough in their own walks. For Solon, when he was asked whether he had given his citizens the best laws, answered wisely, *Yea of such as they would receive:* and Plato, finding that his own heart could not agree with the corrupt manners of his country, refused to bear place or office; saying, *That a man's country was to be used as his parents were, that is, with humble persuasions, and not with contestations:* and Cæsar's counsellor put in the same caveat, *Non ad vetera instituta revocans quæ jampridem corruptis moribus ludibrio sunt:* [not to attempt to bring things back to the original institution, now that by reason of the corruption of manners the ancient simplicity and purity had fallen into contempt:] and Cicero noteth this error directly in Cato the second, when he writes to his friend Atticus; *Cato optime sentit, sed nocet interdum reipublicæ; loquitur enim tanquam in republica Platonis, non tanquam in fæce Romuli:* [Cato means excellently well; but he does hurt sometimes to the state; for he talks as if it were Plato's republic that we are living in, and not the dregs of Romulus:] and the same Cicero doth excuse and expound the philosophers for going too far and being too exact in their prescripts, when he saith, *Isti ipsi præceptores virtutis et magistri videntur fines officiorum paulo longius quam natura vellet protulisse, ut cum ad ultimum animo contendissemus, ibi tamen, ubi oportet, consisteremus:* [that they had set the points of duty somewhat higher than nature would well bear; meaning belike to allow for shortcomings, and that our endeavours aiming beyond the mark and falling short, should light at the right place:] and yet himself might have said, *Monitis sum minor ipse meis,* [that he fell short of his own precepts]; for it was his own fault, though not in so extreme a degree.

Another fault likewise much of this kind hath been incident to learned men; which is, that they have esteemed the preservation, good, and honour of their countries or masters before their own fortunes or safeties. For so saith Demosthenes unto the Athenians: *If it please you to note it, my counsels unto you are not such whereby I should grow great amongst you, and you become little amongst the Grecians: but they be of that nature, as they are sometimes not good for me to give, but are always good for you to follow.* And so Seneca, after he had consecrated that *Quinquennium Neronis* to the eternal glory of learned governors, held on his honest and loyal course of good and free counsel, after his master grew extremely corrupt in his government. Neither can this point otherwise be; for learning endueth men's minds with a true sense of the frailty of their persons, the casualty of their fortunes, and the dignity of their soul and vocation; so that it is impossible for them to esteem that any greatness of their own fortunes can be a true or worthy end of their being and ordainment; and therefore are desirous to give their account to God, and so likewise to their masters under God (as kings and the states that they serve), in these words; *Ecce tibi lucrefeci,* and not *Ecce mihi lucrefeci,* ['Lo, I have gained for thee,' not 'Lo, I have gained for myself:'] whereas the corrupter sort of mere politiques, that have not their thoughts established by learning in the love and apprehension of duty, nor never look abroad into universality, do refer all things to themselves, and thrust themselves into the centre of the world, as if all lines should meet in them and their fortunes; never caring in all tempests what becomes of the ship of estates, so they may save themselves in the cockboat of their own fortune; whereas men that feel the weight of duty, and know the limits of self-love, use to make good their places and duties, though with peril. And if they stand in seditious and violent alterations, it is rather the reverence which many times both adverse parts do give to honesty, than any versatile advantage of their own carriage. But for this point of tender sense and fast obligation of duty, which learning doth endue the mind withal, howsoever fortune may tax it and many in the depth of their corrupt principles may despise it, yet it will receive an open allowance, and therefore needs the less disproof or excusation.

Another fault incident commonly to learned men,

which may be more probably defended than truly denied, is that they fail sometimes in applying themselves to particular persons; which want of exact application ariseth from two causes; the one, because the largeness of their mind can hardly confine itself to dwell in the exquisite observation or examination of the nature and customs of one person: for it is a speech for a lover and not for a wise man, *Satis magnum alter alteri theatrum sumus,* [each is to other a theatre large enough]. Nevertheless I shall yield, that he that cannot contract the sight of his mind as well as disperse and dilate it, wanteth a great faculty. But there is a second cause, which is no inability but a rejection upon choice and judgment. For the honest and just bounds of observation by one person upon another extend no farther but to understand him sufficiently, whereby not to give him offence, or whereby to be able to give him faithful counsel, or whereby to stand upon reasonable guard and caution in respect of a man's self: but to be speculative into another man, to the end to know how to work him or wind him or govern him, proceedeth from a heart that is double and cloven, and not entire and ingenuous; which as in friendship it is want of integrity, so towards princes or superiors is want of duty. For the custom of the Levant, which is, that subjects do forbear to gaze or fix their eyes upon princes, is in the outward ceremony barbarous; but the moral is good: for men ought not by cunning and bent observations to pierce and penetrate into the hearts of kings, which the Scripture hath declared to be inscrutable.

There is yet another fault (with which I will conclude this part) which is often noted in learned men, that they do many times fail to observe decency and discretion in their behaviour and carriage, and commit errors in small and ordinary points of action; so as the vulgar sort of capacities do make a judgment of them in greater matters by that which they find wanting in them in smaller. But this consequence doth oft deceive men; for which I do refer them over to that which was said by Themistocles, arrogantly and uncivilly being applied to himself out of his own mouth, but being applied to the general state of this question pertinently and justly; when being invited to touch a lute, he said *he could not fiddle but he could make a small town a great state.* So no doubt many may be well seen in the passages of government and policy, which are to seek in little and punctual occasions. I refer them also to that which Plato said of his master Socrates, whom he compared to the gally-pots of apothecaries, which on the outside had apes and owls and antiques, but contained within sovereign and precious liquors and confections; acknowledging that to an external report he was not without superficial levities and deformities, but was inwardly replenished with excellent virtues and powers. And so much touching the point of manners of learned men.

But in the mean time I have no purpose to give allowance to some conditions and courses base and unworthy, wherein diverse professors of learning have wronged themselves and gone too far; such as were those trencher philosophers, which in the later age of the Roman state were usually in the houses of great persons, being little better than solemn parasites; of which kind, Lucian maketh a merry description of the philosopher that the great lady took to ride with her in her coach, and would needs have him carry her little dog, which he doing officiously and yet uncomely, the page scoffed, and said, *That he doubted the philosopher of a Stoic would turn to be a Cynic.* But above all the rest, the gross and palpable flattery whereunto many (not unlearned) have abased and abused their wits and pens, turning (as Du Bartas saith) Hecuba into Helena and Faustina into Lucretia, hath most diminished the price and estimation of learning. Neither is the moral dedication of books and writings, as to patrons, to be commended; for that books (such as are worthy the name of books) ought to have no patrons but truth and reason; and the ancient custom was to dedicate them only to private and equal friends, or to intitle the books with their names; or if to kings and great persons, it was to some such as the argument of the book was fit and proper for. But these and the like courses may deserve rather reprehension than defence.

Not that I can tax or condemn the morigeration or application of learned men to men in fortune. For the answer was good that Diogenes made to one that asked him in mockery, *How it came to pass that philosophers were the followers of rich men, and not rich men of philosophers?* He answered soberly, and yet sharply, *Because the one sort knew what they had need of, and the other did not.* And of the like nature was the answer which Aristippus made, when having a petition to Dionysius and no ear given to him, he fell down at his feet, whereupon Dionysius staid and gave him the hearing and granted it; and afterward some person tender on the behalf of philosophy, reproved Aristippus that he would offer the profession of philosophy such an indignity, as for a private suit to fall at a tyrant's feet: but he answered, *It was not his fault, but it was the fault of Dionysius, that had his ears in his feet.* Neither was it accounted weakness, but discretion, in him that would not dispute his best with Adrianus Cæsar; excusing himself, *That it was reason to yield to him that commanded thirty legions.*

These and the like applications and stooping to points of necessity and convenience cannot be disallowed; for though they may have some outward baseness, yet in a judgment truly made they are to be accounted submissions to the occasions and not to the person.

Now I proceed to those errors and vanities which have intervened amongst the studies themselves of the learned; which is that which is principal and proper to the present argument; wherein my purpose is not to make a justification of the errors, but, by a censure and separation of the errors, to make a justification of that which is good and sound, and to deliver that from the aspersion of the other. For we see that it is the manner of men to scandalize and deprave that which retaineth the state and virtue, by taking advantage upon that which is corrupt and degenerate: as the Heathens in the primitive church used to blemish and taint the Christians with the faults and corruptions of heretics. But nevertheless I have no meaning at this time to make any exact animadversion of the errors and impediments in matters of learning which are more secret and remote from vulgar opinion; but only to speak unto such as do fall under, or near unto, a popular observation.

There be therefore chiefly three vanities in studies, whereby learning hath been most traduced. For those things we do esteem vain, which are either false or frivolous, those which either have no truth or no use: and those persons we esteem vain, which are either credulous or curious; and curiosity is either in matter or words: so that in reason as well as in experience, there fall out to be these three distempers (as I may term them) of learning; the first, fantastical learning; the second, contentious learning; and the last, delicate learning; vain imaginations, vain altercations, and vain affectations; and with the last I will begin. Martin Luther, conducted (no doubt) by an higher Providence, but in discourse of reason finding what a province he had undertaken against the Bishop of Rome and the degenerate traditions of the church, and finding his own solitude being no ways aided by the opinions of his own time, was enforced to awake all antiquity, and to call former times to his succors, to make a party against the present time; so that the ancient authors, both in divinity and in humanity, which had long time slept in libraries, began generally to be read and revolved. This by consequence did draw on a necessity of a more exquisite travail in the languages original wherein those authors did write, for the better understanding of those authors and the better advantage of pressing and applying their words. And thereof grew again a delight in their manner of style and phrase, and an admiration of that kind of writing; which was much furthered and precipitated by the enmity and opposition that the propounders of those (primitive but seeming new) opinions had against the schoolmen; who were generally of the contrary part, and whose writings were altogether in a differing style and form; taking liberty to coin and frame new terms of art to express their own sense and to avoid circuit of speech, without regard to the pureness, pleasantness, and (as I may call it) lawfulness of the phrase or word. And again, because the great labour then was with the people (of whom the Pharisees were wont to say, *Execrabilis ista turba, quæ non novit legem,*) [the wretched crowd that has not known the law,] for the winning and persuading of them, there grew of necessity in chief price and request eloquence and variety of discourse, as the fittest and forciblest access into the capacity of the vulgar sort. So that these four causes concurring, the admiration of ancient authors, the hate of the schoolmen, the exact study of languages, and the efficacy of preaching, did bring in an affectionate study of eloquence and copie of speech, which then began to flourish. This grew speedily to an excess; for men began to hunt more after words than matter; and more after the choiceness of the phrase, and the round and clean composition of the sentence, and the sweet falling of the clauses, and the varying and illustration of their works with tropes and figures, than after the weight of matter, worth of subject, soundness of argument, life of invention, or depth of judgment. Then grew the flowing and watery vein of Osorius, the Portugal bishop, to be in price. Then did Sturmius spend such infinite and curious pains upon Cicero the orator and Hermogenes the rhetorician, besides his own books of periods and imitation and the like. Then did Car of Cambridge, and Ascham, with their lectures and writings, almost deify Cicero and Demosthenes, and allure all young men that were studious unto that delicate and polished kind of learning. Then did Erasmus take occasion to make the scoffing echo; *Decem annos consumpsi in legendo Cicerone,* [I have spent ten years in reading Cicero:] and the echo answered in Greek, *one, Asine.* Then grew the learning of the schoolmen to be utterly despised as barbarous. In sum, the whole inclination and bent of those times was rather towards copie than weight.

Here therefore [is] the first distemper of learning, when men study words and not matter: whereof though I have represented an example of late times, yet it has been and will be *secundum majus et minus* in all time. And how is it possible but this should have an operation to discredit learning, even with vulgar capacities, when they see learned men's works like the first letter of a patent or limned book; which though it hath large flourishes, yet it is but a letter? It seems to me that Pygmalion's frenzy is a good emblem or portraiture of this vanity: for words are but the images of matter; and except they have life of reason and invention, to fall in love with them is all one as to fall in love with a picture.

But yet notwithstanding it is a thing not hastily to be condemned, to clothe and adorn the obscurity even of philosophy itself with sensible and plausible elocution. For hereof we have great examples in Xenophon, Cicero, Seneca, Plutarch, and of Plato also in some degree; and hereof likewise there is great use; for surely to the severe inquisition of truth, and the deep progress into philosophy, it is some hinderance; because it is too early satisfactory to the mind of man, and quencheth the desire of further search, before we come to a just period; but then if a man be to have any use of such knowledge in civil occasions, of conference, counsel, persuasion, discourse, or the like; then shall he find it prepared to his hands in those authors which write in that manner. But the excess of this is so justly contemptible, that as Hercules, when he saw the image of Adonis, Venus' minion, in a temple, said in disdain, *Nil sacri es,* [you are no divinity;] so there is none of Hercules' followers in learning, that is, the more severe and laborious sort of inquiries into truth, but will despise those delicacies and affectations, as indeed capable of no divineness. And thus much of the first disease or distemper of learning.

The second, which followeth, is in nature worse than the former; for as substance of matter is better than beauty of words, so contrariwise vain matter is worse than vain words: wherein it seemeth the reprehension of St. Paul was not only proper for those times, but prophetical for the times following; and not only respective to divinity, but extensive to all knowledge: *Devita profanas vocum novitates, et oppositiones falsi nominis scientæ:* [shun profane novelties of terms and oppositions of science falsely so called]. For he assigneth two marks and badges of suspected and falsified science; the one, the novelty and strangeness of terms; the other, the strictness of positions, which of necessity doth induce oppositions, and so questions and altercations. Surely, like as many substances in nature which are solid do putrefy and corrupt into worms, so it is the property of good and sound knowledge to putrefy and dissolve into a number of subtile, idle, unwholesome, and (as I may term them) vermiculate questions, which have indeed a kind of quickness and life of spirit, but no soundness of matter or goodness of quality. This kind of degenerate learning did chiefly reign amongst the schoolmen; who having sharp and strong wits, and abundance of leisure, and small variety of reading; but their wits being shut up in the cells of a few authors (chiefly Aristotle their dictator) as their persons were shut up in the cells of monasteries and colleges; and knowing little history, either of nature or time; did out of no great quantity of matter, and infinite agitation of wit, spin out unto us those laborious webs of learning which are extant in their books. For the wit and mind of man, if it work upon matter, which is the contemplation of the creatures of God, worketh according to the stuff, and is limited thereby; but if it work upon itself, as the spider worketh his web, then it is endless, and brings forth indeed cobwebs of learning, admirable for the fineness of thread and work, but of no substance or profit.

This same unprofitable subtility or curiosity is of two

sorts; either in the subject itself that they handle, when it is a fruitless speculation or controversy, (whereof there are no small number both in divinity and philosophy,) or in the manner or method of handling of a knowledge; which amongst them was this; upon every particular position or assertion to frame objections, and to those objections, solutions; which solutions were for the most part not confutations, but distinctions: whereas indeed the strength of all sciences is, as the strength of the old man's faggot, in the bond. For the harmony of a science, supporting each part the other, is and ought to be the true and brief confutation and suppression of all the smaller sort of objections; but on the other side, if you take out every axiom, as the sticks of the faggot, one by one, you may quarrel with them and bend them and break them at your pleasure: so that as was said of Seneca, *Verborum minutiis rerum frangit pondera,* [that he broke up the weight and mass of the matter by verbal points and niceties;] so a man may truly say of the schoolmen, *Quæstionum minutiis scientiarum frangunt soliditatem;* [they broke up the solidity and coherency of the sciences by the minuteness and nicety of their questions]. For were it not better for a man in a fair room to set up one great light, or branching candlestick of lights, than to go about with a small watch candle into every corner? And such is their method, that rests not so much upon evidence of truth proved by arguments, authorities, similitudes, examples, as upon particular confutations and solutions of every scruple, cavillation, and objection; breeding for the most part one question as fast it solveth another; even as in the former resemblance, when you carry the light into one corner, you darken the rest: so that the fable and fiction of Scylla seemeth to be a lively image of this kind of philosophy or knowledge; which was transformed into a comely virgin for the upper parts; but then *Candida succinctam latrantibus inguina monstris,* [there were barking monsters all about her loins:] so the generalities of the schoolmen are for a while good and proportionable; but then when you descend into their distinctions and decisions, instead of a fruitful womb for the use and benefit of man's life, they end in monstrous altercations and barking questions. So as it is not possible but this quality of knowledge must fall under popular contempt, the people being apt to contemn truth upon occasion of controversies and altercations, and to think they are all out of their way which never meet: and when they see such digladiation about subtilities and matter of no use nor moment, they easily fall upon that judgment of Dionysius of Syracusa, *Verba ista sunt senum otiosorum,* [it is the talk of old men that have nothing to do].

Notwithstanding certain it is, that if those schoolmen to their great thirst of truth and unwearied travail of wit had joined variety and universality of reading and contemplation, they had proved excellent lights, to the great advancement of all learning and knowledge. But as they are, they are great undertakers indeed, and fierce with dark keeping; but as in the inquiry of the divine truth their pride inclined to leave the oracle of God's word and to vanish in the mixture of their own inventions, so in the inquisition of nature they ever left the oracle of God's works and adored the deceiving and deformed images which the unequal mirror of their own minds or a few received authors or principles did represent unto them. And thus much for the second disease of learning.

For the third vice or disease of learning, which concerneth deceit or untruth, it is of all the rest the foulest; as that which doth destroy the essential form of knowledge, which is nothing but a representation of truth: for the truth of being and the truth of knowing are one, differing no more than the direct beam and the beam reflected. This vice therefore buncheth itself into two sorts; delight in deceiving, and aptness to be deceived; imposture and credulity; which, although they appear to be of a diverse nature, the one seeming to proceed of cunning, and the other of simplicity, yet certainly they do for the most part concur: for as the verse noteth,

Percontatorem fugito, nam garrulus idem est,

an inquisitive man is a prattler, so upon the like reason a credulous man is a deceiver: as we see it in fame, that he that will easily believe rumours will as easily augment rumours and add somewhat to them of his own; which Tacitus wisely noteth, when he saith, *Fingunt simul creduntque,* [as fast as they believe one tale they make another:] so great an affinity hath fiction and belief.

This facility of credit, and accepting or admitting things weakly authorized or warranted, is of two kinds, according to the subject: for it is either a belief of history (as the lawyers speak, matter of fact), or else of matter of art and opinion. As to the former, we see the experience and inconvenience of this error in ecclesiastical history; which hath too easily received and registered reports and narrations of miracles wrought by martyrs, hermits, or monks of the desert, and other holy men, and their relics, shrines, chapels, and images: which though they had a passage for a time, by the ignorance of the people, the superstitious simplicity of some, and the politic toleration of others, holding them but as divine poesies; yet after a period of time, when the mist began to clear up, they grew to be esteemed but as old wives' fables, impostures of the clergy, illusions of spirits, and badges of antichrist, to the great scandal and detriment of religion.

So in natural history, we see there hath not been that choice and judgment used as ought to have been; as may appear in the writings of Plinius, Cardanus, Albertus, and divers of the Arabians; being fraught with much fabulous matter, a great part not only untried but notoriously untrue, to the great derogation of the credit of natural philosophy with the grave and sober kind of wits. Wherein the wisdom and integrity of Aristotle is worthy to be observed; that having made so diligent and exquisite a history of living creatures, hath mingled it sparingly with any vain or feigned matter; and yet on the other side hath cast all prodigious narrations which he thought worthy the recording into one book; excellently discerning that matter of manifest truth, such whereupon observation and rule was to be built, was not to be mingled or weakened with matter of doubtful credit; and yet again that rareties and reports that seem uncredible are not to be suppressed or denied to the memory of men.

And as for the facility of credit which is yielded to arts and opinions, it is likewise of two kinds; either when too much belief is attributed to the arts themselves, or to certain authors in any art. The sciences themselves which have had better intelligence and confederacy with the imagination of men than with his reason, are three in number; Astrology, Natural Magic, and Alchemy; of which sciences nevertheless the ends or pretences are noble. For astrology pretendeth to discover that correspondence or concatenation which is between the superior globe and the inferior: natural magic pretendeth to call and reduce natural philosophy from variety of speculations to the magnitude of works: and alchemy pretendeth to make separation of all the unlike parts of bodies which in mixtures of nature are incorporate. But the derivations and prosecutions to these ends, both in the theories and in the practices are full of error and vanity; which the great professors themselves have sought to veil over and conceal by enigmatical writings, and referring themselves to auricular traditions, and such other devices to save the credit of impostures. And yet surely to alchemy this right is due, that it may be compared to the husbandman whereof Æsop makes the fable, that when he died told his sons that he had left unto them gold buried under ground in his vineyard; and they digged over all the ground, and gold they found none, but by reason of their stirring and digging the mould about the roots of their vines, they had a great vintage the year following: so assuredly the search and stir to make gold hath brought to light a great number of good and fruitful inventions and experiments, as well for the disclosing of nature as for the use of man's life.

And as for the overmuch credit that hath been given unto authors in sciences, in making them dictators, that their words should stand, and not counsels to give advice; the damage is infinite that sciences have received thereby, as the principal cause that hath kept them low, at a stay without growth or advancement. For hence it hath comen that in arts mechanical the first deviser comes shortest, and time addeth and perfecteth; but in sciences the first author goeth furthest, and time leeseth and corrupteth. So we see, artillery, sailing, printing, and the like, were grossly managed at the first, and by time accommodated and refined; but contrariwise the philosophies and sciences of Aristotle, Plato, Democritus, Hippocrates, Euclides, Archimedes, of most vigour at the first, and by time degenerate and imbased; whereof the reason is no other, but that in the former many wits and industries have contributed in one; and in the later many wits and industries have been spent about the wit of some one, whom many times they have rather depraved than illustrated. For as water will not ascend higher than the level of the first spring-head from whence it descendeth, so knowledge derived from Aristotle, and exempted from liberty of examination, will not rise again higher than the knowledge of Aristotle. And therefore, although the position be good, *Oportet discentem credere,* [a man who is learning must be content to believe what he is told,] yet it must be coupled with this, *Oportet edoctum judicare,* [when he has learned it he must exercise his judgment and see whether it be worthy of belief;] for disciples do owe unto masters only a temporary belief and a suspension of their own judgment until they be fully instructed, and not an absolute resignation or perpetual captivity: and therefore to conclude this point, I will say no more but, so let great authors have their due, as time which is the author of authors be not deprived of his due, which is further and further to discover truth. Thus have I gone over these three diseases of learning; besides the which, there are some other rather peccant humours than formed diseases, which nevertheless are not so secret and intrinsic but that they fall under a popular observation and traducement, and therefore are not to be passed over.

The first of these is the extreme affecting of two extremities; the one Antiquity, the other Novelty: wherein it seemeth the children of time do take after the nature and malice of the father. For as he devoureth his children, so one of them seeketh to devour and suppress the other; while antiquity envieth there should be new additions, and novelty cannot be content to add but it must deface. Surely the advice of the prophet is the true direction in this matter, *State super vias antiquas, et videte quænam sit via recta et bona, et ambulate in ea:* [stand ye in the old ways, and see which is the good way, and walk therein]. Antiquity deserveth that reverence, that men should make a stand thereupon, and discover what is the best way; but when the discovery is well taken, then to make progression. And to speak truly, *Antiquitas sæculi juventus mundi.* These times are the ancient times, when the world is ancient, and not those which we account ancient *ordine retrogrado,* by a computation backward from ourselves.

Another error, induced by the former, is a distrust that any thing should be now to be found out, which the world should have missed and passed over so long time; as if the same objection were to be made to time that Lucian maketh to Jupiter and other the heathen gods, of which he wondereth that they begot so many children in old time and begot none in his time, and asketh whether they were become septuagenary, or whether the law *Pappia,* made against old men's marriages, had restrained them. So it seemeth men doubt lest time is become past children and generation; wherein contrariwise we see commonly the levity and unconstancy of men's judgments, which, till a matter be done, wonder that it can be done; and as soon as it is done, wonder again that it was no sooner done; as we see in the expedition of Alexander into Asia, which at first was prejudged as a vast and impossible enterprise; and yet afterwards it pleaseth Livy to make no more of it than this, *Nil aliud quàm bene ausus vana contemnere:* [it was but taking courage to despise vain apprehensions]. And the same happened to Columbus in the western navigation. But in intellectual matters it is much more common; as may be seen in most of the propositions of Euclid, which till they be demonstrate, they seem strange to our assent; but being demonstrate, our mind accepteth of them by a kind of relation (as the lawyers speak) as if we had known them before.

Another error, that hath also some affinity with the former, is a conceit that of former opinions or sects, after variety and examination, the best hath still prevailed and suppressed the rest; so as if a man should begin the labour of a new search, he were but like to light upon somewhat formerly rejected, and by rejection brought into oblivion: as if the multitude, or the wisest for the multitude's sake, were not ready to give passage rather to that which is popular and superficial than to that which is substantial and profound; for the truth is, that time seemeth to be of the nature of a river or stream, which carrieth down to us that which is light and blown up, and sinketh and drowneth that which is weighty and solid.

Another error, of a diverse nature from all the former, is the over-early and peremptory reduction of knowledge into arts and methods; from which time commonly sciences receive small or no augmentation. But as young men, when they knit and shape perfectly, do seldom grow to a further stature; so knowledge, while it is in aphorisms and observations, it is in growth; but when it once is comprehended in exact methods, it may perchance be further polished and illustrate, and accommodated for use and practice; but it increaseth no more in bulk and substance.

Another error, which doth succeed that which we

last mentioned, is that after the distribution of particular arts and sciences, men have abandoned universality, or *philosophia prima;* which cannot but cease and stop all progression. For no perfect discovery can be made upon a flat or a level: neither is it possible to discover the more remote and deeper parts of any science, if you stand but upon the level of the same science, and ascend not to a higher science.

Another error hath proceeded from too great a reverence, and a kind of adoration of the mind and understanding of man; by means whereof men have withdrawn themselves too much from the contemplation of nature and the observations of experience, and have tumbled up and down in their own reason and conceits. Upon these intellectualists, which are notwithstanding commonly taken for the most sublime and divine philosophers, Heraclitus gave a just censure, saying, *Men sought truth in their own little worlds, and not in the great and common world;* for they disdain to spell and so by degrees to read in the volume of God's works; and contrariwise by continual meditation and agitation of wit do urge and as it were invocate their own spirits to divine and give oracles unto them, whereby they are deservedly deluded.

Another error that hath some connexion with this later is, that men have used to infect their meditations, opinions, and doctrines, with some conceits which they have most admired, or some sciences which they have most applied; and given all things else a tincture according to them, utterly untrue and unproper. So hath Plato intermingled his philosophy with theology, and Aristotle with logic, and the second school of Plato, Proclus and the rest, with the mathematics. For these were the arts which had a kind of primogeniture with them severally. So have the alchemists made a philosophy out of a few experiments of the furnace; and Gilbertus, our countryman, hath made a philosophy out of the observations of a loadstone. So Cicero, when, reciting the several opinions of the nature of the soul, he found a musician that held the soul was but a harmony, saith pleasantly, *Hic ab arte sua non recessit, &c.* [he was constant to his own art]. But of these conceits Aristotle speaketh seriously and wisely, when he saith, *Qui respiciunt ad pauca de facili pronunciant:* [they who take only a few points into account find it easy to pronounce judgment].

Another error is an impatience of doubt, and haste to assertion without due and mature suspension of judgment. For the two ways of contemplation are not unlike the two ways of action commonly spoken of by the ancients; the one plain and smooth in the beginning, and in the end impassable; the other rough and troublesome in the entrance, but after a while fair and even. So it is in contemplation; if a man will begin with certainties, he shall end in doubts; but if he will be content to begin with doubts, he shall end in certainties.

Another error is in the manner of the tradition and delivery of knowledge, which is for the most part magistral and peremptory, and not ingenuous and faithful; in a sort as may be soonest believed, and not easiliest examined. It is true that in compendious treatises for practice that form is not to be disallowed. But in the true handling of knowledge, men ought not to fall either on the one side into the vein of Velleius the Epicurean, *Nil tam metuens, quàm ne dubitare aliqua de re videretur,* [who feared nothing so much as the seeming to be in doubt about anything,] nor on the other side into Socrates his ironical doubting of all things; but to propound things sincerely, with more or less asseveration, as they stand in a man's own judgment proved more or less.

Other errors there are in the scope that men propound to themselves, whereunto they bend their endeavours; for whereas the more constant and devote kind of professors of any science ought to propound to themselves to make some additions to their science, they convert their labours to aspire to certain second prizes; as to be a profound interpreter or commenter, to be a sharp champion or defender, to be a methodical compounder or abridger; and so the patrimony of knowledge cometh to be sometimes improved, but seldom augmented.

But the greatest error of all the rest is the mistaking or misplacing of the last or furthest end of knowledge. For men have entered into a desire of learning and knowledge, sometimes upon a natural curiosity and inquisitive appetite; sometimes to entertain their minds with variety and delight; sometimes for ornament and reputation; and sometimes to enable them to victory of wit and contradiction; and most times for lucre and profession; and seldom sincerely to give a true account of their gift of reason, to the benefit and use of men: as if there were sought in knowledge a couch, whereupon to rest a searching and restless spirit; or a terrace, for a wandering and variable mind to walk up and down with a fair prospect; or a tower of state, for a proud mind to raise itself upon; or a fort or commanding ground, for strife and contention; or a shop, for profit or sale; and not a rich storehouse, for the glory of the Creator and the relief of man's estate. But this is that which will indeed dignify and exalt knowledge, if contemplation and action may be more nearly and straitly conjoined and united together than they have been; a conjunction like unto that of the two highest planets, Saturn the planet of rest and contemplation, and Jupiter the planet of civil society and action. Howbeit, I do not mean, when I speak of use and action, that end before-mentioned of the applying of knowledge to lucre and profession: for I am not ignorant how much that diverteth and interrupteth the prosecution and advancement of knowledge; like unto the golden ball thrown before Atalanta, which while she goeth aside and stoopeth to take up, the race is hindered,

Declinat cursus, aurumque volubile tollit.

Neither is my meaning, as was spoken of Socrates, to call philosophy down from heaven to converse upon the earth; that is, to leave natural philosophy aside, and to apply knowledge only to manners and policy. But as both heaven and earth do conspire and contribute to the use and benefit of man, so the end ought to be, from both philosophies to separate and reject vain speculations and whatsoever is empty and void, and to preserve and augment whatsoever is solid and fruitful; that knowledge may not be as a curtesan, for pleasure and vanity only, or as a bond-woman, to acquire and gain to her master's use; but as a spouse, for generation, fruit, and comfort.

Thus have I described and opened, as by a kind of dissection, those peccant humours (the principal of them) which have not only given impediment to the proficience of learning, but have given also occasion to the traducement thereof: wherein if I have been too plain, it must be remembered *Fidelia vulnera amantis, sed dolosa oscula malignantis:* [faithful are the wounds of a friend, but the kisses of an enemy are deceitful]. This I think I have gained, that I ought to be the better believed in that which I shall say pertaining to commendation, because I have proceeded so freely in that which concerneth censure. And yet I have no purpose to enter into a laudative of learning, or to make a hymn to the muses, (though I am of the opinion that it is long since their rights were duly celebrated:) but my intent is, without varnish or amplification, justly to weigh the dignity of knowledge in the balance with other things, and to take the true value thereof by testimonies and arguments divine and human.

First therefore, let us seek the dignity of knowledge in the arch-type or first platform, which is in the attributes and acts of God, as far as they are revealed to man and may be observed with sobriety; wherein we may not seek it by the name of learning; for all learning is knowledge acquired, and all knowledge in God is original: and therefore we must look for it by another name, that of wisdom or sapience, as the Scriptures call it.

It is so then, that in the work of the creation we see a double emanation of virtue from God; the one referring more properly to power, the other to wisdom; the one expressed in making the subsistence of the matter, and the other in disposing the beauty of the form. This being supposed, it is to be observed, that for any thing which appeareth in the history of the creation, the confused mass and matter of heaven and earth was made in a moment, and the order and disposition of that chaos or mass was the work of six days; such a note of difference it pleased God to put upon the works of power and the works of wisdom; wherewith concurreth, that in the former it is not set down that God said, *Let there be heaven and earth,* as it is set down of the works following; but actually, that God made heaven and earth: the one carrying the style of a manufacture, and the other of a law, decree, or counsel.

To proceed to that which is next in order, from God to spirits; we find, as far as credit is to be given to the celestial hierarchy of that supposed Dionysius the senator of Athens, the first place or degree is given to the angels of love, which are termed Seraphim; the second to the angels of light, which are termed Cherubim; and the third and so following places to thrones, principalities, and the rest, which are all angels of power and ministry; so as the angels of knowledge and illumination are placed before the angels of office and domination.

To descend from spirits and intellectual forms to sensible and material forms; we read the first form that was created was light, which hath a relation and correspondence in nature and corporal things, to knowledge in spirits and incorporal things.

So in the distribution of days, we see the day wherein God did rest and contemplate his own works, was blessed above all the days wherein he did effect and accomplish them.

After the creation was finished, it is set down unto us that man was placed in the garden to work therein; which work so appointed to him could be no other than work of contemplation; that is, when the end of work is but for exercise and experiment, not for necessity, for there being then no reluctation of the creature, nor sweat of the brow, man's employment must of consequence have been matter of delight in the experiment, and not a matter of labour for the use. Again, the first acts which man performed in Paradise consisted of the two summary parts of knowledge; the view of creatures, and the imposition of names. As for the knowledge which induced the fall, it was, as was touched before, not the natural knowledge of creatures, but the moral knowledge of good and evil; wherein the supposition was, that God's commandments or prohibitions were not the originals of good and evil, but that they had other beginnings, which man aspired to know, to the end to make a total defection from God, and to depend wholly upon himself.

To pass on: in the first event or occurrence after the fall of man, we see (as the Scriptures have infinite mysteries, not violating at all the truth of the story or letter,) an image of the two estates, the contemplative state and the active state, figured in the two persons of Abel and Cain, and in the two simplest and most primitive trades of life; that of the shepherd, (who, by reason of his leisure, rest in a place, and living in view of heaven, is a lively image of a contemplative life,) and that of the husbandman: where we see again the favour and election of God went to the shepherd, and not to the tiller of the ground.

So in the age before the flood, the holy records within those few memorials which are there entered and registered have vouchsafed to mention and honour the name of the inventors and authors of music and works in metal. In the age after the flood, the first great judgment of God upon the ambition of man was the confusion of tongues; whereby the open trade and intercourse of learning and knowledge was chiefly imbarred. . . .[1]

As for human proofs, it is so large a field, as in a discourse of this nature and brevity it is fit rather to use choice of those things which we shall produce, than to embrace the variety of them. First therefore, in the degrees of human honour amongst the heathen

[1] Additional testimonies taken from the Scriptures and the Church Fathers are here omitted. *Editor.*

it was the highest, to obtain to a veneration and adoration as a God. This unto the Christians is as the forbidden fruit. But we speak now separately of human testimony: according to which that which the Grecians call *apotheosis,* and the Latins *relatio inter divos,* was the supreme honour which man could attribute unto man; specially when it was given, not by a formal decree or act of state, as it was used among the Roman emperors, but by an inward assent and belief; which honour being so high, had also a degree or middle term; for there were reckoned above human honours, honours heroical and divine; in the attribution and distribution of which honours we see antiquity made this difference: that whereas founders and uniters of states and cities, lawgivers, extirpers of tyrants, fathers of the people, and other eminent persons in civil merit, were honoured but with the titles of worthies or demi-gods; such as were Hercules, Theseus, Minos, Romulus, and the like; on the other side, such as were inventors and authors of new arts, endowments, and commodities towards man's life, were ever consecrated amongst the gods themselves; as was Ceres, Bacchus, Mercurius, Apollo, and others; and justly; for the merit of the former is confined within the circle of an age or a nation; and is like fruitful showers, which though they be profitable and good, yet serve but for that season, and for a latitude of ground where they fall; but the other is indeed like the benefits of heaven, which are permanent and universal. The former again is mixed with strife and perturbation; but the latter hath the true character of divine presence, coming in *aura leni,* without noise or agitation.

Neither is certainly that other merit of learning, in repressing the inconveniences which grow from man to man, much inferior to the former, of relieving the necessities which arise from nature; which merit was lively set forth by the ancients in that feigned relation of Orpheus theatre; where all beasts and birds assembled, and forgetting their several appetites, some of prey, some of game, some of quarrel, stood all sociably together listening unto the airs and accords of the harp; the sound whereof no sooner ceased, or was drowned by some louder noise, but every beast returned to his own nature: wherein is aptly described the nature and condition of men; who are full of savage and unreclaimed desires, of profit, of lust, of revenge, which as long as they give ear to precepts, to laws, to religion, sweetly touched with eloquence and persuasion of books, of sermons, of harangues, so long is society and peace maintained; but if these instruments be silent, or that sedition and tumult make them not audible, all things dissolve into anarchy and confusion.

But this appeareth more manifestly, when kings themselves, or persons of authority under them, or other governors in commonwealths and popular estates, are endued with learning. For although he might be thought partial to his own profession, that said *Then should people and estates be happy, when either kings were philosophers, or philosophers kings;* yet so much is verified by experience, that under learned princes and governors there have been ever the best times: for howsoever kings may have their imperfections in their passions and customs, yet if they be illuminate by learning, they have those notions of religion, policy, and morality, which do preserve them and refrain them from all ruinous and peremptory errors and excesses; whispering evermore in their ears, when counsellors and servants stand mute and silent. And senators or counsellors likewise which be learned, do proceed upon more safe and substantial principles than counsellors which are only men of experience; the one sort keeping dangers afar off, whereas the other discover them not till they come near hand, and then trust to the agility of their wit to ward or avoid them.

Which felicity of times under learned princes (to keep still the law of brevity, by using the most eminent and selected examples) doth best appear in the age which passed from the death of Domitianus the emperor until the reign of Commodus; comprehending a succession of six princes, all learned or singular favourers and advancers of learning; which age, for temporal respects, was the most happy and flourishing that ever the Roman empire (which then was a model of the world) enjoyed: a matter revealed and prefigured unto Domitian in a dream the night before he was slain; for he thought there was grown behind upon his shoulders a neck and a head of gold, which came accordingly to pass in those golden times which succeeded: of which princes we will make some commemoration; wherein although the matter will be vulgar, and be thought fitter for a declamation than agreeable to a treatise infolded as this is, yet because it is pertinent to the point in hand, *neque semper arcum tendit, Apollo,* [and Apollo does not keep his bow always bent,] and to name them only were too naked and cursory, I will not omit it altogether. . . .[1]

But for a table or picture of smaller volume, (not presuming to speak of your Majesty that liveth,) in my judgment the most excellent is that of queen Elizabeth, your immediate predecessor in this part of Britain; a prince that, if Plutarch were now alive to write lives by parallels, would trouble him, I think, to find

[1] Testimonies from the learned among the Roman Emperors are here omitted. *Editor.*

for her a parallel amongst women. This lady was endued with learning in her sex singular, and rare even amongst masculine princes; whether we speak of learning of language or of science; modern or ancient; divinity or humanity. And unto the very last year of her life she accustomed to appoint set hours for reading, scarcely any young student in an university more daily or more duly. As for her government, I assure myself I shall not exceed if I do affirm that this part of the island never had forty-five years of better times; and yet not through the calmness of the season, but through the wisdom of her regiment. For if there be considered of the one side, the truth of religion established; the constant peace and security; the good administration of justice; the temperate use of the prerogative, not slackened, nor much strained; the flourishing state of learning, sortable to so excellent a patroness; the convenient estate of wealth and means, both of crown and subject; the habit of obedience, and the moderation of discontents; and there be considered on the other side, the differences of religion, the troubles of neighbour countries, the ambition of Spain, and opposition of Rome; and then that she was solitary and of herself: these things I say considered, as I could not have chosen an instance so recent and so proper, so I suppose I could not have chosen one more remarkable or eminent, to the purpose now in hand; which is concerning the conjunction of learning in the prince with felicity in the people.

Neither hath learning an influence and operation only upon civil merit and moral virtue, and the arts or temperature of peace and peaceable government; but likewise it hath no less power and efficacy in enablement towards martial and military virtue and prowess; as may be notably represented in the examples of Alexander the Great and Cæsar the Dictator, mentioned before, but now in fit place to be resumed; of whose virtues and acts in war there needs no note or recital, having been the wonders of time in that kind; but of their affections towards learning, and perfections in learning, it is pertinent to say somewhat. . . .[1]

To proceed now from imperial and military virtue to moral and private virtue: first, it is an assured truth which is contained in the verses,

> Scilicet ingenuas didicisse fideliter artes
> Emollit mores, nec sinit esse feros;

[a true proficiency in liberal learning softens and humanises the manners]. It taketh away the wildness and barbarism and fierceness of men's minds: but indeed the accent had need be upon *fideliter:* [it must be a *true* proficiency:] for a little superficial learning doth rather work a contrary effect. It taketh away all levity, temerity, and insolency, by copious suggestion of all doubts and difficulties, and acquainting the mind to balance reasons on both sides, and to turn back the first offers and conceits of the mind, and to accept of nothing but examined and tried. It taketh away vain admiration of any thing, which is the root of all weakness. For all things are admired, either because they are new, or because they are great. For novelty, no man that wadeth in learning or contemplation throughly, but will find that printed in his heart *Nil novi super terram:* [there is nothing new under the sun]. Neither can any man marvel at the play of puppets, that goeth behind the curtain and adviseth well of the motion. And for magnitude, as Alexander the Great after that he was used to great armies and the great conquests of the spacious provinces in Asia, when he received letters out

[1] The eulogies of Alexander and of Caesar are here omitted. *Editor.*

of Greece of some fights and services there, which were commonly for a passage or a fort or some walled town at the most, he said, *It seemed to him that he was advertised of the battles of the frogs and the mice, that the old tales went of:* so certainly if a man meditate much upon the universal frame of nature, the earth with men upon it (the divineness of souls except) will not seem much other than an ant-hill, whereas some ants carry corn, and some carry their young, and some go empty, and all to and fro a little heap of dust. It taketh away or mitigateth fear of death or adverse fortune; which is one of the greatest impediments of virtue and imperfections of manners. For if a man's mind be deeply seasoned with the consideration of the mortality and corruptible nature of things, he will easily concur with Epictetus, who went forth one day and saw a woman weeping for her pitcher of earth that was broken, and went forth the next day and saw a woman weeping for her son that was dead; and thereupon said, *Heri vidi fragilem frangi, hodie vidi mortalem mori:* [yesterday I saw a brittle thing broken, to-day a mortal dead]. And therefore Virgil did excellently and profoundly couple the knowledge of causes and the conquest of all fears together, as *concomitantia.*

> Felix qui potuit rerum cognoscere causas,
> Quique metus omnes et inexorabile fatum
> Subjecit pedibus, strepitumque Acherontis avari.
>
> [Happy the man who doth the causes know
> Of all that is: serene he stands, above
> All fears; above the inexorable Fate,
> And that insatiate gulph that roars below.]

It were too long to go over the particular remedies which learning doth minister to all the diseases of the mind; sometimes purging the ill humours, sometimes opening the obstructions, sometimes helping digestion, sometimes increasing appetite, sometimes healing the wounds and exulcerations thereof, and the like; and therefore I will conclude with that which hath *rationem totius;* which is, that it disposeth the constitution of the mind not to be fixed or settled in the defects thereof, but still to be capable and susceptible of growth and reformation. For the unlearned man knows not what it is to descend into himself or to call himself to account, nor the pleasure of that *suavissima vita, indies sentire se fieri meliorem,* [to feel himself each day a better man than he was the day before]. The good parts he hath he will learn to shew to the full and use them dexterously, but not much to increase them: the faults he hath he will learn how to hide and colour them, but not much to amend them; like an ill mower, that mows on still and never whets his scythe: whereas with the learned man it fares otherwise, that he doth ever intermix the correction and amendment of his mind with the use and employment thereof. Nay further, in general and in sum, certain it is that *veritas* and *bonitas* differ but as the seal and the print; for truth prints goodness, and they be the clouds of error which descend in the storms of passions and perturbations.

From moral virtue let us pass on to matter of power and commandment, and consider whether in right reason there be any comparable with that wherewith knowledge investeth and crowneth man's nature. We see the dignity of the commandment is according to the dignity of the commanded: to have commandment over beasts, as herdsmen have, is a thing contemptible; to have commandment over children, as school-masters have, is a matter of small honour; to have commandment over galley-slaves is a disparagement rather than an honour. Neither is the commandment of tyrants much better, over people which have put off the generosity of their minds: and therefore it was ever holden that honours in free monarchies and commonwealths had a sweetness more than in tyrannies; because the commandment extendeth more over the wills of men, and not only over their deeds and services. And therefore when Virgil putteth himself forth to attribute to Augustus Cæsar the best of human honours, he doth it in these words:

> victorque volentes
> Per populos dat jura, viamque affectat Olympo:
>
> [Moving in conquest onward, at his will
> To willing peoples he gives laws, and shapes
> Through worthiest deeds on earth his course to Heaven.]

But yet the commandment of knowledge is yet higher than the commandment over the will; for it is a commandment over the reason, belief, and understanding of man, which is the highest part of the mind, and giveth law to the will itself. For there is no power on earth which setteth up a throne or chair of estate in the spirits and souls of men, and in their cogitations, imaginations, opinions, and beliefs, but knowledge and learning. And therefore we see the detestable and extreme pleasure that arch-heretics and false prophets and impostors are transported with, when they once find in themselves that they have a superiority in the faith and conscience of men; so great, that if they have once tasted of it, it is seldom seen that any torture or persecution can make them relinquish or abandon it. But as this is that which the author of the Revelation calleth the depth or profoundness of Satan; so by argument of contraries, the just and lawful sovereignty over men's understanding, by force of truth rightly interpreted, is that which approacheth nearest to the similitude of the divine rule.

As for fortune and advancement, the beneficence of learning is not so confined to give fortune only to states and commonwealths, as it doth not likewise give fortune to particular persons. For it was well noted long ago, that Homer hath given more men their livings than either Sylla or Cæsar or Augustus ever did, notwithstanding their great largesses and donatives and distributions of lands to so many legions. And no doubt it is hard to say whether arms or learning have advanced greater numbers. And in case of sovereignty, we see that if arms or descent have carried away the kingdom, yet learning hath carried the priesthood, which ever hath been in some competition with empire.

Again, for the pleasure and delight of knowledge and learning, it far surpasseth all other in nature: for shall the pleasures of the affections so exceed the senses, as much as the obtaining of desire or victory exceedeth a song or a dinner; and must not of consequence the pleasures of the intellect or understanding exceed the pleasures of the affections? We see in all other pleasures there is satiety, and after they be used, their verdure departeth; which sheweth well they be but deceits of pleasure, and not pleasures; and that it was the novelty which pleased, and not the quality. And therefore we see that voluptuous men turn friars, and ambitious princes turn melancholy. But of knowledge there is no satiety, but satisfaction and appetite are perpetually interchangeable; and therefore appeareth to be good in itself simply, without fallacy or accident. Neither is that pleasure of small efficacy and contentment to the mind of man, which the poet Lucretius describeth elegantly,

Suave mari magno, turbantibus æquora ventis, &c.

It is a view of delight (saith he) *to stand or walk*

upon the shore side, and to see a ship tossed with tempest upon the sea; or to be in a fortified tower, and to see two battles join upon a plain. But it is a pleasure incomparable, for the mind of man to be settled, landed, and fortified in the certainty of truth; and from thence to descry and behold the errors, perturbations, labours, and wanderings up and down of other men.

Lastly, leaving the vulgar arguments, that by learning man excelleth man in that wherein man excelleth beasts; that by learning man ascendeth to the heavens and their motions, where in body he cannot come; and the like; let us conclude with the dignity and excellency of knowledge and learning in that whereunto man's nature doth most aspire; which is immortality or continuance; for to this tendeth generation, and raising of houses and families; to this buildings, foundations, and monuments; to this tendeth the desire of memory, fame, and celebration; and in effect, the strength of all other human desires. We see then how far the monuments of wit and learning are more durable than the monuments of power or of the hands. For have not the verses of Homer continued twenty-five hundred years or more, without the loss of a syllable or letter; during which time infinite palaces, temples, castles, cities, have been decayed and demolished? It is not possible to have the true pictures or statuaes of Cyrus, Alexander, Cæsar, no nor of the kings or great personages of much later years; for the originals cannot last, and the copies cannot but leese of the life and truth. But the images of men's wits and knowledges remain in books, exempted from the wrong of time and capable of perpetual renovation. Neither are they fitly to be called images, because they generate still, and cast their seeds in the minds of others, provoking and causing infinite actions and opinions in succeeding ages. So that if the invention of the ship was thought so noble, which carrieth riches and commodities from place to place, and consociateth the most remote regions in participation of their fruits, how much more are letters to be magnified, which as ships pass through the vast seas of time, and make ages so distant to participate of the wisdom, illuminations, and inventions, the one of the other? Nay further, we see some of the philosophers which were least divine and most immersed in the senses and denied generally the immortality of the soul, yet came to this point, that whatsoever motions the spirit of man could act and perform without the organs of the body they thought might remain after death; which were only those of the understanding, and not of the affection; so immortal and incorruptible a thing did knowledge seem unto them to be. But we, that know by divine revelation that not only the understanding but the affections purified, not only the spirit but the body changed, shall be advanced to immortality, do disclaim in these rudiments of the senses. But it must be remembered both in this last point, and so it may likewise be needful in other places, that in probation of the dignity of knowledge or learning I did in the beginning separate divine testimony from human; which method I have pursued, and so handled them both apart.

Nevertheless I do not pretend, and I know it will be impossible for me by any pleading of mine, to reverse the judgment, either of Æsop's cock, that preferred the barleycorn before the gem; or of Midas, that being chosen judge between Apollo president of the Muses, and Pan god of the flocks, judged for plenty; or of Paris, that judged for beauty and love against wisdom and power; or of Agrippina, *occidat matrem, modo imperet,* [let him kill his mother so he be emperor,] that preferred empire with condition never so detestable; or of Ulysses, *qui vetulam prætulit immortalitati,* [that preferred an old woman to an immortality,] being a figure of those which prefer custom and habit before all excellency; or of a number of the like popular judgments. For these things continue as they have been: but so will that also continue whereupon learning hath ever relied, and which faileth not: *Justificata est sapientia a filiis suis:* [wisdom is justified of her children].

THE

SECOND BOOK OF FRANCIS BACON

OF THE

PROFICIENCE AND ADVANCEMENT OF LEARNING

DIVINE AND HUMAN.

TO THE KING.

It might seem to have more convenience, though it come often otherwise to pass, (excellent King,) that those which are fruitful in their generations, and have in themselves the foresight of immortality in their descendants, should likewise be more careful of the good estate of future times; unto which they know they must transmit and commend over their dearest pledges. Queen Elizabeth was a sojourner in the world in respect of her unmarried life; and was a blessing to her own times; and yet so as the impression of her good government, besides her happy memory, is not without some effect which doth survive her. But to your Majesty, whom God hath already blessed with so much royal issue, worthy to continue and represent you for ever, and whose youthful and fruitful bed doth yet promise many the like renovations, it is proper and agreeable to be conversant not only in the transitory parts of good government, but in those acts also which are in their nature permanent and perpetual. Amongst the which (if affection do not transport me) there is not any more worthy than the further endowment of the world with sound and fruitful knowledge: for why should a few received authors stand up like Hercules' Columns, beyond which there should be no sailing or discovering, since we have so bright and benign a star as your Majesty to conduct and prosper us? To return therefore where we left, it remaineth to consider of what kind those acts are, which have been undertaken and performed by kings and others for the increase and advancement of learning: wherein I purpose to speak actively without digressing or dilating.

Let this ground therefore be laid, that all works are overcomen by amplitude of reward, by soundness of direction, and by the conjunction of labours. The first multiplieth endeavour, the second preventeth error, and the third supplieth the frailty of man. But the principal of these is direction: for *claudus in via antevertit cursorem extra viam;* [the cripple that keeps the way gets to the end of the journey sooner than the runner who goes aside;] and Salomon excellently setteth it down, *If the iron be not sharp, it requireth more strength; but wisdom is that which prevaileth;* signifying that the invention or election of the mean is more effectual than any inforcement or accumulation of endeavours. This I am induced to speak, for that (not derogating from the noble intention of any that have been deservers towards the state of learning) I do observe nevertheless that their works and acts are rather matters of magnificence and memory than of progression and proficience, and tend rather to augment the mass of learning in the multitude of learned men than to rectify or raise the sciences themselves.

The works or acts of merit towards learning are conversant about three objects; the places of learning, the books of learning, and the persons of the learned. For as water, whether it be the dew of heaven or the springs of the earth, doth scatter and leese itself in the ground, except it be collected into some receptacle, where it may by union comfort and sustain itself; and from that cause the industry of man hath made and framed spring-heads, conduits, cisterns, and pools, which men have accustomed likewise to beautify and adorn with accomplishments of magnificence and state, as well as of use and necessity; so this excellent liquor of knowledge, whether it descend from divine inspiration or spring from human sense, would soon perish and vanish to oblivion, if it were not preserved in books, traditions, conferences, and places appointed, as universities, colleges, and schools, for the receipt and comforting of the same.

The works which concern the seats and places of learning are four; foundations and buildings, endowments with revenues, endowments with franchises and privileges, institutions and ordinances for government; all tending to quietness and privateness of life, and discharge of cares and troubles; much like the stations which Virgil prescribeth for the hiving of bees:

> Principio sedes apibus statioque petenda,
> Quo neque sit ventis aditus, &c.
> [First for thy bees a quiet station find,
> And lodge them under covert of the wind.]

The works touching books are two: first libraries, which are as the shrines where all the relics of the ancient saints, full of true virtue and that without delusion or imposture, are preserved and reposed; secondly, new editions of authors, with more correct impressions, more faithful translations, more profitable glosses, more diligent annotations, and the like.

The works pertaining to the persons of learned men (besides the advancement and countenancing of them in general) are two: the reward and designation of readers in sciences already extant and invented; and the reward and designation of writers and inquirers concerning any parts of learning not sufficiently laboured and prosecuted.

These are summarily the works and acts, wherein the merits of many excellent princes and other worthy personages have been conversant. As for any particular commemorations, I call to mind what Cicero said, when he gave general thanks; *Difficile non aliquem, ingratum quenquam præterire:* [it were hard to remember all, and yet ungracious to forget any]. Let us rather, according to the Scriptures, look unto that part of the race which is before us than look back to that which is already attained.

First therefore, amongst so many great foundations of colleges in Europe, I find it strange that they are all dedicated to professions, and none left free to arts and sciences at large. For if men judge that learning should be referred to action, they judge well; but in this they fall into the error described in the ancient fable; in which the other parts of the body did suppose the stomach had been idle, because it neither performed the office of motion, as the limbs do, nor of sense, as the head doth; but yet notwithstanding it is the stomach that digesteth and distributeth to all the rest. So if any man think philosophy and universality to be idle studies, he doth not consider that all professions are from thence served and supplied. And this I take to be a great cause that hath hindered the progression of learning, because these fundamental knowledges have been studied but in passage. For if you will have a tree bear more fruit than it hath used to do, it is not any thing you can do to the boughs, but it is the stirring of the earth and putting new mould about the roots that must work it. Neither is it to be forgotten that this dedicating of foundations and dotations to professory learning hath not only had a malign aspect and influence upon the growth of sciences, but hath also been prejudicial to states and governments. For hence it proceedeth that princes find a solitude in regard of able men to serve them in causes of estate, because there is no education collegiate which is free; where such as were so disposed might give themselves to histories, modern languages, books of policy and civil discourse, and other the like enablements unto service of estate.

And because founders of colleges do plant and founders of lectures do water, it followeth well in order to speak of the defect which is in public lectures; namely, in the smallness and meanness of the salary or reward which in most places is assigned unto them; whether they be lectures of arts, or of professions. For it is necessary to the progression of sciences that readers be of the most able and sufficient men; as those which are ordained for generating and propagating of sciences, and not for transitory use. This cannot be, except their condition and endowment be such as may content the ablest man to appropriate his whole labour and continue his whole age in that function and attendance; and therefore must have a proportion answerable to that mediocrity or competency of advancement which may be expected from a profession or the practice of a profession. So as, if you will have sciences flourish, you must observe David's military law, which was, *That those which staid with the carriage should have equal part with those which were in the action;* else will the carriages be ill attended: So readers in sciences are indeed the guardians of the stores and provisions of sciences whence men in active courses are furnished, and therefore ought to have equal entertainment with them; otherwise if the fathers in sciences be of the weakest sort or be ill-maintained,

Et patrum invalidi referent jejunia nati:

[the poor keeping of the parents will appear in the poor constitution of the offspring.]

Another defect I note, wherein I shall need some alchemist to help me, who call upon men to sell their books and to build furnaces; quitting and forsaking Minerva and the Muses as barren virgins, and relying upon Vulcan. But certain it is that unto the deep, fruitful, and operative study of many sciences, specially natural philosophy and physic, books be not only the instrumentals; wherein also the beneficence of men hath not been altogether wanting; for we see spheres, globes, astrolabes, maps, and the like, have been provided as appurtenances to astronomy and cosmography, as well as books: we see likewise that some places instituted for physic have annexed the commodity of gardens for simples of all sorts, and do likewise command the use of dead bodies for anatomies. But these do respect but a few things. In general, there will hardly be any main proficience in the disclosing of nature, except there be some allowance for expenses about experiments; whether they be experiments appertaining to Vulcanus or Dædalus, furnace or engine, or any other kind; and therefore as secretaries and spials of princes and states bring in bills for intelligence, so you must allow the spials and intelligencers of nature to bring in their bills, or else you shall be ill advertised.

And if Alexander made such a liberal assignation to Aristotle of treasure for the allowance of hunters, fowlers, fishers, and the like, that he might compile an History of nature, much better do they deserve it that travail in Arts of nature.

Another defect which I note, is an intermission or neglect in those which are governors in universities of consultation, and in princes or superior persons of visitation; to enter into account and consideration, whether the readings, exercises, and other customs appertaining unto learning, anciently begun and since continued, be well instituted or no; and thereupon to ground on amendment or reformation in that which shall be found inconvenient. For it is one of your Majesty's own most wise and princely maxims, *that in all usages and precedents, the times be considered wherein they first began; which if they were weak or ignorant, it derogateth from the authority of the usage, and leaveth it for suspect.* And therefore in as much as most of the usages and orders of the universities were derived from more obscure times, it is the more requisite they be re-examined. In this kind I will give an instance or two for example sake, of things that are the most obvious and familiar. The one is a matter which though it be ancient and general, yet I hold to be an error; which is, that scholars in universities come too soon and too unripe to logic and rhetoric; arts fitter for graduates than children and novices: for these two, rightly taken, are the gravest of sciences; being the arts of arts, the one for judgment, the other for ornament; and they be the rules and directions how to set forth and dispose matter; and therefore for minds empty and unfraught with matter, and which have not gathered that which

Cicero calleth *sylva* and *supellex,* stuff and variety, to begin with those arts, (as if one should learn to weigh or to measure or to paint the wind), doth work but this effect, that the wisdom of those arts, which is great and universal, is almost made contemptible, and is degenerate into childish sophistry and ridiculous affectation. And further, the untimely learning of them hath drawn on by consequence the superficial and unprofitable teaching and writing of them, as fitteth indeed to the capacity of children. Another is a lack I find in the exercises used in the universities, which do make too great a divorce between invention and memory; for their speeches are either premeditate *in verbis conceptis,* where nothing is left to invention, or merely *extemporal,* where little is left to memory: whereas in life and action there is least use of either of these, but rather of intermixtures of premeditation and invention, notes and memory; so as the exercise fitteth not the practice, nor the image the life; and it is ever a true rule in exercises, that they be framed as near as may be to the life of practice; for otherwise they do pervert the motions and faculties of the mind, and not prepare them. The truth whereof is not obscure, when scholars come to the practices of professions, or other actions of civil life; which when they set into, this want is soon found by themselves, and sooner by others. But this part, touching the amendment of the institutions and orders of universities, I will conclude with the clause of Cæsar's letter to Oppius and Balbus, *Hoc quemadmodum fieri possit, nonnulla mihi in mentem veniunt, et multa reperiri possunt; de iis rebus rogo vos ut cogitationem suscipiatis:* [how this may be done, some things occur to me and more may be thought of. I would have you take these matters into consideration.]

Another defect which I note, ascendeth a little higher

than the precedent. For as the proficience of learning consisteth much in the orders and institutions of universities in the same states and kingdoms, so it would be yet more advanced, if there were more intelligence mutual between the universities of Europe than now there is. We see there be many orders and foundations, which though they be divided under several sovereignties and territories, yet they take themselves to have a kind of contract, fraternity, and correspondence one with the other, insomuch as they have Provincials and Generals. And surely as nature createth brotherhood in families, and arts mechanical contract brotherhoods in communalties, and the anointment of God superinduceth a brotherhood in kings and bishops; so in like manner there cannot but be a fraternity in learning and illumination, relating to that paternity which is attributed to God, who is called the Father of illuminations or lights.

The last defect which I will note is, that there hath not been, or very rarely been, any public designation of writers or inquirers concerning such parts of knowledge as may appear not to have been already sufficiently laboured or undertaken; unto which point it is an inducement, to enter into a view and examination what parts of learning have been prosecuted, and what omitted; for the opinion of plenty is amongst the causes of want, and the great quantity of books maketh a shew rather of superfluity than lack; which surcharge nevertheless is not to be remedied by making no more books, but by making more good books, which, as the serpent of Moses, might devour the serpents of the enchanters.

The removing of all the defects formerly enumerate, except the last, and of the active part also of the last, (which is the designation of writers,) are *opera basilica,* [works for a king;] towards which the endeavours of a private man may be but as an image in a crossway, that may point at the way but cannot go it. But the inducing part of the latter (which is the survey of learning) may be set forward by private travel. Wherefore I will now attempt to make a general and faithful perambulation of learning, with an inquiry what parts thereof lie fresh and waste, and not improved and converted by the industry of man; to the end that such a plot made and recorded to memory may both minister light to any public designation, and also serve to excite voluntary endeavours; wherein nevertheless my purpose is at this time to note only omissions and deficiencies, and not to make any redargution of errors or incomplete prosecutions; for it is one thing to set forth what ground lieth unmanured, and another thing to correct ill husbandry in that which is manured.

In the handling and undertaking of which work I am not ignorant what it is that I do now move and attempt, nor insensible of mine own weakness to sustain my purpose; but my hope is that if my extreme love to learning carry me too far, I may obtain the excuse of affection; for that *it is not granted to man to love and to be wise*. But I know well I can use no other liberty of judgment than I must leave to others; and I for my part shall be indifferently glad either to perform myself or accept from another that day of humanity, *Nam qui erranti comiter monstrat viam,* &c. [to put the wanderer in the right way]. I do foresee likewise that of those things which I shall enter and register as deficiencies and omissions, many will conceive and censure that some of them are already done and extant; others to be but curiosities, and things of no great use; and others to be of too great difficulty and almost impossibility to be compassed and effected. But for the two first, I refer myself to the particulars. For the last, touching impossibility, I take it those things are to be held possible which may be done by some person, though not by every one; and which may be done by many, though not by any one; and which may be done in succession of ages, though not within the hourglass of one man's life; and which may be done by public designation, though not by private endeavour. But notwithstanding, if any man will take to himself rather that of Salomon, *Dicit piger, Leo est in via,* [the slothful man saith there is a lion in the path,] than that of Virgil, *Possunt quia posse videntur,* [they find it possible because they think it possible,] I shall be content that my labours be esteemed but as the better sort of wishes; for as it asketh some knowledge to demand a question not impertinent, so it requireth some sense to make a wish not absurd.

The parts of human learning have reference to the three parts of Man's Understanding, which is the seat of learning: History to his Memory, Poesy to his Imagination, and Philosophy to his Reason. Divine learning receiveth the same distribution; for the spirit of man is the same, though the revelation of oracle and sense be diverse: so as theology consisteth also of History of the Church; of Parables, which is divine poesy; and of holy Doctrine or precept. For as for that part which seemeth supernumerary, which is Prophecy, it is but divine history; which hath that prerogative over human, as the narration may be before the fact as well as after.

History is Natural, Civil, Ecclesiastical, and Literary; whereof the three first I allow as extant, the fourth I note as deficient. For no man hath propounded to himself the general state of learning to be described and represented from age to age, as many have done the works of nature and the state civil and ecclesiastical; without which the history of the world seemeth to me to be as the statua of Polyphemus with his eye out; that part being wanting which doth most shew the spirit and life of the person. And yet I am not ignorant that in divers particular sciences, as of the jurisconsults, the mathematicians, the rhetoricians, the philosophers, there are set down some small memorials of the schools, authors, and books; and so likewise some barren relations touching the invention of arts or usages. But a just story of learning, containing the antiquities and originals of knowledges, and their sects; their inventions, their traditions; their diverse administrations and managings; their flourishings, their oppositions, decays, depressions, oblivions, removes; with the causes and occasions of them, and all other events concerning learning, throughout the ages of the world; I may truly affirm to be wanting. The use and end of which work I do not so much design for curiosity, or satisfaction of those that are the lovers of learning; but chiefly for a more serious and grave purpose, which is this in few words, that it will make learned men wise in the use and administration of learning. For it is not St. Augustine's nor St. Ambrose' works that will make so wise a divine, as ecclesiastical history throughly read and observed; and the same reason is of learning.

History of Nature is of three sorts; of nature in course, of nature erring or varying, and of nature altered or wrought; that is, history of Creatures, history of Marvels, and history of Arts. The first of these no doubt is extant, and that in good perfection; the two later are handled so weakly and unprofitably, as I am moved to note them as deficient. For I find no sufficient or competent collection of the works of nature which have a digression and deflexion from the ordinary course of generations, productions, and motions; whether they be singularities of place and region, or the strange events of time and chance, or the effects of yet unknown proprieties, or the instances of exception to general kinds. It is true, I find a number of books of fabulous experiments and secrets, and frivolous impostures for pleasure and strangeness. But a substantial and severe collection of the Heteroclites or Irregulars of nature, well examined and described, I find not; specially not with due rejection of fables and popular errors: for as things now are, if an untruth in nature be once on foot, what by reason of the neglect of examination and countenance of antiquity, and what by reason of the use of the opinion in similitudes and ornaments of speech, it is never called down.

The use of this work, honoured with a precedent in Aristotle, is nothing less than to give contentment to the appetite of curious and vain wits, as the manner of Mirabilaries is to do; but for two reasons, both of great weight; the one to correct the partiality of axioms and opinions, which are commonly framed only upon common and familiar examples; the other because from the wonders of nature is the nearest intelligence and passage towards the wonders of art: for it is no more but by following and as it were hounding Nature in her wanderings, to be able to lead her afterwards to the same place again. Neither am I of opinion, in this History of Marvels, that superstitious narrations of sorceries, witchcrafts, dreams, divinations, and the like, where there is an assurance and clear evidence of the fact, be altogether excluded. For it is not yet known in what cases, and how far, effects attributed to superstition do participate of natural causes; and therefore howsoever the practice of such things is to be condemned, yet from the speculation and consideration of them light may be taken, not only for the discerning of the offences, but for the further disclosing of nature. Neither ought a man to make scruple of entering into these things for inquisition of truth, as your Majesty hath shewed in your own example; who with the two clear eyes of religion and natural philosophy have looked deeply and wisely into these shadows, and yet proved yourself to be of the nature of the sun, which passeth through pollutions and itself remains as pure as before. But this I hold fit, that these narrations which have mixture with superstition be sorted by themselves, and not to be mingled with the narrations which are merely and sincerely natural. But as for the narrations touching the prodigies and miracles of religions, they are either not true or not natural; and therefore impertinent for the story of nature.

For History of Nature Wrought or Mechanical, I find some collections made of agriculture, and likewise of manual arts; but commonly with a rejection of experiments familiar and vulgar. For it is esteemed a kind of dishonour unto learning to descend to inquiry or meditation upon matters mechanical, except they be such as may be thought secrets, rarities, and special subtilties; which humour of vain and supercilious arrogancy is justly derided in Plato; where he brings in Hippias, a vaunting sophist, disputing with Socrates, a true and unfeigned inquisitor of truth; where the subject being touching beauty, Socrates, after his wandering manner of inductions, put first an example of a fair virgin, and then of a fair horse, and then of a fair pot well glazed, whereat Hippias was offended, and said, *More than for courtesy's sake, he did think much to dispute with any that did allege such base and sordid instances:* whereunto Socrates answereth: *You have reason, and it becomes you well, being a man so trim in your vestments,* &c. and so goeth on in an irony. But the truth is, they be not the highest instances that give the securest information; as may be well expressed in the tale so common of the philosopher, that while he gazed upwards to the stars fell into the water; for if he had looked down he might have seen the stars in the water, but looking aloft he could not see the water in the stars. So it cometh often to pass that mean and small things discover great better than great can discover the small; and therefore Aristotle noteth well, *that the nature of every thing is best seen in his smallest portions,* and for that cause he inquireth the nature of a commonwealth, first in a family, and the simple conjugations of man and wife, parent and child, master and servant, which are in every cottage: even so likewise the nature of this great city of the world and the policy thereof must be first sought in mean concordances and small portions. So we see how that secret of nature, of the turning of iron touched with the loadstone towards the north, was found out in needles of iron, not in bars of iron.

But if my judgment be of any weight, the use of History Mechanical is of all others the most radical and fundamental towards natural philosophy; such natural philosophy as shall not vanish in the fume of subtile, sublime, or delectable speculation, but such as shall be operative to the endowment and benefit of man's life: for it will not only minister and suggest for the present many ingenious practices in all trades, by a connexion and transferring of the observations of one art to the use of another, when the experiences of several mysteries shall fall under the consideration of one man's mind; but further it will give a more true and real illumination concerning causes and axioms than is hitherto attained. For like as a man's disposition is never well known till he be crossed, nor Proteus ever changed shapes till he was straitened and held fast; so the passages and variations of nature cannot appear so fully in the liberty of nature, as in the trials and vexations of art.

For Civil History, it is of three kinds; not unfitly to be compared with the three kinds of pictures or images. For of pictures or images, we see some are unfinished, some are perfect, and some are defaced. So of histories we may find three kinds, Memorials, Perfect Histories, and Antiquities; for Memorials are history unfinished, or the first or rough draughts of history, and Antiquities are history defaced, or some remnants of history which have casually escaped the shipwrack of time.

Memorials, or Preparatory History, are of two sorts; whereof the one may be termed Commentaries, and the other Registers. Commentaries are they which set down a continuance of the naked events and actions, without the motives or designs, the counsels, the speeches, the pretexts, the occasions, and other passages of action: for this is the true nature of a Commentary; though Cæsar, in modesty mixed with greatness, did for his pleasure apply the name of a Commentary to the best history of the world. Registers are collections of public acts, as decrees of council, judicial proceedings, declarations and letters of estate, orations, and the like, without a perfect continuance or contexture of the thread of the narration.

Antiquities or Remnants of History are as was said, *tanquam tabula naufragii,* [like the planks of a shipwreck;] when industrious persons by an exact and scrupulous diligence and observation, out of monuments, names, words, proverbs, traditions, private records and evidences, fragments of stories, passages of books that concern not story, and the like, do save and recover somewhat from the deluge of time.

In these kinds of unperfect histories I do assign no deficience, for they are *tanquam imperfecte mista,* [things imperfectly compounded;] and therefore any deficience in them is but their nature. As for the corruptions and moths of history, which are Epitomes, the use of them deserveth to be banished as all men of sound judgment have confessed; as those that have fretted and corroded the sound bodies of many excellent histories, and wrought them into base and unprofitable dregs.

History which may be called Just and Perfect History is of three kinds, according to the object which it propoundeth, or pretendeth to represent: for it either representeth a Time, or a Person, or an Action. The first we call Chronicles, the second Lives, and the third Narrations or Relations. Of these, although the first be the most complete and absolute kind of history and hath most estimation and glory, yet the second excelleth it in profit and use, and the third in verity and sincerity. For History of Times representeth the magnitude of actions and the public faces and deportments of persons, and passeth over in silence the smaller passages and motions of men and matters. But such being the workmanship of God as he doth hang the greatest weight upon the smallest wires, *maxima e minimis suspendens,* it comes therefore to pass, that such histories do rather set forth the pomp of business than the true and inward resorts thereof. But Lives, if they be well written, propounding to themselves a person to represent in whom actions both greater and smaller, public and private, have a commixture, must of necessity contain a more true, native, and lively representation. So again Narrations and Relations of actions, as the War of Peloponnesus, the Expedition of Cyrus Minor, the Conspiracy of Catiline, cannot but be more purely and exactly true than Histories of Times, because they may choose an argument comprehensible within the notice and instructions of the writer: whereas he that undertaketh the story of a time, especially of any length, cannot but meet with many blanks and spaces which he must be forced to fill up out of his own wit and conjecture.

For the History of Times, (I mean of civil history) the providence of God hath made the distribution: for it hath pleased God to ordain and illustrate two exemplar states of the world, for arms, learning, moral virtue, policy, and laws; the state of Græcia, and the state of Rome; the histories whereof occupying the middle part of time, have more ancient to them, histories which may by one common name be termed the Antiquities of the World; and after them, histories which may be likewise called by the name of Modern History.

Now to speak of the deficiencies. As to the Heathen Antiquities of the world, it is in vain to note them for deficient. Deficient they are no doubt, consisting most of the fables and fragments; but the deficience cannot be holpen; for antiquity is like fame, *caput inter nubila condit,* her head is muffled from our sight. For the History of the Exemplar States, it is extant in good perfection. Not but I could wish there were a perfect course of history for Græcia from Theseus to Philopœmen, (what time the affairs of Græcia drowned and extinguished in the affairs of Rome;) and for Rome from Romulus to Justinianus, who may be truly said to be *ultimus Romanorum.* In which sequences of story the text of Thucydides and Xenophon in the one, and the texts of Livius, Polybius, Sallustius, Cæsar, Appianus, Tacitus, Herodianus in the other, to be kept entire without any diminution at all, and only to be supplied and continued. But this is matter of magnificence, rather to be commended than required: and we speak now of parts of learning supplemental, and not of supererogation.

But for Modern Histories, whereof there are some few very worthy, but the greater part beneath mediocrity, leaving the care of foreign stories to foreign states, because I will not be *curiosus in aliena republica,* [a meddler in other nations' matters,] I cannot fail to represent to your Majesty the unworthiness of the history of England in the main continuance thereof, and the partiality and obliquity of that of Scotland in the latest and largest author that I have seen; supposing that it would be honour for your Majesty and a work very memorable, if this island of Great Britain, as it is now joined in monarchy for the ages to come, so were joined in one history for the times passed; after the manner of the sacred history which draweth down the story of the Ten Tribes and of the Two Tribes as twins together. And if it shall seem that the greatness of this work may make it less exactly performed, there is an excellent period of a much smaller compass of time, as to the story of England; that is to say, from the Uniting of the Roses to the Uniting of the Kingdoms; a portion of time, wherein to my understanding, there hath been the rarest varieties that in like number of successions of any hereditary monarchy hath been known. For it beginneth with the mixed adeption of a crown, by arms and title; an entry by battle, an establishment by marriage; and therefore times answerable, like waters after a tempest, full of working and swelling, though without extremity of storm; but well passed through by the wisdom of the pilot, being one of the most sufficient kings of all the number. Then followeth the reign of a king, whose actions, howsoever conducted, had much intermixture with the affairs of Europe, balancing and inclining them variably; in whose time also began that great alteration in the state ecclesiastical, an action which seldom cometh upon the stage: then the reign of a minor: then an offer of an usurpation, though it was but as *febris ephemera,* [a diary ague:] then the reign of a queen matched with a foreigner: then of a queen that lived solitary and unmarried, and yet her government so masculine as it had greater impression and operation upon the states abroad than it any ways received from thence: and now last, this most happy and glorious event, that this island of Britain, divided from all the world, should be united in itself; and that oracle of rest given to Æneas, *Antiquam exquirite matrem,* [seek out your ancient mother,] should now be performed and fulfilled upon the nations of England and Scotland being now reunited in the ancient mother name of Britain, as a full period of all instability and peregrinations: so that as it cometh to pass in massive bodies, that they have certain trepidations and waverings before they fix and settle; so it seemeth that by the providence of God this monarchy, before it was to settle in your Majesty and your generations, (in which I hope it is now established for ever,) it had these prelusive changes and varieties.

For Lives, I do find strange that these times have so little esteemed the virtues of the times, as that the writing of lives should be no more frequent. For although there be not many sovereign princes or absolute commanders, and that states are most collected into monarchies, yet are there many worthy personages that deserve better than dispersed report or barren elogies. For herein the invention of one of the late poets is proper, and doth well enrich the ancient fiction: for he feigneth that at the end of the thread or web of every man's life there was a little medal containing the person's name, and that Time waited upon the shears, and as soon as the thread was cut, caught the medals and carried them to the river of Lethe; and about the bank there were many birds flying up and down, that would get the medals and carry them in their beak a little while, and then let them fall into the river: only there were a few swans, which if they got a name, would carry it to a temple where it was consecrate. And although many men more mortal in their affections than in their bodies, do esteem desire of name and memory but as a vanity and ventosity,

Animi nil magnæ laudis egentes;

[souls that have no care for praise;] which opinion cometh from that root, *non prius laudes contempsimus, quam laudanda facere desivimus;* [men hardly despise praise till they have ceased to deserve it;] yet that will not alter Salomon's judgment, *Memoria justi cum laudibus, at impiorum nomen putrescet;* [the memory of the just is blessed; but the name of the wicked shall rot;] the one flourisheth, the other either consumeth to present oblivion, or turneth to an ill odour. And therefore in that style or addition, which is and hath been long well received and brought in use, *felicis memoriæ, piæ memoriæ, bonæ memoriæ,* [of happy, of pious, of good memory,] we do acknowledge that which Cicero saith, borrowing it from Demosthenes, that *bona fama propria possessio defunctorum;* [good fame is all that a dead man can possess;] which possession I cannot but note that in our times it lieth much waste, and that therein there is a deficience.

For Narrations and Relations of particular actions,

there were also to be wished a greater diligence therein; for there is no great action but hath some good pen which attends it. And because it is an ability not common to write a good history, as may well appear by the small number of them; yet if particularity of actions memorable were but tolerably reported as they pass, the compiling of a complete History of Times might be the better expected, when a writer should arise that were fit for it: for the collection of such relations might be as a nursery garden, whereby to plant a fair and stately garden when time should serve.

There is yet another portion of history which Cornelius Tacitus maketh, which is not to be forgotten, specially with that application which he accoupleth it withal, Annals and Journals: appropriating to the former matters of estate, and to the later acts and accidents of a meaner nature. For giving but a touch of certain magnificent buildings, he addeth, *Cum ex dignitate populi Romani repertum sit, res illustres annalibus, talia diurnis urbis actis mandare:* [that it had been thought suitable to the dignity of the Roman people to enter in their *annals* only matters of note and greatness; leaving such things as these to the *journal records* of the city.] So as there is a kind of contemplative heraldry, as well as civil. And as nothing doth derogate from the dignity of a state more than confusion of degrees; so it doth not a little embase the authority of an history, to intermingle matters of triumph or matters of ceremony or matters of novelty with matters of state. But the use of a Journal hath not only been in the history of times, but likewise in the history of persons, and chiefly of actions; for princes in ancient time had, upon point of honour and policy both, journals kept of what passed day by day: for we see the Chronicle which was read before Ahasuerus, when he could not take rest, contained matter of affairs indeed, but such as had passed in his own time, and very lately before: but the Journal of Alexander's house expressed every small particularity, even concerning his person and court; and it is yet an use well received in enterprises memorable, as expeditions of war, navigations, and the like, to keep diaries of that which passeth continually.

I cannot likewise be ignorant of a form of writing which some grave and wise men have used, containing a scattered history of those actions which they have thought worthy of memory, with politic discourse and observation thereupon; not incorporate into the history, but separately, and as the more principal in their intention; which kind of Ruminated History I think more fit to place amongst books of policy, whereof we shall hereafter speak, than amongst books of history; for it is the true office of history to represent the events themselves together with the counsels, and to leave the observations and conclusions thereupon to the liberty and faculty of every man's judgment. But mixtures are things irregular, whereof no man can define.

So also is there another kind of history manifoldly mixed, and that is History of Cosmography: being compounded of natural history, in respect of the regions themselves; of history civil, in respect of the habitations, regiments, and manners of the people; and the mathematics, in respect of the climates and configurations towards the heavens: which part of learning of all others in this latter time hath obtained most proficience. For it may be truly affirmed to the honour of these times and in a virtuous emulation with antiquity, that this great building of the world had never throughlights made in it, till the age of us and our fathers; for although they had knowledge of the antipodes,

> Nosque ubi primus equis oriens afflavit anhelis,
> Illic sera rubens accendit lumina Vesper:
> [And while on us the fresh East breathes from far,
> For them the red West lights her evening star:]

yet that might be by demonstration, and not in fact; and if by travel, it requireth the voyage but of half the globe. But to circle the earth, as the heavenly bodies do, was not done nor enterprised till these later times: and therefore these times may justly bear in their word, not only *plus ultra,* in precedence of the ancient *non ultra,* and *imitabile fulmen* in precedence of the ancient *non imitabile fulmen,*

> Demens qui nimbos et non imitabile fulmen &c.

but likewise *imitabile cœlum;* in respect of the many memorable voyages, after the manner of heaven, about the globe of the earth.

And this proficience in navigation and discoveries may plant also an expectation of the further proficience and augmentation of all sciences; because it may seem they are ordained by God to be coevals, that is, to meet in one age. For so the prophet Daniel speaking of the latter times fortelleth, *Plurimi pertransibunt, et multiplex erit scientia:* [many shall pass to and fro, and knowledge shall be multiplied:] as if the openness and through passage of the world and the increase of knowledge were appointed to be in the same ages; as we see it is already performed in great part; the learning of these later times not much giving place to the former two periods or returns of learning, the one of the Grecians, the other of the Romans.

History Ecclesiastical receiveth the same divisions with History Civil: but further in the propriety thereof may be divided into History of the Church, by a general name; History of Prophecy; and History of Providence. The first describeth the times of the militant church; whether it be fluctuant, as the ark of Noah; or moveable, as the ark in the wilderness; or at rest, as the ark in the temple; that is, the state of the church in persecution, in remove, and in peace. This part I ought in no sort to note as deficient; only I would that the virtue and sincerity of it were according to the mass and quantity. But I am not now in hand with censures, but with omissions.

The second, which is History of Prophecy, consisteth of two relatives, the prophecy and the accomplishment; and therefore the nature of such a work ought to be, that every prophecy of the scripture be sorted with the event fulfilling the same, throughout the ages of the world; both for the better confirmation of faith, and for the better illumination of the church touching those parts of prophecies which are yet unfulfilled; allowing nevertheless that latitude which is agreeable and familiar unto divine prophecies; being of the nature of their author, with whom a thousand years are but as one day; and therefore are not fulfilled punctually at once, but have springing and germinant accomplishment throughout many ages, though the height or fulness of them may refer to some one age. This is a work which I find deficient, but is to be done with wisdom, sobriety, and reverence, or not at all.

The third, which is History of Providence, containeth that excellent correspondence which is between God's revealed will and his secret will; which though it be so obscure as for the most part it is not legible to the natural man; no, nor many times to those that behold it from the tabernacle; yet at some times it pleaseth God, for our better establishment and the confuting of those which are as without God in the world, to write it in such text and capital letters that, as the prophet saith, *he that runneth by may read it;* that is, mere sensual persons, which hasten by God's judgments and never bend or fix their cogitations upon them, are nevertheless in their passage and race urged to discern it. Such are the notable events and examples of God's judgments, chastisements, deliverances, and blessings. And this is a work which hath passed through the labour of many, and therefore I cannot present as omitted.

There are also other parts of learning which are Appendices to history. For all the exterior proceedings of man consist of words and deeds; whereof history doth properly receive and retain in memory the deeds, and if words, yet but as inducements and passages to deeds; so are there other books and writings, which are appropriate to the custody and receit of words only; which likewise are of three sorts; Orations, Letters, and Brief Speeches or Sayings. Orations are pleadings, speeches of counsel; laudatives, invectives, apologies, reprehensions; orations of formality or ceremony, and the like. Letters are according to all the variety of occasions; advertisements, advices, directions, propositions, petitions, commendatory, expostulatory, satisfactory, of compliment, of pleasure, of discourse, and all other passages of action. And such as are written from wise men are, of all the words of man, in my judgment the best; for they are more natural than orations and public speeches, and more advised than conferences or present speeches. So again letters of affairs from such as manage them or are privy to them are of all others the best instructions for history, and to a diligent reader the best histories in themselves. For Apophthegms, it is a great loss of that book of Cæsar's; for as his history and those few letters of his which we have and those apophthegms which were of his own excel all men's else, so I suppose would his collection of Apophthegms have done; for as for those which are collected by others, either I have no taste in such matters, or else their choice hath not been happy. But upon these three kinds of writings I do not insist, because I have no deficiencies to propound concerning them.

Thus much therefore concerning History; which is that part of learning which answereth to one of the cells, domiciles, or offices of the mind of man; which is that of the Memory.

Poesy is a part of learning in measure of words for the most part restrained, but in all other points extremely licensed, and doth truly refer to the Imagination; which, being not tied to the laws of matter, may at pleasure join that which nature hath severed, and sever that which nature hath joined, and so make unlawful matches and divorces of things: *Pictoribus atque poetis*, &c. [Painters and Poets have always been allowed to take what liberties they would.] It is taken in two senses, in respect of words or matter. In the first sense it is but a character of style, and belongeth to arts of speech, and is not pertinent for the present. In the later, it is (as hath been said) one of the principal portions of learning, and is nothing else but Feigned History, which may be styled as well in prose as in verse.

The use of this Feigned History hath been to give some shadow of satisfaction to the mind of man in those points wherein the nature of things doth deny it; the world being in proportion inferior to the soul; by reason whereof there is agreeable to the spirit of man a more ample greatness, a more exact goodness, and a more absolute variety, than can be found in the nature of things. Therefore, because the acts or events of true history have not that magnitude which satisfieth the mind of man, poesy feigneth acts and events greater and more heroical; because true history propoundeth the successes and issues of actions not so agreeable to the merits of virtue and vice, therefore poesy feigns them more just in retribution, and more according to revealed providence; because true history representeth actions and events more ordinary and less interchanged, therefore poesy endueth them with more rareness, and more unexpected and alternative variations. So as it appeareth that poesy serveth and conferreth to magnanimity, morality, and to delectation. And therefore it was ever thought to have some participation of divineness, because it doth raise and erect the mind, by submitting the shews of things to the desires of the mind; whereas reason doth buckle and bow the mind unto the nature of things. And we see that by these insinuations and congruities with man's nature and pleasure, joined also with the agreement and consort it hath with music, it hath had access and estimation in rude times and barbarous regions, where other learning stood excluded.

The division of poesy which is aptest in the propriety thereof, (besides those divisions which are common unto it with history, as feigned chronicles, feigned lives; and the appendices of history, as feigned epistles, feigned orations, and the rest;) is into Poesy Narrative, Representative, and Allusive. The Narrative is a mere imitation of history, with the excesses before remembered; choosing for subject commonly wars and love, rarely state, and sometimes pleasure or mirth. Representative is as a visible history, and is an image of actions as if they were present, as history is of actions in nature as they are, (that is) past. Allusive or Parabolical is a narration applied only to express some special purpose or conceit. Which later kind of parabolical wisdom was much more in use in the ancient times, as by the fables of Æsop and the brief sentences of the Seven and the use of hieroglyphics may appear. And the cause was, for that it was then of necessity to express any point of reason which was more sharp or subtile than the vulgar in that manner; because men in those times wanted both variety of examples and subtilty of conceit: and as hieroglyphics were before letters, so parables were before arguments: and nevertheless now and at all times they do retain much life and vigour, because reason cannot be so sensible, nor examples so fit.

But there remaineth yet another use of Poesy Parabolical, opposite to that which we last mentioned: for that tendeth to demonstrate and illustrate that which is taught or delivered, and this other to retire and obscure it: that is when the secrets and mysteries of religion, policy, or philosophy are involved in fables or parables. Of this in divine poesy we see the use is authorized. In heathen poesy we see the exposition of fables doth fall out sometimes with great felicity; as in the fable that the giants being overthrown in their war against the gods, the Earth their mother in revenge thereof brought forth Fame:

> Illam Terra parens, irâ irritata deorum,
> Extremam, ut perhibent, Cœo Enceladoque sororem
> Progenuit:

expounded that when princes and monarchs have suppressed actual and open rebels, then the malignity of people (which is the mother of rebellion) doth bring forth libels and slanders and taxations of the state, which is of the same kind with rebellion, but more feminine. So in the fable that the rest of the gods having conspired to bind Jupiter, Pallas called Briareus with his hundred hands to his aid: expounded that monarchies need not fear any curbing of their absoluteness by mighty subjects, as long as by wisdom they keep the hearts of the people, who will be sure to come in on their side. So in the fable that Achilles was brought up under Chiron the Centaur, who was part a man and part a beast: expounded ingeniously but corruptly by Machiavel, that it belongeth to the education and discipline of princes to know as well how to play the part of the lion in violence and the fox in guile, as of the man in virtue and justice. Nevertheless in many the like encounters, I do rather think that the fable was first, and the exposition devised, than that the moral was first, and thereupon the fable framed. For I find it was an ancient vanity in Chrysippus, that troubled himself with great contention to fasten the assertions of the Stoics upon the fictions of the ancient poets. But yet that all the fables and fictions of the poets were but pleasure and not figure, I interpose no opinion. Surely of those poets which are now extant, even Homer himself, (notwithstanding he was made a kind of Scripture by the later schools of the Grecians,) yet I should without any difficulty pronounce that his fables had no such inwardness in his own meaning; but what they might have upon a more original tradition, is not easy to affirm; for he was not the inventor of many of them.

In this third part of learning, which is poesy, I can report no deficience. For being as a plant that cometh of the lust of the earth, without a formal seed, it hath sprung up and spread abroad more than any other kind. But to ascribe unto it that which is due; for the expressing of affections, passions, corruptions, and customs, we are beholding to poets more than to the philosophers' works; and for wit and eloquence not much less than to orators' harangues. But it is not good to stay too long in the theatre. Let us now pass on to the judicial place or palace of the mind, which we are to approach and view with more reverence and attention.

The knowledge of man is as the waters, some descending from above, and some springing from beneath; the one informed by the light of nature, the other inspired by divine revelation. The light of nature consisteth in the notions of the mind and the reports of the senses; for as for knowledge which man receiveth by teaching, it is cumulative and not original; as in a water that besides his own spring-head is fed with other springs and streams. So then according to these two differing illuminations or originals, knowledge is first of all divided into Divinity and Philosophy.

In Philosophy, the contemplations of man do either penetrate unto God, or are circumferred to Nature, or are reflected or reverted upon Himself. Out of which several inquiries there do arise three knowledges, Divine philosophy, Natural philosophy, and Human philosophy or Humanity. For all things are marked and stamped with this triple character, of the power of God, the difference of nature, and the use of man. But because the distributions and partitions of knowledge are not like several lines that meet in one angle, and so touch but in a point; but are like branches of a tree that meet in a stem, which hath a dimension and quantity of entireness and continuance, before it come to discontinue and break itself into arms and boughs; therefore it is good, before we enter into the former distribution, to erect and constitute one universal science, by the name of *Philosophia Prima,* Primitive or Summary Philosophy, as the main and common way, before we come where the ways part and divide themselves; which science whether I should report as deficient or no, I stand doubtful. For I find a certain rhapsody of Natural Theology, and of divers parts of Logic; and of that part of Natural Philosophy which concerneth the Principles, and of that other part of Natural Philosophy which concerneth the Soul or Spirit; all these strangely commixed and confused; but being examined, it seemeth to me rather a depredation of other sciences, advanced and exalted unto some height of terms, than any thing solid or substantive of itself. Nevertheless I cannot be ignorant of the distinction which is current, that the same things are handled but in several respects; as for example, that logic considereth of many things as they are in notion, and this philosophy as they are in nature; the one in appearance, the other in existence. But I find this difference better made than pursued. For if they had considered Quantity, Similitude, Diversity, and the rest of those Extern Characters of things, as philosophers, and in nature, their inquiries must of force have been of a far other kind than they are. For doth any of them, in handling Quantity, speak of the force of union, how and how far it multiplieth virtue? Doth any give the reason, why some things in nature are so common and in so great mass, and others so rare and in so small quantity? Doth any, in handling Similitude and Diversity, assign the cause why iron should not move to iron, which is more like, but move to the loadstone, which is less like? Why in all diversities of things there should be certain participles in nature, which are almost ambiguous to which kind they should be referred? But there is a mere and deep silence touching the nature and operation of those Common Adjuncts of things, as in nature; and only a resuming and repeating of the force and use of them in speech or argument. Therefore, because in a writing of this nature I avoid all subtility, my meaning touching this original or universal philosophy is thus, in a plain and gross description by negative: *That it be a receptacle for all such profitable observations and axioms as fall not within the compass of any of the special parts of philosophy or sciences, but are more common and of a higher stage.*

Now that there are many of that kind need not be doubted. For example; is not the rule, *Si inæqualibus æqualia addas, omnia erunt inæqualia,* [if equals be added to unequals, the wholes will be unequal,] an axiom as well of justice as of the mathematics? And is there not a true coincidence between commutative and distributive justice, and arithmetical and geometrical proportion? Is not that other rule, *Quæ in eodem tertio conveniunt, et inter se conveniunt,* [things that are equal to the same are equal to each other,] a rule taken from the mathematics, but so potent in logic as all syllogisms are built upon it? Is not the observation, *Omnia mutantur, nil interit,* [all things change, but nothing is lost,] a contemplation in philosophy thus, That the *quantum* of nature is eternal? in natural theology thus, That it requireth the same omnipotence to make somewhat nothing, which at the first made nothing somewhat? according to the scripture, *Didici quod omnia opera quae fecit Deus perseverent in perpetuum; non possumus eis quicquam addere nec auferre:* [I know that whatsoever God doeth, it shall be for ever; nothing can be put to it, nor anything taken from it]. Is not the ground, which Machiavel wisely and largely discourseth concerning governments, that the way to establish and preserve them is to reduce them *ad principia,* a rule in religion and nature as well as in civil administration? Was not the Persian Magic a reduction or correspondence of the principles and architectures of nature to the rules and policy of governments? Is not the precept of a musician, to fall from a discord or harsh accord upon a concord or sweet accord, alike true in affection? Is not the trope of music, to avoid or slide from the close or cadence, common with the trope of rhetoric of deceiving expectation? Is not the delight of the quavering upon a stop in music the same with the playing of light upon the water?

> Splendet tremulo sub lumine pontus:
> [Beneath the trembling light glitters the sea.]

Are not the organs of the senses of one kind with the organs of reflexion, the eye with a glass, the ear with a cave or strait determined and bounded? Neither are these only similitudes, as men of narrow observation may conceive them to be, but the same footsteps of nature, treading or printing upon several subjects or matters. This science therefore (as I understand it) I may justly report as deficient; for I see sometimes the profounder sort of wits, in handling some particular argument, will now and then draw a bucket of water out of this well for their present use; but the springhead thereof seemeth to me not to have been visited, being of so excellent use both for the disclosing of nature and the abridgment of art.

This science being therefore first placed as a common parent, like unto Berecynthia, which had so much heavenly issue,

> Omnes cœlicolas, omnes supera alta tenentes:
> [All dwellers in the heaven and upper sky:]

we may return to the former distribution of the three philosophies; Divine, Natural, and Human. And as concerning Divine Philosophy or Natural Theology, it is that knowledge or rudiment of knowledge concerning God which may be obtained by the contemplation of his creatures; which knowledge may be truly termed divine in respect of the object, and natural in respect of the light. The bounds of this knowledge are, that it sufficeth to convince atheism, but not to inform religion: and therefore there was never miracle wrought by God to convert an atheist, because the light of nature might have led him to confess a God: but miracles have been wrought to convert idolaters and the superstitious, because no light of nature extended to declare the will and true worship of God. For as all works do shew forth the power and skill of the workman, and not his image; so it is of the works of God; which do shew the omnipotency and wisdom of the maker, but not his image: and therefore therein the heathen opinion differeth from the sacred truth; for they supposed the world to be the image of God, and man to be an extract or compendious image of the world; but the Scriptures never vouchsafe to attribute to the world that honour, as to be the image of God, but only *the work of his hands;* neither do they speak of any other image of God, but man. Wherefore by the contemplation of nature to induce and inforce the acknowledgment of God, and to demonstrate his power, providence, and goodness, is an excellent argument, and hath been excellently handled by divers. But on the other side, out of the contemplation of nature, or ground of human knowledges, to induce any verity or persuasion concerning the points of faith, is in my judgment not safe: *Da fidei quæ fidei sunt:* [give unto Faith that which is Faith's]. For the Heathen themselves conclude as much in that excellent and divine fable of the golden chain: *That men and gods were not able to draw Jupiter down to the earth; but contrariwise, Jupiter was able to draw them up to heaven.* So as we ought not to attempt to draw down or submit the mysteries of God to our reason; but contrariwise to raise and advance our reason to the divine truth. So as in this part of knowledge touching divine philosophy, I am so far from noting any deficience, as I rather note an excess: whereunto I have digressed, because of the extreme prejudice which both religion and philosophy hath received and may receive by being commixed together; as that which undoubtedly will make an heretical religion, and an imaginary and fabulous philosophy.

Otherwise it is of the nature of angels and spirits, which is an appendix of theology both divine and natural, and is neither inscrutable nor interdicted; for although the Scripture saith, *Let no man deceive you in sublime discourse touching the worship of angels, pressing into that he knoweth not,* &c. yet notwithstanding if you observe well that precept, it may appear thereby that there be two things only forbidden, adoration of them, and opinion fantastical of them; either to extol them further than appertaineth to the degree of a creature, or to extol a man's knowledge of them further than he hath ground. But the sober and grounded inquiry which may arise out of the passages of holy Scriptures, or out of the gradations of nature, is not restrained. So of degenerate and revolted spirits, the conversing with them or the employment of them is prohibited, much more any veneration towards them. But the contemplation or science of their nature, their power, their illusions, either by Scripture or reason, is a part of spiritual wisdom. For so the apostle saith, *We are not ignorant of his stratagems;* and it is no more unlawful to inquire the nature of evil spirits than to enquire the force of poisons in nature, or the nature of sin and vice in morality. But this part touching angels and spirits, I cannot note as deficient, for many have occupied themselves in it; I may rather challenge it, in many of the writers thereof, as fabulous and fantastical.

Leaving therefore Divine Philosophy or Natural Theology (not Divinity or Inspired Theology, which we reserve for the last of all, as the haven and sabbath of all man's contemplations), we will now proceed to Natural Philosophy. If then it be true that Democritus said, *That the truth of nature lieth hid in certain deep mines and caves;* and if it be true likewise that the Alchemists do so much inculcate, that Vulcan is a second nature, and imitateth that dexterously and compendiously which nature worketh by ambages and length of time; it were good to divide natural philosophy into the mine and the furnace, and to make two professions or occupations of natural philosophers, some to be pioners and some smiths; some to dig, and some to refine and hammer. And surely I do best allow of a division of that kind, though in more familiar and scholastical terms; namely, that these be the two parts of natural philosophy,—the Inquisition of Causes, and the Production of Effects; Speculative, and Operative; Natural Science, and Natural Prudence. For as in civil matters there is a wisdom of discourse and a wisdom of direction; so is it in natural. And here I will make a request, that for the latter (or at least for a part thereof) I may revive and reintegrate the misapplied and abused name of Natural Magic; which in the true sense is but Natural Wisdom, or Natural Prudence; taken according to the ancient acception, purged from vanity and superstition. Now although it be true, and I know it well, that there is an intercourse between Causes and Effects, so as both these knowledges, Speculative and Operative, have a great connexion between themselves; yet because all true and fruitful Natural Philosophy hath a double scale or ladder, ascendent and descendent; ascending from experiments to the invention of causes and descending from causes to the invention of new experiments; therefore I judge it most requisite that these two parts be severally considered and handled.

Natural Science or Theory is divided into Physic and Metaphysic: wherein I desire it may be conceived that I use the word Metaphysic in a differing sense from that that is received: and in like manner I doubt not but it will easily appear to men of judgment that in this and other particulars, wheresoever my conception and notion may differ from the ancient, yet I am studious to keep the ancient terms. For hoping well to deliver myself from mistaking by the order and perspicuous expressing of that I do propound, I am otherwise zealous and affectionate to recede as little from antiquity, either in terms or opinions, as may stand with truth and the proficience of knowledge. And herein I cannot a little marvel at the philosopher Aristotle, that did proceed in such a spirit of difference and contradiction towards all antiquity; undertaking not only to frame new words of science at pleasure, but to confound and extinguish all ancient wisdom; insomuch as he never nameth or mentioneth an ancient author or opinion, but to confute and reprove; wherein for glory, and drawing followers and disciples, he took the right course. For certainly there cometh to pass and hath place in human truth, that which was noted and pronounced in the highest truth: *Veni in nomine Patris, nec recipitis me; si quis venerit in nomine suo, eum recipietis;* [I have come in my Father's name, and ye receive me not; if one come in his own name, him ye will receive]. But in this divine aphorism (considering to whom it was applied, namely to Antichrist, the highest deceiver,) we may discern well that *the coming in a man's own name,* without regard of antiquity or paternity, is no good sign of truth; although it be joined with the fortune and success of an

Eum recipietis. But for this excellent person Aristotle, I will think of him that he learned that humour of his scholar, with whom it seemeth he did emulate, the one to conquer all opinions, as the other to conquer all nations. Wherein nevertheless, it may be, he may at some men's hands that are of a bitter disposition get a like title as his scholar did;

> Felix terrarum prædo, non utile mundo
> Editus exemplum, &c.

[a fortunate robber, who made prize of nations]; so

> Felix doctrinæ prædo,

[a fortunate robber, who made prize of learning]. But to me on the other side that do desire, as much as lieth in my pen, to ground a sociable intercourse between antiquity and proficience, it seemeth best to keep way with antiquity *usque ad aras,* [as far as may be without violating higher obligations;] and therefore to retain the ancient terms, though I sometimes alter the uses and definitions; according to the moderate proceeding in civil government, where although there be some alteration, yet that holdeth which Tacitus wisely noteth *eadem magistratuum vocabula,* [the name of the magistracies are not changed].

To return therefore to the use and acception of the term Metaphysic, as I do now understand the word: It appeareth by that which hath been already said, that I intend Philosophia Prima, Summary Philosophy, and Metaphysic, which heretofore have been confounded as one, to be two distinct things. For the one I have made as a parent or common ancestor to all knowledge, and the other I have now brought in as a branch or descendent of Natural Science. It appeareth likewise that I have assigned to Summary Philosophy the common principles and axioms which are promiscuous and indifferent to several sciences. I have assigned unto it likewise the inquiry *touching the operation of the relative and adventive characters of essences, as Quantity, Similitude, Diversity, Possibility,* and the rest; with this distinction and provision; that they be handled as they have efficacy in nature, and not logically. It appeareth likewise that Natural Theology, which heretofore hath been handled confusedly with Metaphysic, I have inclosed and bounded by itself. It is therefore now a question, what is left remaining for Metaphysic; wherein I may without prejudice preserve thus much of the conceit of antiquity, that Physic should contemplate that which is inherent in matter and therefore transitory, and Metaphysic that which is abstracted and fixed. And again that Physic should handle that which supposeth in nature only a being and moving, and Metaphysic should handle that which supposeth further in nature a reason, understanding, and platform. But the difference, perspicuously expressed, is most familiar and sensible. For as we divided Natural Philosophy in general into the Inquiry of Causes and Productions of Effects; so that part which concerneth the Inquiry of Causes we do subdivide, according to the received and sound division of Causes; the one part, which is Physic, enquireth and handleth the Material and Efficient Causes; and the other, which is Metaphysic, handleth the Formal and Final Causes.

Physic (taking it according to the derivation, and not according to our idiom for Medicine) is situate in a middle term or distance between Natural History and Metaphysic. For Natural History describeth the *variety of things;* Physic, the causes, but *variable or respective causes;* and Metaphysic, the *fixed and constant causes.*

> Limus ut hic durescit, et hæc ut cera liquescit,
> Uno eodemque igni:
> [As the same fire which makes the soft clay hard
> Makes hard wax soft:]

Fire is the cause of induration, but respective to clay; fire is the cause of colliquation, but respective to wax: but fire is no constant cause either of induration or colliquation. So then the physical causes are but the efficient and the matter. Physic hath three parts; whereof two respect nature *united* or *collected,* the third contemplateth nature *diffused* or *distributed.* Nature is collected either into one entire *total,* or else into the same *principles* or *seeds.* So as the first doctrine is touching the Contexture or Configuration of things, as *de mundo, de universitate rerum.* The second is the doctrine concerning the Principles or Originals of things. The third is the doctrine concerning all Variety and Particularity of things, whether it be of the differing substances, or their differing qualities and natures; whereof there needeth no enumeration, this part being but as a gloss or paraphrase, that attendeth upon the text of Natural History. Of these three I cannot report any as deficient. In what truth or perfection they are handled, I make not now any judgment: but they are parts of knowledge not deserted by the labour of man.

For Metaphysic, we have assigned unto it the inquiry of Formal and Final Causes; which assignation, as to the former of them, may seem to be nugatory and void, because of the received and inveterate opinion that the inquisition of man is not competent to find out *essential forms* or *true differences:* of which opinion we will take this hold; that the invention of Forms is of all other parts of knowledge the worthiest to be sought, if it be possible to be found. As for the possibility, they are ill discoverers that think there is no land when they can see nothing but sea. But it is manifest that Plato in his opinion of Ideas, as one that had a wit of elevation situate as upon a cliff, did descry *that forms were the true object of knowledge;* but lost the real fruit of his opinion, by considering of forms as absolutely abstracted from matter, and not confined and determined by matter; and so turning his opinion upon Theology, wherewith all his natural philosophy is infected. But if any man shall keep a continual watchful and severe eye upon action, operation, and the use of knowledge, he may advise and take notice what are the Forms, the disclosures whereof are fruitful and important to the state of man. For as to the Forms of substances—Man only except, of whom it is said, *Formavit hominem de limo terræ, et spiravit in faciem ejus spiraculum vitæ,* [He formed man of the dust of the ground, and breathed into his nostrils the breath of life,] and not as of all other creatures, *Producant aquæ, producat terra,* [let the waters bring forth, let the earth bring forth,]—the Forms of Substances I say (as they are now by compounding and transplanting multiplied) are so perplexed, as they are not to be enquired; no more than it were either possible or to purpose to seek in gross *the forms of those sounds which make words,* which by composition and transposition of letters are infinite. But on the other side, to enquire *the form of those sounds or voices which make simple letters* is easily comprehensible, and being known, induceth and manifesteth the forms of all words, which consist and are compounded of them. In the same manner to enquire the Form of a lion, of an oak, of gold, nay of water, of air, is a vain pursuit: but to enquire the Forms of sense, of voluntary motion, of vegetation, of colours, of gravity and levity, of density, of tenuity, of heat, of cold, and all other natures and qualities, which like an alphabet are not many, and of which the essences (upheld by matter) of all creatures do consist; to enquire I say the *true forms* of these, is that part of Metaphysic which we now define of. Not but that Physic doth make inquiry and take consideration of the same natures: but how? Only as to the Material and Efficient Causes of them, and not as to the Forms. For example; if the cause of Whiteness in snow or froth be enquired, and it be rendered thus, *that the subtile intermixture of air and water is the cause*, it is well rendered; but nevertheless, is this the Form of Whiteness? No; but it is the Efficient, which is ever but *vehiculum formæ*, [the carrier of the Form]. This part of Metaphysic I do not find laboured and performed; whereat I marvel not, because I hold it not possible to be invented by that course of invention which hath been used; in regard that men (which is the root of all error) have made too untimely a departure and too remote a recess from particulars.

But the use of this part of Metaphysic which I report as deficient, is of the rest the most excellent in two respects; the one, because it is the duty and virtue of all knowledge to abridge the infinity of individual experience as much as the conception of truth will permit, and to remedy the complaint of *vita brevis, ars longa*, [life is short and art is long;] which is performed by uniting the notions and conceptions of sciences. For knowledges are as pyramides, whereof history is the basis: so of Natural Philosophy the basis is Natural History; the stage next the basis is Physic; the stage next the vertical point is Metaphysic. As for the vertical point, *Opus quod operatur Deus à principio usque ad finem*, [the work which God worketh from the beginning to the end,] the Summary Law of Nature, we know not whether man's inquiry can attain unto it. But these three be the true *stages* of knowledge; and are to them that are depraved no better than the giants' hills, [Pelion, Ossa, and Olympus, piled upon each other,]

> Ter sunt conati imponere Pelio Ossam,
> Scilicet atque Ossæ frondosum involvere Olympum:

but to those which refer all things to the glory of God, they are as the three acclamations, *Sancte, sancte, sancte;* holy in the description or dilatation of his works, holy in the connexion or concatenation of them, and holy in the union of them in a perpetual and uniform law. And therefore the speculation was excellent in Parmenides and Plato, although but a speculation in them, That all things by scale did ascend to unity. So then always that knowledge is worthiest, which is charged with least multiplicity; which appeareth to be Metaphysic; as that which considereth the Simple Forms or Differences of things, which are few in number, and the degrees and co-ordinations whereof make all this variety. The second respect which valueth and commendeth this part of Metaphysic, is that it doth enfranchise the power of man unto the greatest liberty and possibility of works and effects. For Physic carrieth men in narrow and restrained ways, subject to many accidents of impediments, imitating the ordinary flexuous courses of nature; but *latæ undique sunt sapientibus viæ:* to sapience (which was anciently defined to be *rerum divinarum et humanarum scientia,* [the knowledge of things human and divine],) there is ever choice of means. For physical causes give light to new invention *in simili materia;* but whosoever knoweth any *form,* knoweth the utmost possibility of *superinducing that nature upon any variety of matter,* and so is less restrained in operation, either to the basis of the Matter, or the condition of the Efficient: which kind of knowledge, Salomon likewise, though in a more divine sense, elegantly describeth: *Non arctabuntur gressus tui, et currens non habebis offendiculum;* [thy steps shall not be straitened; thou shalt run and not stumble]. The ways of sapience are not much liable either to particularity or chance.

The second part of Metaphysic is the inquiry of *final* causes, which I am moved to report not as omitted, but as misplaced. And yet if it were but a fault in order, I would not speak of it; for order is matter of illustration, but pertaineth not to the substance of sciences: but this misplacing hath caused a deficience, or at least a great improficience in the sciences themselves. For the handling of final causes mixed with the rest in physical inquiries, hath intercepted the severe and diligent inquiry of all real and physical causes, and given men the occasion to stay upon these satisfactory and specious causes, to the great arrest and prejudice of further discovery. For this I find done not only by Plato, who ever anchoreth upon that shore, but by Aristotle, Galen, and others, which do usually likewise fall upon these flats of *discoursing causes.* For to say that *the hairs of the eye-lids are for a quickset and fence about the sight;* or that *the firmness of the skins and hides of living creatures is to defend them from the extremities of heat or cold;* or that *the bones are for the columns or beams, whereupon the frames of the bodies of living creatures are built;* or that *the leaves of trees are for protecting of the fruit;* or that *the clouds are for watering of the earth;* or that *the solidness of the earth is for the station and mansion of living creatures,* and the like, is well enquired and collected in Metaphysic; but in Physic they are impertinent. Nay, they are indeed but remoras and hinderances to stay and slug the ship from further sailing, and have brought this to pass, that the search of the Physical

Causes hath been neglected and passed in silence. And therefore the natural philosophy of Democritus and some others, who did not suppose a mind or reason in the frame of things, but attributed *the form thereof able to maintain itself to infinite essays or proofs of nature,* which they term *fortune,* seemeth to me (as far as I can judge by the recital and fragments which remain unto us) in particularities of physical causes more real and better enquired than that of Aristotle and Plato; whereof both intermingled final causes, the one as a part of theology, and the other as a part of logic, which were the favourite studies respectively of both those persons. Not because those final causes are not true, and worthy to be enquired, being kept within their own province; but because their excursions into the limits of physical causes hath bred a vastness and solitude in that track. For otherwise keeping their precincts and borders, men are extremely deceived if they think there is an enmity or repugnancy, at all between them. For the cause rendered, that *the hairs about the eye-lids are for the safeguard of the sight,* doth not impugn the cause rendered, that *pilosity is incident to orifices of moisture; Muscosi fontes,* [the mossy springs,] &c. Nor the cause rendered, that *the firmness of hides is for the armour of the body against extremities of heat or cold,* doth not impugn the cause rendered, that *contraction of pores is incident to the outwardest parts, in regard of their adjacence to foreign or unlike bodies;* and so of the rest: both causes being true and compatible, the one declaring an intention, the other a consequence only. Neither doth this call in question or derogate from divine providence, but highly confirm and exalt it. For as in civil actions he is the greater and deeper politique, that can make other men the instruments of his will and ends and yet never acquaint them with his purpose, so as they shall do it and yet not know what they do, than he that imparteth his meaning to those he employeth; so is the wisdom of God more admirable, when nature intendeth one thing and providence draweth forth another, than if he had communicated to particular creatures and motions the characters and impressions of his providence. And thus much for Metaphysic; the later part whereof I allow as extant, but wish it confined to its proper place.

Nevertheless there remaineth yet another part of Natural Philosophy, which is commonly made a principal part, and holdeth rank with Physic special and Metaphysic; which is Mathematic; but I think it more agreeable to the nature of things and to the light of order to place it as a branch of Metaphysic; for the subject of it being Quantity; not Quantity indefinite, which is but a relative and belongeth to *philosophia prima* (as hath been said,) but Quantity determined or proportionable; it appeareth to be one of the Essential Forms of things; as that that is causative in nature of a number of effects; insomuch as we see in the schools both of Democritus and of Pythagoras, that the one *did ascribe figure to the first seeds of things,* and the other *did suppose numbers to be the principles and originals of things:* and it is true also that of all other forms (as we understand forms) it is the most abstracted and separable from matter, and therefore most proper to Metaphysic; which hath likewise been the cause why it hath been better laboured and enquired than any of the other forms, which are more immersed into matter. For it being the nature of the mind of man (to the extreme prejudice of knowledge) to delight in the spacious liberty of generalities, as in a champion region, and not in the inclosures of particularity; the Mathematics of all other knowledge were the goodliest fields to satisfy that appetite. But for the placing of this science, it is not much material: only we have endeavoured in these our partitions to observe a kind of perspective, that one part may cast light upon another.

The Mathematics are either Pure or Mixed. To the Pure Mathematics are those sciences belonging which handle Quantity Determinate, merely severed from any axioms of natural philosophy; and these are two, Geometry and Arithmetic; the one handling Quantity continued, and the other dissevered. Mixed hath for subject some axioms or parts of natural philosophy, and considereth Quantity determined, as it is auxiliary and incident unto them. For many parts of nature can neither be invented with sufficient subtilty nor demonstrated with sufficient perspicuity nor accommodated unto use with sufficient dexterity, without the aid and intervening of the Mathematics: of which sort are Perspective, Music, Astronomy, Cosmography, Architecture, Enginery, and divers others. In the Mathematics I can report no deficience, except it be that men do not sufficiently understand the excellent use of the Pure Mathematics, in that they do remedy and cure many defects in the wit and faculties intellectual. For if the wit be too dull, they sharpen it; if too wandering, they fix it; if too inherent in the sense, they abstract it. So that as tennis is a game of no use in itself, but of great use in respect it maketh a quick eye and a body ready to put itself into all postures; so in the Mathematics, that use which is collateral and intervenient is no less worthy than that which is principal and intended. And as for the Mixed Mathematics, I may only make this prediction, that there cannot fail to be more kinds of them, as nature grows further disclosed. Thus much of Natural Science, or the part of nature Speculative.

For Natural Prudence, or the part Operative of Natural Philosophy, we will divide it into three parts, Experimental, Philosophical, and Magical; which three parts active have a correspondence and analogy with the three parts Speculative, Natural History, Physic, and Metaphysic. For many operations have been invented, sometimes by a casual incidence and occurrence, sometimes by a purposed experiment; and of those which have been found by an intentional experiment, some have been found out by varying or extending the same experiment, some by transferring and compounding divers experiments the one into the other, which kind of invention an empiric may manage. Again, by the knowledge of physical causes there cannot fail to follow many indications and designations of new particulars, if men in their speculation will keep one eye upon use and practice. But these are but coastings along the shore, *premendo littus iniquum:* for it seemeth to me there can hardly be discovered any radical or fundamental alterations and innovations in nature, either by the fortune and essays of experiments, or by the light and direction of physical causes. If therefore we have reported Metaphysic deficient, it must follow that we do the like of Natural Magic, which hath relation thereunto. For as for the Natural Magic whereof now there is mention in books, containing certain credulous and superstitious conceits and observations of Sympathies and Antipathies and hidden proprieties, and some frivolous experiments, strange rather by disguisement than in themselves; it is as far differing in truth of nature from such a knowledge as we require, as the story of king Arthur of Britain, or Hugh of Bourdeaux, differs from Cæsar's commentaries in truth of story. For it is manifest that Cæsar did greater things *de vero* than those imaginary heroes were feigned to do. But he did them not in that fabulous manner. Of this kind of learning the fable of Ixion was a figure, who designed to enjoy Juno, the goddess of power; and instead of her had copulation with a cloud, of which mixture were begotten centaurs and chimeras. So whosoever shall entertain high and vaporous imaginations instead of a laborious and sober inquiry of truth, shall beget hopes and beliefs of strange and impossible shapes. And therefore we may note in these sciences which hold so much of imagination and belief, as this degenerate Natural Magic, Alchemy, Astrology, and the like, that in their propositions the description of the means is ever more monstrous than the pretence or end. For it is a thing more probable, that he that knoweth well the natures of Weight, of Colour, of Pliant and Fragile in respect of the hammer, of Volatile and Fixed in respect of the fire, and the rest, may superinduce upon some metal the nature and form of gold by such mechanique as belongeth to the production of the natures afore rehearsed, than that some grains of the medicine projected should in a few moments of time turn a sea of quicksilver or other material into gold. So it is more probable, that he that knoweth the nature of arefaction, the nature of assimilation of nourishment to the thing nourished, the manner of increase and clearing of spirits, the manner of the depredations which spirits make upon the humours and solid parts, shall by ambages of diets, bathings, anointings, medicines, motions, and the like, prolong life or restore some degree of youth or vivacity, than that it can be done with the use of a few drops or scruples of a liquor or receit. To conclude therefore, the true Natural Magic, which is that great liberty and latitude of operation which dependeth upon the knowledge of Forms, I may report deficient, as the relative thereof is. To which part, if we be serious and incline not to vanities and plausible discourse, besides the deriving and deducing the operations themselves from Metaphysic, there are pertinent two points of much purpose, the one by way of preparation, the other by way of caution. The first is, that there be made a *Calendar resembling an inventory* of the estate of man, containing all the inventions (being the works or fruits of nature or art) which are now extant and whereof man is already possessed; out of which doth naturally result a note, what things are yet held impossible, or not invented; which calendar will be the more artificial and serviceable, if to every reputed impossibility you add what thing is extant which cometh the nearest in degree to that impossibility; to the end that by these optatives and potentials man's inquiry may be the more awake in deducing direction of works from the speculation of causes. And secondly, that those experiments be not only esteemed which have an immediate and present use, but those principally which are of most universal consequence for invention of other experiments, and those which give most light to the invention of causes; for the invention of the mariner's needle, which giveth the direction, is of no less benefit for navigation than the invention of the sails, which give the motion.

Thus have I passed through Natural Philosophy, and the deficiences thereof; wherein if I have differed from the ancient and received doctrines, and thereby shall move contradiction; for my part, as I affect not to dissent, so I purpose not to contend. If it be truth,

Non canimus surdis, respondent omnia sylvæ:
[All as we sing the listening woods reply:]

the voice of nature will consent, whether the voice of man do or no. And as Alexander Borgia was wont to say of the expedition of the French for Naples, that they came with chalk in their hands to mark up their lodgings, and not with weapons to fight; so I like better that entry of truth which cometh peaceably with chalk to mark up those minds which are capable to lodge and harbour it, than that which cometh with pugnacity and contention.

But there remaineth a division of Natural Philosophy according to the *report of the inquiry,* and nothing concerning the matter or subject; and that is Positive and Considerative; when the inquiry reporteth either an Assertion or a Doubt. These doubts or *non liquets* are of two sorts, Particular and Total. For the first, we see a good example thereof in Aristotle's Problems, which deserved to have had a better continuance, but so nevertheless as there is one point whereof warning is to be given and taken. The registering of doubts hath two excellent uses: the one, that it saveth philosophy from errors and falsehoods; when that which is not fully appearing is not collected into assertion, whereby error might draw error, but reserved in doubt: the other, that the entry of doubts are as so many suckers or spunges to draw use of knowledge; insomuch as that which if doubts had not preceded a man should never have advised but passed it over without note, by the suggestion and solicitation of doubts is made to be attended and applied. But both these commodities do scarcely countervail an inconvenience which will intrude itself, if it be not debarred; which is, that when a doubt is once received men labour rather how to keep it a doubt still than how to solve it, and accordingly bend their wits. Of this we see the familiar example in lawyers and scholars, both which if they have once admitted a doubt, it goeth ever after authorised for a doubt. But that use of wit and knowledge is to be allowed, which laboureth to make doubtful things certain, and not those which labour to make certain things doubtful. Therefore these *calendars of doubts* I commend as excellent things, so that there be this caution used, that when they be thoroughly sifted and brought to resolution, they be from thenceforth omitted, decarded, and not continued to cherish and encourage men in doubting. To which calendar of doubts or problems, I advise be annexed another calendar, as much or more material, which is *a calendar of popular errors:* I mean chiefly, in natural history such as pass in speech and conceit, and are nevertheless apparently detected and convicted of untruth; that man's knowledge be not weakened nor imbased by such dross and vanity. As for the *doubts or non liquets general or in total,* I understand those differences of opinions touching the principles of nature and the fundamental points of the same, which have caused the diversity of sects, schools, and philosophies; as that of Empedocles, Pythagoras, Democritus, Parmenides, and the rest. For although Aristotle, as though he had been of the race of the Ottomans, thought he could not reign except the first thing he did he killed all his brethren; yet to those that seek truth and not magistrality, it cannot but seem a matter of great profit to see before them the several opinions touching the foundations of nature; not for any exact truth that can be expected in those theories; for as the same phænomena in astronomy are satisfied by the received astronomy of the diurnal motion and the proper motions of the planets with their eccentrics and epicycles and likewise by the theory of Copernicus who supposed the earth to move; and the calculations are indifferently agreeable to both; so the ordinary face and view of experience is many times satisfied by several theories and philosophies; whereas to find the real truth requireth another manner of severity and attention. For as Aristotle saith that children at the first will call every woman mother, but afterward they come to distinguish according to truth; so experience, if it be in childhood, will call every philosophy mother, but when it cometh to ripeness it will discern the true mother. So as in the mean time it is good to see the several glosses and opinions upon nature, whereof it may be every one in some one point hath seen clearer than his fellows. Therefore I wish some collection to be made painfully and understandingly *de antiquis philosophiis,* out of all the possible light which remaineth to us of them. Which kind of work I find deficient. But here I must give warning, that it be done distinctly and severely; the philosophies of every one throughout by themselves; and not by titles packed and faggoted up together, as hath been done by Plutarch. For it is the harmony of a philosophy in itself which giveth it light and credence; whereas if it be singled and broken, it will seem more foreign and dissonant. For as when I read in Tacitus the actions of Nero or Claudius, with circumstances of times, inducements, and occasions, I find them not so strange; but when I read them in Suetonius Tranquillus gathered into titles and bundles, and not in order of time, they seem more monstrous and incredible; so it is of any philosophy reported entire, and dismembered by articles. Neither do I exclude opinions of latter times to be likewise represented in this calendar of sects of philosophy, as that of Theophrastus Paracelsus, eloquently reduced into an harmony by the pen of Severinus the Dane; and that of Telesius, and his scholar Donius, being as a pastoral philosophy, full of sense but of no great depth; and that of Fracastorius, who though he pretended not to make any new philosophy, yet did use the absoluteness of his own sense upon the old; and that of Gilbertus our countryman, who revived, with some alterations and demonstrations, the opinions of Xenophanes; and any other worthy to be admitted.

Thus have we now dealt with two of the three beams of man's knowledge; that is *Radius Directus,* which is referred to nature, *Radius Refractus,* which is referred to God, and cannot report truly because of the inequality of the medium. There resteth *Radius Reflexus* whereby Man beholdeth and contemplateth himself.

We come therefore now to that knowledge whereunto the ancient oracle directeth us, which is *the knowledge of ourselves;* which deserveth the more accurate handling, by how much it toucheth us more nearly. This knowledge, as it is the end and term of natural philosophy in the intention of man, so notwithstanding it is but a portion of natural philosophy in the continent of nature. And generally let this be a rule, that all partitions of knowledges be accepted rather for lines and veins, than for sections and separations; and that the continuance and entireness of knowledge be preserved. For the contrary hereof hath made particular sciences to become barren, shallow, and erroneous; while they have not been nourished and maintained from the common fountain. So we see Cicero the orator complained of Socrates and his school, that he was the first that separated philosophy and rhetoric; whereupon rhetoric became an empty and verbal art. So we may see that the opinion of Copernicus touching the rotation of the earth, which astronomy itself cannot correct because it is not repugnant to any of the phænomena, yet natural philosophy may correct. So we see also that the science of medicine, if it be destituted and forsaken by natural philosophy, it is not much better than an empirical practice. With this reservation therefore we proceed to Human Philosophy or Humanity, which hath two parts: the one considereth man segregate, or distributively; the other congregate, or in society. So as Human Philosophy is either Simple and Particular, or Conjugate and Civil. Humanity Particular consisteth of the same parts whereof man consisteth; that is, of knowledges which respect the Body, and of knowledges that respect the Mind. But before we distribute so far, it is good to constitute. For I do take the consideration in general and at large of Human Nature to be fit to be emancipate and made a knowledge by itself; not so much in regard to those delightful and elegant discourses which have been made of the dignity of man, of his miseries, of his state and life, and the like *adjuncts of his common and undivided nature;* but chiefly in regard of the knowledge concerning the *sympathies and concordances between the mind and body,* which, being mixed, cannot be properly assigned to the sciences of either.

This knowledge hath two branches: for as all leagues and amities consist of mutual Intelligence and mutual Offices, so this league of mind and body hath these two parts; *how the one discloseth the other,* and *how the one worketh upon the other;* Discovery, and Impression. The former of these hath begotten two arts, both of Prediction or Prenotion; whereof the one is honoured with the inquiry of Aristotle, and the other of Hippocrates. And although they have of later time been used to be coupled with superstitious and fantastical arts, yet being purged and restored to their true state, they have both of them a solid ground in nature, and a profitable use in life. The first is Physiognomy, which discovereth the disposition of the mind by the lineaments of the body. The second is the Exposition of Natural Dreams, which discovereth the state of the body by the imaginations of the mind. In the former of these I note a deficience. For Aristotle hath very ingeniously and diligently handled the factures of the body, but not the gestures of the body, which are no less comprehensible by art, and of greater use and advantage. For the Lineaments of the body do disclose the disposition and inclination of the mind in general; but the Motions of the countenance and parts do not only so, but do further disclose the present humour and state of the mind and will. For as your Majesty saith most aptly and elegantly, *As the tongue speaketh to the ear, so the gesture speaketh to the eye.* And therefore a number of subtile persons, whose eyes do dwell upon the faces and fashions of men, do well know the advantage of this observation, as being most part of their ability; neither can it be denied but that it is a great discovery of dissimulations, and a great direction in business.

The latter branch, touching Impression, hath not been collected into art, but hath been handled dispersedly; and it hath the same relation or antistrophe that the former hath. For the consideration is double: Either *how, and how far the humours and effects of the body do alter or work upon the mind;* or again, *how and how far the passions or apprehensions of the mind do alter or work upon the body.* The former of these hath been inquired and considered as a part and appendix of Medicine, but much more as a part of Religion or Superstition. For the physician prescribeth cures of the mind in phrensies and melancholy passions; and pretendeth also to exhibit medicines to exhilarate the mind, to confirm the courage, to clarify the wits, to corroborate the memory, and the like; but the scruples and superstitions of diet and other regiment of the body in the sect of the Pythagoreans, in the heresy of the Manicheans, and in the law of Mahomet, do exceed. So likewise the ordinances in the Ceremonial Law, interdicting the eating of the blood and the fat, distinguishing between beasts clean and unclean for meat, are many and strict. Nay the faith itself being clear and serene from all clouds of Ceremony, yet retaineth the use of fastings, abstinences, and other macerations and humiliations of the body, as things real, and not figurative. The root and life of all which prescripts is, (besides the ceremony,) the consideration of that dependency which the affections of the mind are submitted unto upon the state and disposition of the body. And if any man of weak judgment do conceive that this suffering of the mind from the body doth either question the immortality or derogate from the sovereignty of the soul, he may be taught in easy instances, that the infant in the mother's womb is compatible with the mother and yet separable; and the most absolute monarch is sometimes led by his servants and yet without subjection. As for the reciprocal knowledge, which is the operation of the conceits and passions of the mind upon the body, we see all wise physicians in the prescriptions of their regiments to their patients do ever consider *accidentia animi,* as of great force to further or hinder remedies or recoveries; and more specially it is an inquiry of great depth and worth concerning Imagination, how and how far it altereth the body proper of the imaginant. For although it hath a manifest power to hurt, it followeth not it hath the same degree of power to help; no more than a man can conclude, that because there be pestilent airs, able suddenly to kill a man in health, therefore there should be sovereign airs, able suddenly to cure a man in sickness. But the inquisition of this part is of great use, though it needeth, as Socrates said, *a Delian diver,* being difficult and profound. But unto all this knowledge *de communi vinculo,* of the concordances between the mind and the body, that part of inquiry is most necessary, which considereth of the *seats* and *domiciles* which the several faculties of the mind do take and occupate in the organs of the body; which knowledge hath been attempted, and is controverted, and deserveth to be much better enquired. For the opinion of Plato, who placed *the understanding in the brain, animosity* (which he did unfitly call *anger,* having a greater mixture with *pride*) *in the heart,* and *concupiscence or sensuality in the liver,* deserveth not to be despised; but much less to be allowed. So then we have constituted (as in our own wish and advice) the inquiry *touching human nature entire,* as a just portion of knowledge to be handled apart.

The knowledge that concerneth man's body is divided as the good of man's body is divided, unto which it referreth. The good of man's body is of four kinds, Health, Beauty, Strength, and Pleasure: so the knowledges are Medicine, or art of Cure; art of Decoration, which is called Cosmetic; art of Activity, which is called Athletic; and art Voluptuary, which Tacitus truly calleth *eruditus luxus,* [educated luxury.] This subject of man's body is of all other things in nature most susceptible of remedy; but then that remedy is most susceptible of error. For the same subtility of the subject doth cause large possibility and easy failing; and therefore the inquiry ought to be the more exact.

To speak therefore of Medicine, and to resume that we have said, ascending a little higher: The ancient opinion that man was Microcosmus, an abstract or model of the world, hath been fantastically strained by Paracelsus and the alchemists, as if there were to be found in man's body certain correspondences and parallels, which should have respect to all varieties of things, as stars, planets, minerals, which are extant in the great world. But thus much is evidently true, that of all substances which nature hath produced, man's body is the most extremely compounded. For we see herbs and plants are nourished by earth and water; beasts for the most part by herbs and fruits; man by the flesh of beasts, birds, fishes, herbs, grains, fruits, water, and the manifold alterations, dressings, and preparations of these several bodies, before they come to be his food and aliment. Add hereunto that beasts have a more simple order of life, and less change of affections to work upon their bodies; whereas man in his mansion, sleep, exercise, passions, hath infinite variations; and it cannot be denied but that the Body of man of all other things is of the most compounded mass. The Soul on the other side is the simplest of substances, as is well expressed,

Purumque reliquit
Æthereum sensum atque auraï simplicis ignem:
[Pure and unmixed
The etherial sense is left—mere air and fire.]

So that it is no marvel though the soul so placed enjoy no rest, if that principle be true that *Motus rerum est rapidus extra locum, placidus in loco;* [things move rapidly to their place and calmly in their place]. But to the purpose. This variable composition of man's body hath made it as an instrument easy to distemper; and therefore the poets did well to conjoin Music and Medicine in Apollo: because the office of medicine is but to tune this curious harp of Man's body and to reduce it to harmony. So then the subject being so variable hath made the art by consequent more conjectural; and the art being conjectural hath made so much the more place to be left for imposture. For almost all other arts and sciences are judged by acts or masterpieces, as I may term them, and not by the successes and events. The lawyer is judged by the virtue of his pleading, and not by the issue of the cause. The master in the ship is judged by the directing his course aright, and not by the fortune of the voyage. But the physician, and perhaps the politique, hath no particular acts demonstrative of his ability, but is judged most by the event; which is ever but as it is taken: for who can tell, if a patient die or recover, or if a state be preserved or ruined, whether it be art or accident? And therefore many times the impostor is prized, and the man of virtue taxed. Nay, we see [the] weakness and credulity of men is such, as they will often prefer a montabank or witch before a learned physician. And therefore the poets were clear-sighted in discerning this extreme folly, when they made Æsculapius and Circe brother and sister, both children of the sun, as in the verses,

> Ipse repertorem medicinæ talis et artis
> Fulmine *Phœbigenam* Stygais detrusit at undas:
> [*Apollo's son* from whom that art did grow
> Jove struck with thunder to the shades below].

And again,

> Dives inaccessos ubi *Solis filia* lucos, &c.
> [Now by the shelves of Circe's coast they run,—
> Circe the rich, the *daughter of the sun*.]

For in all times, in the opinion of the multitude, witches and old women and impostors have had a competition with physicians. And what followeth? Even this, that physicians say to themselves, as Salomon expresseth it upon an higher occasion; *If it befal to me as befalleth to the fools, why should I labour to be more wise?* And therefore I cannot much blame physicians, that they use commonly to intend some other art or practice, which they fancy, more than their profession. For you shall have of them antiquaries, poets, humanists, statesmen, merchants, divines, and in every of these better seen than in their profession; and no doubt upon this ground, that they find that mediocrity and excellency in their art maketh no difference in profit or reputation towards their fortune; for the weakness of patients and sweetness of life and nature of hope maketh men depend upon physicians with all their defects. But nevertheless these things which we have spoken of are courses begotten between a little occasion and a great deal of sloth and default; for if we will excite and awake our observation, we shall see in familiar instances what a predominant faculty the *subtilty of spirit* hath over the *variety of matter or form.* Nothing more variable than faces and countenances; yet men can bear in memory the infinite distinctions of them; nay, a painter with a few shells of colours, and the benefit of his eye and habit of his imagination, can imitate them all that ever have been, are, or may be, if they were brought before him. Nothing more variable than voices; yet men can likewise discern them personally; nay, you shall have a *buffon* or *pantomimus* will express as many as he pleaseth. Nothing more variable than the differing sounds of words; yet men have found the way to reduce them to a few simple letters. So that it is not *the insufficiency or incapacity of man's mind,* but it is *the remote standing or placing thereof,* that breedeth these mazes and incomprehensions: for as the sense afar off is full of mistaking but is exact at hand, so is it of the understanding; the remedy whereof is not to quicken or strengthen the organ, but to go nearer to the object; and therefore there is no doubt but if the physicians will learn and use the true approaches and avenues of nature, they may assume as much as the poet saith:

> Et quoniam variant morbi, variabimus artes;
> Mille mali species, mille salutis erunt:

[varying their arts according to the variety of diseases,—for a thousand forms of sickness a thousand methods of cure]. Which that they should do, the nobleness of their art doth deserve; well shadowed by the poets, in that they made Æsculapius to be the son of the Sun, the one being the fountain of life, the other as the second stream; but infinitely more honoured by the example of our Saviour, who made the body of man the object of his miracles, as the soul was the object of his doctrine. For we read not that ever he vouchsafed to do any miracle about honour, or money (except that one for giving tribute to Cæsar), but only about the preserving, sustaining, and healing the body of man.

Medicine is a science which hath been (as we have said) more professed than laboured, and yet more laboured than advanced; the labour having been, in my judgment, rather in circle than in progression. For I find much iteration, but small addition. It considereth *causes of diseases,* with the *occasions or impulsions;* the *diseases themselves,* with the *accidents;* and the *cures,* with the *preservations.* The deficiencies which I think good to note, being a few of many, and those such as are of a more open and manifest nature, I will enumerate, and not place.

The first is the discontinuance of the ancient and serious diligence of Hippocrates, which used to set down a narrative of the special cases of his patients, and how they proceeded, and how they were judged by recovery or death. Therefore having an example proper in the father of the art, I shall not need to allege an example foreign, of the wisdom of the lawyers, who are careful to report new cases and decisions for the direction of future judgments. This continuance of Medicinal History I find deficient; which I understand neither to be so infinite as to extend to every common case, nor so reserved as to admit none but wonders: for many things are new in the manner which are not new in the kind; and if men will intend to observe, they shall find much worthy to observe.

In the inquiry which is made by Anatomy I find much deficience: for they inquire of the *parts,* and their *substances, figures,* and *collocations;* but they inquire not of the *diversities of the parts,* the *secrecies of the passages,* and the *seats or nestling of the humours,* nor much of the *footsteps and impressions of diseases:* the reason of which omission I suppose to be, because the first inquiry may be satisfied in the view of one or a few anatomies; but the latter, being comparative and casual, must arise from the view of many. And as to the diversity of parts, there is no doubt but the facture or framing of the inward parts is as full of difference as the outward, and in that is the *cause continent* of many diseases; which not being observed, they quarrel many times with the humours, which are not in fault; the fault being in the very frame and mechanic of the part, which cannot be removed by medicine alterative, but must be accommodate and palliate by diets and medicines familiar. And for the passages and pores, it is true which was anciently noted, that the more subtle of them appear not in anatomies, because they are shut and latent in dead bodies, though they be open and manifest in live: which being supposed, though the inhumanity of *anatomia vivorum* [anatomy of the living subject] was by Celsus justly reproved yet in regard of the great use of this observation, the inquiry needed not by him so slightly to have been relinquished altogether, or referred to the casual practices of surgery; but might have been well diverted upon the dissection of beasts alive, which notwithstanding the dissimilitude of their parts, may sufficiently satisfy this inquiry. And for the humours, they are commonly passed over in anatomies as purgaments; whereas it is most necessary to observe what cavities, nests, and receptacles the humours do find in the parts, with the differing kind of the humour so lodged and received. And as for the footsteps of diseases, and their devastations of the inward parts, imposthumations, exulcerations, discontinuations, putrefactions, consumptions, contractions, extensions, convulsions, dislocations, obstructions, repletions, together with all preternatural substances, as stones, carnosities, excrescences, worms, and the like; they ought to have been exactly observed by multitude of anatomies and the contribution of men's several experiences, and carefully set down both historically according to the appearances, and artificially with a reference to the diseases and symptoms which resulted from them, in case where the anatomy is of a defunct patient; whereas now upon opening of bodies they are passed over slightly and in silence.

In the inquiry of diseases, they do abandon the cures of many, some as in their nature incurable, and others as past the period of cure; so that Sylla and the triumvirs never proscribed so many men to die, as they do by their ignorant edicts; whereof numbers do escape with less difficulty than they did in the Roman proscriptions. Therefore I will not doubt to note as a deficience, that they inquire not the perfect cures of many diseases, or extremities of diseases, but pronouncing them incurable do enact a law of neglect, and exempt ignorance from discredit.

Nay further, I esteem it the office of a physician not only to restore health, but to mitigate pain and dolors; and not only when such mitigation may conduce to recovery, but when it may serve to make a fair and easy passage: for it is no small felicity which Augustus Cæsar was wont to wish to himself, that same *Euthanasia;* and which was specially noted in the death of Antoninus Pius, whose death was after the fashion and semblance of a kindly and pleasant sleep. So it is written of Epicurus, that after his disease was judged desperate, he drowned his stomach and senses with a large draught and ingurgitation of wine; whereupon the epigram was made, *Hinc stygias ebrius hausit aquas;* he was not sober enough to taste any bitterness of the Stygian water. But the physicians contrariwise do make a kind of scruple and religion to stay with the patient after the disease is deplored; whereas, in my judgment, they ought both to enquire the skill and to give the attendance for the facilitating and assuaging of the pains and agonies of death.

In the consideration of the Cures of diseases, I find a deficience in the receipts of propriety respecting the particular cures of diseases: for the physicians have frustrated the fruit of tradition and experience by their magistralities, in adding and taking out and changing *quid pro quo* in their receipts, at their pleasures; commanding so over the medicine as the medicine cannot command over the disease. For except it be treacle and mithridatum, and of late *diascordium,* and a few more, they tie themselves to no receipts severely and religiously: for as to the confections of sale which are in the shops, they are for readiness and not for propriety; for they are upon general intentions of purging, opening, comforting, altering, and not much appropriate to particular diseases: and this is the cause why empirics and old women are more happy many times in their cures than learned physicians, because they are more religious in holding their medicines. Therefore here is the deficience which I find, that physicians have not, partly out of their own practice, partly out of the constant probations reported in books, and partly out of the traditions of empirics, set down and delivered over certain *experimental medicines* for the cure of particular diseases, besides their own *conjectural* and *magistral descriptions.* For as they were the men of the best composition in the state of Rome, which either being consuls inclined to the people, or being tribunes inclined to the senate; so in the matter we now handle, they be the best physicians, which being learned incline to the traditions of experience, or being empirics incline to the methods of learning.

In preparation of Medicines, I do find strange, specially considering how mineral medicines have been extolled, and that they are safer for the outward than inward parts, that no man hath sought to make an imitation by art of Natural Baths and Medicinable Fountains; which nevertheless are confessed to receive their virtues from minerals: and not so only, but discerned and distinguished from what particular mineral they receive tinctures, as sulphur, vitriol, steel, or the like; which nature if it may be reduced to compositions of art, both the variety of them will be increased, and the temper of them will be more commanded.

But lest I grow to be more particular than is agreeable either to my intention or to proportion, I will conclude this part with the note of one deficience more, which seemeth to me of greatest consequence; which is, that the prescripts in use are too compendious to attain their end: for, to my understanding, it is a vain and flattering opinion to think any medicine can be so sovereign or so happy, as that the receit or use of it can work any great effect upon the body of man. It were a strange speech which spoken, or spoken oft, should reclaim a man from a vice to which he were by nature subject. It is order, pursuit, sequence, and interchange of application, which is mighty in nature; which although it require more exact knowledge in prescribing and more precise obedience in observing, yet is recompensed with the magnitude of effects. And although a man would think, by the daily visitations of the physicians, that there were a pursuance in the cure; yet let a man look into their prescripts and ministrations, and he shall find them but inconstancies and every day's devices, without any settled providence or project. Not that every scrupulous or superstitious prescript is effectual, no more than every straight way is the way to heaven; but the *truth of the direction* must precede *severity of observance.*

For Cosmetic, it hath parts civil, and parts effeminate: for cleanness of body was ever esteemed to proceed from a due reverence to God, to society, and to ourselves. As for artificial decoration, it is well worthy of the deficiencies which it hath; being neither fine enough to deceive, nor handsome to use, nor wholesome to please.

For Athletic, I take the subject of it largely; that

is to say, for any point of ability whereunto the body of man may be brought, whether it be of *activity* or of *patience;* whereof activity hath two parts, *strength* and *swiftness;* and patience likewise hath two parts, *hardness against wants and extremities,* and *indurance of pain or torment:* whereof we see the practices in tumblers, in savages, and in those that suffer punishment: nay, if there be any other faculty which falls not within any of the former divisions, as in those that dive, that obtain a strange power of containing respiration, and the like, I refer it to this part. Of these things the practices are known, but the philosophy that concerneth them is not much enquired; the rather, I think, because they are supposed to be obtained either by an aptness of nature, which cannot be taught, or only by continual custom, which is soon prescribed; which though it be not true, yet I forbear to note any deficiencies; for the Olympian Games are down long since, and the mediocrity of these things is for use; as for the excellency of them, it serveth for the most part but for mercenary ostentation.

For Arts of Pleasure Sensual, the chief deficience in them is of laws to repress them. For as it hath been well observed that the arts which flourish in times while virtue is in growth, are military; and while virtue is in state, are liberal; and while virtue is in declination, are voluptuary; so I doubt that this age of the world is somewhat upon the descent of the wheel. With arts *voluptuary* I couple practices *joculary;* for the deceiving of the senses is one of the pleasures of the senses. As for games of recreation, I hold them to belong to civil life and education. And thus much of that particular Human Philosophy which concerns the Body, which is but the tabernacle of the mind.

For Human Knowledge which concerns the Mind, it hath two parts; the one that enquireth of *the substance or nature of the soul or mind,* the other that enquireth of *the faculties or functions thereof.* Unto the first of these, the considerations of *the original of the soul,* whether it be *native or adventive,* and *how far it is exempted from laws of matter,* and of the *immortality thereof,* and many other points, do appertain: which have been not more laboriously enquired than variously reported; so as the travail therein taken seemeth to have been rather in a maze than in a way. But although I am of opinion that this knowledge may be more really and soundly enquired, even in nature, than it hath been; yet I hold that in the end it must be bounded by religion, or else it will be subject to deceit and delusion; for as the substance of the soul in the creation was not extracted out of the mass of heaven and earth by the benediction of a *producat,* but was immediately inspired from God; so it is not possible that it should be (otherwise than by accident) subject to *the laws of heaven and earth,* which are *the subject of philosophy;* and therefore the true knowledge of the nature and state of the soul, must come by the same inspiration that gave the substance. Unto this part of knowledge touching the soul there be two appendices; which, as they have been handled, have rather vapoured forth fables than kindled truth; Divination and Fascination.

Divination hath been anciently and fitly divided into *artificial* and *natural;* whereof *artificial* is when the mind maketh a prediction by argument, concluding upon signs and tokens; *natural* is when the mind hath a presentation by an internal power, without the inducement of a sign. Artificial is of two sorts; either when the argument is coupled with a derivation of causes, which is *rational;* or when it is only grounded upon a coincidence of the effect, which is *experimental:* whereof the later for the most part is superstitious; such as where the heathen observations upon the inspection of sacrifices, the flights of birds, the swarming of bees; and such as was the Chaldean Astrology, and the like. For *artificial divination,* the several kinds thereof are distributed amongst particular knowledges. The Astronomer hath his predictions, as of conjunctions, aspects, eclipses, and the like. The Physician hath his predictions, of death, of recovery, of the accidents and issues of diseases. The Politique hath his predictions; *O urbem venalem, et cito perituram, si emptorem invenerit!* [a city in which all things are for sale and which will fall to the first purchaser,] which stayed not long to be performed, in Sylla first, and after in Cæsar. So as these predictions are now impertinent, and to be referred over. But the divination which springeth from the internal nature of the soul, is that which we now speak of; which hath been made to be of two sorts, *primitive* and by *influxion.* Primitive is grounded upon the supposition that the mind, when it is withdrawn and collected into itself and not diffused into the organs of the body, hath some extent and latitude of prenotion; which therefore appeareth most in sleep, in extasies, and near death; and more rarely in waking apprehensions; and is induced and furthered by those abstinences and observances which make the mind most to consist in itself. By influxion, is grounded upon the conceit that the mind, as a mirror or glass, should take illumination from the foreknowledge of God and spirits; unto which the same regiment doth likewise conduce. For the retiring of the mind within itself is the state which is most susceptible of divine influxions; save that it is accompanied in this case with a fervency and elevation (which the ancients noted by *fury*), and not with a repose and quiet, as it is in the other.

Fascination is the power and act of imagination, intensive upon other bodies than the body of the imaginant: for of that we spake in the proper place: wherein the school of Paracelsus and the disciples of pretended Natural Magic have been so intemperate, as they have exalted the power of the imagination to be much one with the power of miracle-working faith; others that draw nearer to probability, calling to their view the secret passages of things, and especially of the contagion that passeth from body to body, do conceive it should likewise be agreeable to nature that there should be some transmissions and operations from spirit to spirit, without the mediation of the senses; whence the conceits have grown (now almost made civil) of the Mastering Spirit, and the force of confidence, and the like. Incident unto this is the inquiry how to raise and fortify the imagination; for if the imagination fortified have power, then it is material to know how to fortify and exalt it. And herein comes in crookedly and dangerously a palliation of a great part of Ceremonial Magic. For it may be pretended that Ceremonies, Characters, and Charms, do work not by any tacit or sacramental contract with evil spirits, but serve only to strengthen the imagination of him that useth it; as images are said by the Roman church to fix the cogitations and raise the devotions of them that pray before them. But for mine own judgment, if it be admitted that imagination hath power, and that Ceremonies fortify imagination, and that they be used sincerely and intentionally for that purpose; yet I should hold them unlawful, as opposing to that first edict which God gave unto man, *In sudore vultus comedes panem tuum,* [in the sweat of thy brow shalt thou eat bread]. For they propound those noble effects which God hath set forth unto man to be bought at the price of labour, to be attained by a few easy and slothful observances. Deficiences in these knowledges I will report none, other than the general deficience, that it is not known how much of them is verity and how much vanity.

The knowledge which respecteth the Faculties of the Mind of man is of two kinds; the one respecting his Understanding and Reason, and the other his Will, Appetite, and Affection; whereof the former produceth Position or Decree, the later Action or Execution. It is true that the Imagination is an agent or *nuncius* in both provinces, both the judicial and the ministerial. For Sense sendeth over to Imagination before Reason have judged: and Reason sendeth over to Imagination before the Decree can be acted; for Imagination ever precedeth Voluntary Motion: saving that this Janus of Imagination hath differing faces; for the face towards Reason hath the print of Truth, but the face towards Action hath the print of Good; which nevertheless are faces,

Quales decet esse sororum,—

[sister-faces]. Neither is the Imagination simply and only a messenger; but is invested with or at leastwise usurpeth no small authority in itself, besides the duty of the message. For it was well said by Aristotle, *That the mind hath over the body that commandment, which the lord hath over a bondman; but that reason hath over the imagination that commandment which a magistrate hath over a free citizen;* who may come also to rule in his turn. For we see that in matters of Faith and Religion we raise our Imagination above our Reason; which is the cause why Religion sought ever access to the mind by similitudes, types, parables, visions, dreams. And again in all persuasions that are wrought by eloquence and other impression of like nature, which do paint and disguise the true appearance of things, the chief recommendation unto Reason is from the Imagination. Nevertheless, because I find not any science that doth properly or fitly pertain to the Imagination, I see no cause to alter the former division. For as for Poesy, it is rather a pleasure or play of imagination, than a work or duty thereof. And if it be a work, we speak not now of such parts of learning as the Imagination produceth, but of such sciences as handle and consider of the Imagination; no more than we shall speak now of such knowledges as Reason produceth, (for that extendeth to all philosophy,) but of such knowledges as do handle and inquire of the faculty of Reason: so as Poesy had his true place. As for the power of the Imagination in nature, and the manner of fortifying the same, we have mentioned it in the doctrine *De Anima,* whereunto most fitly it belongeth. And lastly, for Imaginative or Insinuative Reason, which is the subject of Rhetoric, we think it best to refer it to the Arts of Reason. So therefore we content ourselves with the former division, that Human Philosophy which respecteth the faculties of the mind of man hath two parts, Rational and Moral.

The part of Human Philosophy which is rational, is of all knowledges, to the most wits, the least delightful; and seemeth but a net of subtility and spinosity. For as it was truly said, that knowledge is *pabulum animi,* [the food of the mind;] so in the nature of men's appetite to this food, most men are of the taste and stomach of the Israelites in the desert, that would fain have returned *ad ollas carnium,* [to the flesh-pots,] and were weary of manna; which, though it were celestial, yet seemed less nutritive and comfortable. So generally men taste well knowledges that are drenched in flesh and blood, Civil History, Morality, Policy, about the which men's affections, praises, fortunes, do turn and are conversant; but this same *lumen siccum,* [this dry light,] doth parch and offend most men's watery and soft natures. But to speak truly of things as they are in worth, Rational Knowledges are the keys of all other arts; for as Aristotle saith aptly and elegantly, *That the hand is the Instrument of Instruments, and the mind is the Form of Forms:* so these be truly said to be the Art of Arts: neither do they only direct, but likewise confirm and strengthen; even as the habit of shooting doth not only enable to shoot a nearer shoot, but also to draw a stronger bow.

The Arts Intellectual are four in number; divided according to the ends whereunto they are referred: for man's labour is to *invent* that which is *sought* or *propounded;* or to *judge* that which is *invented;* or to *retain* that which is *judged;* or to *deliver over* that which is *retained.* So as the arts must be four; Art of Inquiry or Invention: Art of Examination or Judgment; Art of Custody or Memory; and the Art of Elocution or Tradition.

Invention is of two kinds, much differing; the one, of Arts and Sciences; and the other, of Speech and Arguments. The former of these I do report deficient; which seemeth to me to be such a deficience as if in the making of an inventory touching the estate of a defunct it should be set down *that there is no ready money*. For as money will fetch all other commodities, so this knowledge is that which should purchase all the rest. And like as the West-Indies had never been discovered if the use of the mariner's needle had not been first discovered, though the one be vast regions and the other a small motion; so it cannot be found strange if sciences be no further discovered, if the art itself of invention and discovery hath been passed over.

That this part of knowledge is wanting, to my judgment standeth plainly confessed: for first, Logic doth not pretend to invent Sciences or the Axioms of Sciences, but passeth it over with a *cuique in sua arte credendum,* [the knowledge that pertains to each art must be taken on trust from those that profess it]. And Celsus acknowledgeth it gravely, speaking of the empirical and dogmatical sects of physicians, *That medicines and cures were first found out, and then after the reasons and causes were discoursed; and not the causes first found out, and by light from them the medicines and cures discovered.* And Plato in his Theætetus noteth well, *That particulars are infinite, and the higher generalities give no sufficient direction; and that the pith of all sciences, which maketh the arts-man differ from the inexpert, is in the middle propositions, which in every particular knowledge are taken from tradition and experience.* And therefore we see that they which discourse of the inventions and originals of things, refer them rather to chance than to art, and rather to beasts, birds, fishes, serpents, than to men.

> Dictamnum genetrix Cretæa carpit ab Ida,
> Puberibus caulem foliis et flore comantem
> Purpureo: non illa feris incognita capris
> Gramina, cum tergo volucres hæsere sagittæ.
> [A sprig of dittany his mother brought,
> Gathered by Cretan Ide; a stalk it is
> Of woolly leaf, crested with purple flower;
> Which well the wild-goat knows when in his side
> Sticks the winged shaft.]

So that it was no marvel (the manner of antiquity being to consecrate inventors) that the Ægyptians had so few human idols in their temples, but almost all brute:

Omnigenumque Deum monstra, et latrator Anubis,
Contra Neptunum et Venerem, contraque Minervam, &c.
[All kinds and shapes of Gods, a monstrous host,
The dog Anubis foremost, stood arrayed
'Gainst Neptune, Venus, Pallas, &c.]

And if you like better the tradition of the Grecians, and ascribe the first inventions to men, yet you will rather believe that Prometheus first struck the flints, and marvelled at the spark, than that when he first struck the flints he expected the spark; and therefore we see the West-Indian Prometheus had no intelligence with the European, because of the rareness with them of flint, that gave the first occasion. So as it should seem that hitherto men are rather beholden to a wild goat for surgery, or to a nightingale for music, or to the Ibis for some part of physic, or to the pot lid that flew open for artillery, or generally to chance or anything else, than to Logic, for the invention of arts and sciences. Neither is the form of invention which Virgil describeth much other:

Ut varias usus meditando extunderet artes
Paulatim:

[that practice with meditation might by degrees hammer out the arts]. For if you observe the words well, it is no other method than that which brute beasts are capable of, and do put in ure; which is *a perpetual intending or practising some one thing, urged and imposed by an absolute necessity of conservation of being:* for so Cicero saith very truly, *Usus uni rei deditus et naturam et artem sæpe vincet:* [practice applied constantly to one thing will often do more than either nature or art can]. And therefore if it be said of men,

Labor omnia vincit
Improbus, et duris urgens in rebus egestas,
[Stern labour masters all,
And want in poverty importunate,]

it is likewise said of beasts, *Quis psittaco docuit suum χαῖρε?* [who taught the parrot to say how d'ye do?] Who taught the raven in a drowth to throw pebbles into a hollow tree where she spied water, that the water might rise so as she might come to it? Who taught the bee to sail through such a vast sea of air, and to find the way from a field in flower a great way off to her hive? Who taught the ant to bite every grain of corn that she burieth in her hill, lest it should take root and grow? Add then the word *extundere,* which importeth the extreme difficulty, and the word *paulatim,* which importeth the extreme slowness, and we are where we were, even amongst the Ægyptians' gods; there being little left to the faculty of Reason, and nothing to the duty of Art, for matter of invention.

Secondly, the induction which the logicians speak of and which seemeth familiar with Plato, whereby the Principles of sciences may be pretended to be invented, and so the middle propositions by derivation from the principles,—their form of induction, I say, is utterly vicious and incompetent: wherein their error is the fouler, because it is the duty of Art to perfect and exalt Nature; but they contrariwise have wronged, abused, and traduced nature. For he that shall attentively observe how the mind doth gather this excellent dew of knowledge, like unto that which the poet speaketh of, *Aërei mellis cœlestia dona,* [the gift of heaven, aëriel honey,] distilling and contriving it out of particulars natural and artificial, as the flowers of the field and garden, shall find that the mind of herself by nature doth manage and act an induction much better than they describe it. For to conclude *upon an enumeration of particulars without instance contradictory* is no conclusion, but a conjecture; for who can assure (in many subjects) upon those particulars which appear of a side, that there are not other on the contrary side which appear not? As if Samuel should have rested upon those sons of Issay which were brought before him, and failed of David, which was in the field. And this form (to say truth) is so gross, as it had not been possible for wits so subtile as have managed these things to have offered it to the world, but that they hastened to their *theories* and *dogmaticals,* and were imperious and scornful toward particulars; which their manner was to use but as *lictores* and *viatores,* for sergeants and whiffiers, *ad summovendam turbam,* to make way and make room for their opinions, rather than in their true use and service. Certainly it is a thing may touch a man with a religious wonder, to see how the footsteps of seducement are the very same in divine and human truth: for as in divine truth man cannot endure to become as a child; so in human, they reputed the attending the Inductions (wherof we speak) as if it were a second infancy or childhood.

Thirdly, allow some Principles or Axioms were rightly induced, yet nevertheless certain it is that Middle Propositions cannot be deduced from them in subject of nature by Syllogism, that is, *by touch and reduction of them to principles in a middle term.* It is true that in sciences popular, as moralities, laws, and the like, yea and divinity (because it pleaseth God to apply himself to the capacity of the simplest), that form may have use; and in natural philosophy likewise, by way of argument or satisfactory reason, *quæ assensum parit, operis effœta est,* [which procures assent but can do no work:] but the subtilty of nature and operations will not be enchained in those bonds: for Arguments consist of Propositions, and Propositions of Words; and Words are but the current tokens or marks of Popular Notions of things; which notions, if they be grossly and variably collected out of particulars, it is not the laborious examination either of consequences of arguments or of the truth of propositions, that can ever correct that error; being (as the physicians speak) in the first digestion: and therefore it was not without cause, that so many excellent philosophers became Sceptics and Academics, and denied any certainty of knowledge or comprehension, and held opinion that the knowledge of man extended only to appearances and probabilities. It is true that in Socrates it was supposed to be but a form of irony, *Scientiam dissimulando simulavit,* [an affectation of knowledge under pretence of ignorance:] for he used to disable his knowledge, to the end to enhance his knowledge; like the humour of Tiberius in his beginnings, that would reign, but who would not acknowledge so much; and in the later Academy, which Cicero embraced, this opinion also of *acatalepsia* (I doubt) was not held sincerely: for that all those which excelled in copie of speech seem to have chosen that sect, as that which was fittest to give glory to their eloquence and variable discourses; being rather like progresses of pleasure than journeys to an end. But assuredly many scattered in both Academies did hold it in subtilty and integrity. But here was their chief error; they charged the deceit upon the Senses; which in my judgment (notwithstanding all their cavillations) are very sufficient to certify and report truth, though not always immediately, yet by comparison, by help of instrument, and by producing and urging such things as are too subtile for the sense to some effect comprehensible by the sense, and other like assistance. But they ought to have charged the deceit upon *the weakness of the intellectual powers, and upon the man-*

ner of collecting and concluding upon the reports of the senses. This I speak not to disable the mind of man, but to stir it up to seek help: for no man, be he never so cunning or practised, can make a straight line or perfect circle by steadiness of hand, which may be easily done by help of a ruler or compass.

This part of invention, concerning the invention of sciences, I purpose (if God give me leave) hereafter to propound; having digested it into two parts; whereof the one I term *Experientia literata,* and the other *Interpretatio Naturæ:* the former being but a degree and rudiment of the latter. But I will not dwell too long, nor speak too great upon a promise.

The invention of speech or argument is not properly an invention: for to invent is to discover that we know not, and not to recover or resummon that which we already know; and the use of this invention is no other but *out of the knowledge whereof our mind is already possessed, to draw forth or call before us that which may be pertinent to the purpose which we take into our consideration.* So as, to speak truly, it is no *Invention,* but a *Remembrance* or *Suggestion,* with an application; which is the cause why the schools do place it after judgment, as subsequent and not precedent. Nevertheless, because we do account it a Chase as well of deer in an inclosed park as in a forest at large, and that it hath already obtained the name, let it be called invention: so as it be perceived and discerned, that the scope and end of this invention is readiness and present use of our knowledge, and not addition or amplification thereof.

To procure this ready use of knowledge there are two courses, Preparation and Suggestion. The former of these seemeth scarcely a part of Knowledge, consisting rather of diligence than of any artificial erudition. And herein Aristotle wittily, but hurtfully, doth deride the sophists near his time, saying, *they did as if one that professed the art of shoe-making should not teach how to make up a shoe, but only exhibit in a readiness a number of shoes of all fashions and sizes.* But yet a man might reply, that if a shoe-maker should have no shoes in his shop, but only work as he is bespoken, he should be weakly customed. But our Saviour, speaking of Divine Knowledge, saith, *that the kingdom of heaven is like a good householder, that bringeth forth both new and old store;* and we see the ancient writers of rhetoric do give it in precept, that pleaders should have the Places whereof they have most continual use ready handled in all the variety that may be; as that, to speak for the literal interpretation of the law against equity, and contrary; and to speak for presumptions and inferences against testimony, and contrary. And Cicero himself, being broken unto it by great experience, delivereth it plainly, that whatsoever a man shall have occasion to speak of, (if he will take the pains) he may have it in effect premeditate, and handled *in thesi;* so that when he cometh to a particular, he shall have nothing to do but to put to names and times and places, and such other circumstances of individuals. We see likewise the exact diligence of Demosthenes; who, in regard of the great force that the entrance and access into causes hath to make a good impression, had ready framed a number of prefaces for orations and speeches. All which authorities and precedents may overweigh Aristotle's opinion, that would have us change a rich wardrobe for a pair of shears.

But the nature of the collection of this provision or preparatory store, though it be common both to logic and rhetoric, yet having made an entry of it here, where it came first to be spoken of, I think fit to refer over the further handling of it to rhetoric.

The other part of Invention, which I term Suggestion, doth assign and direct us to certain *marks* or *places,* which may excite our mind to return and produce such knowledge as it hath formerly collected, to the end we may make use thereof. Neither is this use (truly taken) only to furnish argument to dispute probably with others, but likewise to minister unto our judgment to conclude aright within ourselves. Neither may these Places serve only to apprompt our invention, but also to direct our inquiry. For a faculty of wise interrogating is half a knowledge. For as Plato saith, *Whosoever seeketh, knoweth that which he seeketh for in a general notion; else how shall he know it when he hath found it?* And therefore the larger your Anticipation is, the more direct and compendious is your search. But the same Places which will help us what to produce of that which we know already, will also help us, if a man of experience were before us, what questions to ask; or if we have books and authors to instruct us, what points to search and revolve: so as I cannot report that this part of invention, which is that which the schools call Topics, is deficient.

Nevertheless Topics are of two sorts, *general* and *special.* The general we have spoken to; but the particular hath been touched by some, but rejected generally as inartificial and variable. But leaving the humour which hath reigned too much in the schools, (which is to be vainly subtile in a few things which are within their command, and to reject the rest,) I do receive particular Topics, that is places or directions of invention and inquiry in every particular knowledge, as things of great use; being mixtures of Logic with the matter of sciences; for in these it holdeth,

Ars inveniendi adolescit cum inventis, [every act of discovery advances the art of discovery;] for as in going of a way we do not only gain that part of the way which is passed, but we gain the better sight of that part of the way which remaineth; so every degree of proceeding in a science giveth a light to that which followeth; which light if we strengthen, by drawing it forth into questions or places of inquiry, we do greatly advance our pursuit.

Now we pass unto the arts of Judgment, which handle the natures of Proofs and Demonstrations; which as to Induction hath a coincidence with Invention; *for in all inductions, whether in good or vicious form, the same action of the mind which inventeth, judgeth; all one as in the sense;* but otherwise it is in proof by syllogism; for the proof being not immediate but by mean, *the invention of the mean* is one thing, and the *judgment of the consequence* is another; the one exciting only, the other examining. Therefore for the real and exact form of judgment we refer ourselves to that which we have spoken of *Interpretation of Nature.*

For the other judgment by Syllogism, as it is a thing most agreeable to the mind of man, so it hath been vehemently and excellently laboured. For the nature of man doth extremely covet to have somewhat in his understanding fixed and immoveable, and as a rest and support of the mind. And therefore as Aristotle endeavoreth to prove that in all motion there is some point quiescent; and as he elegantly expoundeth the ancient fable of Atlas (that stood fixed and bare up the heaven from falling) to be meant of the poles or axle-tree of heaven, whereupon the conversion is accomplished; so assuredly men have a desire to have an Atlas or axle-tree within to keep them from fluctuation, which is like to a perpetual peril of falling;

therefore men did hasten to set down some Principles about which the variety of their disputations might turn.

So then this art of Judgment is but *the reduction of propositions to principles in a middle term:* the Principles to be agreed by all and exempted from argument; the Middle Term to be elected at the liberty of every man's invention; the Reduction to be of two kinds, direct and inverted; the one when the proposition is reduced to the principle, which they term a *Probation ostensive;* the other when the contradictory of the proposition is reduced to the contradictory of the principle, which is that which they call *per incommodum,* or *pressing an absurdity;* the number of middle terms to be as the proposition standeth degrees more or less removed from the principle.

But this art hath two several methods of doctrine; the one by way of direction, the other by way of caution: the former frameth and setteth down a true form of consequence, by the variations and deflexions from which errors and inconsequences may be exactly judged; toward the composition and structure of which form, it is incident to handle the parts thereof, which are propositions, and the parts of propositions, which are simple words; and this is that part of logic which is comprehended in the Analytics.

The second method of doctrine was introduced for expedite use and assurance sake; discovering the more subtile forms of sophisms and illaqueations with their redargutions, which is that which is termed *Elenches.* For although in the more gross sorts of fallacies it happeneth (as Seneca maketh the comparison well) as in juggling feats, which though we know not how they are done, yet we know well it is not as it seemeth to be; yet the more subtile sort of them doth not only put a man besides his answer, but doth many times abuse his judgment.

This part concerning *Elenches* is excellently handled by Aristotle in precept, but more excellently by Plato in example, not only in the persons of the Sophists, but even in Socrates himself; who professing to affirm nothing, but to infirm that which was affirmed by another, hath exactly expressed all the forms of objection, fallace, and redargution. And although we have said that the use of this doctrine is for redargution, yet it is manifest the degenerate and corrupt use is for caption and contradiction; which passeth for a great faculty, and no doubt is of very great advantage: though the difference be good which was made between orators and sophisters, that the one is as the greyhound, which hath his advantage in the race, and the other as the hare, which hath her advantage in the turn, so as it is the advantage of the weaker creature.[1] . . .

The custody or retaining of knowledge is either in Writing or Memory; whereof Writing hath two parts, the nature of the *character,* and the order of the *entry.* For the art of *character,* or other visible notes of words or things, it hath nearest conjugation with grammar, and therefore I refer it to the due place. For the *disposition* and *collocation* of that knowledge which we preserve in writing, it consisteth in a good digest of common-places; wherein I am not ignorant of the prejudice imputed to the use of common-place books, as causing a retardation of reading, and some sloth or relaxation of memory. But because it is but a counterfeit thing in knowledges to be forward and pregnant, except a man be deep and full, I hold the entry of

[1] The doctrine of *Elenches,* containing the first sketch of the Idols, is here omitted since the Idols, are treated in final form in the *Novum Organum. Editor.*

common-places to be a matter of great use and essence in studying; as that which assureth copie of invention, and contracteth judgment to a strength. But this is true, that of the *methods* of common-places that I have seen, there is none of any sufficient worth; all of them carrying merely the face of a *school,* and not of a *world;* and referring to vulgar matters and pedantical divisions without all life or respect to action.

For the other principal part of the custody of knowledge, which is Memory, I find that faculty in my judgment weakly enquired of. An art there is extant of it; but it seemeth to me that there are better precepts than that art, and better practices of that art than those received. It is certain the art (as it is) may be raised to points of ostentation prodigious: but in use (as it is now managed) it is barren; not burdensome nor dangerous to natural memory, as is imagined, but barren; that is, not dexterous to be applied to the serious use of business and occasions. And therefore I make no more estimation of repeating a great number of names or words upon once hearing, or the pouring forth of a number of verses or rhymes *ex tempore,* or the making of a satirical simile of every thing, or the turning of every thing to a jest, or the falsifying or contradicting of every thing by cavil, or the like, (whereof in the faculties of the mind there is a great copie, and such as by device and practice may be exalted to an extreme degree of wonder,) than I do of the tricks of tumblers, funambuloes, baladines; the one being the same in the mind that the other is in the body; matters of strangeness without worthiness.

This art of Memory is but built upon two intentions; the one Prenotion, the other Emblem. Prenotion dischargeth the indefinite seeking of that we would remember, and directeth us to seek in a narrow compass; that is, somewhat that hath congruity with our *place of memory.* Emblem reduceth conceits intellectual to images sensible, which strike the memory more; out of which axioms may be drawn much better practique than that in use; and besides which axioms, there are divers moe touching help of memory, not inferior to them. But I did in the beginning distinguish, not to report those things deficient, which are but only ill managed.

There remaineth the fourth kind of Rational Knowledge, which is transitive, concerning the expressing or transferring our knowledge to others; which I will term by the general name of Tradition or Delivery. Tradition hath three parts; the first concerning the *organ* of tradition; the second concerning the *method* of tradition; and the third concerning the *illustration* of tradition.

For the organ of tradition, it is either Speech or Writing: for Aristotle saith well, *Words are the images of cogitations, and letters are the images of words;* but yet it is not of necessity that cogitations be expressed by the medium of words. For *whatsoever is capable of sufficient differences, and those perceptible by the sense, is in nature competent to express cogitations.* And therefore we see in the commerce of barbarous people that understand not one another's language, and in the practice of divers that are dumb and deaf, that men's minds are expressed in gestures, though not exactly, yet to serve the turn. And we understand further that it is the use of China and the kingdoms of the high Levant to write in Characters Real, which express neither letters nor words in gross, but Things or Notions; insomuch as countries and provinces, which understand not one another's language, can nevertheless read one another's writings, because the characters are accepted more generally than the languages do extend; and therefore they have a vast multitude of characters; as many, I suppose, as radical words.

These Notes of Cogitations are of two sorts; the one when the note hath some similitude or congruity with the notion; the other *ad placitum,* having force only by contract or acceptation. Of the former sort are Hieroglyphics and Gestures. For as to Hieroglyphics, (things of ancient use, and embraced chiefly by the Ægyptians, one of the most ancient nations,) they are but as continued impresses and emblems. And as for Gestures, they are as transitory Hieroglyphics, and are to Hieroglyphics as words spoken are to words written, in that they abide not; but they have evermore, as well as the other, an affinity with the things signified: as Periander, being consulted with how to preserve a tyranny newly usurped, bid the messenger attend and report what he saw him do; and went into his garden and topped all the highest flowers; signifying, that it consisted in the cutting off and keeping low of the nobility and *grandes. Ad placitum* are the Characters Real before mentioned, and Words: although some have been willing by curious inquiry, or rather by apt feigning, to have derived imposition of names from reason and intendment; a speculation elegant, and, by reason it searcheth into antiquity, reverent; but sparingly mixed with truth, and of small fruit. This portion of knowledge, touching the Notes of Things and cogitations in general, I find not enquired, but deficient. And although it may seem of no great use, considering that words and writings by letters do far excel all the other ways; yet because this part concerneth as it were the mint of knowledge, (for words are the tokens current and accepted for conceits, as moneys are for values, and that it is fit men be not ignorant that moneys may be of another kind than gold and silver,) I thought good to propound it to better enquiry.

Concerning Speech and Words, the consideration of them hath produced the science of Grammar: for man still striveth to reintegrate himself in those benedictions, from which by his fault he hath been deprived; and as he hath striven against the first general curse by the invention of all other arts, so hath he sought to come forth of the second general curse (which was the confusion of tongues) by the art of Grammar: whereof the use in a mother tongue is small; in a foreign tongue more; but most in such foreign tongues as have ceased to be vulgar tongues, and are turned only to learned tongues. The duty of it is of two natures; the one popular, which is for the speedy and perfect attaining languages, as well for intercourse of speech as for understanding of authors; the other philosophical, examining the power and nature of words as they are the footsteps and prints of reason: which kind of analogy between words and reason is handled *sparsim*, brokenly, though not entirely; and therefore I cannot report it deficient, though I think it very worthy to be reduced into a science by itself.

Unto Grammar also belongeth, as an appendix, the consideration of the Accidents of Words; which are measure, sound, and elevation or accent, and the sweetness and harshness of them; whence hath issued some curious observations in Rhetoric, but chiefly Poesy, as we consider it in respect of the verse and not of the argument: wherein though men in learned tongues do tie themselves to the ancient measures, yet in modern languages it seemeth to me as free to make new measures of verses as of dances; for a dance is a measured pace, as a verse is a measured speech. In these things the sense is better judge than the art;

Cœnæ fercula nostræ
Mallem convivis quam placuisse cocis:

[the dinner is to please the guests that eat it, not the cook that dresses it.] And of the servile expressing antiquity in an unlike and an unfit subject, it is well said, *Quod tempore antiquum videtur, id incongruitate est maxime novum;* [there is nothing more new than an old thing that has ceased to fit].

For Ciphers, they are commonly in letters or alphabets, but may be in words. The kinds of Ciphers (besides the simple ciphers with changes and intermixtures of nulls and non-significants) are many, according to the nature or rule of the infolding; Wheel-ciphers, Key-ciphers, Doubles, &c. But the virtues of them, whereby they are to be preferred, are three; that they be not laborious to write and read; that they be impossible to decipher; and, in some cases, that they be without suspicion. The highest degree whereof is to write *omnia per omnia;* which is undoubtedly possible, with a proportion quintuple at most of the writing infolding to the writing infolded, and no other restraint whatsoever. This art of Ciphering, hath for relative an art of Discipering; by supposition unprofitable; but, as things are, of great use. For suppose that ciphers were well managed, there be multitudes of them which exclude the discipherer. But in regard of the rawness and unskilfulness of the hands through which they pass, the greatest matters are many times carried in the weakest ciphers.

In the enumeration of these private and retired arts, it may be thought I seek to make a great muster-roll of sciences; naming them for shew and ostentation, and to little other purpose. But let those which are skilful in them judge whether I bring them in only for appearance, or whether in that which I speak of them (though in few marks) there be not some seed of proficience. And this must be remembered, that as there be many of great account in their countries and provinces, which when they come up to the Seat of the Estate are but of mean rank and scarcely regarded; so these arts being here placed with the principal and supreme sciences, seem petty things; yet to such as have chosen them to spend their studies in them, they seem great matters.

For the Method of Tradition, I see it hath moved a controversy in our time. But as in civil business, if there be a meeting and men fall at words there is commonly an end of the matter for that time and no proceeding at all; so in learning, where there is much controversy there is many times little inquiry. For this part of knowledge of Method seemeth to me so weakly enquired as I shall report it deficient.

Method hath been placed, and that not amiss, in Logic, as a part of Judgment: for as the doctrine of Syllogisms comprehendeth the rules of judgment upon that which is invented, so the doctrine of Method containeth the rules of judgment upon that which is to be delivered; for judgment precedeth Delivery, as it followeth Invention. Neither is the method or the nature of the tradition material only to the *use* of knowledge, but likewise to the *progression* of knowledge: for since the labour and life of one man cannot attain to perfection of knowledge, the wisdom of the Tradition is that which inspireth the felicity of continuance and proceeding. And therefore the most real diversity of method is of method referred to Use, and method referred to Progression; whereof the one may be termed Magistral, and the other of Probation.

The later whereof seemeth to be *via deserta et interclusa,* [a way that is abandoned and stopped up]. For as knowledges are now delivered, there is a kind of contract of error between the deliverer and the receiver: for he that delivereth knowledge desireth to deliver it in such form as may be best believed, and not as may be best examined; and he that receiveth knowledge desireth rather present satisfaction than expectant inquiry; and so rather not to doubt than not to err: glory making the author not to lay open his weakness, and sloth making the disciple not to know his strength.

But knowledge that is delivered as a thread to be spun on, ought to be delivered and intimated, if it were possible, *in the same method wherein it was invented;* and so is it possible of knowledge induced. But in this same anticipated and prevented knowledge, no man knoweth how he came to the knowledge which he hath obtained. But yet nevertheless, *secundum majus et minus,* a man may revisit and descend unto the foundations of his knowledge and consent; and so transplant it into another as it grew in his own mind. For it is in knowledges as it is in plants: if you mean to use the plant, it is no matter for the roots; but if you mean to remove it to grow, then it is more assured to rest upon roots than slips. So the delivery of knowledges (as it is now used) is as of fair bodies of trees without the roots; good for the carpenter, but not for the planter; but if you will have science grow, it is less matter for the shaft or body of the tree, so you look well to the taking up of the roots. Of which kind of delivery the method of the mathematiques, in that subject, hath some shadow; but generally I see it neither put in ure nor put in inquisition, and therefore note it for deficient.

Another diversity of Method there is, which hath some affinity with the former, used in some cases by the discretion of the ancients, but disgraced since by the impostures of many vain persons, who have made it as a false light for their counterfeit merchandise; and that is, Enigmatical and Disclosed. The pretence whereof is to remove the vulgar capacities from being admitted to the secrets of knowledges, and to reserve them to selected auditors, or wits of such sharpness as can pierce the veil.

Another diversity of Method, whereof the consequence is great, is the delivery of knowledge in Aphorisms, or in Methods; wherein we may observe that it hath been too much taken into custom, out of a few Axioms or observations upon any subject to make a solemn and formal art; filling it with some discourses, and illustrating it with examples, and digesting it into a sensible Method; but the writing in Aphorisms hath many excellent virtues, whereto the writing in Method doth not approach.

For first, it trieth the writer, whether he be superficial or solid: for Aphorisms, except they should be ridiculous, cannot be made but of the pith and heart of sciences; for discourse of illustration is cut off; recitals of examples are cut off; discourse of connexion and order is cut off; descriptions of practice are cut off; so there remaineth nothing to fill the Aphorisms but some good quantity of observation: and therefore no man can suffice, nor in reason will attempt, to write Aphorisms, but he that is sound and grounded. But in Methods,

Tantum series juncturaque, pollet
Tantum de medio sumptis accedit honoris,

[the arrangement and connexion and joining of the parts has so much effect,] as a man shall make a great shew of an art, which if it were disjointed would come to little. Secondly, Methods are more fit to win consent or belief, but less fit to point to action; for they carry a kind of demonstration in orb or circle, one part illuminating another, and therefore satisfy; but particulars, being dispersed, do best agree with dispersed directions. And lastly, Aphorisms, representing a knowledge broken, do invite men to enquire farther; whereas Methods, carrying the shew of a total, do secure men, as if they were at furthest.

Another diversity of Method, which is likewise of great weight, is the handling of knowledge by Assertions and their Proofs, or by Questions and their Determinations; the latter kind whereof, if it be immoderately followed, is as prejudicial to the proceeding of learning, as it is to the proceeding of an army to go about to besiege every little fort or hold. For if the field be kept and the sum of the enterprise pursued, those smaller things will come in of themselves: indeed a man would not leave some important piece enemy at his back. In like manner, the use of confutation in the delivery of sciences ought to be very sparing; and to serve to remove strong preoccupations and prejudgments, and not to minister and excite disputations and doubts.

Another diversity of Methods is *according to the subject or matter which is handled;* for there is a great difference in delivery of the Mathematics, which are the most abstracted of knowledges, and Policy, which is the most immersed: and howsoever contention hath been moved touching an uniformity of method in multiformity of matter, yet we see how that opinion, besides the weakness of it, hath been of ill desert towards learning, as that which taketh the way to reduce learning to certain empty and barren generalities; being but the very husks and shells of sciences, all the kernel being forced out and expulsed with the torture and press of the method; and therefore as I did allow well of particular Topics for invention, so I do allow likewise of particular Methods of tradition.

Another diversity of judgment in the delivery and teaching of knowledge is *according unto the light and presuppositions of that which is delivered;* for that knowledge which is new and foreign from opinions received, is to be delivered in another form than that that is agreeable and familiar; and therefore Aristotle, when he thinks to tax Democritus, doth in truth commend him, where he saith, *If we shall indeed dispute, and not follow after similitudes,* &c. For those whose conceits are seated in popular opinions, need only but to prove or dispute; but those whose conceits are beyond popular opinions, have a double labour; the one to make themselves conceived, and the other to prove and demonstrate; so that it is of necessity with them to have recourse to similitudes and translations to express themselves. And therefore in the infancy of learning, and in rude times, when those conceits which are now trivial were then new, the world was full of Parables and Similitudes; for else would men either have passed over without mark or else rejected for paradoxes that which was offered, before they had understood or judged. So in divine learning we see how frequent Parables and Tropes are: for it is a rule, *That whatsoever science is not consonant to presuppositions, must pray in aid of similitudes.*

There be also other diversities of Methods, vulgar and received; as that of Resolution or Analysis, of Constitution or Systasis, of Concealment or Cryptic,

&c. which I do allow well of; though I have stood upon those which are least handled and observed. All which I have remembered to this purpose, because I would erect and constitute one general inquiry, which seems to me deficient, touching the Wisdom of Tradition.

But unto this part of knowledge concerning Method doth further belong not only the Architecture of the whole frame of a work, but also the several beams and columns thereof; not as to their stuff, but as to their quantity and figure; and therefore Method considereth not only the disposition of the Argument or Subject, but likewise the Propositions; not as to their truth or matter, but as to their limitation and manner. For herein Ramus merited better a great deal in reviving the good rules of Propositions, Καθόλου πρῶτον, κατὰ παντός, &c. than he did in introducing the canker of Epitomes; and yet (as it is the condition of human things that, according to the ancient fables, *The most precious things have the most pernicious keepers;*) it was so, that the attempt of the one made him fall upon the other. For he had need be well conducted that should design to make Axioms *convertible,* if he make them not withal *circular,* and *non-promovent,* or *incurring into themselves:* but yet the intention was excellent.

The other considerations of Method concerning Propositions are chiefly touching the utmost propositions, which limit the dimensions of sciences; for every knowledge may be fitly said, besides the profundity, (which is the truth and substance of it, that makes it solid,) to have a longitude and a latitude; accounting the latitude towards other sciences, and the longitude towards action; that is, from the greatest generality to the most particular precept: the one giveth rule how far one knowledge ought to intermeddle within the province of another, which is the rule they call Καθαυτὸ; the other giveth rule unto what degree of particularity a knowledge should descend: which latter I find passed over in silence, being in my judgment the more material; for certainly there must be somewhat left to practice; but how much is worthy the inquiry. We see remote and superficial generalities do but offer knowledge to scorn of practical men; and are no more aiding to practice, than an Ortelius' universal map is to direct the way between London and York. The better sort of rules have been not unfitly compared to glasses of steel unpolished, where you may see the images of things, but first they must be filed: so the rules will help, if they be laboured and polished by practice. But how chrystalline they may be made at the first, and how far forth they may be polished aforehand, is the question; the inquiry whereof seemeth to me deficient.

There hath been also laboured and put in practice a method, which is not a lawful method, but a method of imposture; which is to deliver knowledges in such manner, as men may speedily come to make a shew of learning who have it not: such was the travail of Raymundus Lullius, in making that art which bears his name; not unlike to some books of Typocosmy which have been made since; being nothing but a mass of words of all arts, to give men countenance that those which use the terms might be thought to understand the art; which collections are much like a fripper's or broker's shop, that hath ends of every thing, but nothing of worth.

Now we descend to that part which concerneth the Illustration of Tradition, comprehended in that science which we call Rhetoric, or Art of Eloquence; a science excellent, and excellently well laboured. For although in true value it is inferior to wisdom, as it is said by God to Moses, when he disabled himself for want of this faculty, *Aaron shall be thy speaker, and thou shalt be to him as God;* yet with people it is the more mighty: for so Salomon saith, *Sapiens corde appellabitur prudens, sed dulcis eloquio majora reperiet,* [the wise in heart shall be called prudent, but he that is sweet of speech shall compass greater things;] signifying that profoundness of wisdom will help a man to a name or admiration, but that it is eloquence that prevaileth in an active life. And as to the labouring of it, the emulation of Aristotle with the rhetoricians of his time, and the experience of Cicero, hath made them in their works of Rhetorics exceed themselves. Again, the excellency of examples of eloquence in the orations of Demosthenes and Cicero, added to the perfection of the precepts of eloquence, hath doubled the progression in this art; and therefore the deficiencies which I shall note will rather be in some collections which may as handmaidens attend the art, than in the rules or use of the art itself.

Notwithstanding, to stir the earth a little about the roots of this science, as we have done of the rest: The duty and office of Rhetoric is *to apply Reason to Imagination* for the better moving of the will. For we see Reason is disturbed in the administration thereof by three means; by Illaqueation or Sophism, which pertains to Logic; by Imagination or Impression, which pertains to Rhetoric; and by Passion or Affection, which pertains to Morality. And as in negotiation with others men are wrought by cunning, by importunity, and by the vehemency; so in this negotiation within ourselves men are undermined by Inconsequences, solicited and importuned by Impressions or Observations, and transported by Passions. Neither is the nature of man so unfortunately built, as that those powers and arts should have force to disturb reason, and not to establish and advance it: for the end of Logic is to teach a form of argument to secure reason, and not to entrap it; the end of Morality is to procure the affections to obey reason, and not to invade it; the end of Rhetoric is to fill the imagination to second reason, and not to oppress it: for these abuses of arts come in but *ex obliquo,* for caution.

And therefore it was great injustice in Plato, though springing out of a just hatred of the rhetoricians of his time, to esteem of Rhetoric but as a voluptuary art, resembling it to cookery, that did mar wholesome meats, and help unwholesome by variety of sauces to the pleasure of the taste. For we see that speech is much more conversant in adorning that which is good than in colouring that which is evil; for there is no man but speaketh more honestly than he can do or think: and it was excellently noted by Thucydides in Cleon, that because he used to hold on the bad side in causes of estate, therefore he was ever inveighing against eloquence and good speech; knowing that no man can speak fair of courses sordid and base. And therefore as Plato said elegantly, *That virtue, if she could be seen, would move great love and affection;* so seeing that she cannot be shewed to the Sense by corporal shape, the next degree is to shew her to the Imagination in lively representation: for to shew her to Reason only in subtilty of argument, was a thing ever derided in Chrysippus and many of the Stoics; who thought to thrust virtue upon men by sharp disputations and conclusions, which have no sympathy with the will of man.

Again, if the affections in themselves were pliant and obedient to reason, it were true there should be no great use of persuasions and insinuations to the will, more than of naked proposition and proofs; but in regard of the continual mutinies and seditions of the affections,

> Video meliora, proboque;
> Deteriora sequor:

[whereby they who not only see the better course, but approve it also, nevertheless follow the worse,] reason would become captive and servile, if Eloquence of Persuasions did not practice and win the Imagination from the Affection's part, and contract a confederacy between the Reason and Imagination against the Affections. For the affections themselves carry ever an appetite to good, as reason doth; the difference is, that *the affection beholdeth merely the present; reason beholdeth the future and sum of time;* and therefore the present filling the imagination more, reason is commonly vanquished; but after that force of eloquence and persuasion hath made things future and remote appear as present, then upon the revolt of the imagination reason prevaileth.

We conclude therefore, that Rhetoric can be no more charged with the colouring of the worse part, than Logic with Sophistry, or Morality with Vice. For we know the doctrines of contraries are the same, though the use be opposite. It appeareth also that Logic differeth from Rhetoric, not only as the fist from the palm, the one close the other at large; but much more in this, that Logic handleth reason exact and in truth, and Rhetoric handleth it as it is planted in popular opinions and manners. And therefore Aristotle doth wisely place Rhetoric as between Logic on the one side and moral or civil knowledge on the other, as participating of both: for the proofs and demonstrations of Logic are toward all men indifferent and the same; but the proofs and persuasions of Rhetoric ought to differ according to the auditors:

> Orpheus in sylvis, inter delphinas Arion:

[to be in the woods an Orpheus, among the dolphins an Arion:] which application, in perfection of idea, ought to extend so far, that if a man should speak of the same thing to several persons, he should speak to them all respectively and several ways: though this *politic part of eloquence in private speech* it is easy for the greatest orators to want, whilst by the observing their well-graced forms of speech they leese the volubility of application: and therefore it shall not be amiss to recommend this to better inquiry; not being curious whether we place it here, or in that part which concerneth policy. . . .[1]

We proceed now to that knowledge which considereth of the Appetite and Will of Man; whereof Salomon saith, *Ante omnia, fili, custodi cor tuum; nam inde procedunt actiones vitæ* [keep thy heart with all diligence, for thereout come the actions of thy life]. In the handling of this science, those which have written seem to me to have done as if a man that professeth to teach to write did only exhibit fair copies of alphabets and letters joined, without giving any precepts or directions for the carriage of the hand and framing of the letters. So have they made good and fair exemplars and copies, carrying the draughts and portraitures of Good, Virtue, Duty, Felicity; propounding them well described as the true objects and scopes of man's will and desires; but how to attain these excellent marks, and how to frame and subdue the will of man to become true and conformable to these pursuits, they pass it over altogether or slightly and unprofitably. For

[1] The treatment of sophisms is here omitted. *Editor.*

it is not the disputing *that moral virtues are in the mind of man by habit and not by nature,* or the distinguishing *that generous spirits are won by doctrines and persuasions, and the vulgar sort by reward and punishment,* and the like scattered glances and touches, that can excuse the absence of this part.

The reason of this omission I suppose to be that hidden rock whereupon both this and many other barks of knowledge have been cast away; which is, that men have despised to be conversant in ordinary and common matters; the judicious direction whereof nevertheless is the wisest doctrine (for life consisteth not in novelties or subtilities); but contrariwise they have compounded sciences chiefly of a certain resplendent or lustrous mass of matter, chosen to give glory either to the subtility of disputations or to the eloquence of discourses. But Seneca giveth an excellent check to eloquence; *Nocet illis eloquentia, quibus non rerum cupiditatum facit, sed sui:* [eloquence does mischief when it draws men's attention away from the matter to fix it on itself]. Doctrines should be such as should make men in love with the lesson, and not with the teacher; being directed to the auditor's benefit, and not to the author's commendation: and therefore those are of the right kind which may be concluded as Demosthenes concludes his counsel, *Quæ si feceritis, non oratorem duntaxat in præsentia laudabitis, sed vosmetipsos etiam non ita multo post statu rerum vestrarum meliore:* [if you follow this advice you will do a grace to yourselves no less than to the speaker,—to him by your vote today, to yourselves by the improvement which you will presently find in your affairs].

Neither needed men of so excellent parts to have despaired of a fortune which the poet Virgil promised himself, (and indeed obtained,) who got as much glory of eloquence, wit, and learning in the expressing of the observations of husbandry, as of the heroical acts of Æneas:—

> Nec sum animi dubius, verbis ea vincere magnum
> Quam sit, et angustis his addere rebus honorem.
> [How hard the task alas full well I know
> With charm of words to grace a theme so low.]

And surely if the purpose be in good earnest not to write at leisure that which men may read at leisure, but really to instruct and suborn action and active life, these Georgics of the mind, concerning the husbandry and tillage thereof, are no less worthy than the heroical descriptions of Virtue, Duty, and Felicity. Wherefore the main and primitive division of moral knowledge seemeth to be into the Exemplar or Platform of Good, and the Regiment or Culture of the Mind; the one describing the nature of good, the other prescribing rules how to subdue, apply, and accommodate the will of man thereunto.

The doctrine touching the Platform or Nature of Good considereth it either Simple or Compared; either the kinds of good, or the degrees of good: in the later whereof those infinite disputations which were touching the supreme degree thereof, which they term felicity, beatitude, or the highest good, the doctrines concerning which were as the heathen divinity, are by the Christian faith discharged. And as Aristotle saith, *That young men may be happy, but not otherwise but by hope;* so we must all acknowledge our minority, and embrace the felicity which is by hope of the future world.

Freed therefore and delivered from this doctrine of the philosophers' heaven, whereby they feigned an higher elevation of man's nature than was, (for we see in what an height of style Seneca writeth, *Vere magnum, habere fragilitatem hominis, securitatem Dei,* [it is true greatness to have in one the frailty of a man and the security of a God,]) we may with more sobriety and truth receive the rest of their inquiries and labours. Wherein for the Nature of Good Positive or Simple, they have set it down excellently, in describing the forms of Virtue and Duty, with their situations and postures, in distributing them into their kinds, parts, provinces, actions, and administrations, and the like: nay farther, they have commended them to man's nature and spirit with great quickness of argument and beauty of persuasions; yea, and fortified and intrenched them (as much as discourse can do) against corrupt and popular opinions. Again, for the Degrees and Comparative Nature of Good, they have also excellently handled it in their triplicity of Good, in the comparisons between a contemplative and an active life, in the distinction between virtue with reluctation and virtue secured, in their encounters between honesty and profit, in their balancing of virtue with virtue, and the like; so as this part deserveth to be reported for excellently laboured.

Notwithstanding, if before they had comen to the popular and received notions of virtue and vice, pleasure and pain, and the rest, they had stayed a little longer upon the inquiry concerning the roots of good and evil, and the strings of those roots, they had given, in my opinion, a great light to that which followed; and specially if they had consulted with nature, they had made their doctrines less prolix and more profound; which being by them in part omitted and in part handled with much confusion, we will endeavor to resume and open in a more clear manner.

There is formed in every thing a double nature of good: the one, as every thing is a total or substantive in itself; the other, as it is a part or member of a greater body; whereof the later is in degree the greater and the worthier, because it tendeth to the conservation of a more general form. Therefore we see the iron in particular sympathy moveth to the loadstone; but yet if it exceed a certain quantity, it forsaketh the affection to the loadstone, and like a good patriot moveth to the earth, which is the region and country of massy bodies; so may we go forward, and see that water and massy bodies move to the centre of the earth; but rather than to suffer a divulsion in the continuance of nature, they will move upwards from the centre of the earth, forsaking their duty to the earth in regard of their duty to the world. This double nature of good, and the comparative thereof, is much more engraven upon man, if he degenerate not; unto whom the conservation of duty to the public ought to be much more precious than the conservation of life and being: according to that memorable speech of Pompeius Magnus, when being in commission of purveyance for a famine at Rome, and being dissuaded with great vehemency and instance by his friends about him that he should not hazard himself to sea in an extremity of weather, he said only to them, *Necesse est ut eam, non ut vivam:* [it is needful that I go, not that I live]. But it may be truly affirmed that there was never any philosophy, religion, or other discipline, which did so plainly and highly exalt the good which is communicative, and depress the good which is private and particular, as the Holy Faith; well declaring, that it was the same God that gave the Christian law to men, who gave those laws of nature to inanimate creatures that we spake of before; for we read that the elected saints of God have wished themselves anathematized and razed out of the book of life, in an ecstasy of charity and infinite feeling of communion.

This being set down and strongly planted, doth judge and determine most of the controversies wherein Moral Philosophy is conversant. For first it decideth the question touching the preferment of the contemplative or active life, and decideth it against Aristotle. For all the reasons which he bringeth for the contemplative are private, and respecting the pleasure and dignity of a man's self, (in which respects no question the contemplative life hath the pre-eminence:) not much unlike to that comparison which Pythagoras made for the gracing and magnifying of philosophy and contemplation; who being asked what he was, answered, *That if Hiero were ever at the Olympian games, he knew the manner, that some came to try their fortune for the prizes, and some came as merchants to utter their commodities, and some came to make good cheer and meet their friends, and some came to look on; and that he was one of them that came to look on.* But men must know, that in this theatre of man's life it is reserved only for God and Angels to be lookers on. Neither could the like question ever have been received in the church, notwithstanding their *Pretiosa in oculis Domini mors sanctorum ejus,* [precious in the sight of the Lord is the death of his saints,] by which place they would exalt their civil death and regular professions, but upon this defence, that the monastical life is not simple contemplative, but performeth the duty either of incessant prayers and supplications, which hath been truly esteemed as an office in the church, or else of writing or taking instructions for writing concerning the law of God, as Moses did when he abode so long in the mount. And so we see Henoch the seventh from Adam, who was the first Contemplative and walked with God, yet did also endow the church with prophecy, which St. Jude citeth. But for contemplation which should be finished in itself without casting beams upon society, assuredly divinity knoweth it not.

It decideth also the controversies between Zeno and Socrates and their schools and successions on the one side, who placed felicity in virtue simply or attended; the actions and exercises whereof do chiefly embrace and concern society; and on the other side, the Cyrenaics and Epicureans, who placed it in pleasure, and made virtue (as it is used in some comedies of errors, wherein the mistress and the maid change habits,) to be but as a servant, without which pleasure cannot be served and attended; and the reformed school of the Epicureans, which placed it in serenity of mind and freedom from perturbation; as if they would have deposed Jupiter again, and restored Saturn and the first age, when there was no summer nor winter, spring nor autumn, but all after one air and season; and Herillus, which placed felicity in extinguishment of the disputes of the mind, making no fixed nature of good and evil, esteeming things according to the clearness of the desires, or the reluctation; which opinion was revived in the heresy of the Anabaptists, measuring things according to the motions of the spirit, and the constancy or wavering of belief: all which are manifest to tend to private repose and contentment, and not to point of society.

It censureth also the philosophy of Epictetus, which presupposeth that felicity must be placed in those things which are in our power, lest we be liable to fortune and disturbance: as if it were not a thing much more happy to fail in good and virtuous ends for the public, than to obtain all that we can wish to ourselves in our proper fortune; as Consalvo said to his soldiers, shewing them Naples, and protesting he had rather die one foot forwards than to have his life secured for long by one foot of retreat; whereunto the wisdom of that heavenly leader hath signed, who hath affirmed that *a good conscience is a continual feast:* shewing plainly that the conscience of good intentions, howsoever succeeding, is a more continual joy to nature than all the provision which can be made for security and repose.

It censureth likewise that abuse of philosophy which grew general about the time of Epictetus, in converting it into an occupation or profession; as if the purpose had been, not to resist and extinguish perturbations, but to fly and avoid the causes of them, and to shape a particular kind and course of life to that end; introducing such an health of mind, as was that health of body of which Aristotle speaketh of Herodicus, who did nothing all his life long but intend his health: whereas if men refer themselves to duties of society, as that health of body is best which is ablest to endure all alterations and extremities, so likewise that health of mind is most proper which can go through the greatest temptations and perturbations. So as Diogenes' opinion is to be accepted, who commended not them which abstained, but them which sustained, and could refrain their mind *in præcipitio,* and could give unto the mind (as is used in horsemanship) the shortest stop or turn.

Lastly, it censureth the tenderness and want of application in some of the most ancient and reverend philosophers and philosophical men, that did retire too easily from civil business, for avoiding of indignities and perturbations; whereas the resolution of men truly moral ought to be such as the same Consalvo said the honour of a soldier should be, *e telâ crassiore,* [of a stouter web,] and not so fine as that every thing should catch in it and endanger it.

To resume Private or Particular Good, it falleth into the division of Good Active and Passive: for this difference of Good (not unlike to that which amongst the Romans was expressed in the familiar or household terms of Promus and Condus) is formed also in all things; and is best disclosed in the two several appetites in creatures, the one to preserve or continue themselves, and the other to dilate or multiply themselves; whereof the later seemeth to be the worthier. For in nature, the heavens, which are the more worthy, are the agent; and the earth, which is the less worthy, is the patient. In the pleasures of living creatures, that of generation is greater than that of food. In divine doctrine, *Beatius est dare quam accipere:* [it is more blessed to give than to receive]. And in life, there is no man's spirit so soft, but esteemeth the affecting of somewhat that he hath fixed in his desire more than sensuality. Which priority of the Active Good is much upheld by the consideration of our estate to be mortal and exposed to fortune; for if we might have a perpetuity and certainty in our pleasures, the *state* of them would advance their price; but when we see it is but *Magni æstimamus mori tardius,* [we think it a great matter to be a little longer in dying,] and *Ne glorieris de crastino, nescis partum diei,* [boast not thyself of tomorrow, thou knowest not what the day may bring forth,] it maketh us to desire to have somewhat secured and exempted from time; which are only our deeds and works; as it is said *Opera eorum sequantur eos:* [their works follow them]. The pre-eminence likewise of this Active Good is upheld by the affection which is natural in man towards variety and proceeding; which in the pleasures of the sense (which is the principal part of Passive Good) can have no great latitude: *Cogita quamdiu eadem feceris; cibus, somnus, ludus; per hunc circulum curritur; mori velle non tantum fortis, aut miser, aut prudens, sed etiam fastidiosus potest:* [if you consider, says Seneca, how often you do the same thing over and over; food, sleep, exercise, and then food, sleep, exercise again, and so round and round: you will think that there needs neither fortitude nor misery nor wisdom to reconcile a man to death; one might wish to die for mere weariness of being alive]. But in enterprises, pursuits, and purposes of life, there is much variety; whereof men are sensible with pleasure in their inceptions, progressions, recoils, reintegrations, approaches, and attainings to their ends: so as it was well said, *Vita sine proposito languida et vaga est:* [life without an object to pursue is a languid and tiresome thing.] Neither hath this Active Good any identity with the good of society, though in some case it hath an incidence into it: for although it do many times bring forth acts of beneficence, yet it is with a respect private to a man's own power, glory, amplification, continuance; as appeareth plainly when it findeth a contrary subject. For that gigantine state of mind which possesseth the troublers of the world, such as was Lucius Sylla, and infinite other in smaller model, who would have all men happy or unhappy as they were their friends or enemies, and would give form to the world according to their own humours, (which is the true Theomachy,) pretendeth and aspireth to active good, though it recedeth furthest from good of society, which we have determined to be the greater.

To resume Passive Good, it receiveth a subdivision of Conservative and Perfective. For let us take a brief review of that which we have said: we have spoken first of the Good of Society, the intention whereof embraceth the form of Human Nature, whereof we are members and portions, and not our own proper and individual form; we have spoken of Active Good, and supposed it as a part of Private and Particular Good;

and rightly; for there is impressed upon all things a triple desire or appetite proceeding from love to themselves; one of preserving and continuing their form; another of advancing and perfecting their form; and a third of multiplying and extending their form upon other things; whereof the multiplying or signature of it upon other things is that which we handled by the name of Active Good. So as there remaineth the conserving of it, and perfecting or raising of it; which later is the highest degree of Passive Good. For to preserve in state is the less, to preserve with advancement is the greater. So in man,

> Igneus est ollis vigor, et cœlestis origo.
> [The living fire that glows those seeds within
> Remembers its celestial origin.]

His approach or assumption to divine or angelical nature is the perfection of his form; the error or false imitation of which good is that which is the tempest of human life; while man, upon the instinct of an advancement formal and essential, is carried to seek an advancement local. For as those which are sick, and find no remedy, do tumble up and down and change place, as if by a remove local they could obtain a remove internal; so it is with men in ambition, when failing of the mean to exalt their nature, they are in a perpetual estuation to exalt their place. So then Passive Good is, as was said, either Conservative or Perfective.

To resume the good of Conservation or Comfort, which consisteth *in the fruition of that which is agreeable to our natures;* it seemeth to be the most pure and natural of pleasures, but yet the softest and the lowest. And this also receiveth a difference, which hath neither been well judged of nor well enquired. For the good of fruition or contentment is placed either in the sincereness of the fruition, or in the quickness and vigour of it; the one superinduced by the equality, the other by vicissitude; the one having less mixture of evil, the other more impression of good. Whether of these is the greater good, is a question controverted; but whether man's nature may not be capable of both, is a question not enquired.

The former question being debated between Socrates and a Sophist, Socrates placing felicity in an equal and constant peace of mind, and the Sophist in much desiring and much enjoying, they fell from argument to ill words: the Sophist saying that Socrates' felicity was the felicity of a block or stone; and Socrates saying that the Sophist's felicity was the felicity of one that had the itch, who did nothing but itch and scratch. And both these opinions do not want their supports. For the opinion of Socrates is much upheld by the general consent even of the Epicures themselves, that virtue beareth a great part in felicity; and if so, certain it is that virtue hath more use in clearing perturbations than in compassing desires. The Sophist's opinion is much favoured by the assertion we last spake of, that good of advancement is greater than good of simple preservation; because every obtaining a desire hath a shew of advancement, as motion though in a circle hath a shew of progression.

But the second question, decided the true way, maketh the former superfluous. For can it be doubted but that there are some who take more pleasure in enjoying pleasures than some other, and yet nevertheless are less troubled with the loss or leaving of them? so as this same *Non uti ut non appetas, non appetere ut non metuas, sunt animi pusilli et diffidentis:* [to abstain from the use of a thing that you may not feel a want of it;

to shun the want that you may not fear the loss of it; are the precautions of pusillanimity and cowardice]. And it seemeth to me, that most of the doctrines of the philosophers are more fearful and cautionary than the nature of things requireth. So have they increased the fear of death in offering to cure it. For when they would have a man's whole life to be but a discipline or preparation to die, they must needs make men think that it is a terrible enemy against whom there is no end of preparing. Better saith the poet:

> Qui finem vitæ extremum inter munera ponat
> Naturæ:

[the end of life is to be counted among the boons of nature]. So have they sought to make men's minds too uniform and harmonical, by not breaking them sufficiently to contrary motions: the reason whereof I suppose to be, because they themselves were men dedicated to a private, free, and unapplied course of life. For as we see, upon the lute or like instrument, a *ground,* though it be sweet and have shew of many changes, yet breaketh not the hand to such strange and hard stops and passages as a *set song* or *voluntary;* much after the same manner was the diversity between a philosophical and a civil life. And therefore men are to imitate the wisdom of jewellers; who, if there be a grain or a cloud or an ice which may be ground forth without taking too much of the stone, they help it; but if it should lessen and abate the stone too much, they will not meddle with it: so ought men so to procure serenity as they destroy not magnanimity.

Having therefore deduced the Good of Man which is Private and Particular as far as seemeth fit, we will now return to that good of man which respecteth and beholdeth society, which we may term Duty; because the term of Duty is more proper to a mind well framed and disposed towards others, as the term of Virtue is applied to a mind well formed and composed in itself; though neither can a man understand Virtue without some relation to society, nor Duty without an inward disposition. This part may seem at first to pertain to science civil and politic; but not if it be well observed. For it concerneth the regiment and government of every man over himself, and not over others. And as in architecture the direction of framing the posts, beams, and other parts of building, is not the same with the manner of joining them and erecting the building; and in mechanicals, the direction how to frame an instrument or engine, is not the same with the manner of setting it on work and employing it; and yet nevertheless in expressing of the one you incidently express the aptness towards the other; so the doctrine of conjugation of men in society differeth from that of their conformity thereunto.

This part of Duty is subdivided into two parts; the common duty of every man, as a man or member of a state; the other, the respective or special duty of every man, in his profession, vocation, and place. The first of these is extant and well laboured, as hath been said. The second likewise I may report rather dispersed than deficient; which manner of dispersed writing in this kind of argument I acknowledge to be best. For who can take upon him to write of the proper duty, virtue, challenge, and right of every several vocation, profession and place? For although sometimes a looker on may see more than a gamester, and there be a proverb more arrogant than sound, *That the vale best discovereth the hill;* yet there is small doubt but that men can write best and most really and materially in their own professions; and that the writing of speculative men of active matter for the most part doth seem to men of experience, as Phormio's argument of the wars seemed to Hannibal, to be but dreams and dotage. Only there is one vice which accompanieth them that write in their own professions, that they magnify them in excess. But generally it were to be wished (as that which would make learning indeed solid and fruitful) that active men would or could become writers.

In which kind I cannot but mention, *honoris causa,* your Majesty's excellent book touching the duty of a king: a work richly compounded of divinity, morality, and policy, with great aspersion of all other arts; and being in mine opinion one of the most sound and healthful writings that I have read; not distempered in the heat of invention, nor in the coldness of negligence; not sick of dizziness, as those are who leese themselves in their order; nor of convulsions, as those which cramp in matters impertinent; not savouring of perfumes and paintings, as those do who seek to please the reader more than nature beareth; and chiefly well disposed in the spirts thereof, being agreeable to truth and apt for action; and far removed from that natural infirmity, whereunto I noted those that write in their own professions to be subject, which is, that they exalt it above measure. For your Majesty hath truly described, not a king of Assyria or Persia in their extern glory, but a Moses or a David, pastors of their people. Neither can I ever leese out of my remembrance what I heard your Majesty in the same sacred spirit of government deliver in a great cause of judicature, which was, *That Kings ruled by their laws as God did by the laws of nature, and ought as rarely to put in use their supreme prerogative as God doth his power of working miracles.* And yet notwithstanding, in your book of a free monarchy, you do well give men to understand, that you know the plenitude of the power and right of a King, as well as the circle of his office and duty. Thus have I presumed to allege this excellent writing of your Majesty, as a prime or eminent example of tractates concerning special and respective duties; wherein I should have said as much, if it had been written a thousand years since. Neither am I moved with certain courtly decencies, which esteem it flattery to praise in presence. No, it is flattery to praise in absence; that is, when either the virtue is absent, or the occasion is absent; and so the praise is not natural, but forced, either in truth or in time. But let Cicero be read in his oration *pro Marcello,* which is nothing but an excellent table of Cæsar's virtue, and made to his face; besides the example of many other excellent persons, wiser a great deal than such observers; and we will never doubt, upon a full occasion, to give just praise to present or absent.

But to return: there belongeth further to the handling of this part touching the duties of professions and vocations, a Relative or opposite, touching the frauds, cautels, impostures, and vices of every profession; which hath been likewise handled: but how? rather in a satire and cynically, than seriously and wisely: for men have rather sought by wit to deride and traduce much of that which is good in professions, than with judgment to discover and sever that which is corrupt. For, as Salomon saith, He that cometh to seek after knowledge with a mind to scorn and censure, shall be sure to find matter for his humour, but no matter for his instruction: *Quærenti derisori scientiam ipsa se abscondit; sed studioso fit obviam.* But the managing of this argument with integrity and truth, which I note as deficient, seemeth to me to be one of the best fortifications for honesty and virtue that can be planted. For as the fable goeth of the Basilisk, that if he see you first you die for it, but if you see him first he dieth; so is it with deceits and evil arts; which if they be first espied they leese their life, but if they prevent they endanger. So that we are much beholden to Machiavel and others, that write what men do and not what they ought to do. For it is not possible to join serpentine wisdom with the columbine innocency, except men know exactly all the conditions of the serpent; his baseness and going upon his belly, his volubility and lubricity, his envy and sting, and the rest; that is, all forms and natures of evil. For without this, virtue lieth open and unfenced. Nay an honest man can do no good upon those that are wicked to reclaim them, without the help of the knowledge of evil. For men of corrupted minds presuppose that honesty groweth out of simplicity of manners, and believing of preachers, school-masters, and men's exterior language: so as, except you can make them perceive that you know the utmost reaches of their own corrupt opinions, they despise all morality. *Non recipit stultus verba prudentiæ, nisi ea dixeris quæ versantur in corde ejus:* [the fool will not listen to the words of the wise, unless you first tell him what is in his own heart].

Unto this part touching Respective Duty doth also appertain the duties between husband and wife, parent and child, master and servant: so likewise the laws of friendship and gratitude, the civil bond of companies, colleges, and politic bodies, of neighbourhood, and all other proportionate duties; not as they are parts of government and society, but as to the framing of the mind of particular persons.

The knowledge concerning good respecting Society doth handle it also not simply alone, but comparatively;

whereunto belongeth the weighing of duties between person and person, case and case, particular and public: as we see in the proceeding of Lucius Brutus against his own sons, which was so much extolled; yet what was said?

Infelix, utcunque ferent ea facta minores;

[unhappy man! whatever judgment posterity shall pass upon that deed, &c.]. So the case was doubtful, and had opinion on both sides. Again, we see when M. Brutus and Cassius invited to a supper certain whose opinions they meant to feel, whether they were fit to be made their associates, and cast forth the question touching the killing of a tyrant being an usurper, they were divided in opinion; some holding that servitude was the extreme of evils, and others that tyranny was better than a civil war: and a number of the like cases there are of comparative duty. Amongst which that of all others is the most frequent, where the question is of a great deal of good to ensue of a small injustice. Which Jason of Thessalia determined against the truth; *Aliqua sunt injuste facienda, ut multa juste fieri possint:* [that there may be justice in many things there must be injustice in some]. But the reply is good, *Authorem præsentis justitiæ habes, sponsorem futuræ non habes:* [the justice that is to be done now is in your power, but where is your security for that which is to be done hereafter?] Men must pursue things which are just in present, and leave the future to the divine Providence. So then we pass on from this general part touching the exemplar and description of good.

Now therefore we have spoken of this fruit of life, it remaineth to speak of the husbandry that belongeth thereunto; without which part the former seemeth to be no better than a fair image or statua, which is beautiful to contemplate, but is without life and motion: whereunto Aristotle himself subscribeth in these words: *Necesse est scilicet de virtute dicere, et quid sit, et ex quibus gignatur. Inutile enim fere fuerit virtutem quidem nosse, acquirendæ autem ejus modos et vias ignorare. Non enim de virtute tantum, qua specie sit, quærendum est, sed et quomodo sui copiam faciat: utrumque enim volumus, et rem ipsam nosse, et ejus compotes fieri: hoc autem ex voto non succedet, nisi sciamus et ex quibus et quomodo:* [it is necessary to determine concerning Virtue not only what it is but whence it proceeds. For there would be no use in knowing Virtue without knowing the ways and means of acquiring it. For we have to consider not only what it is, but how it is to be had. For we want both to know virtue and to be virtuous; which we cannot be without knowing both the whence and the how]. In such full words and with such iteration doth he inculcate this part. So saith Cicero in great commendation of Cato the second, that he had applied himself to philosophy *non ita disputandi causa, sed ita vivendi:* [not that he might talk like a philosopher, but that he might live like one]. And although the neglect of our times, wherein few men do hold any consultations touching the reformation of their life, (as Seneca excellently saith, *De partibus vitæ quisque deliberat, de summâ nemo,*) [every man takes thought about the parts of his life, no man about the whole,] may make this part seem superfluous; yet I must conclude with that aphorism of Hippocrates, *Qui gravi morbo correpti dolores non sentiunt, iis mens ægrotat;* [they that are sick and yet feel no pain are sick in their minds;] they need medicine not only to assuage the disease but to awake the sense. And if it be said that the cure of men's minds belongeth to sacred Divinity, it is most true: but yet Moral

Philosophy may be preferred unto her as a wise servant and humble handmaid. For as the Psalm saith, *that the eyes of the handmaid look perpetually towards the mistress,* and yet no doubt many things are left to the discretion of the handmaid to discern of the mistress' will; so ought Moral Philosophy to give a constant attention to the doctrines of Divinity, and yet so as it may yield of herself (within due limits) many sound and profitable directions.

This part therefore, because of the excellency thereof, I cannot but find exceeding strange that it is not reduced to written inquiry; the rather because it consisteth of much matter wherein both speech and action is often conversant, and such wherein the common talk of men (which is rare, but yet cometh sometimes to pass) is wiser than their books. It is reasonable therefore that we propound it in the more particularity, both for the worthiness, and because we may acquit ourselves for reporting it deficient; which seemeth almost incredible, and is otherwise conceived and presupposed by those themselves that have written. We will therefore enumerate some heads or points thereof, that it may appear the better what it is, and whether it be extant.

First therefore, in this, as in all things which are practical, we ought to cast up our account, what is in our power and what not; for the one may be dealt with by way of alteration, but the other by way of application only. The husbandman cannot command neither the nature of the earth nor the season of the weather; no more can the physician the constitution of the patient nor the variety of accidents. So in the culture and cure of the mind of man, two things are without our command; points of nature, and points of fortune; for to the basis of the one, and the conditions of the other, our work is limited and tied. In these things therefore it is left unto us to proceed by application:

Vincenda est omnis fortuna ferendo:

[all fortune may be overcome by endurance or suffering;] and so likewise,

Vincenda est omnis natura ferendo:

[all nature may be overcome by suffering]. But when that we speak of suffering, we do not speak of a dull and neglected suffering, but of a wise and industrious suffering, which draweth and contriveth use and advantage out of that which seemeth adverse and contrary; which is that property which we call Accommodating or Applying. Now the wisdom of application resteth principally in the exact and distinct knowledge of the precedent state or disposition unto which we do apply: for we cannot fit a garment, except we first take measure of the body.

So then the first article of this knowledge is to set down sound and true distributions and descriptions of the several characters and tempers of men's natures and dispositions, specially having regard to those differences which are most radical in being the fountains and causes of the rest, or most frequent in concurrence or commixture; wherein it is not the handling of a few of them in passage, the better to describe the mediocrities of virtues, that can satisfy this intention; for if it deserve to be considered, *that there are minds which are proportioned to great matters, and others to small,* (which Aristotle handleth or ought to have handled by the name of Magnanimity,) doth it not deserve as well to be considered, *that there are minds proportional to intend many matters, and others to few?* so that some can divide themselves, others can perchance do exactly well, but it must be but in a few things at once; and so there cometh to be a *narrowness of mind,* as well as a *pusillanimity.* And again, *that some minds are proportioned to that which may be dispatched at once, or within a short return of time; others to that which begins afar off, and is to be won with length of pursuit;*

Jam tum tenditque fovetque;

[he begins to attend and nurse his project while it is yet in the cradle;] so that there may be fitly said to be a *longanimity;* which is commonly also ascribed to God as a *magnanimity.* So further deserved it to be considered by Aristotle, *that there is a disposition in conversation (supposing it in things which do in no sort touch or concern a man's self) to soothe and please, and a disposition contrary to contradict and cross;* and deserveth it not much better to be considered, *that there is a disposition, not in conversation or talk but in matter of more serious nature, (and supposing it still in things merely indifferent,) to take pleasure in the good of another, and a disposition contrariwise to take distaste at the good of another;* which is that property which we call good-nature or ill-nature, benignity or malignity? And therefore I cannot sufficiently marvel that this part of knowledge touching the several characters of natures and dispositions should be omitted both in morality and policy, considering it is of so great ministery and suppeditation to them both. A man shall find in the traditions of astrology some pretty and apt divisions of men's natures, according to the predominances of the planets; *lovers of quiet, lovers of action, lovers of victory, lovers of honour, lovers of pleasure, lovers of arts, lovers of change,* and so forth. A man shall find in the wisest sort of these Relations which the Italians make touching Conclaves, the natures of the several Cardinals handsomely and lively painted forth. A man shall meet with in every day's conference the denominations of *sensitive, dry, formal, real, humorous, certain, huomo di prima impressione, huomo di ultima impressione,* and the like; and yet nevertheless this kind of observations wandereth in words, but is not fixed in inquiry. For the distinctions are found (many of them), but we conclude no precepts upon them; wherein our fault is the greater, because both history, poesy, and daily experience are as goodly fields where these observations grow; whereof we make a few posies to hold in our hands, but no man bringeth them to the confectionary, that receits might be made of them for use of life.

Of much like kind are those impressions of nature, which are imposed upon the mind *by the sex, by the age, by the region, by health and sickness, by beauty and deformity,* and the like, which are inherent and not extern; and again those which are caused by extern fortune; as *sovereignty, nobility, obscure birth, riches, want, magistracy, privateness, prosperity, adversity, constant fortune, variable fortune, rising per saltum, per gradus,* and the like. And therefore we see that Plautus maketh it a wonder to see an old man beneficent; *benignitas hujus ut adolescentuli est:* [he is generous as if he were a young man:] St. Paul concludeth that severity of discipline was to be used to the Cretans, *Increpa eos durè,* [rebuke them sharply,] upon the disposition of their country; *Cretenses semper mendaces, malæ bestiæ, ventres pigri:* [the Cretans are alway liars, evil beasts, slow bellies:] Sallust noteth that it is usual with Kings to desire contradictories; *Sed plerumque regiæ voluntates, ut vehementes sunt, sic mobiles, sæpeque ipsæ sibi adversæ:* [royal desires, as they are violent, so are they changeable, and often incompatible with each other:] Tacitus observeth how rarely raising of the fortune mendeth the disposition; *Solus Vespasianus mutatus in melius:* [Vespasian the only one of the emperors that changed for the better:] Pindarus maketh an observation that great and sudden fortune for the most part defeateth men; *Qui magnum felicitatem concoquere non possunt:* [that cannot digest great felicity:] so the Psalm sheweth it is more easy to keep a measure in the enjoying of fortune than in the increase of fortune; *Divitiæ si affluant, nolite cor apponere:* [if riches increase set not your heart upon them]. These observations and the like I deny not but are touched a little by Aristotle as in passage in his Rhetorics, and are handled in some scattered discourses; but they were never incorporate into Moral Philosophy, to which they do essentially appertain; as the knowledge of the diversity of grounds and moulds doth to agriculture, and the knowledge of the diversity of complexions and constitutions doth to the physician; except we mean to follow the indiscretion of empirics, which minister the same medicines to all patients.

Another article of this knowledge is the inquiry touching the affections; for as in medicining of the body it is in order first to know the divers complexions and constitutions, secondly the diseases, and lastly the cures; so in medicining of the mind, after knowledge of the divers characters of men's natures, it followeth in order to know the diseases and infirmities of the mind, which are no other than the perturbations and distempers of the affections. For as the ancient politiques in popular estates were wont to compare the people to the sea and the orators to the winds, because as the sea would of itself be calm and quiet if the winds did not move and trouble it, so the people would be peaceable and tractable if the seditious orators did not set them in working and agitation; so it may be fitly said, that the mind in the nature thereof would be temperate and stayed, if the affections, as winds, did not put it into tumult and perturbation. And here again I find strange, as before, that Aristotle should have written divers volumes of Ethics, and never handled the affections, which is the principal subject thereof; and yet in his Rhetorics, where they are considered but collaterally and in a second degree (*as they may be moved by speech*), he findeth place for them, and handleth them well for the quantity; but where their true place is, he pretermitteth them. For it is not his disputations about pleasure and pain that can satisfy this inquiry, no more than he that should generally handle the nature of light can be said to handle the nature of colours; for pleasure and pain are to the particular affections as light is to particular colours. Better travails I suppose had the Stoics taken in this argument, as far as I can gather by that which we have at second hand: but yet it is like it was after their manner, rather in subtilty of definitions (which in a subject of this nature are but curiosities) than in active and ample descriptions and observations. So likewise I find some particular writings of an elegant nature touching some of the affections; as of *anger*, of *comfort upon adverse accidents*, of *tenderness of countenance*, and other. But the poets and writers of histories are the best doctors of this knowledge; where we may find painted forth with great life, how affections are kindled and incited; and how pacified and refrained; and how again contained from act and further degree; how they disclose themselves, how they work, how they vary, how they gather and fortify, how they are inwrapped one within another, and how they do fight and encounter one with another, and other the like particularities: amongst the which this last is of special use in moral and civil matters; how (I say) to set affection against affection, and to master one by another; even as we use to hunt beast with beast and fly bird with bird, which otherwise percase we could not so easily recover: upon which foundation is erected that excellent use of the *præmium* and *pœna,* whereby civil states consist; employing the predominant affections of *fear* and *hope,* for the suppressing and bridling the rest. For as in the government of states it is sometimes necessary to bridle one faction with another, so it is in the government within.

Now come we to those points which are within our own command, and have force and operation upon the mind to affect the will and appetite and to alter manners: wherein they ought to have handled *custom, exercise, habit, education, example, imitation, emulation, company, friends, praise, reproof, exhortation, fame, laws, books, studies:* these as they have determinate use in moralities, from these the mind suffereth, and of these are such receipts and regiments compounded and described, as may seem to recover or preserve the health and good estate of the mind, as far as pertaineth to human medicine: of which number we will visit upon some one or two as an example of the rest, because it were too long to prosecute all; and therefore we do resume Custom and Habit to speak of.

The opinion of Aristotle seemeth to me a negligent opinion, that of those things which consist by nature nothing can be changed by custom; using for example, that if a stone be thrown ten thousand times up, it will not learn to ascend; and that by often seeing or hearing, we do not learn to see or hear the better. For though this principle be true in things wherein nature is *peremptory,* (the reason whereof we cannot now stand to discuss,) yet it is otherwise in things wherein nature admitteth *a latitude.* For he might see that a strait glove will come more easily on with use, and that a wand will by use bend otherwise than it grew, and that by use of the voice we speak louder and stronger, and that by use of enduring heat or cold we endure it the better, and the like: which later sort have a nearer resemblance unto that subject of manners he handleth than those instances which he allegeth. But allowing his conclusion, *that virtues and vices consist in habit,* he ought so much the more to have taught the manner of superinducing that habit: for there be many precepts of the wise ordering the exercises of the mind, as there is of ordering the exercises of the body; whereof we will recite a few.

The first shall be, that we beware we take not at the first either too *high* a strain or too *weak:* for if too high, in a diffident nature you discourage; in a confident nature you breed an opinion of facility, and so a sloth; and in all natures you breed a further expectation that can hold out, and so an insatisfaction on the end: if too weak of the other side, you may not look to perform and overcome any great task.

Another precept is, to practise all things chiefly at two several times, the one when the mind is best disposed, the other when it is worst disposed; that by the one you may gain a great step, by the other you may work out the knots and stonds of the mind, and make the middle times the more easy and pleasant.

Another precept is, that which Aristotle mentioneth by the way, which is to bear ever towards the contrary extreme of that whereunto we are by nature inclined: like unto the rowing against the stream, or making a wand straight by bending him contrary to his natural crookedness.

Another precept is, that the mind is brought to any thing better, and with more sweetness and happiness, if that whereunto you pretend be not first in the intention, but *tanquam aliud agendo,* because of the natural hatred of the mind against necessity and constraint. Many other axioms there are touching the managing of *Exercise* and *Custom;* which being so conducted, doth prove indeed another nature; but being governed by chance, doth commonly prove but an ape of nature, and bringeth forth that which is lame and counterfeit.

So if we should handle *books* and *studies,* and what influence and operation they have upon manners, are there not divers precepts of great caution and direction appertaining thereunto? Did not one of the fathers in great indignation call Poesy *vinum dæmonum,* because it increaseth temptations, perturbations, and vain opinions? Is not the opinion of Aristotle worthy to be regarded, wherein he saith that young men are no fit auditors of moral philosophy, because they are not settled from the boiling heat of their affections, nor attempered with time and experience? And doth it not hereof come, that those excellent books and discourses of the ancient writers (whereby they have persuaded unto virtue most effectually, by representing her in state and majesty, and popular opinions against virtue in their parasites' coats, fit to be scorned and derided,) are of so little effect towards honesty of life, because they are not read and revolved by men in their mature and settled years, but confined almost to boys and beginners? But is it not true also, that much less young men are fit auditors of matters of policy, till they have been throughly seasoned in religion and morality; lest their judgments be corrupted, and made apt to think that there are no true differences of things, but according to utility and fortune; as the verse describes it,

Prosperum et felix scelus virtus vocatur; [a crime that is successful is called a virtue;] and again, *Ille crucem pretium sceleris tuli, hic diadema;* [the same crime is rewarded in one man with a gibbet and in another with a crown;] which the poets do speak satirically, and in indignation on virtue's behalf; but books of policy do speak it seriously and positively; for so it pleaseth Machiavel to say, *that if Cæsar had been overthrown he would have been more odious than ever was Catiline;* as if there had been no difference but in fortune, between a very fury of lust and blood, and the most excellent spirit (his ambition reserved) of the world? Again, is there not a caution likewise to be given of the doctrines of moralities themselves (some kinds of them,) lest they make men too precise, arrogant, incompatible; as Cicero saith of Cato, *In Marco Catone hæc bona quæ videmus divina et egregia, ipsius scitote esse propria; quæ nonnunquam requirimus, ea sunt omnia non a naturâ, sed a magistro:* [his excellencies were his own, his defects came from the school-master?] Many other axioms and advices there are touching those proprieties and effects which studies do infuse and instil into manners. And so likewise is there touching the use of all those other points, of company, fame, laws, and the rest, which we recited in the beginning in the doctrine of morality.

But there is a kind of Culture of the Mind that seemeth yet more accurate and elaborate than the rest, and is built upon this ground; that the minds of all men are at some times in a state more perfect, and at other times in a state more depraved. The purpose therefore of this practice is to fix and cherish the good hours of the mind, and to obliterate and take forth the evil. The fixing of the good hath been practised by two means; vows or constant resolutions; and observances or exercises; which are not to be regarded so much in themselves, as because they keep the mind in continual obedience. The obliteration of the evil hath been practised by two means; some kind of redemption or expiation of that which is past; and an inception or account *de novo* for the time to come. But this part seemeth sacred and religious, and justly; for all good Moral Philosophy (as was said) is but an handmaid to religion.

Wherefore we will conclude with that last point which is of all other means the most compendious and summary, and again the most noble and effectual, to the reducing of the mind unto virtue and good estate; which is the electing and propounding unto a man's self good and virtuous ends of his life, such as may be in a reasonable sort within his compass to attain. For if these two things be supposed, that a man set before him honest and good ends, and again that he be resolute, constant, and true unto them, it will follow that he shall mould himself into all virtue at once. And this is indeed like the work of nature; whereas the other course is like the work of the hand. For as when a carver makes an image, he shapes only that part whereupon he worketh; as if he be upon the face, that part which shall be the body is but a rude stone still, till such times as he comes to it; but contrariwise when nature makes a flower or living creature, she formeth rudiments of all the parts at one time; so in obtaining virtue by *habit,* while a man practiseth temperance, he doth not profit much to fortitude, nor the like; but when he dedicateth and applieth himself to *good ends,* look what virtue soever the pursuit and passage towards those ends doth commend unto him, he is invested of a precedent disposition to conform himself thereunto; which state of mind Aristotle doth excellently express himself, that it ought not to be called *virtuous,* but *divine:* his words are these: *Immanitati autem consentaneum est opponere eam, quæ supra humanitatem, est, heroicam sive divinam virtutem:* and a little after, *Nam ut feræ neque vitium neque virtus est, sic neque Dei: sed hic quidem status altius quiddam virtute est, ille aliud quiddam a vitio:* [that which answers to the brutal degree of vice is the heroical or divine degree of virtue. . . . For as neither virtue nor vice can be predicated of a brute, so neither can it of a God: the divine condition being something higher than virtue, the brutal something different from vice]. And therefore we may see what celsitude of honour Plinus Secundus attributeth to Trajan in his funeral oration, where he said, *that men needed to make no other prayers to the gods, but that they would continue as good lords to them as Trajan had been;* as if he had not been only an imitation of divine nature, but a pattern of it. But these be heathen and profane passages, having but a shadow of that divine state of mind which religion and the holy faith doth conduct men unto, by imprinting upon their souls Charity, which is excellently called the bond of Perfection, because it comprehendeth and fasteneth all virtues together. And as it is elegantly said by Menander of vain love, which is but a false imitation of divine love, *Amor melior sophista lævo ad humanam vitam,* that love teacheth a man to carry himself better than the sophist or preceptor, which he calleth *left-handed,* because with all his rules and preceptions he cannot form a man so *dexterously,* nor with that facility to prize himself and govern himself, as love can do; so certainly if a man's mind be truly inflamed with charity, it doth work him suddenly into greater perfection than all the doctrine of morality can do, which is but a sophist in comparison of the other. Nay further, as Xenophon observed truly that all other affections, though they raise the mind, yet they do it by distorting and uncomeliness of ecstasies or excesses; but only love doth exalt the mind, and nevertheless at the same instant doth settle and compose it; so in all other excellencies, though they advance nature, yet they are subject to excess; only charity admitteth no excess: for so we see, aspiring to be like God in power, the angels transgressed and fell; *Ascendam, et ero similis Altissimo;* [I will ascend and be like unto the Highest:] by aspiring to be like God in knowledge, man transgressed and fell; *Eritis sicut Dii, scientes bonum et malum;* [ye shall be as Gods, knowing good and evil;] but by aspiring to a similitude of God in goodness or love, neither man nor angel ever transgressed or shall transgress. For unto that imitation we are called: *Diligite inimicos vestros, benefacite eis qui oderunt vos, et orate pro persequentibus et calumniantibus vos, ut sitis filii Patris vestri qui in cœlis est, qui solem suum oriri facit super bonos et malos, et pluit super justos et injustos;* [love your enemies, do good to them that hate you, and pray for them which despitefully use you and persecute you; that ye may be the children of your Father which is in Heaven, who maketh his sun to rise on the evil and on the good, and sendeth rain on the just and on the unjust]. So in the first platform of the divine nature itself, the heathen religion speaketh thus, *Optimus Maximus,* [Best and Greatest:] and the sacred Scriptures thus, *Misericordia ejus super omnia opera ejus,* [his mercy is over all his works].

Wherefore I do conclude this part of moral knowledge, concerning the Culture and Regiment of the Mind; wherein if any man, considering the parts thereof which I have enumerated, do judge that my labour is but to collect into an Art or Science that which hath been pretermitted by others as matter of common sense and experience, he judgeth well. But as Philocrates sported with Demosthenes, *You may not marvel (Athenians,) that Demosthenes and I do differ, for he drinketh water, and I drink wine;* and like as we read of an ancient parable of the *two gates of sleep,*

> Sunt geminæ somni portæ: quarum altera fertur
> Cornea, qua veris facilis datur exitus umbris:
> Altera candenti perfecta nitens elephanto,
> Sed falsa ad cœlum mittunt insomnia manes:
> [Two gates there are of sleep; of horn the one,
> By which the true shades pass; of ivory
> Burnished and white the other, but through it
> Into the upper world false dreams are sent:]

so if we put on sobriety and attention, we shall find it a sure maxim in knowledge, that the more pleasant liquor (*of wine*) is the more vaporous, and the braver gate (*of ivory*) sendeth forth the falser dreams.

But we have now concluded *that general part of Human Philosophy, which contemplateth man segregate, and as he consisteth of body and spirit.* Wherein we may further note, that there seemeth to be a relation or conformity between the good of the mind and the good of the body. For as we divided the good of the body into *health, beauty, strength,* and *pleasure;* so the good of the mind, inquired in rational and moral knowledges, tendeth to this, to make the mind *sound,* and without perturbation; *beautiful,* and graced with decency; and *strong* and *agile* for all duties of life. These three, as in the body so in the mind, seldom meet, and commonly sever. For it is easy to observe that many have strength of wit and courage, but have neither health from perturbations, nor any beauty or decency in their doings: some again have an elegancy and fineness of carriage, which have neither soundness of honesty, nor substance of sufficiency: and some again have honest and reformed minds, that can neither become themselves nor manage business: and sometimes two of them meet, and rarely all three. As for pleasure, we have likewise determined that the mind ought not to be reduced to stupid, but to retain pleasure; confined rather in the subject of it, than in the strength and vigour of it.

Civil Knowledge is conversant about a subject which of all others is most immersed in matter, and hardliest reduced to axiom. Nevertheless, as Cato the censor said, *That the Romans were like sheep, for that a man might better drive a flock of them, than one of them; for in a flock, if you could get but some few go right, the rest would follow:* so in that respect moral philosophy is more difficile than policy. Again, moral philosophy propoundeth to itself the framing of internal goodness; but civil knowledge requireth only an external goodness; for that as to society sufficeth; and therefore it cometh oft to pass that there be evil times in good governments: for so we find in the holy story, when the kings were good, yet it is added, *Sed adhuc populus non direxerat cor suum ad Dominum Deum patrum suorum;* [but as yet the people had not turned their hearts towards the Lord God of their fathers]. Again, States, as great engines, move slowly, and are not so soon put out of frame: for as in Egypt the seven good years sustained the seven bad, so governments for a time well grounded do bear out errors following: but the resolution of particular persons is more suddenly subverted. These respects do somewhat qualify the extreme difficulty of civil knowledge.

This knowledge hath three parts, according to the three summary actions of society; which are Conversation, Negotiation, and Government. For man seeketh in society comfort, use, and protection: and they be three wisdoms of divers natures, which do often sever; wisdom of the behaviour, wisdom of business, and wisdom of state.

The wisdom of Conversation ought not to be over much affected, but much less despised; for it hath not only an honour in itself, but an influence also into business and government. The poet saith,

Nec vultu destrue verba tuo:

a man may destroy the force of his words with his countenance: so may he of his deeds, saith Cicero; recommending to his brother affability and easy access; *Nil interest habere ostium apertum, vultum clausum;* it is nothing won to admit men with an open door, and to receive them with a shut and reserved countenance. So we see Atticus, before the first interview between Cæsar and Cicero, the war depending, did seriously advise Cicero touching the composing and ordering of his countenance and gesture. And if the government of the countenance be of such effect, much more is that of the speech, and other carriage appertaining to conversation; the true model whereof seemeth to me well expressed by Livy, though not meant for this purpose; *Ne aut arrogans videar, aut obnoxius; quorum alterum est alienæ libertatis obliti, alterum suæ:* the sum of behaviour is to retain a man's own dignity, without intruding upon the liberty of others. On the other side, if behaviour and outward carriage be intended too much, first it may pass into affection, and then *quid deformius quam scenam in vitam transferre,* [what more unseemly than to be always playing a part;] to act a man's life? But although it proceed not to that extreme, yet it consumeth time, and employeth the mind too much. And therefore as we use to advise young students from company keeping, by saying, *Amici fures temporis,* [friends are thieves of time;] so certainly the intending of the discretion of behaviour is a great thief of meditation. Again, such as are accomplished in that honor of urbanity please themselves in name, and seldom aspire to higher virtue; whereas those that have defect in it do seek comeliness by reputation: for where reputation is, almost every thing becometh; but where that is not, it must be supplied by *puntos* and compliments. Again, there is no greater impediment of action than an over-curious observance of decency, and the guide of decency, which is time and season. For as Salomon sayeth, *Qui respicit ad ventos, non seminat; et qui respicit ad nubes, non metet;* [he that looketh to the winds doth not sow, and he that regardeth the clouds shall not reap:] a man must make his opportunity, as oft as find it. To conclude: Behaviour seemeth to me as a garment of the mind, and to have the conditions of a garment. For it ought to be made in fashion; it ought not to be too curious; it ought to be shaped so as to set forth any good making of the mind, and hide any deformity; and above all, it ought not to be too strait or restrained for exercise or motion. But this part of civil knowledge hath been elegantly handled, and therefore I cannot report it for deficient.

The wisdom touching Negotiation or Business hath not been hitherto collected into writing, to the great derogation of learning and the professors of learning. For from this root springeth chiefly that note or opinion, which by us is expressed in adage to this effect, that there is no great concurrence between learning and wisdom. For of the three wisdoms which we have set down to pertain to civil life, for wisdom of Behaviour, it is by learned men for the most part despised, as an inferior to virtue and an enemy to meditation; for wisdom of Government, they acquit themselves well when they are called to it, but that happeneth to few; but for the wisdom of Business, wherein man's life is most conversant, there be no books of it, except some few scattered advertisements, that have no proportion to the magnitude of this subject. For if books were written of this as the other, I doubt not but learned men with mean experience would far excel men of long experience without learning, and outshoot them in their own bow.

Neither needeth it at all to be doubted that this knowledge should be so variable as it falleth not under precept; for it is much less infinite than science of Government, which we see is laboured and in some part reduced. Of this wisdom it seemeth some of the ancient Romans in the saddest and wisest times were professors; for Cicero reporteth that it was then in use for senators that had name and opinion for general wise men, as Coruncanius, Curius, Lælius, and many others, to walk at certain hours in the Place, and to give audience to those that would use their advice; and that the particular citizens would resort unto them, and consult with them of the marriage of a daughter, or of the employing of a son, or of a purchase or bargain, or of an accusation, and every other occasion incident to man's life; so as there is a wisdom of counsel and advice even in private causes, arising out of an universal insight into the affairs of the world; which is used indeed upon particular cases propounded, but is gathered by general observation of causes of like nature. For so we see in the book which Q. Cicero writeth to his brother *De petitione consulatus* (being the only book of business that I know written by the ancients), although it concerned a particular action then on foot, yet the substance thereof consisteth of many wise and politic axioms, which contain not a temporary but a perpetual direction in the case of popular elections. But chiefly we may see in those aphorisms which have place amongst divine writings, composed by Salomon the king, of whom the Scriptures testify that his heart was as the sands of the sea, encompassing the world and all worldly matters; we see, I say, not a few profound and excellent cautions, precepts, positions, extending to much variety of occasions; whereupon we will stay awhile, offering to consideration some number of examples.

Sed et cunctis sermonibus qui dicuntur ne accomodes aurem tuam, ne forte audias servum tuum maledicentem tibi. [Hearken not unto all words that are spoken, lest thou hear thy servant curse thee.] Here is concluded the provident stay of inquiry of that which we would be loth to find: as it was judged great wisdom in Pompeius Magnus that he burned Sertorius' papers unperused.

Vir sapiens si cum stulto contenderit, sive irascatur sive rideat, non inveniet requiem. [A wise man if he contend with a fool, whether he be angry or whether he laugh, shall find no rest:.] Here is described the great disadvantage which a wise man hath in undertaking a lighter person than himself; which is such an engagement as whether a man turn the matter to jest, or turn it to heat, or howsoever he change copy, he can no ways quit himself well of it.

Qui delicatè a pueritia nutrit servum suum, postea sentiet eum contumacem. [He that delicately bringeth up his servant from a child shall have him become froward at the length.] Here is signified, that if a man begin too high a pitch in his favours, it doth commonly end in unkindness and unthankfulness.

Vidisti virum velocem in opere suo? Coram regibus

stabit, nec erit inter ignobiles. [Seest thou a man that is quick in his business? He shall stand before kings; his place shall not be among mean men.] Here is observed that, of all virtues for rising to honour, quickness of dispatch is the best; for superiors many times love not to have those they employ too deep or too sufficient, but ready and diligent.

Vidi cunctos viventes qui ambulant sub sole, cum adolescente secundo qui consurgit pro eo. [I beheld all the living which walk under the sun, with the second youth that shall stand in his place.] Here is expressed that which was noted by Sylla first, and after him by Tiberius: *Plures adorant solem orientem quam occidentem vel meridianum,* [there be more than worship the rising sun than the sun setting or at mid-day.]

Si spiritus potestatem habentis ascenderit super te, locum tuum ne dimiseris; quia curatio faciet cessare peccata maxima. [If the spirit of the ruler rise up against thee, leave not thy place; for observance will remove great offences.] Here caution is given that upon displeasure, retiring is of all courses the unfittest; for a man leaveth things at worst, and depriveth himself of means to make them better.

Erat civitas parva, et pauci in ea viri: venit contra eam rex magnus, et vadavit eam, intruxitque munitiones per gyrum, et perfecta est obsidio: inventusque est in ea vir pauper et sapiens, et liberavit eam per sapientiam suam; et nullus deinceps recordatus est hominis illus pauperis. [There was a little city and few men within it; and there came a great king against it and besieged it and raised great bulwarks round about it: and there was found in it a poor wise man, and he by his wisdom delivered the city; yet no man remembered that same poor man.] Here the corruption of states is set forth, that esteem not virtue or merit longer than they have use of it.

Mollis responsio frangit iram. [A soft answer defeateth wrath.] Here is noted that silence or rough answer exasperateth; but an answer present and temperate pacifieth.

Iter pigrorum quasi sepes spinarum. [The way of the slothful is as an hedge of thorne.] Here is lively represented how laborious sloth proveth in the end; for when things are deferred till the last instant and nothing prepared beforehand, every step findeth a brier of an impediment, which catcheth or stoppeth.

Melior est finis orationis quam principium. [Better is the end of a speech than the beginning thereof.] Here is taxed the vanity of formal speakers, that study more about prefaces and inducements than upon the conclusions and issues of speech.

Qui cognoscit in judicio faciem, non bene facit; iste et pro buccella panis deseret veritatem. [He that respecteth persons in judgment doth not well; even for a piece of bread will that man depart from the truth.] Here is noted, that a judge were better be a briber than a respecter of persons; for a corrupt judge offendeth not so lightly as a facile.

Vir pauper calumnians pauperes similis est imbri vehementi, in quo paratur fames. [A poor man that beareth witness against the poor is like a sweeping rain which leaveth no food.] Here is expressed the extremity of necessitous extortions, figured in the ancient fable of the full and hungry horse-leech.

Fons turbatus pede, et vena corrupta, est justus cadens coram impio. [A righteous man falling down before the wicket is as a troubled fountain and a corrupt spring.] Here is noted, that one judicial and exemplar iniquity in the face of the world, doth trouble the fountains of justice more than many particular injuries passed over by connivance.

Qui subtrahit aliquid a patre et a matre, et dicit hoc non esse peccatum, particeps est homicidii. [Whoso robbeth his father and his mother, and saith it is no transgression, is the companion of a destroyer.] Here is noted, that whereas men in wronging their best friends use to extenuate their fault, as if they might presume or be bold upon them, it doth contrariwise indeed aggravate their fault, and turneth it from injury to impiety.

Noli esse amicus homini iracundo, nec ambulato cum homine furioso. [Make no friendship with an angry man, neither go with a furious man.] Here caution is given, that in the election of our friends we do principally avoid those which are impatient, as those that will espouse us to many factions and quarrels.

Qui conturbat domum suam, possidebit ventum. [He that troubleth his own house shall inherit the wind.] Here is noted, that in domestical separations and breaches men do promise to themselves quieting of their mind and contentment; but still they are deceived of their expectation, and it turneth to wind.

Filius sapiens lætificat patrem: filius vero stultus mœstitia est matri suæ. [A wise son maketh a glad father, but a foolish son is the heaviness of his mother.] Here is distinguished, that fathers have most comfort of the good proof of their sons; but mothers have most discomfort of their ill proof, because women have little discerning of virtue, but of fortune.

Qui celat delictum, quærit amicitiam; sed qui altero sermone repetit, separat fœderatos. [He that covereth a transgression seeketh love, but he that repeateth a matter separateth very friends.] Here caution is given, that reconcilement is better managed by an *amnesty*, and passing over that which is past, than by apologies and excusations.

In omni opere bono erit abundantia; ubi autem verba sunt plurima, ibi frequenter egestas. [In every good work there shall be abundance, but where there are many words there is penury.] Here is noted that words and discourse abound most where there is idleness and want.

Primus in sua causa justus; sed venit altera pars, et inquirit in eum. [He that is first in his own cause seemeth just; but the other party cometh and searcheth him.] Here is observed, that in all causes the first tale possesseth much; in sort that the prejudice thereby wrought will be hardly removed, except some abuse or falsity in the information be detected.

Verba bilinguis quasi simplicia, et ipsa perveniunt ad interiora ventris. [The words of the double-tongued man which seem artless are they that go down to the innermost parts of the belly.] Here is distinguished, that flattery and insinuation which seemeth set and artificial sinketh not far; but that entereth deep which hath shew of nature, liberty, and simplicity.

Qui erudit derisorem, ipse sibi injuriam facit; et qui arguit impium, sibi maculam generat. [He that reproveth a scorner doth himself wrong, and he that rebuketh a wicked man getteth himself a blot.] Here caution is given how we tender reprehension to arrogant and scornful natures, whose manner is to esteem it for contumely, and accordingly to return it.

Da sapienti occasionem, et addetur ei sapientia. [Give opportunity to a wise man, and he will be yet wiser.] Here is distinguished the wisdom brought into habit, and that which is but verbal and swimming only in conceit; for the one upon the occasion presented is quickened and redoubled, the other is amazed and confused.

Quomodo in aquis resplendent vultus prospicientium, sic corda hominum manifesta sunt prudentibus. [As the face of one that looketh upon the water is reflected therein, so the hearts of men are mànifest unto the wise.] Here the mind of a wise man is compared to a glass, wherein the images of all diversity of natures and customs are represented; from which representation proceedeth that application,

Qui sapit, innumeris moribus aptus erit:

[a wise man will know how to apply himself to all sorts of characters].

Thus have I staid somewhat longer upon these sentences politic of Salomon than is agreeable to the proportion of an example; led with a desire to give authority to this part of knowledge, which I noted as deficient, by so excellent a precedent; and have also attended them with brief observations, such as to my understanding offer no violence to the sense, though I know they may be applied to a more divine use: but it is allowed even in divinity, that some interpretations, yea and some writings, have more of the Eagle than others. But taking them as instructions for life, they might have received large discourse, if I would have broken them and illustrated them by deducements and examples.

Neither was this in use only with the Hebrews; but it is generally to be found in the wisdom of the more ancient times, that as men found out any observation that they thought was good for life, they would gather it and express it in parable or aphorism or fable. But for fables, they were viceregents and supplies where examples failed: now that the times abound with history, the aim is better when the mark is alive. And therefore the form of writing which of all others is fittest for this variable argument of negotiation and occasions is that which Machiavel chose wisely and aptly for government; namely, *discourse upon histories or examples.* For knowledge drawn freshly and in our view out of particulars, knoweth the way best to particulars again. And it hath much greater life for practice when the discourse attendeth upon the example, than when the example attendeth upon the discourse. For this is no point of order, as it seemeth at first, but of substance. For when the example is the ground, being set down in an history at large, it is set down with all circumstances, which may sometimes control the discourse thereupon made and sometimes supply it, as a very pattern for action; whereas the examples alleged for the discourse's sake are cited succinctly and without particularity, and carry a servile aspect toward the discourse which they are brought in to make good.

But this difference is not amiss to be remembered, that as history of Times is the best ground for discourse of government, such as Machiavel handleth, so histories of Lives is the most proper for discourse of business, as more conversant in private actions. Nay there is a ground of discourse for this purpose fitter than them both, which is *discourse upon letters,* such as are wise and weighty, as many are of Cicero *ad Atticum* and others. For letters have a great and more particular representation of business than either Chronicles or Lives. Thus have we spoken both of the matter and form of this part of civil knowledge touching Negotiation, which we note to be deficient.

But yet there is another part of this part, which differeth as much from that whereof we have spoken as *sapere and sibi sapere,* [*to be wise* and *to be wise for oneself,*] the one moving as it were to the circumference, the other to the centre. For there is a wisdom of counsel, and again there is a wisdom of pressing a man's own fortune; and they do sometimes meet, and often sever. For many are wise in their own ways that are weak for government or counsel; like ants, which is a wise creature for itself, but very hurtful for the garden. This wisdom the Romans did take much knowledge of: *Nam pol sapiens* (saith the comical poet) *fingit fortunam sibi,* [the wise man fashions his fortune for himself;] and it grew to an adage, *Faber quisque fortunæ propriæ,* [every man has tools to make his own fortune with,] and Livy attributeth it to Cato, the first, *In hoc vire tanta vis animi et ingenii inerat, ut quocunque loco natus esset, sibi ipse fortunam facturus videretur,* [such was his force of mind and genius that in whatever state he had been born he would have made himself a fortune].

This conceit or position if it be too much declared and professed, hath been thought a thing impolitic and unlucky; as was observed in Timotheus the Athenian; who having done many great services to the estate in his government, and giving an account thereof to the people as the manner was, did conclude every particular with this clause, and in this fortune had no part. And it came so to pass that he never prospered in any thing he took in hand afterward: for this is too high and too arrogant, savouring of that which Ezekiel saith of Pharoah, *Dicis, Fluvius est meus, et ego feci memet ipsum,* [thou sayest the river is mine, and I made myself;] or of that which another prophet speaketh, that men offer sacrifices to their nets and snares; and that which the poet expresseth,

> Dextra mihi Deus, et telum quod missile libro,
> Nunc adsint!

[my right hand and my spear are the God I trust in].

For these confidences were ever unhallowed, and unblessed. And therefore those that were great politiques indeed ever ascribed their successes to their felicity, and not to their skill or virtue. For so Sylla surnamed himself *Felix,* not *Magnus,* [the Fortunate, not the Great]. So Cæsar said to the master of the ship, *Cæsarem portas et fortunam ejus,* [you carry Cæsar and his fortune].

But yet nevertheless these positions, *Faber quisque fortunæ suæ; Sapiens dominabitur astris; Invia virtuti nulla est via;* [Every man should be the maker of his own fortune; the wise man will command his stars; nothing impossible to virtue:] and the like, being taken and used as spurs to industry, and not as stirrups to insolency, rather for resolution than for presumption or outward declaration, have been ever thought sound and good, and are no question imprinted in the greatest minds; who are so sensible of this opinion as they can scarce contain it within. As we see in Augustus Cæsar, (who was rather diverse from his uncle than inferior in virtue,) how when he died, he desired his friends about him to give him a *Plaudite;* as if he were conscient to himself that he had played his part well upon the stage. This part of knowledge we do report also as deficient: not but that it is practised too much, but it hath not been reduced to writing. And therefore lest it should seem to any that it is not comprehensible by axiom, it is requisite, as we did in the former, that we set down some heads or passages of it.

Wherein it may appear at the first a new and unwonted argument to teach men how to raise and make their fortune; a doctrine wherein every man perchance will be ready to yield himself a disciple, till he see the difficulty: for Fortune layeth as heavy impositions as Virtue; and it is as hard and severe a thing to be a true politique, as to be truly moral. But the handling hereof concerneth learning greatly, both in honour and in substance: in honour, because pragmatical men may not go away with an opinion that learning is like a lark, that can mount and sing and please herself, and nothing else; but may know that she holdeth as well of the hawk, that can soar aloft, and can also descend and strike upon the prey: in substance, because it is the perfect law of inquiry of truth, *that nothing be in the globe of matter, which should not be likewise in the globe of crystal, or form;* that is that there be not any thing in being and action, which should not be drawn and collected into contemplation and doctrine. Neither doth learning admire or esteem of this architecture of fortune otherwise than as of an inferior work: for no man's fortune can be an end worthy of his being, and many times the worthiest men do abandon their fortune willingly for better respects: but nevertheless fortune as an organ of virtue and merit deserveth the consideration.

First therefore, the precept which I conceive to be most summary towards the prevailing in fortune, is to obtain that window which Momus did require, who seeing in the frame of man's heart such angles and recesses, found fault there was not a window to look into them; that is, to procure good informations of particulars touching persons, their natures, their desires and ends, their customs and fashions, their helps and advantages, and whereby they chiefly stand; so again their weaknesses and disadvantages, and where they lie most open and obnoxious; their friends, factions, dependances; and again their opposites, enviers, competitors, their moods and times, *Sola viri molles aditus et tempora noras;* their principles, rules and observations, and the like: and this not only of persons, but of actions; what are on foot from time to time, and how they are conducted, favoured, opposed; and how they import, and the like. For the knowledge of present actions is not only material in itself, but without it also the knowledge of persons is very erroneous: for men change with the actions; and whiles they are in pursuit they are one, and when they return to their nature they are another. These informations of particulars touching persons and actions are as the minor propositions in every active syllogism; for no excellency of observations (which are as the major propositions) can suffice to ground a conclusion, if there be error and mistaking in the minors.

That this knowledge is possible, Salomon is our surety; who saith, *Consilium in corde viri tanquam aqua profunda; sed vir prudens exhauriet illud,* [counsel in the heart of man is like deep water; but a man of understanding will draw it out]. And although the knowledge itself falleth not under precept, because it is of individuals, yet the instructions for the obtaining of it may.

We will begin therefore with this precept, according to the ancient opinion, that the sinews of wisdom are slowness of belief and distrust; that more trust be given to countenances and deeds than to words; and in words, rather to sudden passages and surprised words, than to set and purposed words. Neither let that be feared which is said, *fronti nulla fides,* [no trusting to the face:] which is meant of a general outward behaviour, and not of the private and subtile motions and labours of the countenance and gesture; which as Q. Cicero elegantly saith, is *animi janua,* the gate of the mind. None more close than Tiberius, and yet Tacitus saith of Gallus, *Etenim vultu offensionem conjectaverat,* [he had seen displeasure in his countenance]. So again, noting the differing character and manner of his commending Germanicus and Drusus in the senate, he saith touching his fashion wherein he carried his speech of Germanicus, thus; *Magis in speciem adornatis verbis, quam ut penitus sentire videretur,* [it was in words too laboured and specious to be taken for what he really felt;] but of Drusus thus; *Paucioribus, sed intentior, et fida oratione,* [he said less, but more earnestly, and in a style of sincerity]; and in another place, speaking of his character of speech when he did any thing that was gracious and popular, he saith that in other things he was *velut eluctantium verborum,* [of a kind of struggling speech;] but then again, *solutius loquebatur quando subveniret;* [he spoke with more freedom when he was speaking in a man's favour]. So that there is no such artificer of dissimulation, nor no such commanded countenance (*vultus jussus*) that can sever from a feigned tale some of these fashions, either a more slight and careless fashion, or more set and formal, or more tedious and wandering, or coming from a man more drily and hardly.

Neither are *deeds* such assured pledges, as that they may be trusted without a judicious consideration of their magnitude and nature: *Fraus sibi in parvis fidem præstruit, ut majore emolumento fallat,* [it is a trick of treachery to win itself credit at the first by fidelity in small things, that being thereupon trusted in greater it may deceive with more advantage;] and the Italian thinketh himself upon the point to be bought and sold, when he is better used than he was wont to be without manifest cause. For small favours, they do but lull men asleep, both as to caution and as to industry, and are as Demosthenes calleth them, *Alimenta socordiæ,* [sops to feed sloth]. So again we see how false the nature of some deeds are, in that particular which Mutianus practised upon Antonius Primus, upon that hollow and unfaithful reconcilement which was made between them; whereupon Mutianus advanced many of the friends of Antonius: *simul amicis ejus præfecturas et tribunatus largitur,* [making them prefects and tribunes:] wherein under pretence to strengthen him, he did desolate him, and won from him his dependances.

As for *words,* (though they be like waters to physicians, full of flattery and uncertainty,) yet they are not to be despised, specially with the advantage of passion and affection. For so we see Tiberius upon a stinging and incensing speech of Agrippina came a step forth of his dissimulation, when he said, *You are hurt because you do not reign;* of which Tacitus saith, *Audita hæc raram occulti pectoris vocem elicuere; correptamque Græco versus admonuit, ideo lædi quia non regnaret,* [these words drew from Tiberius the voice, so rarely heard, of his secret heart: he retorted upon her with a Greek verse, that she was hurt, &c.]. And therefore the poet doth elegantly call passions tortures, that urge men to confess their secrets:

Vino tortus et ira.

And experience sheweth, there are few men so true to themselves and so settled, but that, sometimes upon heat, sometimes upon bravery, sometimes upon kindness, sometimes upon trouble of mind and weakness, they open themselves; specially if they be put to it with a counter-dissimulation, according to the proverb of Spain, *Di mentira, y sacaras verdad, Tell a lie and find a truth.*

As for the knowing of men which is at second hand from reports; men's weaknesses and faults are best known from their enemies, their virtues and abilities from their friends, their customs and times from their servants, their conceits and opinions from their familiar friends with whom they discourse most. General fame is light, and the opinions conceived by superiors or equals are deceitful; for to such men are more masked: *Verior fama e domesticis emanat,* [the truer kind of report comes from those who see them at home].

But the soundest disclosing and expounding of men is by their natures and ends; wherein the weakest sort of men are best interpreted by their natures, and the wisest by their ends. For it was both pleasantly and wisely said (though I think very untruly) by a nuncio of the pope, returning from a certain nation where he served as lieger; whose opinion being asked touching the appointment of one to go in his place, he wished that in any case they did not send one that was too wise; because no very wise man would ever imagine what they in that country were like to do. And certainly it is an error frequent for men to shoot over, and to suppose deeper ends and more compass reaches than are: the Italian proverb being elegant, and for the most part true:

> Di danari, di senno, e di fede,
> Cè nè manco che non credi:

There is commonly less money, less wisdom, and less good faith, than men do account upon.

But Princes upon a far other reason are best interpreted by their natures, and private persons by their ends; for princes being at the top of human desires, they have for the most part no particular ends whereto they aspire, by distance from which a man might take measure and scale of the rest of their actions and desires; which is one of the causes that maketh their hearts more inscrutable. Neither is it sufficient to inform ourselves in men's ends and natures of the variety of them only, but also of the predominancy, what humour reigneth most, and what end is principally sought. For so we see, when Tigellinus saw himself outstripped by Petronius Turpilianus in Nero's humours of pleasures, *metus ejus rimatur,* he wrought upon Nero's fears, whereby he brake the other's neck.

But to all this part of inquiry the most compendious way resteth in three things. The first, to have general acquaintance and inwardness with those which have general acquaintance and look most into the world; and specially according to the diversity of business and the diversity of persons, to have privacy and conversation with some one friend at least which is perfect and well intelligenced in every several kind. The second is to keep a good mediocrity in liberty of speech and secrecy; in most things liberty; secrecy where it importeth; for liberty of speech inviteth and provoketh liberty to be used again, and so bringeth much to a man's knowledge; and secrecy, on the other side, induceth trust and inwardness. The last is the reducing of a man's self to this watchful and serene habit, as to make account and purpose, in every conference and action, as well to observe as to act. For as Epictetus would have a philosopher in every particular action to say to himself, *Et hoc volo, et etiam institutum servare,* [I would do this and keep my course too;] so a politic man in every thing should say to himself, *Et hoc volo, ac etiam aliquid addiscere,* [I would do it and also learn something from it]. I have stayed the longer upon this precept of obtaining good information, because it is a main part by itself, which answereth to all the rest. But, above all things, caution must be taken that men have a good stay and hold of themselves, and that this much knowledge do not draw on much meddling; for nothing is more unfortunate than light and rash intermeddling in many matters; so that this variety of knowledge tendeth in conclusion but only to this, to make a better and freer choice of those actions which may concern us, and to conduct them with the less error and the more dexterity.

The second precept concerning this knowledge is, for men to take good information touching their own person, and well to understand themselves; knowing that, as St. James saith, though men look oft in a glass, yet they do suddenly forget themselves; wherein as the divine glass is the word of God, so the politic glass is the state of the world or times wherein we live; in the which we are to behold ourselves.

For men ought to take an unpartial view of their own abilities and virtues; and again of their wants and impediments; accounting these with the most, and those other with the least; and from this view and examination to frame the considerations following.

First, to consider how the constitution of their nature sorteth with the general state of the times; which if they find agreeable and fit, then in all things to give themselves more scope and liberty; but if differing and dissonant, then in the whole course of their life to be more close, retired, and reserved: as we see in Tiberius, who was never seen at a play and came not into the senate in twelve of his last years; whereas Augustus Cæsar lived ever in men's eyes, which Tacitus observeth: *Alia Tiberio morum via,* [Tiberius's ways were different].

Secondly, to consider how their nature sorteth with professions and courses of life, and accordingly to make election, if they be free; and, if engaged, to make the departure at the first opportunity: as we see was done by duke Valentine, that was designed by his father to a sacerdotal profession, but quitted it soon after in regard of his parts and inclination; being such nevertheless, as a man cannot tell well whether they were worse for a prince or for a priest.

Thirdly, to consider how they sort with those whom they are like to have competitors and concurrents, and to take that course wherein there is most solitude, and themselves like to be most eminent: as Cæsar Julius did, who at first was an orator or pleader; but when he saw the excellency of Cicero, Hortensius, Catulus, and others, for eloquence, and saw there was no man of reputation for the wars but Pompeius, upon whom the state was forced to rely, he forsook his course begun toward a civil and popular greatness, and transferred his designs to a martial greatness.

Fourthly, in the choice of their friends and dependances, to proceed according to the composition of their own nature; as we may see in Cæsar, all whose friends and followers were men active and effectual, but not solemn or of reputation.

Fifthly, to take special heed how they guide themselves by examples, in thinking they can do as they see others do; whereas perhaps their natures and carriages are far differing; in which error it seemeth Pompey was, of whom Cicero saith, that he was wont often to say, *Sylla potuit, ego non potero?* [Sylla could do it, why not I?] wherein he was much abused, the natures and proceedings of himself and his example being the unlikest in the world; the one being fierce, violent, and pressing the fact; the other solemn, and full of majesty and circumstance, and therefore the less effectual.

But this precept touching the politic knowledge of ourselves hath many other branches whereupon we cannot insist.

Next to the well understanding and discerning of a man's self, there followeth the well opening and revealing a man's self; wherein we see nothing more usual than for the more able man to make the less shew.

For there is a great advantage in the well setting forth of a man's virtues, fortunes, merits; and again in the artificial covering of a man's weaknesses, defects, disgraces; staying upon the one, sliding from the other; cherishing the one by circumstances, gracing the other by exposition, and the like: wherein we see what Tacitus saith of Mutianus, who was the greatest politique of his time, *Omnium quæ dixerat feceratque arte quâdam ostentator,* [having a certain art of displaying to advantage all he said and did;] which requireth indeed some art, less it turn tedious and arrogant; but yet so as ostentation (though it be to the first degree of vanity) seemeth to me rather a vice in manners than in policy: for as it is said, *Audacter calumniare, semper aliquid hæret,* [slander boldly, there is eversome that sticks;] so, except it be in a ridiculous degree of deformity, *Audacter te vendita, semper aliquid hæret,* [put forward your own pretensions boldly—something always sticks]. For it will stick with the more ignorant and inferior sort of men, though men of wisdom and rank do smile at it and despise it; and yet the authority won with many doth countervail the disdain of a few. But if it be carried with decency and government, as with a natural, pleasant, and ingenious fashion; or at times when it is mixed with some peril and unsafety, (as in military persons;) or at times when others are most envied; or with easy and careless passage to it and from it, without dwelling too long or being too serious; or with an equal freedom of taxing a man's self as well as gracing himself; or by occasion of repelling or putting down others' injury or insolency; it doth greatly add to reputation: and surely not a few solid natures, that want this ventosity and cannot sail in the height of the winds, are not without some prejudice and disadvantage by their moderation.

But for these flourishes and enhancements of virtue, as they are not perchance unnecessary, so it is at least necessary that virtue be not disvalued and imbased under the just price; which is done in three manners: by offering and obtruding a man's self; wherein men think he is rewarded, when he is accepted: by doing too much; which will not give that which is well done leave to settle, and in the end induceth satiety: and by finding too soon the fruit of a man's virtue, in commendation, applause, honour, favour; wherein if a man be pleased with a little, let him hear what is truly said, *Cave ne insuetus rebus majoribus videaris, si hæc te res parva sicuti magna delectat,* [if he take so much delight in a little thing, he will be thought unused to greater things].

But the covering of defects is of no less importance than the valuing of good parts, which may be done likewise in three manners; by Caution, by Colour, and by Confidence. Caution is when men do ingeniously and discreetly avoid to be put into those things for which they are not proper: whereas contrariwise bold and unquiet spirits will thrust themselves into matters without difference, and so publish and proclaim all their wants. Colour is when men make a way for themselves to have a construction made of their faults or wants as proceeding from a better cause, or intended for some other purpose: for of the one it is well said, *Sæpe latet vitium proximitate boni,* [a vice will often hide itself under the shadow of a neighbouring virtue]; and therefore whatsoever want a man hath, he must see that he pretend the virtue that shadoweth it; as if he be dull, he must affect gravity; if a coward, mildness; and so the rest: for the second, a man must frame some probable cause why he should not do his best, and why he should dissemble his abilities; and for that purpose must use to dissemble those abilities which are notorious in him, to give colour that his true wants are but industries and dissimulations. For Confidence, it is the last but the surest remedy; namely, to depress and seem to despise whatsoever a man cannot attain; observing the good principle of the merchants, who endeavour to raise the price of their own commodities, and to beat down the price of others. But there is a confidence that passeth this other; which is, to face out a man's own defects, in seeming to conceive that he is best in those things wherein he is failing; and, to help that again, to seem on the other side that he hath least opinion of himself in those things wherein he is best: like as we shall see it commonly in poets, that if they shew their verses, and you except to any, they will say *that that line cost them more labour than any of the rest;* and presently will seem to disable and suspect rather some other line, which they know well enough to be the best in the number. But above all, in this righting and helping of a man's self in his own carriage, he must take heed he shew not himself dismantled and exposed to scorn and injury, by too much dulceness, goodness, and facility of nature, but shew some sparkles of liberty, spirit, and edge: which kind of fortified carriage, with a ready rescuing of a man's self from scorns, is sometimes of necessity imposed upon men by somewhat in their person or fortune; but it ever succeedeth with good felicity.

Another precept of this knowledge is, by all possible endeavour to frame the mind to be pliant and obedient to occasion; for nothing hindereth men's fortunes so much as this *Idem manebat neque idem decebat,* [continuing the same when the same is no longer fit:] men are where they were, when occasions turn: and therefore to Cato, whom Livy maketh such an architect of fortune, he addeth that he had *versatile ingenium,* [a wit that could turn well]. And thereof it cometh that these grave solemn wits, which must be like themselves and cannot make departures, have more dignity than felicity. But in some it is nature to be somewhat viscous and inwrapped, and not easy to turn. In some it is a conceit that is almost a nature, which is, that men can hardly make themselves believe that they ought to change their course, when they have found good by it in former experience. For Machiavel noteth wisely, how Fabius Maximus would have been temporizing still, according to his old bias, when the nature of the war was altered and required hot pursuit. In some other it is want of point and penetration in their judgment, that they do not discern when things have a period, but come in too late after the occasion; as Demosthenes compareth the people of Athens to country fellows when they play in a fence school, that if they have a blow, then they remove their weapon to that ward, and not before. In some other it is a lothness to leese labours passed, and a conceit that they can bring about occasions to their ply; and yet in the end, when they see no other remedy, then they come to it with disadvantage; as Tarquinius, that gave for the third of Sibylla's books the treble price, when he might at first have had all three for the simple. But from whatsoever root or cause this restiveness of mind proceedeth, it is a thing most prejudicial; and nothing is more politic than to make the wheels of our mind concentric and voluble with the wheels of fortune.

Another precept of this knowledge, which hath some affinity with that we last spake of, but with difference, is that which is well expressed, *Fatis accede Deisque,* [take the way which the Fates and the Gods offer;] that men do not only turn with the occasions but also run with the occasions, and not strain their credit or strength to over hard or extreme points, but choose in their actions that which is most passable: for this will preserve men from foil, not occupy them too much about one matter, win opinion of moderation, please the most, and make a shew of a perpetual felicity in all they undertake; which cannot but mightily increase reputation.

Another part of this knowledge seemeth to have some repugnancy with the former two, but not as I understand it; and it is that which Demosthenes uttereth in high terms; *Et quemadmodum receptum est, ut exercitum ducat imperator, sic et a cordatis viris res ipsæ ducendæ; ut quæ ipsis videntur, ea gerantur, et non ipsi eventus persequi cogantur;* [as the captain leads the army, so should wise men lead affairs; they should get that done which they think good to be done, and not be forced to follow at the heels of events]. For if we observe, we shall find two differing kinds of sufficiency in managing of business: some can make use of occasions aptly and dexterously, but plot little; some can urge and pursue their own plots well, but cannot accommodate nor take in; either of which is very unperfect without the other.

Another part of this knowledge is the observing a good mediocrity in the declaring or not declaring a man's self: for although depth of secrecy, and making way *qualis est via navis in mari,* [like the way of a ship through the water,] (which the French calleth *sourdes menées,* when men set things in work without opening themselves at all,) be sometimes both prosperous and admirable; yet many times *Dissimulatio errores parit qui dissimulatorem ipsum illaqueant,* [dissimulation breeds mistakes in which the dissembler himself is caught]. And therefore we see the greatest politiques have in a natural and free manner professed their desires, rather than been reserved and disguised in them. For so we see that Lucius Sylla made a kind of profession, *that he wished all men happy or unhappy as they stood his friends or enemies.* So Cæsar, when he went first into Gaul, made no scruple to profess *that he had rather be first in a village than second at Rome.* So again as soon as he had begun the war, we see what Cicero saith of him; *Alter* (meaning of Cæsar) *non recusat, sed quodommodo postulat, ut* (*ut est*) *sic appelletur tyrannus,* [he does not refuse, but in a manner demands, to be called what he is—tyrant]. So we may see in a letter of Cicero to Atticus, that Augustus Cæsar in his very entrance into affairs, when he was a dearling of the senate, yet in his harangues to the people would swear *Ita parentis honores consequi liceat,* [as I hope to attain my father's honours;] which was no less than the tyranny, save that, to help it he would stretch forth his hand toward a statua of Cæsar's that was erected in the place: and men laughed and wondered and said Is it possible? or Did you ever hear the like? and yet thought he meant no hurt, he did it so handsomely and ingenuously. And all these were prosperous: whereas Pompey, who tended to the same end but in a more dark and dissembling manner, as Tacitus saith of him, *Occultior non melior,* [having his intentions better concealed but not better,] wherein Sallust concurreth, *ore probo, animo inverecundo,* [an honest tongue but a shameless mind,] made it his design by infinite secret engines to cast the state into an absolute anarchy and confusion, that the state might cast itself into his arms for necessity and protection, and so the sovereign power be put upon him, and he never seen in it: and when he had brought it (as he thought) to that point, when he was chosen consul alone, as never any was, yet he could make no great matter of it, because men understood him not; but was fain in the end to go the beaten track of getting arms into his hands, by colour of the doubt of Cæsar's designs: so tedious, casual, and unfortunate are these deep dissimulations; whereof it seemeth Tacitus made this judgment, that they were a cunning of an inferior form in regard of true policy; attributing the one to Augustus, the other to Tiberius, where speaking of Livia he saith, *Et cum artibus mariti simulatione filii bene composita,* [that she was of a happy composition, uniting the arts of her husband with the dissimulation of her son;] for surely the continual habit of dissimulation is but a weak and sluggish cunning, and not greatly politic.

Another precept of this Architecture of Fortune is to accustom our minds to judge of the proportion or value of things as they conduce and are material to our particular ends; and that to do substantially, and not superficially. For we shall find the logical part (as I may term it) of some men's minds good, but the mathematical part erroneous; that is, they can well judge of consequences, but not of proportions and comparison; preferring things of shew and sense before things of substance and effect. So some fall in love with access to princes, others with popular fame and applause, supposing they are things of great purchase; when in many cases they are but matters of envy, peril, and impediment. So some measure things according to the labour and difficulty or assiduity which are spent about them; and think if they be ever moving, that they must needs advance and proceed; as Cæsar saith in a despising manner of Cato the second, when he describeth how laborious and indefatigable he was to no great purpose; *Hæc omnia magno studio agebat.* So in most things men are ready to abuse themselves in thinking the greatest means to be best, when it should be the fittest.

As for the true marshalling of men's pursuits towards their fortune as they are more or less material, I hold them to stand thus. First the amendment of their own minds; for the remove of the impediments of the mind will sooner clear the passages of fortune, than the obtaining fortune will remove the impediments of the mind. In the second place I set down wealth and means; which I know most men would have placed first, because of the general use which it beareth towards all variety of occasions. But that opinion I may condemn with like reason as Machiavel doth that other, that moneys were the sinews of the wars; whereas (saith he) the true sinews of the wars are the sinews of men's arms, that is, a valiant, populous, and military nation; and he voucheth aptly the authority of Solon, who when Crœsus shewed him his treasury of gold said to him, that if another came that he had better iron he would be master of his gold. In like manner it may be truly affirmed that it is not moneys that are the sinews of fortune, but it is the sinews and steel of men's minds, wit, courage, audacity, resolution, temper, industry, and the like. In third place I set down reputation, because of the peremptory tides and currents it hath; which if they be not taken in their due time are seldom recovered, it being extreme hard to play an after-game of reputation. And lastly I place honour, which is more easily won by any of the other three, much more by all, than any of them can be purchased by honour. To conclude this precept, as there is order and priority in matter, so is there in time, the preposterous placing whereof is one of the commonest errors; while men fly to their ends when they should intend their beginnings, and do not take things in order of time as they come on, but marshal them according to greatness and not according to instance; not observing the good precept, *Quod nunc instat agamus,*

[Despatch we now what stands us now upon].

Another precept of this knowledge is, not to embrace any matters which do occupy too great a quantity of time, but to have that sounding in a man's ears, *Sed fugit interea, fugit irreparabile tempus,* [while he is making ready to do it the time for doing it is gone;] and that is the cause why those which take their course of rising by professions of burden, as lawyers, orators, painful divines, and the like, are not commonly so politic for their own fortune, otherwise than in their ordinary way, because they want time to learn particulars, to wait occasions, and to devise plots.

Another precept of this knowledge is to imitate nature which doth nothing in vain; which surely a man may do, if he do well interlace his business, and bend not his mind too much upon that which he principally intended. For a man ought in every particular action so to carry the motions of his mind, and so to have one thing under another, as if he cannot have that he seeketh in the best degree, yet to have it in a second, or so in a third; and if he can have no part of that which he purposed, yet to turn the use of it to somewhat else; and if he cannot make any thing of it for the present, yet to make it as a seed of somewhat in time to come; and if he can contrive no effect or substance for it, yet to win some good opinion by it, or the like; so that he should exact an account of himself, of every action to reap somewhat, and not to stand amazed and confused if he fail of that he chiefly meant for nothing is more impolitic than to mind actions wholly one by one; for he that doth so leeseth infinite occasions which intervene, and are many times more proper and propitious for somewhat that he shall need afterwards, than for that which he urgeth for the present; and therefore men must be perfect in that rule, *Hæc oportet facere, et illa non omittere,* [these things ought ye to do, and not leave the other undone].

Another precept of this knowledge is, not to engage a man's self peremptorily in any thing, though it seem not liable to accident; but ever to have a window to fly out at, or a way to retire; following the wisdom in the ancient fable of the two frogs, which consulted when their plash was dry whither they should go; and the one moved to go down into a pit, because it was not likely the water would dry there; but the other answered, *True, but if it do, how shall we get out again?*

Another precept of this knowledge is that ancient precept of Bias, construed not to any point of perfidiousness but only to caution and moderation, *Et ama tanquam inimicus futurus, et odi tanquam amaturus,* [love your friend as you would love one who may hereafter be your enemy; hate your enemy as one who may hereafter be your friend;] for it utterly betrayeth all utility for men to embark themselves too far in unfortunate friendships, troublesome spleens, and childish and humorous envies or emulations.

But I continue this beyond the measure of an example; led, because I would not have such knowledges which I note as deficient to be thought things imaginative or in the air, or an observation or two much made of: but things of bulk and mass, whereof an end is hardlier made than a beginning. It must be likewise conceived, that in these points which I mention and set down, they are far from complete tractates of them, but only as small pieces for patterns. And lastly, no man I suppose will think that I mean fortunes are not obtained without all this ado; for I know they come tumbling into some men's laps; and a number obtain good fortunes by diligence in a plain way, little intermeddling, and keeping themselves from gross errors.

But as Cicero, when he setteth down an Idea of a perfect Orator, doth not mean that every pleader should be such; and so likewise, when a Prince or a Courtier hath been described by such as have handled those subjects, the mould hath used to be made according to the perfection of the art, and not according to common practice: so I understand it that it ought to be done in the description of a Politic man; I mean politic for his own fortune.

But it must be remembered all this while, that the precepts which we have set down are of that kind which may be counted and called *bonæ artes,* [honest arts]. As for evil arts, if a man would set down for himself that principle of Machiavel, *that a man seek not to attain virtue itself, but the appearance only thereof; because the credit of virtue is a help, but the use of it is cumber;* or that other of his principles, *that he presuppose that men are not fitly to be wrought otherwise but by fear, and therefore that he seek to have every man obnoxious, low, and in strait,* which the Italians call *seminar spine,* to sow thorns; or that other principle contained in the verse which Cicero citeth, *Cadant amici, dummodo inimici intercidant,* [down with friends so enemies go down with them,] as the Triumvirs, which sold every one to other the lives of their friends for the deaths of their enemies; or that other protestation of L. Catilina, to set on fire and trouble states, to the end to fish in droumy waters, and to unwrap their fortunes; *Ego si quid in fortunis meis excitatum sit incendium, id non aqua sed ruina restinguam,* [if my fortunes be set on fire I will put it out not with water but with demolition:] or that other principle of Lysander *that children are to be deceived with comfits, and men with oaths:* and the like evil and corrupt positions, whereof (as in all things) there are more in number than of the good: certainly with these dispensations from the laws of charity and integrity the pressing of a man's fortune may be more hasty and compendious. But it is in life as it is in ways; the shortest way is commonly the foulest, and surely the fairer way is not much about.

But men if they be in their own power and do bear and sustain themselves, and be not carried away with a whirlwind or tempest of ambition, ought in the pursuit of their own fortune to set before their eyes not only that general map of the world, that *all things are vanity and vexation of spirit,* but many other more particular cards and directions: chiefly that, that Being without well-being is a curse and the greater being the greater curse, and that all virtue is most rewarded and all wickedness most punished in itself: according as the poet saith excellently:

> Quæ vobis, quæ digna, viri, pro laudibus istis
> Præmia posse rear solvi? pulcherrima primum
> Dii *moresque* dabunt vestri:
> [What recompence, O friends, can I hold out
> Worthy such deeds? The best is that ye have,—
> God's blessing and your proper nobleness:]

and so of the contrary. And secondly they ought to look up to the eternal providence and divine judgment, which often subverteth the wisdom of evil plots and imaginations, according to that Scripture, *He hath conceived mischief, and shall bring forth a vain thing.* And although men should refrain themselves from injury and evil arts, yet this incessant and sabbathless pursuit of a man's fortune leaveth not tribute which we owe to God of our time; who (we see) demandeth a tenth of our substance, and a seventh, which is more strict, of our time: and it is too small purpose to have an erected face towards heaven, and a perpetual grovelling spirit upon earth, eating dust as doth the serpent; *Atque affigit humo divinæ particulam auræ,* [fixing to earth the etherial spark divine]. And if any man flatter himself that he will employ his fortune well thought he should obtain it ill, as was said concerning Augustus Cæsar, and after of Septimius Severus, *that either they should never have been born or else they should never have died,* they did so much mischief in the pursuit and ascent of their greatness, and so much good when they were established; yet these compensations and satisfactions are good to be used, but never good to be purposed. And lastly, it is not amiss for men in their race toward their fortune to cool themselves a little with that conceit which is elegantly expressed by the emperor Charles the fifth in his instructions to the king his son, *that fortune hath somewhat of the nature of a woman, that if she be too much wooed she is the farther off.* But this last is but a remedy for those whose tastes are corrupted: let men rather build upon that foundation which is as a corner-stone of divinity and philosophy, wherein they join close, namely that same *Primum quærite.* For divinity saith, *Primum quærite regnum Dei, et ista omnia adjicientur vobis,* [seek ye first the Kingdom of God, and all these things shall be added unto you:] and philosophy saith, *Primum quærite bona animi, cætera aut aderunt aut non oberunt,* [seek ye first the good things of the mind, all other good things will either come or not be wanted]. And although the human foundation hath somewhat of the sand, as we see in M. Brutus when he brake forth into that speech,

Te colui, Virtus, ut rem; at tu nomen inane es;

[I took thee, Virtue, for a reality, but I find thee an empty name;] yet the divine foundation is upon the rock. But this may serve for a taste of that knowledge which I noted as deficient.

Concerning Government, it is a part of knowledge secret and retired, in both these respects in which things are deemed secret; for some things are secret because they are hard to know, and some because they are not fit to utter. We see all governments are obscure and invisible.

> Totamque infusa per artus
> Mens agitat molem, et magno se corpore miscet.
>
> [In every pore diffused the great mind works,
> Stirs all the mass, and thro' the huge frame lives.]

Such is the description of governments. We see the government of God over the world is hidden, insomuch as it seemeth to participate of much irregularity and confusion. The government of the Soul in moving the Body is inward and profound, and the passages thereof hardly to be reduced to demonstration. Again, the wisdom of antiquity (the shadows whereof are in the poets) in the description of torments and pains, next unto the crime of rebellion which was the Giants' offence, doth detest the offence of futility, as in Sisyphus and Tantalus. But this was meant of particulars: nevertheless even unto the general rules and discourses of policy and government there is due a reverent and reserved handling.

But contrariwise in the governors toward the governed all things ought, as far as the frailty of man permitteth, to be manifest and revealed. For so it is expressed in the Scriptures touching the government of God, that this globe, which seemeth to us a dark and shady body, is in the view of God as crystal: *Et in con-*

spectu sedis tanquam mare vitreum simile crystallo, [and before the Throne there was a sea of glass, like unto crystal]. So unto princes and states, and specially towards wise senates and councils, the natures and dispositions of the people, their conditions and necessities, their factions and combinations, their animosities and discontents, ought to be, in regard of the variety of their intelligences, the wisdom of their observations, and the height of their station where they keep sentinel, in great part clear and transparent. Wherefore, considering that I write to a king that is a master of this science, and is so well assisted, I think it decent to pass over this part in silence, as willing to obtain the certificate which one of the ancient philosophers aspired unto; who being silent, when others contended to make demonstration of their abilities by speech, desired it might be certified for his part, *that there was one that knew how to hold his peace.*

Notwithstanding, for the more public part of government, which is Laws, I think good to note only one deficience; which is, that all those which have written of laws, have written either as philosophers or as lawyers, and none as statesmen. As for the philosophers, they make imaginary laws for imaginary commonwealths; and their discourses are as the stars, which give little light because they are so high. For the lawyers, they write according to the states where they live, what is received law, and not what ought to be law: for the wisdom of a lawmaker is one, and of a lawyer is another. For there are in nature certain fountains of justice, whence all civil laws are derived but as streams; and like as waters do take tinctures and tastes from the soils through which they run, so do civil laws vary according to the regions and governments where they are planted, though they proceed from the same fountains.

Again, the wisdom of a lawmaker consisteth not only in a platform of justice, but in the application thereof; taking into consideration by what means laws may be made certain, and what are the causes and remedies of the doubtfulness and incertainty of law; by what means laws may be made apt and easy to be executed, and what are the impediments and remedies in the execution of laws; what influence laws touching private right of *meum* and *tuum* have into the public state, and how they may be made apt and agreeable; how laws are to be penned and delivered, whether in Texts or in Acts; brief or large; with preambles or without; how they are to be pruned and reformed from time to time; and what is the best means to keep them from being too vast in volumes or too full of multiplicity and crossness; how they are to be expounded, when upon causes emergent and judicially discussed, and when upon responses and conferences touching general points or questions; how they are to be pressed, rigorously or tenderly; how they are to be mitigated by equity and good conscience; and whether discretion and strict law are to be mingled in the same courts or kept apart in several courts; again, how the practice, profession, and erudition of law is to be censured and governed; and many other points touching the administration, and (as I may term it) animation of laws. Upon which I insist the less, because I purpose (if God give me leave), having begun a work of this nature in aphorisms, to propound it hereafter noting it in the mean time for deficient.

And for your Majesty's laws of England, I could say much of their dignity, and somewhat of their defect; but they cannot but excel the civil laws in fitness for the government: for the civil law was *non hos quæsitum munus in usus;* it was not made for the countries which it governeth. Hereof I cease to speak, because I will not intermingle matter of action with matter of general learning.

Thus have I concluded this portion of learning touching Civil Knowledge; and with civil knowledge have concluded Human Philosophy; and with human philosophy, Philosophy in General. And being now at some pause, looking back into that I have passed through, this writing seemeth to me, (*si nunquam fallit imago*) as far as a man can judge of his own work, not much better than that noise or sound which musicians make while they are tuning their instruments; which is nothing pleasant to hear, but yet is a cause why the music is sweeter afterwards. So have I been content to tune the instruments of the muses, that they may play that have better hands. And surely, when I set before me the condition of these times, in which learning hath made her third visitation or circuit, in all the qualities thereof; as the excellency and vivacity of the wits of this age; the noble helps and lights which we have by the travails of ancient writers; the art of printing, which communicateth books to men of all fortunes; the openness of the world by navigation, which hath disclosed multitudes of experiments, and a mass of natural history; the leisure wherewith these times abound, not employing men so generally in civil business, as the states of Græcia did in respect of their popularity, and the state of Rome in respect of the greatness of their monarchy; the present disposition of these times at this instant to peace; the consumption of all that ever can be said in controversies of religion, which have so much diverted men from other sciences; the perfection of your Majesty's learning, which as a phœnix may call whole vollies of wits to follow you; and the inseparable propriety of time, which is ever more and more to disclose truth; I cannot but be raised to this persuasion, that this third period of time will far surpass that of the Græcian and Roman learning: only if men will know their own strength and their own weakness both; and take one from the other light of invention, and not fire of contradiction; and esteem of the inquisition of truth as of an enterprise, and not as of a quality or ornament; and employ wit and magnificence to things of worth and excellency, and not to things vulgar and of popular estimation. As for my labours, if any man shall please himself or others in the reprehension of them, they shall make that ancient and patient request, *Verbera sed audi,* [strike me if you will, only hear me;] let men reprehend them, so they observe and weigh them. For the appeal is (lawful though it may be it shall not be needful) from the first cogitations of men to their second, and from the nearer times to the times further off. Now let us come to that learning, which both the former times were not so blessed as to know, sacred and inspired Divinity, the Sabaoth and port of all men's labours and peregrinations. . . .[1]

[1] The treatment of Divinity is here omitted; it is both pompous and insincere. *Editor.*

NOVUM ORGANUM

THE

FIRST PART OF THE INSTAURATION,

WHICH COMPRISES THE

DIVISIONS OF THE SCIENCES,

IS WANTING.

But some account of them will be found in the Second Book of the "Proficience and Advancement of Learning, Divine and Human."

Next comes

THE

SECOND PART OF THE INSTAURATION,

WHICH EXHIBITS

THE ART ITSELF OF INTERPRETING NATURE,

AND OF THE TRUER EXERCISE OF THE INTELLECT;

Not however in the form of a regular Treatise, but only a Summary digested into Aphorisms.

THE

SECOND PART OF THE WORK,

WHICH IS CALLED

THE NEW ORGANON;

OR,

TRUE DIRECTIONS

CONCERNING

THE INTERPRETATION OF NATURE.

PREFACE

Those who have taken upon them to lay down the law of nature as a thing already searched out and understood, whether they have spoken in simple assurance or professional affectation, have therein done philosophy and the sciences great injury. For as they have been successful in inducing belief, so they have been effective in quenching and stopping inquiry; and have done more harm by spoiling and putting an end to other men's efforts than good by their own. Those on the other hand who have taken a contrary course, and asserted that absolutely nothing can be known,—whether it were from hatred of the ancient sophists, or from uncertainty and fluctuation of mind, or even from a kind of fulness of learning, that they fell upon this opinion,—have certainly advanced reasons for it that are not to be despised; but yet they have neither started from true principles nor rested in the just conclusion, zeal and affectation having carried them much too far. The more ancient of the Greeks (whose writings are lost) took up with better judgment a position between these two extremes,—between the presumption of pronouncing on everything, and the despair of comprehending anything; and though frequently and bitterly complaining of the difficulty of inquiry and the obscurity of things, and like impatient horses champing the bit, they did not the less follow up their object and engage with Nature; thinking (it seems) that this very question,—viz. whether or no anything can be known,—was to be settled not by arguing, but by trying. And yet they too, trusting entirely to the force of their understanding, applied no rule, but made everything turn upon hard thinking and perpetual working and exercise of the mind.

Now my method, though hard to practise, is easy to explain; and it is this. I propose to establish progressive stages of certainty. The evidence of the sense, helped and guarded by a certain process of correction, I retain. But the mental operation which follows the act of sense I for the most part reject; and instead of it I open and lay out a new and certain path for the mind to proceed in, starting directly from the simple sensuous perception. The necessity of this was felt no doubt by those who attributed so much importance to Logic; showing thereby that they were in search of helps for the understanding, and had no confidence in the native and spontaneous process of the mind. But this remedy comes too late to do any good, when the mind is already, through the daily intercourse and conversation of life, occupied with unsound doctrines and beset on all sides by vain imaginations. And therefore that art of Logic, coming (as I said) too late to the rescue, and no way able to set matters right again, has had the effect of fixing errors rather than disclosing truth. There remains but one course for the recovery of a sound and healthy condition,—namely, that the entire work of the understanding be commenced afresh, and the mind itself be from the very outset not left to take its own course, but guided at every step; and the business be done as if by machinery. Certainly if in things mechanical men had set to work with their naked hands, without help or force of instruments, just as in things intellectual they have set to work with little else than the naked forces of the understanding, very small would the matters have been which, even with their best efforts applied in conjunction, they could have attempted or accomplished. Now (to pause awhile upon this example and look in it as in a glass) let us suppose that some vast obelisk were (for the decoration of a triumph or some such magnificence) to be removed from its place, and that men should set to work upon it with their naked hands; would not any sober spectator think them mad? And if they should then send for more people, thinking that in that way they might manage it, would he not think them all the madder? And if they then proceeded to make a selection, putting away the weaker hands, and using only the strong and vigorous, would he not think them madder than ever? And if lastly, not content with this, they resolved to call in aid the art of athletics, and required all their men to come with hands, arms, and sinews well anointed and medicated according to the rules of art, would he not cry out that they were only taking pains to show a kind of method and discretion in their madness? Yet just so it is that men proceed in matters intellectual,—with just the same kind of mad effort and useless combination of forces,—when they hope great things either from the number and co-operation or from the excellency and acuteness of individual wits; yea, and when they endeavour by Logic (which may be considered as a kind of athletic art) to strengthen the sinews of the understanding; and yet with all this study and endeavour it is apparent to any true judgment that they are but applying the naked intellect all the time; whereas in every great work to be done by the hand of man it is manifestly impossible, without instruments and machinery, either for the strength of each to be exerted or the strength of all to be united.

Upon these premises two things occur to me of which, that they may not be overlooked, I would have men reminded. First it falls out fortunately as I think for the allaying of contradictions and heart-burnings, that the honour and reverence due to the ancients remains untouched and undiminished; while I may carry out my designs and at the same time reap the fruit of my modesty. For if I should profess that I, going the same road as the ancients, have something better to produce, there must needs have been some comparison or rivalry between us (not to be avoided by any art of words) in respect of excellency or ability of wit; and though in this there would be nothing unlawful or new, (for if there be anything misapprehended by them, or falsely laid down, why may not I, using a liberty common to all, take exception to it?) yet the contest, however just and allowable, would have been an unequal one perhaps, in respect of the measure of my own powers. As it is however,—my object being to open a new way for the understanding, a way by them untried and unknown,—

the case is altered; party zeal and emulation are at an end; and I appear merely as a guide to point out the road; an office of small authority, and depending more upon a kind of luck than upon any ability or excellency. And thus much relates to the persons only. The other point of which I would have men reminded relates to the matter itself.

Be it remembered then that I am far from wishing to interfere with the philosophy which now flourishes, or with any other philosophy more correct and complete than this which has been or may hereafter be propounded. For I do not object to the use of this received philosophy, or others like it, for supplying matter for disputations or ornaments for discourse,—for the professor's lecture and for the business of life. Nay more, I declare openly that for these uses the philosophy which I bring forward will not be much available. It does not lie in the way. It cannot be caught up in passage. It does not flatter the understanding by conformity with preconceived notions. Nor will it come down to the apprehension of the vulgar except by its utility and effects.

Let there be therefore (and may it be for the benefit of both) two streams and two dispensations of knowledge; and in like manner two tribes or kindreds of students in philosophy—tribes not hostile or alien to each other, but bound together by mutual services;—let there in short be one method for the cultivation, another for the invention, of knowledge.

And for those who prefer the former, either from hurry or from considerations of business or for want of mental power to take in and embrace the other (which must needs be most men's case), I wish that they may succeed to their desire in what they are about, and obtain what they are pursuing. But if any man there be who, not content to rest in and use the knowledge which has already been discovered, aspires to penetrate further; to overcome, not an adversary in argument, but nature in action; to seek, not pretty and probable conjectures, but certain and demonstrable knowledge; —I invite all such to join themselves, as true sons of knowledge, with me, that passing by the outer courts of nature, which numbers have trodden, we may find a way at length into her inner chambers. And to make my meaning clearer and to familiarise the thing by giving it a name, I have chosen to call one of these methods or ways *Anticipation of the Mind,* the other *Interpretation of Nature.*

Moreover I have one request to make. I have on my own part made it my care and study that the things which I shall propound should not only be true, but should also be presented to men's minds, how strangely soever preoccupied and obstructed, in a manner not harsh or unpleasant. It is but reasonable however (especially in so great a restoration of learning and knowledge) that I should claim of men one favour in return; which is this; If any one would form an opinion or judgment either out of his own observation, or out of the crowd of authorities, or out of the forms of demonstration (which have now acquired a sanction like that of judicial laws), concerning these speculations of mine, let him not hope that he can do it in passage or by the by; but let him examine the thing thoroughly; let him make some little trial for himself of the way which I describe and lay out; let him familiarise his thoughts with that subtlety of nature to which experience bears witness; let him correct by seasonable patience and due delay the depraved and deep-rooted habits of his mind; and when all this is done and he has begun to be his own master, let him (if he will) use his own judgment.

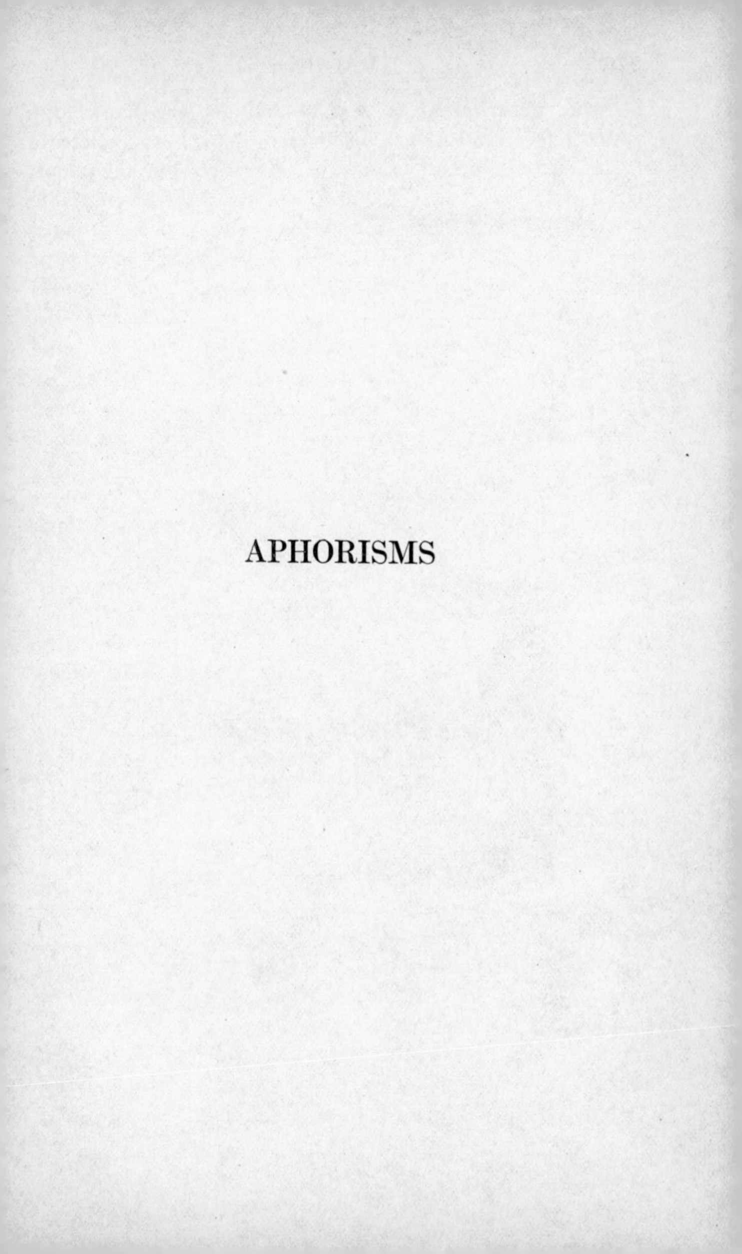

APHORISMS

APHORISMS

CONCERNING

THE INTERPRETATION OF NATURE

AND

THE KINGDOM OF MAN

Aphorism

I.

Man, being the servant and interpreter of Nature, can do and understand so much and so much only as he has observed in fact or in thought of the course of nature: beyond this he neither knows anything nor can do anything.

II.

Neither the naked hand nor the understanding left to itself can effect much. It is by instruments and helps that the work is done, which are as much wanted for the understanding as for the hand. And as the instruments of the hand either give motion or guide it, so the instruments of the mind supply either suggestions for the understanding or cautions.

III.

Human knowledge and human power meet in one; for where the cause is not known the effect cannot be produced. Nature to be commanded must be obeyed; and that which in contemplation is as the cause is in operation as the rule.

IV.

Towards the effecting of works, all that man can do is to put together or put asunder natural bodies. The rest is done by nature working within.

V.

The study of nature with a view to works is engaged in by the mechanic, the mathematician, the physician, the alchemist, and the magician; but by all (as things now are) with slight endeavour and scanty success.

VI.

It would be an unsound fancy and self-contradictory to expect that things which have never yet been done can be done except by means which have never yet been tried.

VII.

The productions of the mind and hand seem very numerous in books and manufactures. But all this variety lies in an exquisite subtlety and derivations from a few things already known; not in the number of axioms.

VIII.

Moreover the works already known are due to chance and experiment rather than to sciences; for the sciences we now possess are merely systems for the nice ordering and setting forth of things already invented; not methods of invention or directions for new works.

IX.

The cause and root of nearly all evils in the sciences is this—that while we falsely admire and extol the powers of the human mind we neglect to seek for its true helps.

X.

The subtlety of nature is greater many times over than the subtlety of the senses and understanding; so that all those specious meditations, speculations, and glosses in which men indulge are quite from the purpose, only there is no one by to observe it.

XI.

As the sciences which we now have do not help us in finding out new works, so neither does the logic which we now have help us in finding out new sciences.

XII.

The logic now in use serves rather to fix and give stability to the errors which have their foundation in commonly received notions than to help the search after truth. So it does more harm than good.

XIII.

The syllogism is not applied to the first principles of sciences, and is applied in vain to intermediate axioms; being no match for the subtlety of nature. It commands assent therefore to the proposition, but does not take hold of the thing.

XIV.

The syllogism consists of propositions, propositions consist of words, words are symbols of notions. Therefore if the notions themselves (which is the root of the matter) are confused and over-hastily abstracted from the facts, there can be no firmness in the superstructure. Our only hope therefore lies in a true induction.

XV.

There is no soundness in our notions whether logical or physical. Substance, Quality, Action, Passion, Essence itself, are not sound notions: much less are Heavy, Light, Dense, Rare, Moist, Dry, Generation, Corruption, Attraction, Repulsion, Element, Matter, Form, and the like; but all are fantastical and ill defined.

XVI.

Our notions of less general species, as Man, Dog, Dove, and of the immediate perceptions of the sense, as Hot, Cold, Black, White, do not materially mislead us; yet even these are sometimes confused by the flux and alteration of matter and the mixing of one thing with another. All the others which men have hitherto adopted are but wanderings, not being abstracted and formed from things by proper methods.

XVII.

Nor is there less of wilfulness and wandering in the construction of axioms than in the formations of notions; not excepting even those very principles which are obtained by common induction; but much more in the axioms and lower propositions educed by the syllogism.

XVIII.

The discoveries which have hitherto been made in the sciences are such as lie close to vulgar notions, scarcely beneath the surface. In order to penetrate into the inner and further recesses of nature, it is necessary that both notions and axioms be derived from things by a more sure and guarded way; and that a method of intellectual operation be introduced altogether better and more certain.

XIX.

There are and can be only two ways of searching into and discovering truth. The one flies from the senses and particulars to the most general axioms, and from these principles, the truth of which it takes for settled and immoveable, proceeds to judgment and to the discovery of middle axioms. And this way is now in fashion. The other derives axioms from the senses and particulars, rising by a gradual and unbroken ascent, so that it arrives at the most general axioms last of all. This is the true way, but as yet untried.

XX.

The understanding left to itself takes the same course (namely, the former) which it takes in accordance with logical order. For the mind longs to spring up to positions of higher generality, that it may find rest there; and so after a little while wearies of experiment. But this evil is increased by logic, because of the order and solemnity of its disputations.

XXI.

The understanding left to itself, in a sober, patient, and grave mind, especially if it be not hindered by received doctrines, tries a little that other way, which is the right one, but with little progress; since the understanding, unless directed and assisted, is a thing unequal, and quite unfit to contend with the obscurity of things.

XXII.

Both ways set out from the senses and particulars, and rest in the highest generalities; but the difference between them is infinite. For the one just glances at experiment and particulars in passing, the other dwells duly and orderly among them. The one, again, begins at once by establishing certain abstract and useless generalities, the other rises by gradual steps to that which is prior and better known in the order of nature.

XXIII.

There is a great difference between the Idols of the human mind and the Ideas of the divine. That is to say, between certain empty dogmas, and the true signatures and marks set upon the works of creation as they are found in nature.

XXIV.

It cannot be that axioms established by argumentation should avail for the discovery of new works; since the subtlety of nature is greater many times over than the subtlety of argument. But axioms duly and orderly formed from particulars easily discover the way to new particulars, and thus render sciences active.

XXV.

The axioms now in use, having been suggested by a scanty and manipular experience and a few particulars of most general occurrence, are made for the most part just large enough to fit and take these in: and therefore it is no wonder if they do not lead to new particulars. And if some opposite instance, not observed or not known before, chance to come in the way, the axiom is rescued and preserved by some frivolous distinction; whereas the truer course would be to correct the axiom itself.

XXVI.

The conclusions of human reason as ordinarily applied in matter of nature, I call for the sake of distinction *Anticipations of Nature* (as a thing rash or premature). That reason which is elicited from facts by a just and methodical process, I call *Interpretation of Nature.*

XXVII.

Anticipations are a ground sufficiently firm for consent; for even if men went mad all after the same fashion, they might agree one with another well enough.

XXVIII.

For the winning of assent, indeed, anticipations are far more powerful than interpretations; because being collected from a few instances, and those for the most part of familiar occurrence, they straightway touch the understanding and fill the imagination; whereas interpretations on the other hand, being gathered here and there from very various and widely dispersed facts, cannot suddenly strike the understanding; and therefore they must needs, in respect of the opinions of the time, seem harsh and out of tune; much as the mysteries of faith do.

XXIX.

In sciences founded on opinions and dogmas, the use of anticipations and logic is good; for in them the object is to command assent to the proposition, not to master the thing.

XXX.

Though all the wits of all the ages should meet together and combine and transmit their labours, yet will no great progress ever be made in science by means of anticipations; because radical errors in the first concoction of the mind are not to be cured by the excellence of functions and remedies subsequent.

XXXI.

It is idle to expect any great advancement in science from the superinducing and engrafting of new things upon old. We must begin anew from the very foundations, unless we would revolve for ever in a circle with mean and contemptible progress.

XXXII.

The honour of the ancient authors, and indeed of all, remains untouched; since the comparison I challenge is not of wits or faculties, but of ways and methods, and the part I take upon myself is not that of a judge, but of a guide.

XXXIII.

This must be plainly avowed: no judgment can be rightly formed either of my method or of the discoveries to which it leads, by means of anticipations (that is to say, of the reasoning which is now in use); since I cannot be called on to abide by the sentence of a tribunal which is itself on its trial.

XXXIV.

Even to deliver and explain what I bring forward is no easy matter; for things in themselves new will yet be apprehended with reference to what is old.

XXXV.

It was said by Borgia of the expedition of the French into Italy, that they came with chalk in their hands to mark out their lodgings, not with arms to force their way in. I in like manner would have my doctrine enter quietly into the minds that are fit and capable of receiving it; for confutations cannot be employed, when the difference is upon first principles and very notions and even upon forms of demonstration.

XXXVI.

One method of delivery alone remains to us; which is simply this: we must lead men to the particulars themselves, and their series and order; while men on their side must force themselves for awhile to lay their notions by and begin to familiarise themselves with facts.

XXXVII.

The doctrine of those who have denied that certainty could be attained at all, has some agreement with my way of proceeding at the first setting out; but they end in being infinitely separated and opposed. For the holders of that doctrine assert simply that nothing can be known; I also assert that not much can be known in nature by the way which is now in use. But then they go on to destroy the authority of the senses and understanding; whereas I proceed to devise and supply helps for the same.

XXXVIII.

The idols and false notions which are now in possession of the human understanding, and have taken deep root therein, not only so beset men's minds that truth can hardly find entrance, but even after entrance obtained, they will again in the very instauration of the sciences meet and trouble us, unless men being forewarned of the danger fortify themselves as far as may be against their assaults.

XXXIX.

There are four classes of Idols which beset men's minds. To these for distinction's sake I have assigned names,—calling the first class *Idols of the Tribe;* the second, *Idols of the Cave;* the third, *Idols of the Market-place;* the fourth, *Idols of the Theatre.*

XL.

The formation of ideas and axioms by true induction is no doubt the proper remedy to be applied for the keeping off and clearing away of idols. To point them out, however, is of great use; for the doctrine of Idols is to the Interpretation of Nature what the doctrine of the refutation of Sophisms is to common Logic.

XLI.

The Idols of the Tribe have their foundation in human nature itself, and in the tribe or race of men. For it is a false assertion that the sense of man is the measure of things. On the contrary, all perceptions as well of the sense as of the mind are according to the measure of the individual and not according to the measure of the universe. And the human understanding is like a false mirror, which, receiving rays irregularly, distorts and discolours the nature of things by mingling its own nature with it.

XLII.

The Idols of the Cave are the idols of the individual man. For every one (besides the errors common to human nature in general) has a cave or den of his own, which refracts and discolours the light of nature; owing either to his own proper and peculiar nature; or to his education and conversation with others; or to the reading of books, and the authority of those whom he esteems and admires; or to the differences of impressions, accordingly as they take place in a mind preoccupied and predisposed or in a mind indifferent and settled; or the like. So that the spirit of man (according as it is meted out to different individuals) is in fact a thing variable and full of perturbation, and governed as it were by chance. Whence it was well observed by Heraclitus that men look for sciences in their own lesser worlds, and not in the greater or common world.

XLIII.

There are also Idols formed by the intercourse and association of men with each other, which I call Idols of the Market-place, on account of the commerce and consort of men there. For it is by discourse that men associate; and words are imposed according to the apprehension of the vulgar. And therefore the ill and unfit choice of words wonderfully obstructs the understanding. Nor do the definitions or explanations wherewith in some things learned men are wont to guard and defend themselves, by any means set the matter right. But words plainly force and overrule the understanding, and throw all into confusion, and lead men away into numberless empty controversies and idle fancies.

XLIV.

Lastly, there are Idols which have immigrated into men's minds from the various dogmas of philosophies, and also from wrong laws of demonstration. These I call Idols of the Theatre; because in my judgment all the received systems are but so many stage-plays, representing worlds of their own creation after an unreal and scenic fashion. Nor is it only of the systems now in vogue, or only of the ancient sects and philosophies, that I speak; for many more plays of the same kind may yet be composed and in like artificial manner set forth; seeing that errors the most widely different have nevertheless causes for the most part alike. Neither again do I mean this only of entire systems, but also of many principles and axioms in science, which by tradition, credulity, and negligence have come to be received.

But of these several kinds of Idols I must speak more largely and exactly, that the understanding may be duly cautioned.

XLV.

The human understanding is of its own nature prone to suppose the existence of more order and regularity in the world than it finds. And though there be many things in nature which are singular and unmatched, yet it devises for them parallels and conjugates and relatives which do not exist. Hence the fiction that all celestial bodies move in perfect circles; spirals and dragons being (except in name) utterly rejected. Hence too the element of Fire with its orb is brought in, to make up the square with the other three which the sense perceives. Hence also the ratio of density of the so-called elements is arbitrarily fixed at ten to one. And so on of other dreams. And these fancies affect not dogmas only, but simple notions also.

XLVI.

The human understanding when it has once adopted an opinion (either as being the received opinion or as being agreeable to itself) draws all things else to support and agree with it. And though there be a greater number and weight of instances to be found on the other side, yet these it either neglects and despises, or else by some distinction sets aside and rejects; in order that by this great and pernicious predetermination the authority of its former conclusions may remain inviolate. And therefore it was a good answer that was made by one who when they showed him hanging in a temple a picture of those who had paid their vows as having escaped shipwreck, and would have him say whether he did not now acknowledge the power of the gods,—"Aye," asked he again, "but where are they painted that were drowned after their vows?" And such is the way of all superstition, whether in astrology, dreams, omens, divine judgments, or the like; wherein men, having a delight in such vanities, mark the events where they are fulfilled, but where they fail, though this happen much oftener, neglect and pass them by. But with far more subtlety does this mischief insinuate itself into philosophy and the sciences; in which the first conclusion colours and brings into conformity with itself all that come after, though far sounder and better. Besides, independently of that delight and vanity which I have described, it is the peculiar and perpetual error of the human intellect to be more moved and excited by affirmatives than by negatives; whereas it ought properly to hold itself indifferently disposed towards both alike. Indeed in the establishment of any true axiom, the negative instance is the more forcible of the two.

XLVII.

The human understanding is moved by those things most which strike and enter the mind simultaneously and suddenly, and so fill the imagination; and then it feigns and supposes all other things to be somehow, though it cannot see how, similar to those few things by which it is surrounded. But for that going to and fro to remote and heterogeneous instances, by which axioms are tried as in the fire, the intellect is altogether slow and unfit, unless it be forced thereto by severe laws and overruling authority.

XLVIII.

The human understanding is unquiet; it cannot stop or rest, and still presses onward, but in vain. Therefore it is that we cannot conceive of any end or limit to the world; but always as of necessity it occurs to us that there is something beyond. Neither again can it be conceived how eternity has flowed down to the present day; for that distinction which is commonly received of infinity in time past and in time to come can by no means hold; for it would thence follow that one infinity is greater than another, and that infinity is wasting away and tending to become finite. The like subtlety arises touching the infinite divisibility of lines, from the same inability of thought to stop. But this inability interferes more mischievously in the discovery of causes: for although the most general principles in nature ought to be held merely positive, as they are discovered, and cannot with truth be referred to a cause; nevertheless the human understanding being unable to rest still seeks something prior in the order of nature. And then it is that in struggling towards that which is further off it falls back upon that which is more nigh at hand; namely, on final causes: which have relation clearly to the nature of man rather than to the nature of the universe; and from this source have strangely defiled philosophy. But he is no less an unskilled and shallow philosopher who seeks causes of that which is most general, than he who in things subordinate and subaltern omits to do so.

XLIX.

The human understanding is no dry light, but receives an infusion from the will and affections; whence proceed sciences which may be called "sciences as one would." For what a man had rather were true he more readily believes. Therefore he rejects difficult things from impatience of research; sober things, because they narrow hope; the deeper things of nature, from superstition; the light of experience, from arrogance and pride, lest his mind should seem to be occupied with things mean and transitory; things not commonly believed, out of deference to the opinion of the vulgar. Numberless in short are the ways, and sometimes imperceptible, in which the affections colour and infect the understanding.

L.

But by far the greatest hindrance and aberration of the human understanding proceeds from the dulness, incompetency, and deceptions of the senses; in that things which strike the sense outweigh things which do not immediately strike it, though they be more important. Hence it is that speculation commonly ceases where sight ceases; insomuch that of things invisible there is little or no observation. Hence all the working of the spirits inclosed in tangible bodies lies hid and unobserved of men. So also all the more subtle changes of form in the parts of coarser substances (which they commonly call alteration, though it is in truth local motion through exceedingly small spaces) is in like manner unobserved. And yet unless these two things just mentioned be searched out and brought to light, nothing great can be achieved in nature, as far as the production of works is concerned. So again the essential nature of our common air, and of all bodies less dense than air (which are very many), is almost unknown. For the sense by itself is a thing infirm and erring; neither can instruments for enlarging or sharpening the senses do much; but all the truer kind of interpretation of nature is effected by instances and experiments fit and apposite; wherein the sense decides touching the experiment only, and the experiment touching the point in nature and the thing itself.

LI.

The human understanding is of its own nature prone to abstractions and gives a substance and reality to things which are fleeting. But to resolve nature into abstractions is less to our purpose than to dissect her into parts; as did the school of Democritus, which went further into nature than the rest. Matter rather than forms should be the object of our attention, its configurations and changes of configuration, and simple action, and law of action or motion; for forms are figments of the human mind, unless you will call those laws of action forms.

LII.

Such then are the idols which I call *Idols of the Tribe;* and which take their rise either from the homogeneity of the substance of the human spirit, or from its preoccupation, or from its narrowness, or from its restless motion, or from an infusion of the affections, or from the incompetency of the senses, or from the mode of impression.

LIII.

The *Idols of the Cave* take their rise in the peculiar constitution, mental or bodily, of each individual; and also in education, habit, and accident. Of this kind there is a great number and variety; but I will instance those the pointing out of which contains the most important caution, and which have most effect in disturbing the clearness of the understanding.

LIV.

Men become attached to certain particular sciences and speculations, either because they fancy themselves the authors and inventors thereof, or because they have bestowed the greatest pains upon them and become most habituated to them. But men of this kind, if they betake themselves to philosophy and contemplations of a general character, distort and colour them in obedience to their former fancies; a thing especially to be noticed in Aristotle, who made his natural philosophy a mere bond-servant to his logic, thereby rendering it contentious and well nigh useless. The race of chemists again out of a few experiments of the furnace have built up a fantastic philosophy, framed with reference to a few things; and Gilbert also, after he had employed himself most laboriously in the study and observation of the loadstone, proceeded at once to construct an entire system in accordance with his favourite subject.

LV.

There is one principal and as it were radical distinction between different minds, in respect of philosophy and the sciences; which is this: that some minds are stronger and apter to mark the differences of things, others to mark their resemblances. The steady and acute mind can fix its contemplations and dwell and fasten on the subtlest distinctions: the lofty and discursive mind recognises and puts together the finest and most general resemblances. Both kinds however easily err in excess, by catching the one at gradations the other at shadows.

LVI.

There are found some minds given to an extreme admiration of antiquity, others to an extreme love and appetite for novelty; but few so duly tempered that they can hold the mean, neither carping at what has been well laid down by the ancients, nor despising what is well introduced by the moderns. This however turns to the great injury of the sciences and philosophy; since these affectations of antiquity and novelty are the humours of partisans rather than judgments; and truth is to be sought for not in the felicity of any age, which is an unstable thing, but in the light of nature and experience, which is eternal. These factions therefore must be abjured, and care must be taken that the intellect be not hurried by them into assent.

LVII.

Contemplations of nature and of bodies in their simple form break up and distract the understanding, while contemplations of nature and bodies in their composition and configuration overpower and dissolve the understanding: a distinction well seen in the school of Leucippus and Democritus as compared with the other philosophies. For that school is so busied with the particles that it hardly attends to the structure; while the others are so lost in admiration of the structure that they do not penetrate to the simplicity of nature. These kinds of contemplation should therefore be alternated and taken by turns; that so the understanding may be rendered at once penetrating and comprehensive, and the inconveniences above mentioned, with the idols which proceed from them, may be avoided.

LVIII.

Let such then be our provision and contemplative prudence for keeping off and dislodging the *Idols of the Cave,* which grow for the most part either out of the predominance of a favourite subject, or out of an excessive tendency to compare or to distinguish, or out of partiality for particular ages, or out of the largeness or minuteness of the objects contemplated. And generally let every student of nature take this as a rule,—that whatever his mind seizes and dwells upon with peculiar satisfaction is to be held in suspicion, and that so much the more care is to be taken in dealing with such questions to keep the understanding even and clear.

LIX.

But the *Idols of the Market-place* are the most troublesome of all: idols which have crept into the understanding through the alliances of words and names. For men believe that their reason governs words; but it is also true that words react on the understanding; and this it is that has rendered philosophy and the sciences sophistical and inactive. Now words, being commonly framed and applied according to the capacity of the vulgar, follow those lines of division which are most obvious to the vulgar understanding. And whenever an understanding of greater acuteness or a more diligent observation would alter those lines to suit the true divisions of nature, words stand in the way and resist the change. Whence it comes to pass that the high and formal discussions of learned men end oftentimes in disputes about words and names; with which (according to the use and wisdom of the mathematicians) it would be more prudent to begin, and so by means of definitions reduce them to order. Yet even definitions cannot cure this evil in dealing with natural and material things; since the definitions themselves consist of words, and those words beget others: so that it is necessary to recur to individual instances, and those in due series and order; as I shall say presently when I come to the method and scheme for the formation of notions and axioms.

LX.

The idols imposed by words on the understanding are of two kinds. They are either names of things which do not exist (for as there are things left unnamed through lack of observation, so likewise are there names which result from fantastic suppositions and to which nothing in reality corresponds), or they are names of things which exist, but yet confused and ill-defined, and hastily and irregularly derived from realities. Of the former kind are Fortune, the Prime Mover, Planetary Orbits, Element of Fire, and like fictions which owe their origin to false and idle theories. And this class of idols is more easily expelled, because to get rid of them it is only necessary that all theories should be steadily rejected and dismissed as obsolete.

But the other class, which springs out of a faulty and unskilful abstraction, is intricate and deeply rooted. Let us take for example such a word as *humid;* and see how far the several things which the word is used to signify agree with each other; and we shall find the word *humid* to be nothing else than a mark loosely and confusedly applied to denote a variety of actions which will not bear to be reduced to any constant meaning. For it both signifies that which easily spreads itself round any other body; and that which in itself is indeterminate and cannot solidise; and that which readily yields in every direction; and that which easily divides and scatters itself; and that which easily unites and collects itself; and that which readily flows and is put in motion; and that which readily clings to another body and wets it; and that which is easily reduced to a liquid, or being solid easily melts. Accordingly when you come to apply the word,—if you take it in one sense, flame is humid; if in another, air is not humid; if in another, fine dust is humid; if in another, glass is humid. So that it is easy to see that the notion is taken by abstraction only from water and common and ordinary liquids, without any due verification.

There are however in words certain degrees of distortion and error. One of the least faulty kinds is that of names of substances, especially of lowest species and well-deduced (for the notion of *chalk* and of *mud* is good, of *earth* bad); a more faulty kind is that of actions, as to *generate, to corrupt, to alter;* the most faulty is of qualities (except such as are the immediate objects of the sense) as *heavy, light, rare, dense,* and the like. Yet in all these cases some notions are of necessity a little better than others, in proportion to the greater variety of subjects that fall within the range of the human sense.

LXI.

But the *Idols of the Theatre* are not innate, nor do they steal into the understanding secretly, but are plainly impressed and received into the mind from the play-books of philosophical systems and the perverted rules of demonstration. To attempt refutations in this case would be merely inconsistent with what I have already said: for since we agree neither upon principles nor upon demonstrations there is no place for argument. And this is so far well, inasmuch as it leaves the honour of the ancients untouched. For they are no wise disparaged—the question between them and me being only as to the way. For as the saying is, the lame man who keeps the right road outstrips the runner who takes a wrong one. Nay it is obvious that when a man runs the wrong way, the more active and swift he is the further he will go astray.

But the course I propose for the discovery of sciences is such as leaves but little to the acuteness and strength of wits, but places all wits and understandings nearly on a level. For as in the drawing of a straight line or a perfect circle, much depends on the steadiness and practice of the hand, if it be done by aim of hand only, but if with the aid of rule or compass, little or nothing; so is it exactly with my plan. But though particular confutations would be of no avail, yet touching the sects and general divisions of such systems I must say something; something also touching the external signs which show that they are unsound; and finally something touching the causes of such great infelicity and of such lasting and general agreement in error; that so the access to truth may be made less difficult, and the human understanding may the more willingly submit to its purgation and dismiss its idols.

LXII.

Idols of the Theatre, or of Systems, are many, and there can be and perhaps will be yet many more. For were it not that now for many ages men's minds have been busied with religion and theology; and were it not that civil governments, especially monarchies, have been averse to such novelties, even in matters speculative; so that men labour therein to the peril and harming of their fortunes,—not only unrewarded, but exposed also to contempt and envy; doubtless there would have arisen many other philosophical sects like to those which in great variety flourished once among the Greeks. For as on the phenomena of the heavens many hypotheses may be constructed, so likewise (and more also) many various dogmas may be set up and established on the phenomena of philosophy. And in the plays of this philosophical theatre you may observe the same thing which is found in the theatre of the poets, that stories invented for the stage are more compact and elegant, and more as one would wish them to be, than true stories out of history.

In general however there is taken for the material of philosophy either a great deal out of a few things, or a very little out of many things; so that on both sides philosophy is based on too narrow a foundation of experiment and natural history, and decides on the authority of too few cases. For the Rational School of philosophers snatches from experience a variety of common instances, neither duly ascertained nor diligently examined and weighed, and leaves all the rest to meditation and agitation of wit.

There is also another class of philosophers, who having bestowed much diligent and careful labour on a few experiments, have thence made bold to educe and construct systems; wresting all other facts in a strange fashion to conformity therewith.

And there is yet a third class, consisting of those who out of faith and veneration mix their philosophy with theology and traditions; among whom the vanity of some has gone so far aside as to seek the origin of sciences among spirits and genii. So that this parent stock of errors—this false philosophy—is of three kinds; the Sophistical, the Empirical, and the Superstitious.

LXIII.

The most conspicuous example of the first class was Aristotle, who corrupted natural philosophy by his logic: fashioning the world out of categories; assigning to the human soul, the noblest of substances, a genus from words of the second intention; doing the business of density and rarity (which is to make bodies of greater or less dimensions, that is, occupy greater or less spaces), by the frigid distinction of act and power; asserting that single bodies have each a single and proper motion, and that if they participate in any other, then this results from an external cause; and imposing countless other arbitrary restrictions on the nature of things; being always more solicitous to provide an answer to the question and affirm something positive in words, than about the inner truth of things; a failing best shown when his philosophy is compared with other systems of note among the Greeks. For the Homœomera of Anaxagoras; the Atoms of Leucippus and Democritus; the Heaven and Earth of Parmenides; the Strife and Friendship of Empedocles; Heraclitus's doctrine how bodies are resolved into the indifferent nature of fire, and remoulded into solids; have all of them some taste of the natural philosopher,—some savour of the nature of things, and experience, and bodies; whereas in the physics of Aristotle you hear hardly anything but the words of logic; which in his metaphysics also, under a more imposing name, and more forsooth as a realist than a nominalist, he has handled over again. Nor let any weight be given to the fact, that in his books on animals and his problems, and other of his treatises, there is frequent dealing with experiments. For he had come to his conclusion before; he did not consult experience, as he should have done, in order to the framing of his decisions and axioms; but having first determined the question according to his will, he then resorts to experience, and bending her into conformity with his placets leads her about like a captive in a procession; so that even on this count he is more guilty than his modern followers, the schoolmen, who have abandoned experience altogether.

LXIV.

But the Empirical school of philosophy gives birth to dogmas more deformed and monstrous than the Sophistical or Rational school. For it has its foundations not in the light of common notions, (which though it be a faint and superficial light, is yet in a manner universal, and has reference to many things,) but in the narrowness and darkness of a few experiments. To those therefore who are daily busied with these experiments, and have infected their imagination with them, such a philosophy seems probable and all but certain; to all men else incredible and vain. Of this there is a notable instance in the alchemists and their dogmas; though it is hardly to be found elsewhere in these times, except perhaps in the philosophy of Gilbert. Nevertheless with regard to philosophies of this kind there is one caution not to be omitted; for I foresee that if ever men are roused by my admonitions to betake themselves seriously to experiment and bid farewell to sophistical doctrines, then indeed through the premature hurry of the understanding to leap or fly to universals and principles of things, great danger may be apprehended from philosophies of this kind; against which evil we ought even now to prepare.

LXV.

But the corruption of philosophy by superstition and an admixture of theology is far more widely spread, and does the greatest harm, whether to entire systems or to their parts. For the human understanding is obnoxious to the influence of the imagination no less than to the influence of common notions. For the contentious and sophistical kind of philosophy ensnares the understanding; but this kind, being fanciful and tumid and half poetical, misleads it more by flattery. For there is in man an ambition of the understanding, no less than of the will, especially in high and lofty spirits.

Of this kind we have among the Greeks a striking example in Pythagoras, though he united with it a coarser and more cumbrous superstition; another in

Plato and his school, more dangerous and subtle. It shows itself likewise in parts of other philosophies, in the introduction of abstract forms and final causes and first causes, with the omission in most cases of causes intermediate, and the like. Upon this point the greatest caution should be used. For nothing is so mischievous as the apotheosis of error; and it is a very plague of the understanding for vanity to become the object of veneration. Yet in this vanity some of the moderns have with extreme levity indulged so far as to attempt to found a system of natural philosophy on the first chapters of Genesis, on the book of Job, and other parts of the sacred writings; seeking for the dead among the living: which also makes the inhibition and repression of it the more important, because from this unwholesome mixture of things human and divine there arises not only a fantastic philosophy but also an heretical religion. Very meet it is therefore that we be sober-minded, and give to faith that only which is faith's.

LXVI.

So much then for the mischievous authorities of systems, which are founded either on common notions, or on a few experiments, or on superstition. It remains to speak of the faulty subject-matter of contemplations, especially in natural philosophy. Now the human understanding is infected by the sight of what takes place in the mechanical arts, in which the alteration of bodies proceeds chiefly by composition or separation, and so imagines that something similar goes on in the universal nature of things. From this source has flowed the fiction of elements, and of their concourse for the formation of natural bodies. Again, when man contemplates nature working freely, he meets with different species of things, of animals, of plants, of minerals; whence he readily passes into the opinion that there are in nature certain primary forms which nature intends to educe, and that the remaining variety proceeds from hindrances and aberrations of nature in the fulfilment of her work, or from the collision of different species and the transplanting of one into another. To the first of these speculations we owe our primary qualities of the elements; to the other our occult properties and specific virtues; and both of them belong to those empty *compendia* of thought wherein the mind rests, and whereby it is diverted from more solid pursuits. It is to better purpose that the physicians bestow their labour on the secondary qualities of matter, and the operations of attraction, repulsion, attenuation, conspissation, dilatation, astriction, dissipation, maturation, and the like; and were it not that by those two compendia which I have mentioned (elementary qualities, to wit, and specific virtues) they corrupted their correct observations in these other matters,—either reducing them to first qualities and their subtle and incommensurable mixtures, or not following them out with greater and more diligent observation to third and fourth qualities, but breaking off the scrutiny prematurely,—they had made much greater progress. Nor are powers of this kind (I do not say the same, but similar) to be sought for only in the medicines of the human body, but also in the changes of all other bodies.

But it is a far greater evil that they make the quiescent principles, *wherefrom*, and not the moving principles, *whereby*, things are produced, the object of their contemplation and inquiry. For the former tend to discourse, the latter to works. Nor is there any value in those vulgar distinctions of motion which are observed in the received system of natural philosophy, as generation, corruption, augmentation, diminution, alteration, and local motion. What they mean no doubt is this:—If a body, in other respects not changed, be moved from its place, *this is local motion;* if without change of place or essence, it be changed in quality, this is *alteration;* if by reason of the change the mass and quantity of the body do not remain the same, this is *augmentation* or *diminution;* if they be changed to such a degree that they change their very essence and substance and turn to something else, this is *generation* and *corruption.* But all this is merely popular, and does not at all go deep into nature; for these are only measures and limits, not kinds of motion. What they intimate is *how far,* not *by what means,* or *from what source.* For they do not suggest anything with regard either to the desires of bodies or to the development of their parts: it is only when that motion presents the thing grossly and palpably to the sense as different from what it was, that they begin to mark the division. Even when they wish to suggest something with regard to the causes of motion, and to establish a division with reference to them, they introduce with the greatest negligence a distinction between motion natural and violent; a distinction which is itself drawn entirely from a vulgar notion, since all violent motion is also in fact natural; the external efficient simply setting nature working otherwise than it was before. But if, leaving all this, any one shall observe (for instance) that there is in bodies a desire of mutual contact, so as not to suffer the unity of nature to be quite separated or broken and a vacuum thus made; or if any one say that there is in bodies a desire of resuming their natural dimensions or tension, so that if compressed within or extended beyond them, they immediately strive to recover themselves, and fall back to their old volume and extent; or if any one say that there is in bodies a desire of congregating towards masses of kindred nature,—of dense bodies, for instance, towards the globe of the earth, of thin and rare bodies towards the compass of the sky; all these and the like are truly physical kinds of motion;—but those others are entirely logical and scholastic, as is abundantly manifest from this comparison.

Nor again is it a less evil, that in their philosophies and contemplations their labour is spent in investigating and handling the first principles of things and the highest generalities of nature; whereas utility and the means of working result entirely from things intermediate. Hence it is that men cease not from abstracting nature till they come to potential and uninformed matter, nor on the other hand from dissecting nature till they reach the atom; things which, even if true, can do but little for the welfare of mankind.

LXVII.

A caution must also be given to the understanding against the intemperance which systems of philosophy manifest in giving or withholding assent; because intemperance of this kind seems to establish Idols and in some sort to perpetuate them, leaving no way open to reach and dislodge them.

This excess is of two kinds: the first being manifest in those who are ready in deciding, and render sciences dogmatic and magisterial; the other in those who deny that we can know anything, and so introduce a wandering kind of inquiry that leads to nothing; of which kinds the former subdues, the latter weakens the understanding. For the philosophy of Aristotle, after having by hostile confutations destroyed all the rest (as the Ottomans serve their brothers), has laid down the law on all points; which done, he proceeds himself to raise new questions of his own suggestion, and dispose of them likewise; so that nothing may remain that is not certain and decided: a practice which holds and is in use among his successors.

The school of Plato, on the other hand, introduced *Acatalepsia,* at first in jest and irony, and in disdain of the older sophists, Protagoras, Hippias, and the rest, who were of nothing else so much ashamed as of seeming to doubt about anything. But the New Academy made a dogma of it, and held it as a tenet. And though theirs is a fairer seeming way than arbitrary decisions; since they say that they by no means destroy all investigation, like Pyrrho and his Refrainers, but allow of some things to be followed as probable, though of none to be maintained as true; yet still when the human mind has once despaired of finding truth, its interest in all things grows fainter; and the result is that men turn aside to pleasant disputations and discourses and roam as it were from object to object, rather than keep on a course of severe inquisition. But, as I said at the beginning and am ever urging, the human senses and understanding, weak as they are, are not to be deprived of their authority, but to be supplied with helps.

LXVIII.

So much concerning the several classes of Idols, and their equipage: all of which must be renounced and put away with a fixed and solemn determination, and the understanding thoroughly freed and cleansed; the entrance into the kingdom of man, founded on the sciences, being not much other than the entrance into the kingdom of heaven, whereinto none may enter except as a little child.

LXIX.

But vicious demonstrations are as the strongholds and defences of Idols; and those we have in logic do little else than make the world the bond-slave of human thought, and human thought the bond-slave of words. Demonstrations truly are in effect the philosophies themselves and the sciences. For such as *they* are, well or ill established, such are the systems of philosophy and the contemplations which follow. Now in the whole of the process which leads from the sense and objects to axioms and conclusions, the demonstrations which we use are deceptive and incompetent. This process consists of four parts, and has as many faults. In the first place, the impressions of the sense itself are faulty; for the sense both fails us and deceives us. But its shortcomings are to be supplied, and its deceptions to be corrected. Secondly, notions are ill drawn from the impressions of the senses, and are indefinite and confused, whereas they should be definite and distinctly bounded. Thirdly, the induction is amiss which infers the principles of sciences by simple enumeration, and does not, as it ought, employ exclusions and solutions (or separations) of nature. Lastly, that method of discovery and proof according to which the most general principles are first established, and then intermediate axioms are tried and proved by them, is the parent of error and the curse of all science. Of these things however, which now I do but touch upon, I will speak more largely, when, having performed these expiations and purgings of the mind, I come to set forth the true way for the interpretation of nature.

LXX.

But the best demonstration by far is experience, if it go not beyond the actual experiment. For if it be transferred to other cases which are deemed similar, unless such transfer be made by a just and orderly process, it is a fallacious thing. But the manner of making experiments which men now use is blind and stupid. And therefore, wandering and straying as they do with no settled course, and taking counsel only from things as they fall out, they fetch a wide circuit and meet with many matters, but make little progress; and sometimes are full of hope, sometimes are distracted; and always find that there is something beyond to be sought. For it generally happens that men make their trials carelessly, and as it were in play; slightly varying experiments already known, and, if the thing does not answer, growing weary and abandoning the attempt. And even if they apply themselves to experiments more seriously and earnestly and laboriously, still they spend their labour in working out some one experiment, as Gilbert with the magnet, and the chemists with gold; a course of proceeding not less unskilful in the design then small in the attempt. For no one successfully investigates the nature of a thing in the thing itself; the inquiry must be enlarged, so as to become more general.

And even when they seek to educe some science or theory from their experiments, they nevertheless almost always turn aside with overhasty and unseasonable eagerness to practice; not only for the sake of the uses and fruits of the practice, but from impatience to obtain in the shape of some new work an assurance for themselves that it is worth their while to go on; and also to show themselves off to the world, and so raise the credit of the business in which they are engaged. Thus, like Atalanta, they go aside to pick up the golden apple, but meanwhile they interrupt their course, and let the victory escape them. But in the true course of experience, and in carrying it on to the effecting of new works, the divine wisdom and order must be our pattern. Now God on the first day of creation created light only, giving to that work an entire day, in which no material substance was created. So must we likewise from experience of every kind first endeavour to discover true causes and axioms; and seek for experiments of Light, not for experiments of Fruit. For axioms rightly discovered and established supply practice with its instruments, not one by one, but in clusters, and draw after them trains and troops of works. Of the paths however of experience, which no less than the paths of judgment are impeded and beset, I will speak hereafter; here I have only mentioned ordinary experimental research as a bad kind of demonstration. But now the order of the matter in hand leads me to add something both as to those *signs* which I lately mentioned,—(signs that the systems of philosophy and contemplation in use are in a bad condition)—and also as to the *causes* of what seems at first so strange and incredible. For a knowledge of the signs prepares assent; an explanation of the causes removes the marvel: which two things will do much to render the extirpation of Idols from the understanding more easy and gentle.

LXXI.

The sciences which we possess come for the most part from the Greeks. For what has been added by Roman, Arabic, or later writers is not much nor of much importance; and whatever it is, it is built on the foundation of Greek discoveries. Now the wisdom of the Greeks was professorial and much given to disputations; a kind of wisdom most adverse to the inquisition of truth. Thus that name of Sophists, which by those who would be thought philosophers was in contempt cast back upon and so transferred to the ancient rhetoricians, Gorgias, Protagoras, Hippias, Polus, does indeed suit the entire class, Plato, Aristotle, Zeno, Epicurus, Theophrastus, and their successors Chrysippus, Carnades, and the rest. There was this difference only, that the former class was wandering and mercenary, going about from town to town, putting up their wisdom to sale, and taking a price for it; while the latter was more pompous and dignified, as composed of men who had fixed abodes, and who opened schools and taught their philosophy without reward. Still both sorts, though in other respects unequal, were professorial; both turned the matter into disputations, and set up and battled for philosophical sects and heresies; so that their doctrines were for the most part (as Dionysius not unaptly rallied Plato) "the talk of idle old men to ignorant youths." But the elder of the Greek philosophers, Empedocles, Anaxagoras, Leucippus, Democritus, Parmenides, Heraclitus, Xenophanes, Philolaus, and the rest (I omit Pythagoras as a mystic), did not, so far as we know, open schools; but more silently and severely and simply,—that is, with less affectation and parade,—betook themselves to the inquisition of truth. And therefore they were in my judgment more successful; only that their works were in the course of time obscured by those slighter persons who had more which suits and pleases the capacity and tastes of the vulgar: time, like a river, bringing down to us things which are light and puffed up, but letting weighty matters sink. Still even they were not altogether free from the failing of their nation; but leaned too much to the ambition and vanity of founding a sect and catching popular applause. But the inquisition of truth must be despaired of when it turns aside to trifles of this kind. Nor should we omit that judgment, or rather divination, which was given concerning the Greeks by the Ægyptian priest,—that "they were always boys, without antiquity of knowledge or knowledge of antiquity." Assuredly they have that which is characteristic of boys; they are prompt to prattle, but cannot generate; for their wisdom abounds in words but is barren of works. And therefore the signs which are taken from the origin and birth-place of the received philosophy are not good.

LXXII.

Nor does the character of the time and age yield much better signs than the character of the country and nation. For at that period there was but a narrow and meagre knowledge either of time or place; which is the worst thing that can be, especially for those who rest all on experience. For they had no history, worthy to be called history, that went back a thousand years; but only fables and rumours of antiquity. And of the regions and districts of the world they knew but a small portion; giving indiscriminately the name of Scythians to all in the North, of Celts to all in the West; knowing nothing of Africa beyond the hither side of Æthiopia, of Asia beyond the Ganges; much less were they acquainted with the provinces of the New World, even by hearsay or any well-founded rumour; nay, a multitude of climates and zones, wherein innumerable nations breathe and live, were pronounced by them to be uninhabitable; and the travels of Democritus, Plato, and Pythagoras, which were rather suburban excursions than distant journeys, were talked of as something great. In our times on the other hand both many parts of the New World and the limits on every side of the Old World are known, and our stock of experience has increased to an infinite amount. Wherefore if (like astrologers) we draw signs from the season of their nativity or birth, nothing great can be predicted of those systems of philosophy.

LXXIII.

Of all signs there is none more certain or more noble than that taken from fruits. For fruits and works are as it were sponsors and sureties for the truth of philosophies. Now, from all these systems of the Greeks, and their ramifications through particular sciences there can hardly after the lapse of so many years be adduced a single experiment which tends to relieve and benefit the condition of man, and which can with truth be referred to the speculations and theories of philosophy. And Celsus ingenuously and wisely owns as much, when he tells us that the experimental part of medicine was first discovered, and that afterwards men philosophised about it, and hunted for and assigned causes; and not by an inverse process that philosophy and the knowledge of causes led to the discovery and development of the experimental part. And therefore it was not strange that among the Ægyptians, who rewarded inventors with divine honours and sacred rites, there were more images of brutes than of men; inasmuch as brutes by their natural instinct have produced many discoveries, whereas men by discussion and the conclusions of reason have given birth to few or none.

Some little has indeed been produced by the industry of chemists; but it has been produced accidentally and in passing, or else by a kind of variation of experiments, such as mechanics use; and not by any art or theory; for the theory which they have devised rather confuses the experiments than aids them. They too who have busied themselves with natural magic, as they call it, have but few discoveries to show, and those trifling and imposture-like. Wherefore, as in religion we are warned to show our faith by works, so in philosophy by the same rule the system should be judged of by its fruits, and pronounced frivolous if it be barren; more especially if, in place of fruits of grape and olive, it bear thorns and briars of dispute and contention.

LXXIV.

Signs also are to be drawn from the increase and progress of systems and sciences. For what is founded on nature grows and increases; while what is founded on opinion varies but increases not. If therefore those doctrines had not plainly been like a plant torn up from its roots, but had remained attached to the womb of nature and continued to draw nourishment from her, that could never have come to pass which we have seen now for twice a thousand years; namely, that the sciences stand where they did and remain almost in the same condition; receiving no noticeable increase, but on the contrary, thriving most under their first founder, and then declining. Whereas in the mechanical arts, which are founded on nature and the light of experience, we see the contrary happen, for these (as long as they are popular) are continually thriving and growing, as having in them a breath of life; at first rude, then convenient, afterwards adorned, and at all times advancing.

LXXV.

There is still another sign remaining (if sign it can be called, when it is rather testimony, nay, of all testimony the most valid); I mean the confession of the very authorities whom men now follow. For even they who lay down the law on all things so confidently, do still in their more sober moods fall to complaints of the subtlety of nature, the obscurity of things, and the weakness of the human mind. Now if this were all they did, some perhaps of a timid disposition might be deterred from further search, while others of a more ardent and hopeful spirit might be whetted and incited to go on farther. But not content to speak for themselves, whatever is beyond their own or their master's knowledge or reach they set down as beyond the bounds of possibility, and pronounce, as if on the authority of their art, that it cannot be known or done; thus most presumptuously and invidiously turning the weakness of their own discoveries into a calumny on nature herself, and the despair of the rest of the world. Hence the school of the New Academy, which held *Acatalepsia* as a tenet and doomed men to perpetual darkness. Hence the opinion that Forms or true differences of things (which are in fact laws of pure act) are past finding out and beyond the reach of man. Hence too those opinions in the department of action and operation; as that the heat of the sun and of fire are quite different in kind,—lest men should imagine that by the operations of fire anything like the works of nature can be educed and formed. Hence the notion that composition only is the work of man, and mixture of none but nature,—lest men should expect from art some power of generating or transforming natural bodies. By this sign, therefore, men will easily take warning not to mix up their fortunes and labours with dogmas not only despaired of but dedicated to despair.

LXXVI.

Neither is this other sign to be omitted;—that formerly there existed among philosophers such great disagreement, and such diversities in the schools themselves; a fact which sufficiently shows that the road from the senses to the understanding was not skilfully laid out, when the same groundwork of philosophy (the nature of things to wit) was torn and split up into such vague and multifarious errors. And although in these times disagreements and diversities of opinion on first principles and entire systems are for the most part extinguished, still on parts of philosophy there remain innumerable questions and disputes, so that it plainly appears that neither in the systems themselves nor in the modes of demonstration is there anything certain or sound.

LXXVII.

And as for the general opinion that in the philosophy of Aristotle at any rate there is great agreement; since after its publication the systems of older philosophers died away, while in the times which followed nothing better was found; so that it seems to have been so well laid and established as to have drawn both ages in its train; I answer in the first place, that the common notion of the falling off of the old systems upon the publication of Aristotle's works is a false one; for long afterwards, down even to the times of Cicero and subsequent ages, the works of the old philosophers still remained. But in the times which followed, when on the inundation of barbarians into the Roman empire human learning had suffered shipwreck, then the systems of Aristotle and Plato, like planks of lighter and less solid material, floated on the waves of time, and were preserved. Upon the point of consent also men are deceived, if the matter be looked into more keenly. For true consent is that which consists in the coincidence of free judgments, after due examination. But far the greater number of those who have assented to the philosophy of Aristotle have addicted themselves thereto from prejudgment and upon the authority of others; so that it is a following and going along together, rather than consent. But even if it had been a real and widespread consent, still so little ought consent to be deemed a sure and solid confirmation, that it is in fact a strong presumption the other way. For the worst of all auguries is from consent in matters intellectual (divinity excepted, and politics where there is right of vote). For nothing pleases the many unless it strikes the imagination, or binds the understanding with the bands of common notions, as I have already said. We may very well transfer therefore from moral to intellectual matters, the saying of Phocion, that if the multitude assent and applaud men ought immediately to examine themselves as to what blunder or fault they may have committed. This sign therefore is one of the most unfavourable. And so much for this point; namely, that the signs of truth and soundness in the received systems and sciences are not good; whether they be drawn from their origin, or from their fruits, or from their progress, or from the confessions of their founders, or from general consent.

LXXVIII.

I now come to the *causes* of these errors, and of so long a continuance in them through so many ages; which are very many and very potent;—that all wonder how these considerations which I bring forward should have escaped men's notice till now, may cease; and the only wonder be, how now at last they should have entered into any man's head and become the subject of his thoughts; which truly I myself esteem as the result of some happy accident, rather than of any excellence of faculty in me; a birth of Time rather than a birth of Wit. Now, in the first place, those so many ages, if you weigh the case truly, shrink into a very small compass. For out of the five and twenty centuries over which the memory and learning of men extends, you can hardly pick out six that were fertile in sciences or favourable to their development. In times no less than in regions there are wastes and deserts. For only three revolutions and periods of learning can properly be reckoned; one among the Greeks, the second among the Romans, and the last among us, that is to say, the nations of Western Europe; and to each of these hardly two centuries can justly be assigned. The intervening ages of the world, in respect of any rich or flourishing growth of the sciences, were unprosperous. For neither the Arabians nor the Schoolmen need be mentioned; who in the intermediate times rather crushed the sciences with a multitude of treatises, than increased their weight. And therefore the first cause of so meagre a progress in the sciences is duly and orderly referred to the narrow limits of the time that has been favourable to them.

LXXIX.

In the second place there presents itself a cause of great weight in all ways; namely, that during those very ages in which the wits and learning of men have flourished most, or indeed flourished at all, the least part of their diligence was given to natural philosophy. Yet this very philosophy it is that ought to be esteemed the great mother of the sciences. For all arts and all sciences, if torn from this root, though they may be polished and shaped and made fit for use, yet they will hardly grow. Now it is well known that after the Christian religion was received and grew strong, by far the greater number of the best wits applied themselves to theology; that to this both the highest rewards were offered, and helps of all kinds most abundantly supplied; and that this devotion to theology chiefly occupied that third portion or epoch of time among us Europeans of the West; and the more so because about the same time both literature began to flourish and religious controversies to spring up. In the age before, on the other hand, during the continuance of the second period among the Romans, the meditations and labours of philosophers were principally employed and consumed on moral philosophy, which to the Heathen was as theology to us. Moreover in those times the greatest wits applied themselves very generally to public affairs; the magnitude of the Roman empire requiring the services of a great number of persons. Again, the age in which natural philosophy was seen to flourish most among the Greeks, was but a brief particle of time; for in early ages the Seven Wise Men, as they were called, (all except Thales) applied themselves to morals and politics; and in later times, when Socrates had drawn down philosophy from heaven to earth, moral philosophy became more fashionable than ever, and diverted the minds of men from the philosophy of nature.

Nay, the very period itself in which inquiries concerning nature flourished, was by controversies and the ambitious display of new opinions corrupted and made useless. Seeing therefore that during those three periods natural philosophy was in a great degree either neglected or hindered, it is no wonder if men made but small advance in that to which they were not attending.

LXXX.

To this it may be added that natural philosophy, even among those who have attended to it, has scarcely ever possessed, especially in these later times, a disengaged and whole man (unless it were some monk studying in his cell, or some gentleman in his country-house), but that it has been made merely a passage and bridge to something else. And so this great mother of the sciences has with strange indignity been degraded to the offices of a servant; having to attend on the business of medicine or mathematics, and likewise to wash and imbue youthful and unripe wits with a sort of first dye, in order that they may be the fitter to receive another afterwards. Meanwhile let no man look for much progress in the sciences—especially in the practical part of them—unless natural philosophy be carried on and applied to particular sciences, and particular sciences be carried back again to natural philosophy. For want of this, astronomy, optics, music, a number of mechanical arts, medicine itself,—nay, what one might more wonder at, moral and political philosophy, and the logical sciences,—altogether lack profoundness, and merely glide along the surface and variety of things; because after these particular sciences have been once distributed and established, they are no more nourished by natural philosophy; which might have drawn out of the true contemplation of motions, rays, sounds, texture and configuration of bodies, affections, and intellectual perceptions, the means of imparting to them fresh strength and growth. And therefore it is nothing strange if the sciences grow not, seeing they are parted from their roots.

LXXXI.

Again there is another great and powerful cause why the sciences have made but little progress; which is this. It is not possible to run a course aright when the goal itself has not been rightly placed. Now the true and lawful goal of the sciences is none other than this: that human life be endowed with new discoveries and powers. But of this the great majority have no feeling, but are merely hireling and professorial; except when it occasionally happens that some workman of acuter wit and covetous of honour applies himself to a new invention; which he mostly does at the expense of his fortunes. But in general, so far are men from proposing to themselves to augment the mass of arts and sciences, that from the mass already at hand they neither take nor look for anything more than what they may turn to use in their lectures, or to gain, or to reputation, or to some similar advantage. And if any one out of all the multitude court science with honest affection and for her own sake, yet even with him the object will be found to be rather the variety of contemplations and doctrines than the severe and rigid search after truth. And if by chance there be one who seeks after truth in earnest, yet even he will propose to himself such a kind of truth as shall yield satisfaction to the mind and understanding in rendering causes for things long since discovered, and not the truth which shall lead to new assurance of works and new light of axioms. If then the end of the sciences has not yet been well placed, it is not strange that men have erred as to the means.

LXXXII.

And as men have misplaced the end and goal of the sciences; so again, even if they had placed it right, yet they have chosen a way to it which is altogether erroneous and impassable. And an astonishing thing it is to one who rightly considers the matter, that no mortal should have seriously applied himself to the opening and laying out of a road for the human understanding direct from the sense, by a course of experiment orderly conducted and well built up; but that all has been left either to the mist of tradition, or the whirl and eddy of argument, or the fluctuations and mazes of chance and of vague and ill-digested experience. Now let any man soberly and diligently consider what the way is by which men have been accustomed to proceed in the investigation and discovery of things; and in the first place he will no doubt remark a method of discovery very simple and inartificial; which is the most ordinary method, and is no more than this. When a man addresses himself to discover something, he first seeks out and sets before him all that has been said about it by others; then he begins to meditate for himself; and so by much agitation and working of the wit solicits and as it were evokes his own spirit to give him oracles: which method has no foundation at all, but rests only upon opinions and is carried about with them.

Another may perhaps call in logic to discover it for him; but that has no relation to the matter except in name. For logical invention does not discover principles and chief axioms, of which arts are composed, but only such things as appear to be consistent with them. For if you grow more curious and importunate and busy, and question her of probations and invention of principles or primary axioms, her answer is well known: she refers you to the faith you are bound to give to the principles of each separate art.

There remains simple experience; which, if taken as it comes, is called accident; if sought for, experiment. But this kind of experience is no better than a broom without its band, as the saying is;—a mere groping, as of men in the dark, that feel all round them for the chance of finding their way; when they had much better wait for daylight, or light a candle, and then go. But the true method of experience on the contrary first lights the candle, and then by means of the candle shows the way; commencing as it does with experience duly ordered and digested, not bungling or erratic, and from it educing axioms, and from established axioms again new experiments; even as it was not without order and method that the divine word operated on the created mass. Let men therefore cease to wonder that the course of science is not yet wholly run, seeing that they have gone altogether astray; either leaving and abandoning experience entirely, or losing their way in it and wandering round and round as in a labyrinth; whereas a method rightly ordered leads by an unbroken route through the woods of experience to the open ground of axioms.

LXXXIII.

This evil however has been strangely increased by an opinion or conceit, which though of long standing is vain and hurtful; namely, that the dignity of the human mind is impaired by long and close intercourse with experiments and particulars, subject to sense and bound in matter; especially as they are laborious to search, ignoble to meditate, harsh to deliver, illiberal to practise, infinite in number, and minute in subtlety. So that it has come at length to this, that the true way is not merely deserted, but shut out and stopped up; experience being, I do not say abandoned or badly managed, but rejected with disdain.

LXXXIV.

Again, men have been kept back as by a kind of enchantment from progress in the sciences by reverence for antiquity, by the authority of men accounted great in philosophy, and then by general consent. Of the last I have spoken above.

As for antiquity, the opinion touching it which men entertain is quite a negligent one, and scarcely consonant with the word itself. For the old age of the world is to be accounted the true antiquity; and this is the attribute of our own times, not of that earlier age of the world in which the ancients lived; and which, though in respect of us it was the elder, yet in respect of the world it was the younger. And truly as we look for greater knowledge of human things and a riper judgment in the old man than in the young, because of his experience and of the number and variety of the things which he has seen and heard and thought of; so in like manner from our age, if it but knew its own strength and chose to essay and exert it, much more might fairly be expected than from the ancient times, inasmuch as it is a more advanced age of the world, and stored and stocked with infinite experiments and observations.

Nor must it go for nothing that by the distant voyages and travels which have become frequent in our times, many things in nature have been laid open and discovered which may let in new light upon philosophy. And surely it would be disgraceful if, while the regions of the material globe,—that is, of the earth, of the sea, and of the stars,—have been in our times laid widely open and revealed, the intellectual globe should remain shut up within the narrow limits of old discoveries.

And with regard to authority, it shows a feeble mind to grant so much to authors and yet deny time his rights, who is the author of authors, nay rather of all authority. For rightly is truth called the daughter of time, not of authority. It is no wonder therefore if those enchantments of antiquity and authority and consent have so bound up men's powers that they have been made impotent (like persons bewitched) to accompany with the nature of things.

LXXXV.

Nor is it only the admiration of antiquity, authority, and consent, that has forced the industry of man to rest satisfied with the discoveries already made; but also an admiration for the works themselves of which the human race has long been in possession. For when a man looks at the variety and the beauty of the provision which the mechanical arts have brought together for men's use, he will certainly be more inclined to admire the wealth of man than to feel his wants: not considering that the original observations and operations of nature (which are the life and moving principle of all that variety) are not many nor deeply fetched, and that the rest is but patience, and the subtle and ruled motion of the hand and instruments; —as the making of clocks (for instance) is certainly a subtle and exact work: their wheels seem to imitate the celestial orbs, and their alternating and orderly motion, the pulse of animals: and yet all this depends on one or two axioms of nature.

Again, if you observe the refinement of the liberal arts, or even that which relates to the mechanical preparation of natural substances; and take notice of such things as the discovery in astronomy of the motions of the heavens, of harmony in music, of the letters of the alphabet (to this day not in use among the Chinese) in grammar: or again in things mechanical, the discovery of the works of Bacchus and Ceres—that is, of the arts of preparing wine and beer, and of making bread; the discovery once more of the delicacies of the table, of distillations and the like; and if you likewise bear in mind the long periods which it has taken to bring these things to their present degree of perfection (for they are all ancient except distillation), and again (as has been said of clocks) how little they owe to observations and axioms of nature, and how easily and obviously and as it were by casual suggestion they may have been discovered; you will easily cease from wondering, and on the contrary will pity the condition of mankind, seeing that in a course of so many ages there has been so great a dearth and barrenness of arts and inventions. And yet these very discoveries which we have just mentioned, are older than philosophy and intellectual arts. So that, if the truth must be spoken, when the rational and dogmatical sciences began the discovery of useful works came to an end.

And again, if a man turn from the workshop to the library, and wonder at the immense variety of books he sees there, let him but examine and diligently inspect their matter and contents, and his wonder will assuredly be turned the other way; for after observing their endless repetitions, and how men are ever saying and doing what has been said and done before, he will pass from admiration of the variety to astonishment at the poverty and scantiness of the subjects which till now have occupied and possessed the minds of men.

And if again he descend to the consideration of those arts which are deemed curious rather than safe, and look more closely into the works of the Alchemists or the Magicians, he will be in doubt perhaps whether he ought rather to laugh over them or to weep. For the Alchemist nurses eternal hope, and when the thing fails, lays the blame upon some error of his own; fearing either that he has not sufficiently understood the words of his art or of his authors (whereupon he turns to tradition and auricular whispers), or else that in his manipulations he has made some slip of a scruple in weight or a moment in time (whereupon he repeats his trials to infinity); and when meanwhile among the chances of experiment he lights upon some conclusions either in aspect new or for utility not contemptible, he takes these for earnest of what is to come, and feeds his mind upon them, and magnifies them to the most, and supplies the rest in hope. Not but that Alchemists have made a good many discoveries, and presented men with useful inventions. But their case may be well compared to the fable of the old man, who bequeathed to his sons gold buried in a vineyard, pretending not to know the exact spot; whereupon the sons applied themselves diligently to the digging of the vineyard, and though no gold was found there, yet the vintage by that digging was made more plentiful.

Again the students of natural magic, who explain everything by Sympathies and Antipathies, have in their idle and most slothful conjectures ascribed to substances wonderful virtues and operations; and if ever they have produced works, they have been such as aim rather at admiration and novelty than at utility and fruit.

In superstitious magic on the other hand (if of this also we must speak), it is especially to be observed that they are but subjects of a certain and definite kind wherein the curious and superstitious arts, in all nations and ages, and religions also, have worked or played. These therefore we may pass. Meanwhile it is nowise strange if opinion of plenty has been the cause of want.

LXXXVI.

Further, this admiration of men for knowledges and arts,—an admiration in itself weak enough, and well-nigh childish,—has been increased by the craft and artifices of those who have handled and transmitted sciences. For they set them forth with such ambition and parade, and bring them into the view of the world so fashioned and masked, as if they were complete in all parts and finished. For if you look at the method of them and the divisions, they seem to embrace and comprise everything which can belong to the subject. And although these divisions are ill filled out and are but as empty cases, still to the common mind they present the form and plan of a perfect science. But the first and most ancient seekers after truth were wont, with better faith and better fortune too, to throw the knowledge which they gathered from the contemplation of things, and which they meant to store up for use, into aphorisms; that is, into short and scattered sentences, not linked together by an artificial method; and did not pretend or profess to embrace the entire art. But as the matter now is, it is nothing strange if men do not seek to advance in things delivered to them as long since perfect and complete.

LXXXVII.

Moreover the ancient systems have received no slight accession of reputation and credit from the vanity and levity of those who have propounded new ones; especially in the active and practical department of natural philosophy. For there have not been wanting talkers and dreamers who, partly from credulity, partly in imposture, have loaded mankind with promises, offering and announcing the prolongation of life, the retardation of age, the alleviation of pain, the repairing of natural defects, the deceiving of the senses; arts of binding and inciting the affections, of illuminating and exalting the intellectual faculties, of transmuting substances, of strengthening and multiplying motions at will, of making impressions and alterations in the air, of bringing down and procuring celestial influences; arts of divining things future, and bringing things distant near, and revealing things secret; and many more. But with regard to these lavish promisers, this judgment would not be far amiss; that there is as much difference in philosophy between their vanities and true arts, as there is in history between the exploits of Julius Cæsar or Alexander the Great, and the exploits of Amadis of Gaul or Arthur of

Britain. For it is true that those illustrious generals really did greater things than these shadowy heroes are even feigned to have done; but they did them by means and ways of action not fabulous or monstrous. Yet surely it is not fair that the credit of true history should be lessened because it has sometimes been injured and wronged by fables. Meanwhile it is not to be wondered at, if a great prejudice is raised against new propositions, especially when works are also mentioned, because of those impostors who have attempted the like; since their excess of vanity, and the disgust it has bred, have their effect still in the destruction of all greatness of mind in enterprises of this kind.

LXXXVIII.

Far more however has knowledge suffered from littleness of spirit and the smallness and slightness of the tasks which human industry has proposed to itself. And what is worst of all, this very littleness of spirit comes with a certain air of arrogance and superiority.

For in the first place there is found in all arts one general device, which has now become familiar,—that the author lays the weakness of his art to the charge of nature: whatever his art cannot attain he sets down on the authority of the same art to be in nature impossible. And truly no art can be condemned if it be judge itself. Moreover the philosophy which is now in vogue embraces and cherishes certain tenets, the purpose of which (if it be diligently examined) is to persuade men that nothing difficult, nothing by which nature may be commanded and subdued, can be expected from art or human labour; as with respect to the doctrine that the heat of the sun and of fire differ in kind, and to that other concerning mixture, has been already observed.

Which things, if they be noted accurately, tend wholly to the unfair circumscription of human power, and to a deliberate and factitious despair; which not only disturbs the auguries of hope, but also cuts the sinews and spur of industry, and throws away the chances of experience itself; and all for the sake of having their art thought perfect, and for the miserable vain glory of making it believed that whatever has not yet been discovered and comprehended can never be discovered or comprehended hereafter.

And even if a man apply himself fairly to facts, and endeavour to find out something new, yet he will confine his aim and intention to the investigation and working out of some one discovery and no more; such as the nature of the magnet, the ebb and flow of the sea, the system of the heavens, and things of this kind, which seem to be in some measure secret, and have hitherto been handled without much success. Whereas it is most unskilful to investigate the nature of any thing in the thing itself; seeing that the same nature which appears in some things to be latent and hidden is in others manifest and palpable; wherefore in the former it produces wonder, in the latter excites no attention; as we find it in the nature of consistency, which in wood or stone is not observed, but is passed over under the appellation of solidity, without further inquiry as to why separation or solution of continuity is avoided; while in the case of bubbles, which form themselves into certain pellicles, curiously shaped into hemispheres, so that the solution of continuity is avoided for a moment, it is thought a subtle matter. In fact what in some things is accounted a secret has in others a manifest and well known nature, which will never be recognised as long as the experiments and thoughts of men are engaged on the former only.

But generally speaking, in mechanics old discoveries pass for new, if a man does but refine or embellish them, or unite several in one, or couple them better with their use, or make the work in greater or less volume than it was before, or the like.

Thus then it is no wonder if noble inventions and worthy of mankind have not been brought to light, when men have been contented and delighted with such trifling and puerile tasks, and have even fancied that in them they have been endeavouring after, if not accomplishing, some great matter.

LXXXIX.

Neither is it to be forgotten that in every age Natural Philosophy has had a troublesome adversary and hard to deal with; namely, superstition, and the blind and immoderate zeal of religion. For we see among the Greeks that those who first proposed to men's then uninitiated ears the natural causes for thunder and for storms, were thereupon found guilty of impiety. Nor was much more forbearance shown by some of the ancient fathers of the Christian church to those who on most convincing grounds (such as no one in his senses would now think of contradicting) maintained that the earth was round, and of consequence asserted the existence of the antipodes.

Moreover, as things now are, to discourse of nature is made harder and more perilous by the summaries and systems of the schoolmen; who having reduced theology into regular order as well as they were able, and fashioned it into the shape of an art, ended in incorporating the contentious and thorny philosophy of Aristotle, more than was fit, with the body of religion.

To the same result, though in a different way, tend the speculations of those who have taken upon them to deduce the truth of the Christian religion from the principles of philosophers, and to confirm it by their authority; pompously solemnising this union of the sense and faith as a lawful marriage, and entertaining men's minds with a pleasing variety of matter, but all the while disparaging things divine by mingling them with things human. Now in such mixtures of theology with philosophy only the received doctrines of philosophy are included; while new ones, albeit changes for the better, are all but expelled and exterminated.

Lastly, you will find that by the simpleness of certain divines, access to any philosophy, however pure, is well nigh closed. Some are weakly afraid lest a deeper search into nature should transgress the permitted limits of sobermindedness; wrongfully wresting and transferring what is said in holy writ against those who pry into sacred mysteries, to the hidden things of nature, which are barred by no prohibition. Others with more subtlety surmise and reflect that if second causes are unknown everything can more readily be referred to the divine hand and rod; a point in which they think religion greatly concerned; which is in fact nothing else but to seek to gratify God with a lie. Others fear from past example that movements and changes in philosophy will end in assaults on religion. And others again appear apprehensive that in the investigation of nature something may be found to subvert or at least shake the authority of religion, especially with the unlearned. But these two last fears seem to me to savour utterly of carnal wisdom; as if men in the recesses and secret thoughts of their hearts doubted and distrusted the strength of religion and the empire of faith over the sense, and therefore feared that the investigation of truth in nature might be dangerous to them. But if the matter be truly considered, natural philosophy is after the word of God at once the surest medicine against superstition, and the most approved nourishment for faith, and therefore she is rightly given to religion as her most faithful handmaid, since the one displays the will of God, the other his power. For he did not err who said "Ye err in that ye know not the Scriptures and the power of God," thus coupling and blending in an indissoluble bond information concerning his will and meditation concerning his power. Meanwhile it is not surprising if the growth of Natural Philosophy is checked, when religion, the thing which has most power over men's minds, has by the simpleness and incautious zeal of certain persons been drawn to take part against her.

XC.

Again, in the customs and institutions of schools, academies, colleges, and similar bodies destined for the abode of learned men and the cultivation of learning, everything is found adverse to the progress of science. For the lectures and exercises there are so ordered, that to think or speculate on anything out of the common way can hardly occur to any man. And if one or two have the boldness to use any liberty of judgment, they must undertake the task all by themselves; they can have no advantage from the company of others. And if they can endure this also, they will find their industry and largeness of mind no slight hindrance to their fortune. For the studies of men in these places are confined and as it were imprisoned in the writings of certain authors, from whom if any man dissent he is straightway arraigned as a turbulent person and an innovator. But surely there is a great distinction between matters of state and the arts; for the danger from new motion and from new light is not the same. In matters of state a change even for the better is distrusted, because it unsettles what is established; these things resting on authority, consent, fame and opinion, not on demonstration. But arts and sciences should be like mines, where the noise of new works and further advances is heard on every side. But though the matter be so according to right reason, it is not so acted on in practice; and the points above mentioned in the administration and government of learning put a severe restraint upon the advancement of the sciences.

XCI.

Nay, even if that jealousy were to cease, still it is enough to check the growth of science, that efforts and labours in this field go unrewarded. For it does not rest with the same persons to cultivate sciences and to reward them. The growth of them comes from great wits; the prizes and rewards of them are in the hands of the people, or of great persons, who are but in very few cases even moderately learned. Moreover this kind of progress is not only unrewarded with prizes and substantial benefits; it has not even the advantage of popular applause. For it is a greater matter than the generality of men can take in, and is apt to be overwhelmed and extinguished by the gales of popular opinions. And it is nothing strange if a thing not held in honour does not prosper.

XCII.

But by far the greatest obstacle to the progress of science and to the undertaking of new tasks and provinces therein, is found in this—that men despair and think things impossible. For wise and serious men are wont in these matters to be altogether distrustful; considering with themselves the obscurity of nature, the shortness of life, the deceitfulness of the senses, the weakness of the judgment, the difficulty of experiment and the like; and so supposing that in the revolution of time and of the ages of the world the sciences have their ebbs and flows; that at one season they grow and flourish, at another wither and decay, yet in such sort that when they have reached a certain point and condition they can advance no further. If therefore any one believes or promises more, they think this comes of an ungoverned and unripened mind, and that such attempts have prosperous beginnings, become difficult as they go on, and end in confusion. Now since these are thoughts which naturally present themselves to grave men and of great judgment, we must take good heed that we be not led away by our love for a most fair and excellent object to relax or diminish the severity of our judgment; we must observe diligently what encouragement dawns upon us and from what quarter; and, putting aside the lighter breezes of hope, we must thoroughly sift and examine those which promise greater steadiness and constancy. Nay, and we must take state-prudence too into our counsels, whose rule is to distrust, and to take the less favourable view of human affairs. I am now therefore to speak touching Hope; especially as I am not a dealer in promises, and wish neither to force nor to ensnare men's judgments, but to lead them by the hand with their good will. And though the strongest means of inspiring hope will be to bring men to particulars; especially to particulars digested and arranged in my Tables of Discovery (the subject partly of the second, but much more of the fourth part of my Instauration), since this is not merely the promise of the thing but the thing itself; nevertheless that everything may be done with gentleness, I will proceed with my plan of preparing men's minds; of which preparation to give hope is no unimportant part. For without it the rest tends rather to make men sad (by giving them a worse and meaner opinion of things as they are than they now have, and making them more fully to feel and know the unhappiness of their own condition) than to induce any alacrity or to whet their industry in making trial. And therefore it is fit that I publish and set forth those conjectures of mine which make hope in this matter reasonable; just as Columbus did, before that wonderful voyage of his across the Atlantic, when he gave the reasons for his conviction that new lands and continents might be discovered besides those which were known before; which reasons, though rejected at first, were afterwards made good by experience, and were the causes and beginnings of great events.

XCIII.

The beginning is from God: for the business which is in hand, having the character of good so strongly impressed upon it, appears manifestly to proceed from God, who is the author of good, and the Father of Lights. Now in divine operations even the smallest beginnings lead of a certainty to their end. And as it was said of spiritual things, "The kingdom of God cometh not with observation," so is it in all the greater works of Divine Providence; everything glides on smoothly and noiselessly, and the work is fairly going on before men are aware that it has begun. Nor should the prophecy of Daniel be forgotten, touching the last ages of the world:—"Many shall go to and fro, and knowledge shall be increased;" clearly intimating that the thorough passage of the world (which now by so many distant voyages seems to be accomplished, or in course of accomplishment), and the advancement of the sciences, are destined by fate, that is, by Divine Providence, to meet in the same age.

XCIV.

Next comes a consideration of the greatest importance as an argument of hope; I mean that drawn from the errors of past time, and of the ways hitherto trodden. For most excellent was the censure once passed upon a government that had been unwisely administered. "That which is the worst thing in reference to the past, ought to be regarded as best for the future. For if you had done all that your duty demanded, and yet your affairs were no better, you would not have even a hope left you that further improvement is possible. But now, when your misfortunes are owing, not to the force of circumstances, but to your own errors, you may hope that by dismissing or correcting these errors, a great change may be made for the better." In like manner, if during so long a course of years men had kept the true road for discovering and cultivating sciences, and had yet been unable to make further progress therein, bold doubtless and rash would be the opinion that further progress is possible. But if the road itself has been mistaken, and men's labour spent on unfit objects, it follows that the difficulty has its rise not in things themselves, which are not in our power, but in the human understanding, and the use and application thereof, which admits of remedy and medicine. It will be of great use therefore to set forth what these errors are; for as many impediments as there have been in times past from this cause, so many arguments are there of hope for the time to come. And although they have been partly touched before, I think fit here also, in plain and simple words, to represent them.

XCV.

Those who have handled sciences have been either men of experiment or men of dogmas. The men of experiment are like the ant; they only collect and use: the reasoners resemble spiders, who make cobwebs out of their own substance. But the bee takes a middle course, it gathers its material from the flowers of the garden and of the field, but transforms and digests it by a power of its own. Not unlike this is the true business of philosophy; for it neither relies solely or chiefly on the powers of the mind, nor does it take the matter which it gathers from natural history and mechanical experiments and lay it up in the memory whole, as it finds it; but lays it up in the understanding altered and digested. Therefore from a closer and purer league between these two faculties, the experimental and the rational, (such as has never yet been made) much may be hoped.

XCVI.

We have as yet no natural philosophy that is pure; all is tainted and corrupted; in Aristotle's school by logic; in Plato's by natural theology; in the second school of Platonists, such as Proclus and others, by mathematics, which ought only to give definiteness to natural philosophy, not to generate or give it birth. From a natural philosophy pure and unmixed, better things are to be expected.

XCVII.

No one has yet been found so firm of mind and purpose as resolutely to compel himself to sweep away all theories and common notions, and to apply the understanding, thus made fair and even, to a fresh examination of particulars. Thus it happens that human knowledge, as we have it, is a mere medley and ill-digested mass, made up of much credulity and much accident, and also of the childish notions which we at first imbibed.

Now if any one of ripe age, unimpaired senses, and well-purged mind, apply himself anew to experience and particulars, better hopes may be entertained of that man. In which point I promise to myself a like fortune to that of Alexander the Great; and let no man tax me with vanity till he have heard the end; for the thing which I mean tends to the putting off of all vanity. For of Alexander and his deeds Æschines spake thus: "Assuredly we do not live the life of mortal men; but to this end were we born, that in after ages wonders might be told of us;" as if what Alexander had done seemed to him miraculous. But in the next age Titus Livius took a better and a deeper view of the matter, saying in effect, that Alexander "had done no more than take courage to despise vain apprehensions." And a like judgment I suppose may be passed on myself in future ages: that I did no great things, but simply made less account of things that were accounted great. In the meanwhile, as I have already said, there is no hope except in a new birth of science; that is, in raising it regularly up from experience and building it afresh; which no one (I think) will say has yet been done or thought of.

XCVIII.

Now for grounds of experience—since to experience we must come—we have as yet had either none or very weak ones; no search has been made to collect a store of particular observations sufficient either in number, or in kind, or in certainty, to inform the understanding, or in any way adequate. On the contrary, men of learning, but easy withal and idle, have taken for the construction or for the confirmation of their philosophy certain rumours and vague fames or airs of experience, and allowed to these the weight of lawful evidence. And just as if some kingdom or state were to direct its counsels and affairs, not by letters and reports from ambassadors and trustworthy messengers, but by the gossip of the streets; such exactly is the system of management introduced into philosophy with relation to experience. Nothing duly investigated, nothing verified, nothing counted, weighed, or measured, is to be found in natural history: and what in observation is loose and vague, is in information deceptive and treacherous. And if any one thinks that this is a strange thing to say, and something like an unjust complaint, seeing that Aristotle, himself so great a man, and supported by the wealth of so great a king, has composed so accurate a history of animals; and that others with greater diligence, though less pretence, have made many additions; while others, again, have compiled copious histories and descriptions of metals, plants, and fossils; it seems that he does not rightly apprehend what it is that we are now about. For a natural history which is composed for its own sake is not like one that is collected to supply the understanding with information for the building up of philosophy. They differ in many ways, but especially in this; that the former contains the variety of natural species only, and not experiments of the mechanical arts. For even as in the business of life a man's disposition and the secret workings of his mind and affections are better discovered when he is in trouble than at other times; so likewise the secrets of nature reveal themselves more readily under the vexations of art than when they go their own way. Good hopes may therefore be conceived of natural philosophy, when natural history, which is the basis and foundation of it, has been drawn up on a better plan; but not till then.

XCIX.

Again, even in the great plenty of mechanical experiments, there is yet a great scarcity of those which are of most use for the information of the understanding. For the mechanic, not troubling himself with the investigation of truth, confines his attention to those things which bear upon his particular work, and will not either raise his mind or stretch out his hand for anything else. But then only will there be good ground of hope for the further advance of knowledge, when there shall be received and gathered together into natural history a variety of experiments, which are of no use in themselves, but simply serve to discover causes and axioms; which I call *"Experimenta lucifera,"* experiments of *light*, to distinguish them from those which I call "*fructifera,*" experiments of *fruit.*

Now experiments of this kind have one admirable property and condition; they never miss or fail. For since they are applied, not for the purpose of producing any particular effect, but only of discovering the natural cause of some effect, they answer the end equally well whichever way they turn out; for they settle the question.

C.

But not only is a greater abundance of experiments to be sought for and procured, and that too of a different kind from those hitherto tried; an entirely different method, order, and process for carrying on and advancing experience must also be introduced. For experience, when it wanders in its own track, is, as I have already remarked, mere groping in the dark, and confounds men rather than instructs them. But when it shall proceed in accordance with a fixed law, in regular order, and without interruption, then may better things be hoped of knowledge.

CI.

But even after such a store of natural history and experience as is required for the work of the understanding, or of philosophy, shall be ready at hand, still the understanding is by no means competent to deal with it off hand and by memory alone; no more than if a man should hope by force of memory to retain and make himself master of the computation of an ephemeris. And yet hitherto more has been done in matter of invention by thinking than by writing; and experience has not yet learned her letters. Now no course of invention can be satisfactory unless it be carried on in writing. But when this is brought into use, and experience has been taught to read and write, better things may be hoped.

CII.

Moreover, since there is so great a number and army of particulars, and that army so scattered and dispersed as to distract and confound the understanding, little is to be hoped for from the skirmishings and slight attacks and desultory movements of the intellect, unless all the particulars which pertain to the subject of inquiry shall, by means of Tables of Discovery, apt, well arranged, and as it were animate, be drawn up and marshalled; and the mind be set to work upon the helps duly prepared and digested which these tables supply.

CIII.

But after this store of particulars has been set out duly and in order before our eyes, we are not to pass at once to the investigation and discovery of new particulars or works; or at any rate if we do so we must not stop there. For although I do not deny that when all the experiments of all the arts shall have been collected and digested, and brought within one man's knowledge and judgment, the mere transferring of the experiments of one art to others may lead, by means of that experience which I term *literate,* to the discovery of many new things of service to the life and state of man, yet it is no great matter that can be hoped from that; but from the new light of axioms, which having been educed from those particulars by a certain method and rule, shall in their turn point out the way again to new particulars, greater things may be looked for.

For our road does not lie on a level, but ascends and descends; first ascending to axioms, then descending to works.

CIV.

The understanding must not however be allowed to jump and fly from particulars to remote axioms and of almost the highest generality (such as the first principles, as they are called, of arts and things), and taking stand upon them as truths that cannot be shaken, proceed to prove and frame the middle axioms by reference to them; which has been the practice hitherto; the understanding being not only carried that way by a natural impulse, but also by the use of syllogistic demonstration trained and inured to it. But then, and then only, may we hope well of the sciences, when in a just scale of ascent, and by successive steps not interrupted or broken, we rise from particulars to lesser axioms; and then to middle axioms, one above the other; and last of all to the most general. For the lowest axioms differ but slightly from bare experience, while the highest and most general (which we now have) are notional and abstract and without solidity. But the middle are the true and solid and living axioms, on which depend the affairs and fortunes of men; and above them again, last of all, those which are indeed the most general; such I mean as are not abstract, but of which those intermediate axioms are really limitations.

The understanding must not therefore be supplied with wings, but rather hung with weights, to keep it from leaping and flying. Now this has never yet been done; when it is done, we may entertain better hopes of the sciences.

CV.

In establishing axioms, another form of induction must be devised than has hitherto been employed; and it must be used for proving and discovering not first principles (as they are called) only, but also the lesser axioms, and the middle, and indeed all. For the induction which proceeds by simple enumeration is childish; its conclusions are precarious, and exposed to peril from a contradictory instance; and it generally decides on too small a number of facts, and on those only which are at hand. But the induction which is to be available for the discovery and demonstration of sciences and arts, must analyse nature by proper rejections and exclusions; and then, after a sufficient number of negatives, come to a conclusion on the affirmative instances: which has not yet been done or even attempted, save only by Plato, who does indeed employ this form of induction to a certain extent for the purpose of discussing definitions and ideas. But in order to furnish this induction or demonstration well and duly for its work, very many things are to be provided which no mortal has yet thought of; insomuch that greater labour will have to be spent in it than has hitherto been spent on the syllogism. And this induction must be used not only to discover axioms, but also in the formation of notions. And it is in this induction that our chief hope lies.

CVI.

But in establishing axioms by this kind of induction, we must also examine and try whether the axiom so established be framed to the measure of those particulars only from which it is derived, or whether it be larger and wider. And if it be larger and wider, we must observe whether by indicating to us new particulars it confirm that wideness and largeness as by a collateral security; that we may not either stick fast in things already known, or loosely grasp at shadows and abstract forms; not at things solid and realised in matter. And when this process shall have come into use, then at last shall we see the dawn of a solid hope.

CVII.

And here also should be remembered what was said above concerning the extending of the range of natural philosophy to take in the particular sciences, and the referring or bringing back of the particular sciences to natural philosophy; that the branches of knowledge may not be severed and cut off from the stem. For without this the hope of progress will not be so good.

CVIII.

So much then for the removing of despair and the raising of hope through the dismissal or rectification of the errors of past time. We must now see what else there is to ground hope upon. And this consideration occurs at once—that if many useful discoveries have been made by accident or upon occasion, when men were not seeking for them but were busy about other things; no one can doubt but that when they apply themselves to seek and make this their business, and that too by method and in order and not by desultory impulses, they will discover far more. For although it may happen once or twice that a man shall stumble on a thing by accident which, when taking great pains to search for it, he could not find; yet upon the whole it unquestionably falls out the other way. And therefore far better things, and more of them, and at shorter intervals, are to be expected from man's reason and industry and direction and fixed application, than from accident and animal instinct and the like, in which inventions have hitherto had their origin.

CIX.

Another argument of hope may be drawn from this, —that some of the inventions already known are such as before they were discovered it could hardly have entered any man's head to think of; they would have been simply set aside as impossible. For in conjecturing what may be men set before them the example of what has been, and divine of the new with an imagination preoccupied and coloured by the old; which way of forming opinions is very fallacious; for streams that are drawn from the springheads of nature do not always run in the old channels.

If, for instance, before the invention of ordnance, a man had described the thing by its effects, and said that there was a new invention, by means of which the strongest towers and walls could be shaken and thrown down at a great distance; men would doubtless have begun to think over all the ways of multiplying the force of catapults and mechanical engines by weights and wheels and such machinery for ramming and projecting; but the notion of a fiery blast suddenly and violently expanding and exploding would hardly have entered into any man's imagination or fancy; being a thing to which nothing immediately analogous had been seen, except perhaps in an earthquake or in lightning, which as *magnalia* or marvels of nature, and by man not imitable, would have been immediately rejected.

In the same way, if before the discovery of silk, any one had said that there was a kind of thread discovered for the purposes of dress and furniture, which far surpassed the thread of linen or of wool in fineness and at the same time in strength, and also in beauty and softness; men would have begun immediately to think of some silky kind of vegetable, or of the finer hair of some animal, or of the feathers and down of birds; but of a web woven by a tiny worm, and that in such abundance, and renewing itself yearly, they would assuredly never have thought. Nay, if any one had said anything about a worm, he would no doubt have been laughed at as dreaming of a new kind of cobwebs.

So again, if before the discovery of the magnet, any one had said that a certain instrument had been invented by means of which the quarters and points of the heavens could be taken and distinguished with exactness; men would have been carried by their imagination to a variety of conjectures concerning the more exquisite construction of astronomical instruments; but that anything could be discovered agreeing so well in its movements with the heavenly bodies, and yet not a heavenly body itself, but simply a substance of metal or stone, would have been judged altogether incredible. Yet these things and others like them lay for so many ages of the world concealed from men, nor was it by philosophy or the rational arts that they were found out at last, but by accident and occasion; being indeed, as I said, altogether different in kind and as remote as possible from anything that was known before; so that no preconceived notion could possibly have led to the discovery of them.

There is therefore much ground for hoping that there are still laid up in the womb of nature many secrets of excellent use, having no affinity or parallelism with any thing that is now known, but lying entirely out of the beat of the imagination, which have not yet been found out. They too no doubt will some time or other, in the course and revolution of many ages, come to light of themselves, just as the others did; only by the method of which we are now treating they can be speedily and suddenly and simultaneously presented and anticipated.

CX.

But we have also discoveries to show of another kind, which prove that noble inventions may be lying at our very feet, and yet mankind may step over without seeing them. For however the discovery of gunpowder, of silk, of the magnet, of sugar, of paper, or the like, may seem to depend on certain properties of things themselves and nature, there is at any rate nothing in the art of printing which is not plain and obvious. Nevertheless for want of observing that although it is more difficult to arrange types of letters than to write letters by the motion of the hand, there is yet this difference between the two, that types once arranged serve for innumerable impressions, but letters written with the hand for a single copy only; or perhaps again for want of observing that ink can be so thickened as to colour without running (particularly when the letters face upwards and the impression is made from above) —for want, I say, of observing these things, men went for so many ages without this most beautiful discovery, which is of so much service in the propagation of knowledge.

But such is the infelicity and unhappy disposition of the human mind in this course of invention, that it first distrusts and then despises itself: first will not believe that any such thing can be found out; and when it is found out, cannot understand how the world should have missed it so long. And this very thing may be justly taken as an argument of hope; namely, that there is a great mass of inventions still remaining, which not only by means of operations that are yet to be discovered, but also through the transferring, comparing, and applying of those already known, by the help of that Learned Experience of which I spoke, may be deduced and brought to light.

CXI.

There is another ground of hope that must not be omitted. Let men but think over their infinite expenditure of understanding, time, and means on matters and pursuits of far less use and value; whereof if but a small part were directed to sound and solid studies, there is no difficulty that might not be overcome. This I thought good to add, because I plainly confess that a collection of history natural and experimental, such as I conceive it and as it ought to be, is a great, I may say a royal work, and of much labour and expense.

CXII.

Meantime, let no man be alarmed at the multitude of particulars, but let this rather encourage him to hope. For the particular phenomena of art and nature are but a handful to the inventions of the wit, when disjoined and separated from the evidence of things. Moreover this road has an issue in the open ground and not far off; the other has no issue at all, but endless entanglement. For men hitherto have made but short stay with experience, but passing her lightly by, have wasted an infinity of time on meditations and glosses of the wit. But if some one were by that could answer our questions and tell us in each case what the fact in nature is, the discovery of all causes and sciences would be but the work of a few years.

CXIII.

Moreover I think that men may take some hope from my own example. And this I say not by way of boasting, but because it is useful to say it. If there be any that despond, let them look at me, that being of all men of my time the most busied in affairs of state, and a man of health not very strong (whereby much time is lost), and in this course altogether a pioneer, following in no man's track, nor sharing these counsels with any one, have nevertheless by resolutely entering on the true road, and submitting my mind to Things, advanced these matters, as I suppose, some little way. And then let them consider what may be expected (after the way has been thus indicated) from men abounding in leisure, and from association of labours, and from successions of ages: the rather because it is not a way over which only one man can pass at a time (as is the case with that of reasoning), but one in which the labours and industries of men (especially as regards the collecting of experience) may with the best effect be first distributed and then combined. For then only will men begin to know their strength, when instead of great numbers doing all the same things, one shall take charge of one thing and another of another.

CXIV.

Lastly, even if the breath of hope which blows on us from that New Continent were fainter than it is and harder to perceive; yet the trial (if we would not bear a spirit altogether abject) must by all means be made. For there is no comparison between that which we may lose by not trying and by not succeeding; since by not trying we throw away the chance of an immense good; by not succeeding we only incur the loss of a little human labour. But as it is, it appears to me from what has been said, and also from what has been left unsaid, that there is hope enough and to spare, not only to make a bold man try, but also to make a sober-minded and wise man believe.

CXV.

Concerning the grounds then for putting away despair, which has been one of the most powerful causes of delay and hindrance to the progress of knowledge, I have now spoken. And this also concludes what I had to say touching the *signs* and *causes* of the errors, sluggishness, and ignorance which have prevailed; especially since the more subtle causes, which do not fall under popular judgment and observation, must be referred to what has been said on the Idols of the human mind.

And here likewise should close that part of my Instauration, which is devoted to pulling down: which part is performed by three refutations; first, by the refutation of the *natural human reason,* left to itself; secondly, by the refutation of the *demonstrations;* and thirdly, by the refutation of the *theories,* or the received systems of philosophy and doctrine. And the refutation of these has been such, as alone it could be: that is to say, by signs and the evidence of causes; since no other kind of confutation was open to me, differing as I do from others both on first principles and on rules of demonstration.

It is time therefore to proceed to the art itself and rule of interpreting nature; still however there remains something to be premised. For whereas in this first book of aphorisms I proposed to prepare men's minds as well for understanding as for receiving what is to follow; now that I have purged and swept and levelled the floor of the mind, it remains that I place the mind in a good position and as it were in a favourable aspect towards what I have to lay before it. For in a new matter, it is not only the strong preoccupation of some old opinion that tends to create a prejudice, but also a false preconception or prefiguration of the new thing which is presented. I will endeavour therefore to impart sound and true opinions as to the things I propose, although they are to serve only for the time and by way of interest (so to speak), till the thing itself, which is the principal, be fully known.

CXVI.

First, then, I must request men not to suppose that after the fashion of ancient Greeks, and of certain moderns, as Telesius, Patricius, Severinus, I wish to found a new sect in philosophy. For this is not what I am about; nor do I think that it matters much to the fortunes of men what abstract notions one may entertain concerning nature and the principles of things; and no doubt many old theories of this kind can be revived and many new ones introduced; just as many theories of the heavens may be supposed, which agree well enough with the phenomena and yet differ with each other.

But for my part I do not trouble myself with any such speculative and withal unprofitable matters. My purpose, on the contrary, is to try whether I cannot in very fact lay more firmly the foundations, and extend more widely the limits, of the power and greatness of man. And although on some special subjects and in an incomplete form I am in possession of results which I take to be far more true and more certain and withal more fruitful than those now received, (and these I have collected into the fifth part of my Instauration,) yet I have no entire or universal theory to propound. For it does not seem that the time is come for such an attempt. Neither can I hope to live to complete the sixth part of the Instauration (which is destined for the philosophy discovered by the legitimate interpretation of nature), but hold it enough if in the intermediate business I bear myself soberly and profitably, sowing in the meantime for future ages the seeds of a purer truth, and performing my part towards the commencement of the great undertaking.

CXVII.

And as I do not seek to found a school, so neither do I hold out offers or promises of particular works. It may be thought indeed, that I who make such frequent mention of works and refer everything to that end, should produce some myself by way of earnest. But my course and method, as I have often clearly stated and would wish to state again, is this,—not to extract works from works or experiments from experiments (as an empiric), but from works and experiments to extract causes and axioms, and again from those causes and axioms new works and experiments, as a legitimate interpreter of nature. And although in my tables of discovery (which compose the fourth part of the Instauration), and also in the examples of particulars (which I have adduced in the second part), and moreover in my observations on the history (which I have drawn out in the third part), any reader of even moderate sagacity and intelligence will everywhere observe indications and outlines of many noble works; still I candidly confess that the natural history which I now have, whether collected from books or from my own investigations, is neither sufficiently copious nor verified with sufficient accuracy to serve the purposes of legitimate interpretation.

Accordingly, if there be any one more apt and better prepared for mechanical pursuits, and sagacious in hunting out works by the mere dealing with experiment, let him by all means use his industry to gather from my history and tables many things by the way, and apply them to the production of works, which may serve as interest until the principal be forthcoming. But for myself, aiming as I do at greater things, I condemn all unseasonable and premature tarrying over such things as these; being (as I often say) like Atalanta's balls. For I do not run off like a child after golden apples, but stake all on the victory of art over nature in the race; nor do I make haste to mow down the moss or the corn in blade, but wait for the harvest in its due season.

CXVIII.

There will be found no doubt, when my history and tables of discovery are read, some things in the experiments themselves that are not quite certain, or perhaps that are quite false; which may make a man think that the foundations and principles upon which my discoveries rest are false and doubtful. But this is of no consequence; for such things must needs happen at first. It is only like the occurrence in a written or printed page of a letter or two mistaken or misplaced; which does not much hinder the reader, because such errors are easily corrected by the sense. So likewise may there occur in my natural history many experiments which are mistaken and falsely set down, and yet they will presently by the discovery of causes and axioms be easily expunged and rejected. It is nevertheless true that if the mistakes in natural history and experiments are important, frequent, and continual, they cannot possibly be corrected or amended by any felicity of wit or art. And therefore, if in my natural history, which has been collected and tested with so much diligence, severity, and I may say religious care, there still lurk at intervals certain falsities or errors in the particulars,—what is to be said of common natural history, which in comparison with mine is so negligent and inexact? and what of the philosophy and sciences built on such a sand (or rather quicksand)? Let no man therefore trouble himself for this.

CXIX.

There will be met with also in my history and experiments many things which are trivial and commonly known; many which are mean and low; many, lastly, which are too subtle and merely speculative, and that seem to be of no use; which kind of things may possibly avert and alienate men's interest.

And first for those things which seem common; let men bear in mind that hitherto they have been accustomed to do no more than refer and adapt the causes of things which rarely happen to such as happen frequently; while of those which happen frequently they never ask the cause, but take them as they are for granted. And therefore they do not investigate the causes of weight, of the rotation of heavenly bodies, of heat, cold, light, hardness, softness, rarity, density, liquidity, solidity, animation, inanimation, similarity, dissimilarity, organisation, and the like; but admitting these as self-evident and obvious, they dispute and decide on other things of less frequent and familiar occurrence.

But I, who am well aware that no judgment can be passed on uncommon or remarkable things, much less anything new brought to light, unless the causes of common things, and the causes of those causes, be first duly examined and found out, am of necessity compelled to admit the commonest things into my history. Nay, in my judgment philosophy has been hindered by nothing more than this,—that things of familiar and frequent occurrence do not arrest and detain the thoughts of men, but are received in passing without any inquiry into their causes; insomuch that information concerning things which are not known is not oftener wanted than attention concerning things which are.

CXX.

And for things that are mean or even filthy,—things which (as Pliny says) must be introduced with an apology,—such things, no less than the most splendid and costly, must be admitted into natural history. Nor is natural history polluted thereby; for the sun enters the sewer no less than the palace, yet takes no pollution. And for myself, I am not raising a capitol or pyramid to the pride of man, but laying a foundation in the human understanding for a holy temple after the model of the world. That model therefore I follow. For whatever deserves to exist deserves also to be known, for knowledge is the image of existence; and things mean and splendid exist alike. Moreover as from certain putrid substances—musk, for instance, and civet—the sweetest odours are sometimes generated, so too from mean and sordid instances there sometimes emanates excellent light and information. But enough and more than enough of this; such fastidiousness being merely childish and effeminate.

CXXI.

But there is another objection which must be more carefully looked to: namely, that there are many things in this History which to common apprehension, or indeed to any understanding accustomed to the present system, will seem to be curiously and unprofitably subtle. Upon this point therefore above all I must say again what I have said already,—that at first and for a time I am seeking for experiments of light, not for experiments of fruit; following therein, as I have often said, the example of the divine creation; which on the first day produced light only, and assigned to it alone one entire day, nor mixed up with it on that day any material work.

To suppose therefore that things like these are of no use is the same as to suppose that light is of no use, because it is not a thing solid or material. And the truth is that the knowledge of simple natures well examined and defined is as light; it gives entrance to all the secrets of nature's workshop, and virtually includes and draws after it whole bands and troops of works, and opens to us the sources of the noblest axioms; and yet in itself it is of no great use. So also the letters of the alphabet in themselves and apart have no use or meaning, yet they are the subject-matter for the composition and apparatus of all discourse. So again the seeds of things are of much latent virtue, and yet of no use except in their development. And the scattered rays of light itself, until they are made to converge, can impart none of their benefit.

But if objection be taken to speculative subtleties, what is to be said of the schoolmen, who have indulged in subtleties to such excess? in subtleties too that were spent on words, or at any rate on popular notions (which is much the same thing), not on facts or nature; and such as were useless not only in their origin but also in their consequences; and not like those I speak of, useless indeed for the present, but promising infinite utility hereafter. But let men be assured of this, that all subtlety of disputation and discourse, if not applied till after axioms are discovered, is out of season and preposterous; and that the true and proper or at any rate the chief time for subtlety is in weighing experience and in founding axioms thereon; for that other subtlety, though it grasps and snatches at nature, yet can never take hold of her. Certainly what is said of opportunity or fortune is most true of nature; she has a lock in front, but is bald behind.

Lastly, concerning the disdain to receive into natural history things either common, or mean, or over-subtle and in their original condition useless, the answer of the poor woman to the haughty prince, who had rejected her petition as an unworthy thing and beneath his dignity, may be taken for an oracle,—"Then leave off being king." For most certain it is that he who will not attend to things like these, as being too paltry and minute, can neither win the kingdom of nature nor govern it.

CXXII.

It may be thought also a strange and a harsh thing that we should at once and with one blow set aside all sciences and all authors; and that too without calling in any of the ancients to our aid and support, but relying on our own strength.

And I know that if I had chosen to deal less sincerely, I might easily have found authority for my suggestions by referring them either to the old times before the Greeks (when natural science was perhaps more flourishing, though it made less noise, not having yet passed into the pipes and trumpets of the Greeks), or even, in part at least, to some of the Greeks themselves; and so gained for them both support and honour; as men of no family devise for themselves by the good help of genealogies the nobility of a descent from some ancient stock. But for my part, relying on the evidence and truth of things, I reject all forms of fiction and imposture; nor do I think that it matters any more to the business in hand, whether the discoveries that shall now be made were long ago known to the ancients, and have their settings and their risings according to the vicissitude of things and course of ages, than it matters to mankind whether the new world be that island of Atlantis with which the ancients were acquainted, or now discovered for the first time. For new discoveries must be sought from the light of nature, not fetched back out of the darkness of antiquity.

And as for the universality of the censure, certainly if the matter be truly considered, such a censure is not only more probable but more modest too, than a partial one would be. For if the errors had not been rooted in primary notions, there must have been some true discoveries to correct the false. But the errors being fundamental, and not so much of false judgment as of inattention and oversight, it is no wonder that men have not obtained what they have not tried for, nor reached a mark which they never set up, nor finished a course which they never entered on or kept.

And as for the presumption implied in it; certainly if a man undertakes by steadiness of hand and power of eye to describe a straighter line or more perfect circle than any one else, he challenges a comparison of abilities; but if he only says that he with the help of a rule or a pair of compasses can draw a straighter line or a more perfect circle than any one else can by eye and hand alone, he makes no great boast. And this remark, be it observed, applies not merely to this first and inceptive attempt of mine, but to all that shall take the work in hand hereafter. For my way of discovering sciences goes far to level men's wits, and leaves but little to individual excellence; because it performs everything by the surest rules and demonstrations. And therefore I attribute my part in all this, as I have often said, rather to good luck than to ability, and account it a birth of time rather than of wit. For certainly chance has something to do with men's thoughts, as well as with their works and deeds.

CXXIII.

I may say then of myself that which one said in jest (since it marks the distinction so truly), "It cannot be that we should think alike, when one drinks water and the other drinks wine." Now other men, as well in ancient as in modern times, have in the matter of sciences drunk a crude liquor like water, either flowing spontaneously from the understanding, or drawn up by logic, as by wheels from a well. Whereas I pledge mankind in liquor strained from countless grapes, from grapes ripe and fully seasoned, collected in clusters, and gathered, and then squeezed in the press, and finally purified and clarified in the vat. And therefore it is no wonder if they and I do not think alike.

CXXIV.

Again, it will be thought, no doubt, that the goal and mark of knowledge which I myself set up (the very point which I object to in others) is not the true or the best; for that the contemplation of truth is a thing worthier and loftier than all utility and magnitude of works; and that this long and anxious dwelling with experience and matter and the fluctuations of individual things, drags down the mind to earth, or rather sinks it to a very Tartarus of turmoil and confusion; removing and withdrawing it from the serene tranquillity of abstract wisdom, a condition far more heavenly. Now to this I readily assent; and indeed this which they point at as so much to be preferred, is the very thing of all others which I am about. For I am building in the human understanding a true model of the world, such as it is in fact, not such as a man's own reason would have it to be; a thing which cannot be done without a very diligent dissection and anatomy of the world. But I say that those foolish and apish images of worlds which the fancies of men have created in philosophical systems, must be utterly scattered to the winds. Be it known then how vast a difference there is (as I said above) between the Idols of the human mind and the Ideas of the divine. The former are nothing more than arbitrary abstractions; the latter are the creator's own stamp upon creation, impressed and defined in matter by true and exquisite lines. Truth therefore and utility are here the very same things: and works themselves are of greater value as pledges of truth than as contributing to the comforts of life.

CXXV.

It may be thought again that I am but doing what has been done before; that the ancients themselves took the same course which I am now taking; and that it is likely therefore that I too, after all this stir and striving, shall come at last to some one of those systems which prevailed in ancient times. For the ancients too, it will be said, provided at the outset of their speculations a great store and abundance of examples and particulars, digested the same into notebooks under heads and titles, from them completed their systems and arts, and afterwards, when they understood the matter, published them to the world,—adding a few examples here and there for proof and illustration; but thought it superfluous and inconvenient to publish their notes and minutes and digests of particulars; and therefore did as builders do,—after the house was built they removed the scaffolding and ladders out of sight. And so no doubt they did. But this objection (or scruple rather) will be easily answered by any one who has not quite forgotten what I have said above. For the form of inquiry and discovery that was in use among the ancients is by themselves professed, and appears on the very face of their writings. And that form was simply this. From a few examples and particulars (with the addition of common notions and perhaps of some portion of the received opinions which have been most popular) they flew at once to the most general conclusions, or first principles of science: taking the truth of these as fixed and immoveable, they proceeded by means of intermediate propositions to educe and prove from them the inferior conclusions; and out of these they framed the art. After that, if any new particulars and examples repugnant to their dogmas were mooted and adduced, either they subtly moulded them into their system by distinctions or explanations of their rules, or else coarsely got rid of them by exceptions; while to such particulars as were not repugnant they laboured to assign causes in conformity with those their principles. But this was not the natural history and experience that was wanted; far from it; and besides, that flying off to the highest generalities ruined all.

CXXVI.

It will also be thought that by forbidding men to pronounce and to set down principles as established until they have duly arrived through the intermediate steps at the highest generalities, I maintain a sort of suspension of the judgment, and bring it to what the Greeks call *Acatalepsia,*—a denial of the capacity of the mind to comprehend truth. But in reality that which I meditate and propound is not *Acatalepsia,* but *Eucatalepsia;* not denial of the capacity to understand, but provision for understanding truly; for I do not take away authority from the senses, but supply them with helps; I do not slight the understanding, but govern it. And better surely it is that we should know all we need to know, and yet think our knowledge imperfect, than that we should think our knowledge perfect, and yet not know anything we need to know.

CXXVII.

It may also be asked (in the way of doubt rather than objection) whether I speak of natural philosophy only, or whether I mean that the other sciences, logic, ethics, and politics, should be carried on by this method. Now I certainly mean what I have said to be understood of them all; and as the common logic, which governs by the syllogism, extends not only to natural but to all sciences; so does mine also, which proceeds by induction, embrace everything. For I form a history and tables of discovery for anger, fear, shame, and the like; for matters political; and again for the mental operations of memory, composition and division, judgment and the rest; not less than for heat and cold, or light, or vegetation, or the like. But nevertheless since my method of interpretation, after the history has been prepared and duly arranged, regards not the working and discourse of the mind only (as the common logic does) but the nature of things also, I supply the mind with such rules and guidance that it may in every case apply itself aptly to the nature of things. And therefore I deliver many and diverse precepts in the doctrine of Interpretation, which in some measure modify the method of invention according to the quality and condition of the subject of the inquiry.

CXXVIII.

On one point not even a doubt ought to be entertained; namely, whether I desire to pull down and destroy the philosophy and arts and sciences which are at present in use. So far from that, I am most glad to see them used, cultivated, and honoured. There is no reason why the arts which are now in fashion should not continue to supply matter for disputation and ornaments for discourse, to be employed for the convenience of professors and men of business; to be in short like current coin, which passes among men by consent. Nay I frankly declare that what I am introducing will be but little fitted for such purposes as these, since it cannot be brought down to common apprehension, save by effects and works only. But how sincere I am in my professions of affection and good will towards the received sciences, my published writings, especially the books on the Advancement of Learning, sufficiently show; and therefore I will not attempt to prove it further by words. Meanwhile I give constant and distinct warning that by the methods now in use neither can any great progress be made in the doctrines and contemplative part of sciences, nor can they be carried out to any magnitude of works.

CXXIX.

It remains for me to say a few words touching the excellency of the end in view. Had they been uttered earlier, they might have seemed like idle wishes; but now that hopes have been raised and unfair prejudices removed, they may perhaps have greater weight. Also if I had finished all myself, and had no occasion to call in others to help and take part in the work, I should even now have abstained from such language, lest it might be taken as a proclamation of my own deserts. But since I want to quicken the industry and rouse and kindle the zeal of others, it is fitting that I put men in mind of some things.

In the first place then, the introduction of famous discoveries appears to hold by far the first place among human actions; and this was the judgment of the former ages. For to the authors of inventions they awarded divine honours; while to those who did good service in the state (such as founders of cities and empires, legislators, saviours of their country from long endured evils, quellers of tyrannies, and the like) they decreed no higher honours than heroic. And certainly if a man rightly compare the two, he will find that this judgment of antiquity was just. For the benefits of discoveries may extend to the whole race of man, civil benefits only to particular places; the latter last not beyond a few ages, the former through all time. Moreover the reformation of a state in civil matters is seldom brought in without violence and confusion; but discoveries carry blessings with them, and confer benefits without causing harm or sorrow to any.

Again, discoveries are as it were new creations, and imitations of God's works; as well sang the poet:—

> "To man's frail race great Athens long ago
> First gave the seed whence waving harvests grow,
> And *re-created* all our life below."

And it appears worthy of remark in Solomon, that though mighty in empire and in gold; in the magnificence of his works, his court, his household, and his fleet; in the lustre of his name and the worship of mankind; yet he took none of these to glory in, but pronounced that "The glory of God is to conceal a thing; the glory of the king to search it out."

Again, let a man only consider what a difference there is between the life of men in the most civilised province of Europe, and in the wildest and most barbarous districts of New India; he will feel it be great enough to justify the saying that "man is a god to man," not only in regard of aid and benefit, but also by a comparison of condition. And this difference comes not from soil, not from climate, not from race, but from the arts.

Again, it is well to observe the force and virtue and consequences of discoveries; and these are to be seen nowhere more conspicuously than in those three which were unknown to the ancients, and of which the origin, though recent, is obscure and inglorious; namely, printing, gunpowder, and the magnet. For these three have changed the whole face and state of things throughout the world; the first in literature, the second in warfare, the third in navigation; whence have followed innumerable changes; insomuch that no empire, no sect, no star seems to have exerted greater power and influence in human affairs than these mechanical discoveries.

Further, it will not be amiss to distinguish the three kinds and as it were grades of ambition in mankind. The first is of those who desire to extend their own power in their native country; which kind is vulgar and degenerate. The second is of those who labour to extend the power of their country and its dominion among men. This certainly has more dignity, though not less covetousness. But if a man endeavour to establish and extend the power and dominion of the human race itself over the universe, his ambition (if ambition it can be called) is without doubt both a more wholesome thing and a more noble than the other two. Now the empire of man over things depends wholly on the arts and sciences. For we cannot command nature except by obeying her.

Again, if men have thought so much of some one particular discovery as to regard him as more than man who has been able by some benefit to make the whole human race his debtor, how much higher a thing to discover that by means of which all things else shall be discovered with ease! And yet (to speak the whole truth), as the uses of light are infinite, in enabling us to walk, to ply our arts, to read, to recognise one another; and nevertheless the very beholding of the light is itself a more excellent and a fairer thing than all the uses of it;—so assuredly the very contemplation of things, as they are, without superstition or imposture, error or confusion, is in itself more worthy than all the fruit of inventions.

Lastly, if the debasement of arts and sciences to purposes of wickedness, luxury, and the like, be made a ground of objection, let no one be moved thereby. For the same may be said of all earthly goods; of wit, courage, strength, beauty, wealth, light itself, and the rest. Only let the human race recover the right over nature which belongs to it by divine bequest, and let power be given it; the exercise thereof will be governed by sound reason and true religion.

CXXX.

And now it is time for me to propound the art itself of interpreting nature; in which, although I conceive that I have given true and most useful precepts, yet I do not say either that it is absolutely necessary (as if nothing could be done without it) or that it is perfect. For I am of opinion that if men had ready at hand a just history of nature and experience, and laboured diligently thereon; and if they could bind themselves to two rules,—the first, to lay aside received opinions and notions; and the second, to refrain the mind for a time from the highest generalisations, and those next to them,—they would be able by the native and genuine force of the mind, without any other art, to fall into my form of interpretation. For interpretation is the true and natural work of the mind when freed from impediments. It is true however that by my precepts everything will be in more readiness, and much more sure.

Nor again do I mean to say that no improvement can be made upon these. On the contrary, I that regard the mind not only in its own faculties, but in its connection with things, must needs hold that the art of discovery may advance as discoveries advance.

THE SECOND BOOK OF APHORISMS

THE SECOND BOOK OF

APHORISMS

CONCERNING

THE INTERPRETATION OF NATURE

AND

THE KINGDOM OF MAN.

Aphorism

I.

On a given body to generate and superinduce a new nature or new natures, is the work and aim of Human Power. Of a given nature to discover the form, or true specific difference, or nature-engendering nature, or source of emanation (for these are the terms which come nearest to a description of the thing), is the work and aim of Human Knowledge. Subordinate to these primary works are two others that are secondary and of inferior mark; to the former, the transformation of concrete bodies, so far as this is possible; to the latter, the discovery, in every case of generation and motion, of the *latent process* carried on from the manifest efficient and the manifest material to the form which is engendered; and in like manner the discovery of the *latent configuration* of bodies at rest and not in motion.

II.

In what an ill condition human knowledge is at the present time, is apparent even from the commonly received maxims. It is a correct position that "true knowledge is knowledge by causes." And causes again are not improperly distributed into four kinds; the material, the formal, the efficient, and the final. But of these the final cause rather corrupts than advances the sciences, except such as have to do with human action. The discovery of the formal is despaired of. The efficient and the material (as they are investigated and received, that is, as remote causes, without reference to the latent process leading to the form) are but slight and superficial, and contribute little, if anything, to true and active science. Nor have I forgotten that in a former passage I noted and corrected as an error of the human mind the opinion that Forms give existence. For though in nature nothing really exists beside individual bodies, performing pure individual acts according to a fixed law, yet in philosophy this very law, and the investigation, discovery, and explanation of it, is the foundation as well of knowledge as of operation. And it is this law, with its clauses, that I mean when I speak of *Forms;* a name which I the rather adopt because it has grown into use and become familiar.

III.

If a man be acquainted with the cause of any nature (as whiteness or heat) in certain subjects only, his knowledge is imperfect; and if he be able to superinduce an effect on certain substances only (of those susceptible of such effect), his power is in like manner imperfect. Now if a man's knowledge be confined to the efficient and material causes (which are unstable causes, and merely vehicles, or causes which convey the form in certain cases) he may arrive at new discoveries in reference to substances in some degree similar to one another, and selected beforehand; but he does not touch the deeper boundaries of things. But whosoever is acquainted with Forms, embraces the unity of nature in substances the most unlike; and is able therefore to detect and bring to light things never yet done, and such as neither the vicissitudes of nature, nor industry in experimenting, nor accident itself, would ever have brought into act, and which would never have occurred to the thought of man. From the discovery of Forms therefore results truth in speculation and freedom in operation.

IV.

Although the roads to human power and to human knowledge lie close together, and are nearly the same, nevertheless on account of the pernicious and inveterate habit of dwelling on abstractions, it is safer to begin and raise the sciences from those foundations which have relation to practice, and to let the active part itself be as the seal which prints and determines the contemplative counterpart. We must therefore consider, if a man wanted to generate and superinduce any nature upon a given body, what kind of rule or direction or guidance he would most wish for, and express the same in the simplest and least abstruse language. For instance, if a man wishes to superinduce upon silver the yellow colour of gold or an increase of weight (observing the laws of matter), or transparency on an opaque stone, or tenacity on glass, or vegetation on some substance that is not vegetable,—we must consider, I say, what kind of rule or guidance he would most desire. And in the first place, he will undoubtedly wish to be directed to something which will not deceive him in the result, nor fail him in the trial. Secondly, he will wish for such a rule as shall not tie him down to certain means and particular modes of operation. For perhaps he may not have those means, nor be able conveniently to procure them. And if there be other means and other methods for producing the required nature (beside the one prescribed) these may perhaps be within his reach; and yet he shall be excluded by the narrowness of the rule, and get no good from them. Thirdly, he will desire something to be shown him, which is not as difficult as the thing proposed to be done, but comes nearer to practice.

For a true and perfect rule of operation then the direction will be *that it be certain, free, and disposing or leading to action.* And this is the same thing with the discovery of the true Form. For the Form of a nature is such, that given the Form the nature infallibly follows. Therefore it is always present when the nature is present, and universally implies it, and is constantly inherent in it. Again, the Form is such, that if it be taken away the nature infallibly vanishes. Therefore it is always absent when the nature is absent, and implies its absence, and inheres in nothing else. Lastly, the true Form is such that it deduces the given nature from some source of being which is inherent in more natures, and which is better known in the natural order of things than the Form itself. For a true and perfect axiom of knowledge then the direction and precept will be, *that another nature be discovered which is convertible with the given nature, and yet is a limitation of a more general nature, as of a true and real genus.*

Now these two directions, the one active the other contemplative, are one and the same thing; and what in operation is most useful, that in knowledge is most true.

V.

The rule or axiom for the transformation of bodies is of two kinds. The first regards a body as a troop or collection of simple natures. In gold, for example, the following properties meet. It is yellow in colour; heavy up to a certain weight; malleable or ductile to a certain degree of extension; it is not volatile, and loses none of its substance by the action of fire; it turns into a liquid with a certain degree of fluidity; it is separated and dissolved by particular means; and so on for the other natures which meet in gold. This kind of axiom, therefore, deduces the thing from the forms of simple natures. For he who knows the forms of yellow, weight, ductility, fixity, fluidity, solution, and so on, and the methods for superinducing them, and their gradations and modes, will make it his care to have them joined together in some body, whence may follow the transformation of that body into gold. And this kind of operation pertains to the first kind of action. For the principle of generating some one simple nature is the same as that of generating many, only that a man is more fettered and tied down in operation, if more are required, by reason of the difficulty of combining into one so many natures; which do not readily meet, except in the beaten and ordinary paths of nature. It must be said however that this mode of operation (which looks to simple natures though in a compound body) proceeds from what in nature is constant and eternal and universal, and opens broad roads to human power, such as (in the present state of things) human thought can scarcely comprehend or anticipate.

The second kind of axiom, which is concerned with the discovery of the *latent process,* proceeds not by simple natures, but by compound bodies, as they are found in nature in its ordinary course. As, for instance, when inquiry is made, from what beginnings, and by what method and by what process, gold or any other metal or stone is generated, from its first menstrua and rudiments up to the perfect mineral; or in like manner by what process herbs are generated, from the first concretion of juices in the ground or from seeds up to the formed plant, with all the successive motions and diverse and continued efforts of nature. So also in the inquiry concerning the process of development in the generation of animals, from coition to birth; and in like manner of other bodies.

It is not however only to the generations of bodies that this investigation extends, but also to other motions and operations of nature. As, for instance, when inquiry is made concerning the whole course and continued action of nutrition, from the first reception of the food to its complete assimilation; or again, concerning the voluntary motion of animals, from the first impression on the imagination and the continued efforts of the spirit up to the bendings and movements of the limbs; or concerning the motion of the tongue and lips and other instruments, and the changes through which it passes till it comes to the utterance of articulate sounds. For these inquiries also relate to natures concrete or combined into one structure, and have regard to what may be called particular and special habits of nature, not to her fundamental and universal laws which constitute Forms. And yet it must be confessed that this plan appears to be readier and to lie nearer at hand and to give more ground for hope than the primary one.

In like manner the operative which answers to this speculative part, starting from the ordinary incidents of nature, extends its operation to things immediately adjoining, or at least not far removed. But as for any profound and radical operations on nature, they depend entirely on the primary axioms. And in those things too where man has no means of operating, but only of knowing, as in the heavenly bodies (for these he cannot operate upon or change or transform), the investigation of the fact itself or truth of the thing, no less than the knowledge of the causes and consents, must come from those primary and catholic axioms concerning simple natures; such as the nature of spontaneous rotation, of attraction or magnetism, and of many others which are of a more general form than the heavenly bodies themselves. For let no one hope to decide the question whether it is the earth or heaven that really revolves in the diurnal motion, until he has first comprehended the nature of spontaneous rotation.

VI.

But this Latent Process, of which I speak, is quite another thing than men, preoccupied as their minds now are, will easily conceive. For what I understand by it is not certain measures or signs or successive steps of process in bodies, which can be seen; but a process perfectly continuous, which for the most part escapes the sense.

For instance; in all generation and transformation of bodies, we must inquire what is lost and escapes; what remains, what is added; what is expanded, what contracted; what is united, what separated; what is continued, what cut off; what propels, what hinders; what predominates, what yields; and a variety of other particulars.

Again, not only in the generation or transformation of bodies are these points to be ascertained, but also in all other alterations and motions it should in like manner be inquired what goes before, what comes after; what is quicker, what more tardy; what produces, what governs motion; and like points; all which nevertheless in the present state of the sciences (the texture of which is as rude as possible and good for nothing) are unknown and unhandled. For seeing that every natural action depends on things infinitely small, or at least too small to strike the sense, no one can hope to govern or change nature until he has duly comprehended and observed them.

VII.

In like manner the investigation and discovery of the *latent configuration* in bodies is a new thing, no less than the discovery of the Latent Process and of the Form. For as yet we are but lingering in the outer courts of nature, nor are we preparing ourselves a way into her inner chambers. Yet no one can endow a given body with a new nature, or successfully and aptly transmute it into a new body, unless he has attained a competent knowledge of the body so to be altered or transformed. Otherwise he will run into methods which, if not useless, are at any rate difficult and perverse and unsuitable to the nature of the body on which he is operating. It is clear therefore that to this also a way must be opened and laid out.

And it is true that upon the anatomy of organised bodies (as of man and animals) some pains have been well bestowed and with good effect; and a subtle thing it seems to be, and a good scrutiny of nature. Yet this kind of anatomy is subject to sight and sense, and has place only in organised bodies. And besides it is a thing obvious and easy, when compared with the true anatomy of the Latent Configuration in bodies which are thought to be of uniform structure; especially in things that have a specific character and their parts, as iron, stone; and again in parts of uniform structure in plants and animals, as the root, the leaf, the flower, flesh, blood, and bones. But even in this kind, human industry has not been altogether wanting; for this is the very thing aimed at in the separation of bodies of uniform structure by means of distillations and other modes of analysis; that the complex structure of the compound may be made apparent by bringing together its several homogeneous parts. And this is of use too, and conduces to the object we are seeking; although too often fallacious in its results, because many natures which are in fact newly brought out and superinduced by fire and heat and other modes of solution are taken to be the effect of separation merely, and to have subsisted in the compound before. And after all, this is but a small part of the work of discovering the true Configuration in the compound body; which Configuration is a thing far more subtle and exact, and such as the operation of fire rather confounds than brings out and makes distinct.

Therefore a separation and solution of bodies must be effected, not by fire indeed, but by reasoning and true induction, with experiments to aid; and by a comparison with other bodies, and a reduction to simple natures and their Forms, which meet and mix in the compound. In a word we must pass from Vulcan to Minerva, if we intend to bring to light the true textures and configurations of bodies; on which all the occult and, as they are called, specific properties and virtues in things depend; and from which too the rule of every powerful alteration and transformation is derived.

For example, we must inquire what amount of spirit there is in every body, what of tangible essence; and of the spirit, whether it be copious and turgid, or meagre and scarce; whether it be fine or coarse, akin to air or to fire, brisk or sluggish, weak or strong, progressive or retrograde, interrupted or continuous, agreeing with external and surrounding objects or disagreeing, &c. In like manner we must inquire into the tangible essence (which admits of no fewer differences than the spirit), into its coats, its fibres, its kinds of texture. Moreover the disposition of the spirit throughout the corporeal frame, with its pores, passages, veins and cells, and the rudiments or first essays of the organised body, fall under the same investigation. But on these inquiries also, and I may say on all the discovery of the Latent Configuration, a true and clear light is shed by the primary axioms, which entirely dispels all darkness and subtlety.

VIII.

Nor shall we thus be led to the doctrine of atoms, which implies the hypothesis of a vacuum and that of the unchangeableness of matter (both false assumptions); we shall be led only to real particles, such as really exist. Nor again is there any reason to be alarmed at the subtlety of the investigation, as if it could not be disentangled; on the contrary, the nearer it approaches to simple natures, the easier and plainer will everything become; the business being transferred from the complicated to the simple; from the incommensurable to the commensurable; from surds to rational quantities; from the infinite and vague to the finite and certain; as in the case of the letters of the alphabet and the notes of music. And inquiries into nature have the best result, when they begin with physics and end in mathematics. Again, let no one be afraid of high numbers or minute fractions. For in dealing with numbers it is as easy to set down or conceive a thousand as one, or the thousandth part of an integer as an integer itself.

IX.

From the two kinds of axioms which have been spoken of, arises a just division of philosophy and the sciences; taking the received terms (which come nearest to express the thing) in a sense agreeable to my own views. Thus, let the investigation of Forms, which are (in the eye of reason at least, and in their essential law) eternal and immutable, constitute *Metaphysics;* and let the investigation of the Efficient Cause, and of Matter, and of the Latent Process, and the Latent Configuration (all of which have reference to the common and ordinary course of nature, not to her eternal and fundamental laws) constitute *Physics.* And to these let there be subordinate two practical divisions: to Physics, *Mechanics;* to Metaphysics, what (in a purer sense of the word) I call *Magic,* on account of the broadness of the ways it moves in, and its greater command over nature.

X.

Having thus set up the mark of knowledge, we must go on to precepts, and that in the most direct and obvious order. Now my directions for the interpretation of nature embrace two generic divisions; the one how to educe and form axioms from experience; the other how to deduce and derive new experiments from axioms. The former again is divided into three ministrations; a ministration to the sense, a ministration to the memory, and a ministration to the mind or reason.

For first of all we must prepare a *Natural and Experimental History,* sufficient and good; and this is the foundation of all; for we are not to imagine or suppose, but to discover, what nature does or may be made to do.

But natural and experimental history is so various and diffuse, that it confounds and distracts the understanding, unless it be ranged and presented to view in a suitable order. We must therefore form *Tables and Arrangements of Instances,* in such a method and order that the understanding may be able to deal with them.

And even when this is done, still the understanding, if left to itself and its own spontaneous movements, is incompetent and unfit to form axioms, unless it be directed and guarded. Therefore in the third place we must use *Induction,* true and legitimate induction, which is the very key of interpretation. But of this, which is the last, I must speak first, and then go back to the other ministrations.

XI.

The investigation of Forms proceeds thus: a nature being given, we must first of all have a muster or presentation before the understanding of all known instances which agree in the same nature, though in substances the most unlike. And such collection must be made in the manner of a history, without premature speculation, or any great amount of subtlety. For example, let the investigation be into the Form of Heat.

Instances Agreeing in the Nature of Heat.

1. The rays of the sun, especially in summer and at noon.

2. The rays of the sun reflected and condensed, as between mountains, or on walls, and most of all in burning-glasses and mirrors.

3. Fiery meteors.

4. Burning thunderbolts.

5. Eruptions of flame from the cavities of mountains.

6. All flame.

7. Ignited solids.

8. Natural warm-baths.

9. Liquids boiling or heated.

10. Hot vapours and fumes, and the air itself, which conceives the most powerful and glowing heat, if confined; as in reverbatory furnaces.

11. Certain seasons that are fine and cloudless by the constitution of the air itself, without regard to the time of year.

12. Air confined and underground in some caverns, especially in winter.

13. All villous substances, as wool, skins of animals, and down of birds, have heat.

14. All bodies, whether solid or liquid, whether dense or rare (as the air itself is), held for a time near the fire.

15. Sparks struck from flint and steel by strong percussion.

16. All bodies rubbed violently, as stone, wood, cloth, &c., insomuch that poles and axles of wheels sometimes catch fire; and the way they kindled fire in the West Indies was by attrition.

17. Green and moist vegetables confined and bruised

together, as roses packed in baskets; insomuch that hay, if damp when stacked, often catches fire.

18. Quick lime sprinkled with water.

19. Iron, when first dissolved by strong waters in glass, and that without being put near the fire. And in like manner tin, &c., but not with equal intensity.

20. Animals, especially and at all times internally; though in insects the heat is not perceptible to the touch by reason of the smallness of their size.

21. Horse-dung and like excrements of animals when fresh.

22. Strong oil of sulphur and of vitriol has the effect of heat in burning linen.

23. Oil of marjoram and similar oils have the effect of heat in burning the bones of the teeth.

24. Strong and well rectified spirit of wine has the effect of heat; insomuch that the white of an egg being put into it hardens and whitens almost as if it were boiled; and bread thrown in becomes dry and crusted like toast.

25. Aromatic and hot herbs, as *dracunculus, nasturtium vetus*, &c., although not warm to the hand (either whole or in powder), yet to the tongue and palate, being a little masticated, they feel hot and burning.

26. Strong vinegar, and all acids, on all parts of the body where there is no epidermis, as the eye, tongue, or on any part when wounded and laid bare of the skin; produce a pain but little differing from that which is created by heat.

27. Even keen and intense cold produces a kind of sensation of burning;

Nec Boreæ penetrabile frigus adurit.[1]

28. Other instances.

This table I call the *Table of Essence and Presence*.

[1] Nor burns the sharp cold of the northern blast.

XII.

Secondly, we must make a presentation to the understanding of instances in which the given nature is wanting; because the Form, as stated above, ought no less to be absent when the given nature is absent, than present when it is present. But to note all these would be endless.

The negatives should therefore be subjoined to the affirmatives, and the absence of the given nature inquired of in those subjects only that are most akin to the others in which it is present and forthcoming. This I call the *Table of Deviation, or of Absence in Proximity.*

Instances in Proximity where the Nature of Heat is Absent.

1. The rays of the moon and of stars and comets are not found to be hot to the touch; indeed the severest colds are observed to be at the full moons.

The larger fixed stars however, when passed or approached by the sun, are supposed to increase and give intensity to the heat of the sun; as is the case when the sun is in the sign Leo, and in the Dog-days.

2. The rays of the sun in what is called the middle region of the air do not give heat; for which there is commonly assigned not a bad reason, viz. that that region is neither near enough to the body of the sun from which the rays emanate, nor to the earth from which they are reflected. And this appears from the fact that on the tops of mountains, unless they are very high, there is perpetual snow. On the other hand it has been observed that on the peak of Teneriffe, and among the Andes of Peru, the very tops of the mountains are

free from snow; which lies only somewhat lower down. Moreover the air itself at the very top is found to be by no means cold, but only rare and keen; insomuch that on the Andes it pricks and hurts the eyes by its excessive keenness, and also irritates the mouth of the stomach, producing vomiting. And it was observed by the ancients that on the top of Olympus the rarity of the air was such that those who ascended it had to carry sponges with them dipped in vinegar and water, and to apply them from time to time to their mouth and nose, the air being from its rarity not sufficient to support respiration; and it was further stated that on this summit the air was so serene, and so free from rain and snow and wind, that letters traced by the finger in the ashes of the sacrifices on the altar of Jupiter remained there till the next year without being at all disturbed. And at this day travellers ascending to the top of the Peak of Teneriffe make the ascent by night and not by day; and soon after the rising of the sun are warned and urged by their guides to come down without delay, on account of the danger they run lest the animal spirits should swoon and be suffocated by the tenuity of the air.

3. The reflexion of the rays of the sun in regions near the polar circles is found to be very weak and ineffective in producing heat; insomuch that the Dutch who wintered in Nova Zembla, and expected their ship to be freed from the obstructions of the mass of ice which hemmed her in by the beginning of July, were disappointed of their expectation, and obliged to take to their boat. Thus the direct rays of the sun seem to have but little power, even on the level ground; nor have the reflex much, unless they are multiplied and combined; which is the case when the sun tends more to the perpendicular; for then the incident rays make acuter

angles, so that the lines of the rays are nearer each other; whereas on the contrary, when the sun shines very obliquely, the angles are very obtuse, and thus the lines of rays are at a greater distance from each other. Meanwhile it should be observed that there may be many operations of the sun, and those too depending on the nature of heat, which are not proportioned to our touch; so that in respect of us their action does not go so far as to produce sensible warmth, but in respect of some other bodies they have the effect of heat.

4. Try the following experiment. Take a glass fashioned in a contrary manner to a common burning-glass, and placing it between your hand and the rays of the sun, observe whether it diminishes the heat of the sun, as a burning-glass increases and strengthens it. For it is evident in the case of optical rays that according as the glass is made thicker or thinner in the middle as compared with the sides, so do the objects seen through it appear more spread or more contracted. Observe therefore whether the same is the case with heat.

5. Let the experiment be carefully tried, whether by means of the most powerful and best constructed burning glasses, the rays of the moon can be so caught and collected as to produce even the least degree of warmth. But should this degree of warmth prove too subtle and weak to be perceived and apprehended by the touch, recourse must be had to those glasses which indicate the state of the atmosphere in respect of heat and cold. Thus, let the rays of the moon fall through a burning-glass on the top of a glass of this kind, and then observe whether there ensues a sinking of the water through warmth.

6. Let a burning-glass also be tried with a heat that does not emit rays or light, as that of iron or stone heated but not ignited, boiling water, and the like; and

observe whether there ensue an increase of the heat, as in the case of the sun's rays.

7. Let a burning-glass also be tried with common flame.

8. Comets (if we are to reckon these too among meteors) are not found to exert a constant or manifest effect in increasing the heat of the season, though it is observed that they are often followed by droughts. Moreover bright beams and pillars and openings in the heavens appear more frequently in winter than in summer time, and chiefly during the intensest cold, but always accompanied by dry weather. Lightning, however, and coruscations and thunder, seldom occur in the winter, but about the time of great heat. Falling stars, as they are called, are commonly supposed to consist rather of some bright and lighted viscous substance, than to be of any strong fiery nature. But on this point let further inquiry be made.

9. There are certain coruscations which give light but do not burn. And these always come without thunder.

10. Eructations and eruptions of flame are found no less in cold than in warm countries, as in Iceland and Greenland. In cold countries too the trees are in many cases more inflammable and more pitchy and resinous than in warm; as the fir, pine, and others. The situations however and the nature of the soil in which eruptions of this kind usually occur have not been carefully enough ascertained to enable us to subjoin a Negative to this Affirmative Instance.

11. All flame is in all cases more or less warm; nor is there any Negative to be subjoined. And yet they say that the *ignis fatuus* (as it is called), which sometimes even settles on a wall, has not much heat; perhaps as much as the flame of spirit of wine, which is mild and soft. But still milder must that flame be, which accord-

ing to certain grave and trustworthy histories has been seen shining about the head and locks of boys and girls, without at all burning the hair, but softly playing round it. It is also most certain that about a horse, when sweating on the road, there is sometimes seen at night, and in clear weather, a sort of luminous appearance without any manifest heat. And it is a well known fact, and looked upon as a sort of miracle, that a few years ago a girl's stomacher, on being slightly shaken or rubbed, emitted sparks; which was caused perhaps by some alum or salts used in the dye, that stood somewhat thick and formed a crust, and were broken by the friction. It is also most certain that all sugar, whether refined or raw, provided only it be somewhat hard, sparkles when broken or scraped with a knife in the dark. In like manner sea and salt water is sometimes found to sparkle by night when struck violently by oars. And in storms too at night time, the foam of the sea when violently agitated emits sparks, and this sparkling the Spaniards call *Sea Lung.* With regard to the heat of the flame which was called by ancient sailors Castor and Pollux, and by moderns St. Elmo's Fire, no sufficient investigation thereof has been made.

12. Every body ignited so as to turn to a fiery red, even if unaccompanied by flame, is always hot; neither is there any Negative to be subjoined to this Affirmative. But that which comes nearest seems to be rotten wood, which shines by night, and yet is not found to be hot; and the putrefying scales of fish, which also shine in the dark, and yet are not warm to the touch; nor again is the body of the glow-worm, or of the fly called *Luciola,* found to be warm to the touch.

13. In what situation and kind of soil warm baths usually spring, has not been sufficiently examined; and therefore no Negative is subjoined.

14. To warm liquids I subjoin the Negative Instance of liquid itself in its natural state. For we find no tangible liquid which is warm in its own nature and remains so constantly; but the warmth is an adventitious nature, superinduced only for the time being; so that the liquids which in power and operation are hottest, as spirit of wine, chemical oil of spices, oil of vitriol and sulphur, and the like, which burn after a while, are at first cold to the touch. The water of natural warm baths on the other hand, if received into a vessel and separated from its springs, cools just like water that has been heated on a fire. But it is true that oily substances are less cold to the touch than watery, oil being less cold than water, and silk than linen. But this belongs to the Table of Degrees of Cold.

15. In like manner to hot vapour I subjoin as a Negative the nature of vapour itself, such as we find it with us. For exhalations from oily substances, though easily inflammable, are yet not found to be warm, unless newly exhaled from the warm body.

16. In like manner I subjoin as a Negative to hot air the nature of air itself. For we do not find here any air that is warm, unless it has either been confined, or compressed, or manifestly warmed by the sun, fire, or some other warm substance.

17. I here subjoin the Negative of colder weather than is suitable to the season of the year, which we find occurs during east and north winds; just as we have weather of the opposite kind with the south and west winds. So a tendency to rain, especially in winter time, accompanies warm weather; while frost accompanies cold.

18. Here I subjoin the Negative of air confined in caverns during the summer. But the subject of air in confinement should by all means be more diligently ex-

amined. For in the first place it may well be matter of doubt what is the nature of air in itself with regard to heat and cold. For air manifestly receives warmth from the influence of the heavenly bodies, and cold perhaps from the exhalations of the earth; and again in the middle region of air, as it is called, from cold vapours and snow; so that no opinion can be formed as to the nature of air from the examination of air that is at large and exposed; but a truer judgment might be made by examining it when confined. It is however necessary for the air to be confined in a vessel of such material as will not itself communicate warmth or cold to the air by its own nature, nor readily admit the influence of the outer atmosphere. Let the experiment therefore be made in an earthen jar wrapped round with many folds of leather to protect it from the outward air, and let the vessel remain tightly closed for three or four days; then open the vessel and test the degree of heat or cold by applying either the hand or a graduated glass.

19. In like manner a doubt suggests itself whether the warmth in wool, skins, feathers, and the like, proceeds from a faint degree of heat inherent in them, as being excretions from animals; or from a certain fat and oiliness, which is of a nature akin to warmth; or simply, as surmised in the preceding article, from the confinement and separation of the air. For all air that is cut off from connexion with the outer air seems to have some warmth. Try the experiment therefore with fibrous substances made of linen; not of wool, feathers, or silk, which are excretions from animals. It should also be observed that all powders (in which there is manifestly air enclosed) are less cold than the whole substances they are made from; as likewise I suppose that all froth (as that which contains air) is less cold than the liquor it comes from.

20. To this no Negative is subjoined. For there is nothing found among us either tangible or spirituous which does not contract warmth when put near fire. There is this difference however, that some substances contract warmth more quickly, as air, oil, and water; others more slowly, as stone and metal. But this belongs to the Table of Degrees.

21. To this Instance I subjoin no Negative, except that I would have it well observed that sparks are produced from flint and steel, or any other hard substance, only when certain minute particles are struck off from the substance of the stone or metal; and that the attrition of the air does not of itself ever produce sparks, as is commonly supposed. And the sparks themselves too, owing to the weight of the ignited body, tend rather downwards than upwards; and on going out become a tangible sooty substance.

22. There is no Negative, I think, to be subjoined to this Instance. For we find among us no tangible body which does not manifestly gain warmth by attrition; insomuch that the ancients fancied that the heavenly bodies had no other means or power of producing warmth than by the attrition of the air in their rapid and hurried revolution. But on this subject we must further inquire whether bodies discharged from engines, as balls from cannon, do not acquire some degrees of heat from the very percussion, so as to be found somewhat warm when they fall. Air in motion, however, rather chills than warms, as appears from wind, bellows, and blowing with the mouth contracted. But motion of this kind is not so rapid as to excite heat, and is the motion of a mass, and not of particles; so that it is no wonder if it does not generate heat.

23. On this Instance should be made more diligent inquiry. For herbs and vegetables when green and moist

seem to contain some latent heat, though so slight that it is not perceptible to the touch when they are single; but only when they are collected and shut up together, so that their spirits may not breathe out into the air, but may mutually cherish each other; whereupon there arises a palpable heat, and sometimes flame in suitable matter.

24. On this Instance too should be made more diligent inquiry. For quick lime sprinkled with water seems to contract heat, either by the concentration of heat before dispersed, as in the above-mentioned case of confined herbs, or because the igneous spirit is irritated and exasperated by the water, so as to cause a conflict and reaction. Which of these two is the real cause will more readily appear if oil be poured on instead of water; for oil will serve equally well with water to concentrate the enclosed spirit, but not to irritate it. We should also extend the experiment both by employing the ashes and rusts of different bodies, and by pouring in different liquids.

25. To this Instance is subjoined the Negative of other metals which are softer and more fusible. For gold-leaf dissolved by *aqua regia* gives no heat to the touch; no more does lead dissolved in *aqua fortis;* neither again does quicksilver (as I remember); but silver itself does, and copper too (as I remember); tin still more manifestly; and most of all iron and steel, which not only excite a strong heat in dissolution, but also a violent ebullition. It appears therefore that the heat is produced by conflict; the strong waters penetrating, digging into, and tearing asunder the parts of the substance, while the substance itself resists. But where the substances yield more easily, there is hardly any heat excited.

26. To the heat of animals no Negative is subjoined,

except that of insects (as above-mentioned), on account of their small size. For in fishes, as compared with land animals, it is rather a low degree than an absence of heat that is noted. But in vegetables and plants there is no degree of heat perceptible to the touch, either in their exudations or in their pith when freshly exposed. In animals however is found a great diversity of heat, both in their parts (there being different degrees of heat about the heart, in the brain, and on the skin) and in their accidents, as violent exercise and fevers.

27. To this Instance it is hard to subjoin a Negative. Indeed the excrements of animals when no longer fresh have manifestly a potential heat, as is seen in the enriching of soil.

28. Liquids, whether waters or oils, which possess a great and intense acridity, act like heat in tearing asunder bodies, and burning them after some time; yet to the touch they are not hot at first. But their operation is relative and according to the porosity of the body to which they are applied. For *aqua regia* dissolves gold but not silver; *aqua fortis,* on the contrary, dissolves silver, but not gold; neither dissolves glass, and so on with others.

29. Let trial be made of spirit of wine on wood; and also on butter, wax, or pitch; and observe whether by its heat it in any degree melts them. For the twenty-fourth instance exhibits a power in it that resembles heat in producing incrustation. In like manner therefore try its power in producing liquefaction. Let trial also be made with a graduated or calendar glass, hollow at the top; pour into the hollow spirit of wine well rectified, cover it up that the spirit may better retain its heat, and observe whether by its heat it makes the water sink.

30. Spices and acrid herbs strike hot on the palate, and much hotter on the stomach. Observe therefore on what other substances they produce the effects of heat. Sailors tell us that when large parcels and masses of spices are, after being long kept close, suddenly opened, those who first stir and take them out run the risk of fever and inflammation. It can also be tried whether such spices and herbs when pounded would not dry bacon and meat hung over them, as smoke does.

31. There is an acridity or pungency both in cold things, as vinegar and oil of vitriol, and in hot, as oil of marjoram and the like. Both alike therefore cause pain in animate substances, and tear asunder and consume the parts in such as are inanimate. To this Instance again there is no Negative subjoined. Moreover we find no pain in animals, save with a certain sensation of heat.

32. There are many actions common both to heat and cold, though in a very different manner. For boys find that snow after a while seems to burn their hands; and cold preserves meat from putrefaction, no less than fire; and heat contracts bodies, which cold does also. But these and similar instances may more conveniently be referred to the inquiry concerning Cold.

XIII.

Thirdly, we must make a presentation to the understanding of instances in which the nature under inquiry is found in different degrees, more or less; which must be done by making a comparison either of its increase and decrease in the same subject, or of its amount in different subjects, as compared one with another. For since the Form of a thing is the very thing itself, and the thing differs from the form no otherwise than as the apparent differs from the real, or the external from the internal, or the thing in reference to man from the thing in reference to the universe; it necessarily follows that no nature can be taken as the true form, unless it always decrease when the nature in question decreases, and in like manner always increase when the nature in question increases. This Table therefore I call the *Table of Degrees* or the *Table of Comparison.*

Table of Degrees or Comparison in Heat.

I will therefore first speak of those substances which contain no degree at all of heat perceptible to the touch, but seem to have a certain potential heat only, or disposition and preparation for hotness. After that I shall proceed to substances which are hot actually, and to the touch, and to their intensities and degrees.

1. In solid and tangible bodies we find nothing which is in its nature originally hot. For no stone, metal, sulphur, fossil, wood, water, or carcass of animal is found to be hot. And the hot water in baths seems to be heated by external causes; whether it be by flame or subterraneous fire, such as is thrown up from Ætna and many other mountains, or by the conflict of bodies, as heat is caused in the dissolutions of iron and tin. There is therefore no degree of heat palpable to the touch in animate substances; but they differ in degree of cold, wood not being equally cold with metal. But this belongs to the Table of Degrees in Cold.

2. As far however as potential heat and aptitude for flame is concerned, there are many inanimate substances found strongly disposed thereto, as sulphur, naphtha, rock oil.

3. Substances once hot, as horse-dung from animal

heat, and lime or perhaps ashes and soot from fire, retain some latent remains of their former heat. Hence certain distillations and resolutions of bodies are made by burying them in horse-dung, and heat is excited in lime by sprinkling it with water, as already mentioned.

4. In the vegetable creation we find no plant or part of plant (as gum or pitch) which is warm to the human touch. But yet, as stated above, green herbs gain warmth by being shut up; and to the internal touch, as the palate or stomach, and even to external parts, after a little time, as in plasters and ointments, some vegetables are perceptibly warm and others cold.

5. In the parts of animals after death or separation from the body, we find nothing warm to the human touch. Not even horse-dung, unless enclosed and buried, retains its heat. But yet all dung seems to have a potential heat, as is seen in the fattening of the land. In like manner carcasses of animals have some such latent and potential heat; insomuch that in burying grounds, where burials take place daily, the earth collects a certain hidden heat, which consumes a body newly laid in it much more speedily than pure earth. We are told too that in the East there is discovered a fine soft texture, made of the down of birds, which by an innate force dissolves and melts butter when lightly wrapped in it.

6. Substances which fatten the soil, as dung of all kinds, chalk, sea-sand, salt, and the like, have some disposition to heat.

7. All putrefaction contains in itself certain elements of a slight heat, though not so much as to be perceived by the touch. For not even those substances which on putrefaction turn to animalculæ, as flesh, cheese, &c., feel warm to the touch; no more does rotten wood, which shines in the dark. Heat however in putrid

substances sometimes betrays itself by foul and powerful odours.

8. The first degree of heat therefore among those substances which feel hot to the touch, seems to be the heat of animals, which has a pretty great extent in its degrees. For the lowest, as in insects, is hardly perceptible to the touch; but the highest scarce equals the sun's heat in the hottest countries and seasons, nor is it too great to be borne by the hand. It is said however of Constantius, and some others of a very dry constitution and habit of body, that in violent fevers they became so hot as somewhat to burn the hand that touched them.

9. Animals increase in heat by motion and exercise, wine, feasting, venus, burning fevers, and pain.

10. When attacked by intermittent fevers, animals are at first seized with cold and shivering, but soon after they become exceedingly hot, which is their condition from the first in burning and pestilential fevers.

11. Let further inquiry be made into the different degrees of heat in different animals, as in fishes, quadrupeds, serpents, birds; and also according to their species, as in the lion, the kite, the man; for in common opinion fish are the least hot internally, and birds the hottest; especially doves, hawks, and sparrows.

12. Let further inquiry be made into the different degrees of heat in the different parts and limbs of the same animal. For milk, blood, seed, eggs, are found to be hot only in a moderate degree, and less hot than the outer flesh of the animal when in motion or agitated. But what the degree of heat is in the brain, stomach, heart, &c. has not yet been in like manner inquired.

13. All animals in winter and cold weather are cold

externally, but internally they are thought to be even hotter.

14. The heat of the heavenly bodies, even in the hottest countries, and at the hottest times of the year and day, is never sufficiently strong to set on fire or burn the driest wood or straw, or even tinder, unless strengthened by burning-glasses or mirrors. It is however able to extract vapour from moist substances.

15. By the tradition of astronomers some stars are hotter than others. Of planets, Mars is accounted the hottest after the sun; then comes Jupiter, and then Venus. Others, again, are set down as cold; the moon, for instance, and above all Saturn. Of fixed stars, Sirius is said to be the hottest, then Cor Leonis or Regulus, then Canicula, and so on.

16. The sun gives greater heat the nearer he approaches to the perpendicular or zenith; and this is probably true of the other planets also, according to the proportion of their heat. Jupiter, for instance, is hotter, probably, to us when under Cancer or Leo than under Capricorn or Aquarius.

17. We must also believe that the sun and other planets give more heat in perigee, from their proximity to the earth, than they do in apogee. But if it happens that in some region the sun is at the same time in perigee and near the perpendicular, his heat must of necessity be greater than in a region where he is also in perigee, but shining more obliquely. And therefore the altitude of the planets in their exaltation in different regions ought to be noted, with respect to perpendicularity or obliquity.

18. The sun and other planets are supposed to give greater heat when nearer to the larger fixed stars. Thus when the sun is in Leo he is nearer Cor Leonis, Cauda Leonis, Spica Virginis, Sirius and Canicula, then when

he is in Cancer, in which sign however he is nearer to the perpendicular. And it must be supposed that those parts of the heavens shed the greatest heat (though it be not at all perceptible to the touch) which are the most adorned with stars, especially of a larger size.

19. Altogether, the heat of the heavenly bodies is increased in three ways; first, by perpendicularity; secondly, by proximity or perigee; thirdly, by the conjunction or combination of stars.

20. The heat of animals, and of the rays of the heavenly bodies also (as they reach us), is found to differ by a wide interval from flame, though of the mildest kind, and from all ignited bodies; and from liquids also, and air itself when highly heated by fire. For the flame of spirit of wine, though scattered and not condensed, is yet sufficient to set paper, straw, or linen on fire; which the heat of animals will never do, or of the sun without a burning-glass or mirror.

21. There are however many degrees of strength and weakness in the heat of flame and ignited bodies. But as they have never been diligently inquired into, we must pass them lightly over. It appears however that of all flame that of spirit of wine is the softest, unless perhaps *ignis fatuus* be softer, and the flames or sparklings arising from the sweat of animals. Next to this, as I suppose, comes flame from light and porous vegetable matter, as straw, reeds, and dried leaves; from which the flame from hairs or feathers does not much differ. Next perhaps comes flame from wood, especially such as contains but little rosin or pitch; with this distinction however, that the flame from small pieces of wood (such as are commonly tied up in fagots) is milder than the flame from trunks and roots of trees. And this you may try any day in furnaces for smelting iron, in which a fire made with fagots and boughs

of trees is of no great use. After this I think comes flame from oil, tallow, wax, and such like fat and oily substances, which have no great acrimony. But the most violent heat is found in pitch and rosin; and yet more in sulphur, camphor, naphtha, rock-oil, and salts (after the crude matter is discharged), and in their compounds, as gunpowder, Greek fire (commonly called wild fire), and its different kinds, which have so stubborn a heat that they are not easily extinguished by water.

22. I think also that the flame which results from some imperfect metals is very strong and eager. But on these points let further inquiry be made.

23. The flame of powerful lightning seems to exceed in strength all the former; for it has even been known to melt wrought iron into drops; which those other flames cannot do.

24. In ignited bodies too there are different degrees of heat, though these again have not yet been diligently examined. The weakest heat of all, I think, is that from tinder, such as we use to kindle flame with; and in like manner that of touchwood or tow, which is used in firing cannon. After this comes ignited wood or coal, and also bricks and the like heated to ignition. But of all ignited substances, the hottest, as I take it, are ignited metals; as iron, copper, &c. But these require further investigation.

25. Some ignited bodies are found to be much hotter than some flames. Ignited iron, for instance, is much hotter and more consuming than flame of spirit of wine.

26. Of substances also which are not ignited but only heated by fire, as boiling water and air confined in furnaces, some are found to exceed in heat many flames and ignited substances.

27. Motion increases heat, as you may see in bellows,

and by blowing; insomuch that the harder metals are not dissolved or melted by a dead or quiet fire, till it be made intense by blowing.

28. Let trial be made with burning-glasses, which (as I remember) act thus. If you place a burning-glass at the distance of (say) a span from a combustible body, it will not burn or consume it so easily as if it were first placed at the distance of (say) half a span, and then moved gradually and slowly to the distance of the whole span. And yet the cone and union of rays are the same; but the motion itself increases the operation of the heat.

29. Fires which break out during a strong wind are thought to make greater progress against than with it; because the flame recoils more violently when the wind gives way than it advances while the wind is driving it on.

30. Flame does not burst out, nor is it generated, unless some hollow space be allowed it to move and play in; except the explosive flame of gunpowder, and the like, where compression and imprisonment increase its fury.

31. An anvil grows very hot under the hammer, insomuch that if it were made of a thin plate it might, I suppose, with strong and continuous blows of the hammer, grow red like ignited iron. But let this be tried by experiment.

32. But in ignited substances which are porous, so as to give the fire room to move, if this motion be checked by strong compression, the fire is immediately extinguished. For instance, when tinder, or the burning wick of a candle or lamp, or even live charcoal or coal, is pressed down with an extinguisher, or with the foot, or any similar instrument, the operation of the fire instantly ceases.

33. Approximation to a hot body increases heat in proportion to the degree of approximation. And this is the case also with light; for the nearer an object is brought to the light, the more visible it becomes.

34. The union of different heats increases heat, unless the hot substances be mixed together. For a large fire and a small fire in the same room increase one another's heat; but warm water plunged into boiling water cools it.

35. The continued application of a hot body increases heat, because heat perpetually passing and emanating from it mingles with the previously existing heat, and so multiplies the heat. For a fire does not warm a room as well in half an hour as it does if continued through the whole hour. But this is not the case with light; for a lamp or candle gives no more light after it has been long lighted, than it did at first.

36. Irritation by surrounding cold increases heat, as you may see in fires during a sharp frost. And this I think is owing not merely to the confinement and contraction of the heat, which is a kind of union, but also to irritation. Thus when air or a stick is violently compressed or bent, it recoils not merely to the point it was forced from, but beyond it on the other side. Let trial therefore be carefully made by putting a stick or some such thing into flame, and observing whether it is not burnt more quickly at the sides than in the middle of the flame.

37. There are many degrees in susceptibility of heat. And first of all it is to be observed how slight and faint a heat changes and somewhat warms even those bodies which are least of all susceptible of heat. Even the heat of the hand communicates some heat to a ball of lead or any metal, if held in it a little while. So readily and so universally is heat transmitted and excited, the body remaining to all appearance unchanged.

38. Of all substances that we are acquainted with, the one which most readily receives and loses heat is air; as is best seen in calendar glasses [air thermoscopes], which are made thus. Take a glass with a hollow belly, a thin and oblong neck; turn it upside down and lower it, with the mouth downwards and the belly upwards, into another glass vessel containing water; and let the mouth of the inserted vessel touch the bottom of the receiving vessel, and its neck lean slightly against the mouth of the other, so that it can stand. And that this may be done more conveniently, apply a little wax to the mouth of the receiving glass, but not so as to seal its mouth quite up; in order that the motion, of which we are going to speak, and which is very facile and delicate, may not be impeded by want of a supply of air.

The lowered glass, before being inserted into the other, must be heated before a fire in its upper part, that is its belly. Now when it is placed in the position I have described, the air which was dilated by the heat will, after a lapse of time sufficient to allow for the extinction of that adventitious heat, withdraw and contract itself to the same extension or dimension as that of the surrounding air at the time of the immersion of the glass; and will draw the water upwards to a corresponding height. To the side of the glass there should be affixed a strip of paper, narrow and oblong, and marked with as many degrees as you choose. You will then see, according as the day is warm or cold, that the air contracts under the action of cold, and expands under the action of heat; as will be seen by the water rising when the air contracts, and sinking when it dilates. But the air's sense of heat and cold is so subtle and exquisite as far to exceed the perception of the human touch, insomuch that a ray of sunshine, or the heat of the breath, much more the heat of one's hand placed on the top of the glass, will cause the water immediately to sink in a perceptible degree. And yet I think that animal spirits have a sense of heat and cold more exquisite still, were it not that it is impeded and deadened by the grossness of the body.

39. Next to air, I take those bodies to be most sensitive of heat which have been recently changed and compressed by cold, as snow and ice; for they begin to dissolve and melt with any gentle heat. Next to them, perhaps, comes quicksilver. After that follow greasy substances, as oil, butter, and the like; then comes wood; then water; and lastly stones and metals, which are slow to heat, especially in the inside. These, however, when once they have acquired heat retain it very long; in so much that an ignited brick, stone, or piece of iron, when plunged into a basin of water, will remain for a quarter of an hour, or thereabouts, so hot that you cannot touch it.

40. The less the mass of a body, the sooner is it heated by the approach of a hot body; which shows that all heat of which we have experience is in some sort opposed to tangible matter.

41. Heat, as far as regards the sense and touch of man, is a thing various and relative; insomuch that tepid water feels hot if the hand be cold, but cold if the hand be hot.

XIV.

How poor we are in history any one may see from the foregoing tables; where I not only insert sometimes mere traditions and reports (though never without a note of doubtful credit and authority) in place of history proved and instances certain, but am also frequently forced to use the words "Let trial be made," or "Let it be further inquired."

XV.

The work and office of these three tables I call the Presentation of Instances to the Understanding. Which presentation having been made, Induction itself must be set at work; for the problem is, upon a review of the instances, all and each, to find such a nature as is always present or absent with the given nature, and always increases and decreases with it; and which is, as I have said, a particular case of a more general nature. Now if the mind attempt this affirmatively from the first, as when left to itself it is always wont to do, the result will be fancies and guesses and notions ill defined and axioms that must be mended every day; unless like the schoolmen we have a mind to fight for what is false; though doubtless these will be better or worse according to the faculties and strength of the understanding which is at work. To God, truly, the Giver and Architect of Forms, and it may be to the angels and higher intelligences, it belongs to have an affirmative knowledge of forms immediately, and from the first contemplation. But this assuredly is more than man can do, to whom it is granted only to proceed at first by negatives, and at last to end in affirmatives, after exclusion has been exhausted.

XVI.

We must make therefore a complete solution and separation of nature, not indeed by fire, but by the mind, which is a kind of divine fire. The first work therefore of true induction (as far as regards the discovery of Forms) is the rejection or exclusion of the several natures which are not found in some instance where the given nature is present, or are found in some instance where the given nature is absent, or are found to increase in some instance when the given nature decreases, or to decrease when the given nature increases. Then indeed after the rejection and exclusion has been duly made, there will remain at the bottom, all light opinions vanishing into smoke, a Form affirmative, solid and true and well defined. This is quickly said; but the way to come at it is winding and intricate. I will endeavour however not to overlook any of the points which may help us towards it.

XVII.

But when I assign so prominent a part to Forms, I cannot too often warn and admonish men against applying what I say to those forms to which their thoughts and contemplations have hitherto been accustomed.

For in the first place I do not at present speak of Compound Forms, which are, as I have remarked, combinations of simple natures according to the common course of the universe; as of the lion, eagle, rose, gold, and the like. It will be time to treat of these when we come to the Latent Processes and Latent Configurations, and the discovery of them, as they are found in what are called substances or natures concrete.

And even in the case of simple natures I would not be understood to speak of abstract forms and ideas, either not defined in matter at all, or ill defined. For when I speak of Forms, I mean nothing more than those laws and determinations of absolute actuality, which govern and constitute any simple nature, as heat, light, weight, in every kind of matter and subject that is susceptible of them. Thus the Form of Heat or the

Form of Light is the same thing as the Law of Heat or the Law of Light. Nor indeed do I ever allow myself to be drawn away from things themselves and the operative part. And therefore when I say (for instance) in the investigation of the form of heat, "reject rarity," or "rarity does not belong to the form of heat," it is the same as if I said, "It is possible to superinduce heat on a dense body;" or, "It is possible to take away or keep out heat from a rare body."

But if any one conceive that my Forms too are of a somewhat abstract nature, because they mix and combine things heterogeneous (for the heat of heavenly bodies and the heat of fire seem to be very heterogeneous; so do the fixed red of the rose or the like, and the apparent red in the rainbow, the opal, or the diamond; so again do the different kinds of death; death by drowning, by hanging, by stabbing, by apoplexy, by atrophy; and yet they agree severally in the nature of heat, redness, death); if any one, I say, be of this opinion, he may be assured that his mind is held in captivity by custom, by the gross appearance of things, and by men's opinions. For it is most certain that these things, however heterogeneous and alien from each other, agree in the Form or Law which governs heat, redness and death; and that the power of man cannot possibly be emancipated and freed from the common course of nature, and expanded and exalted to new efficients and new modes of operation, except by the revelation and discovery of Forms of this kind. And yet, when I have spoken of this union of nature, which is the point of most importance, I shall proceed to the divisions and veins of nature, as well the ordinary as those that are more inward and exact, and speak of them in their place.

XVIII.

I must now give an example of the Exclusion or Rejection of natures which by the Tables of Presentation are found not to belong to the Form of Heat; observing in the meantime that not only each table suffices for the rejection of any nature, but even any one of the particular instances contained in any of the tables. For it is manifest from what has been said that any one contradictory instance overthrows a conjecture as to the Form. But nevertheless for clearness' sake and that the use of the tables may be more plainly shown, I sometimes double or multiply an exclusion.

An Example of Exclusion, or Rejection of Natures from the Form of Heat.

1. On account of the rays of the sun, reject the nature of the elements.

2. On account of common fire, and chiefly subterraneous fires (which are the most remote and most completely separate from the rays of heavenly bodies), reject the nature of heavenly bodies.

3. On account of the warmth acquired by all kinds of bodies (minerals, vegetables, skin of animals, water, oil, air, and the rest) by mere approach to a fire, or other hot body, reject the distinctive or more subtle texture of bodies.

4. On account of ignited iron and other metals, which communicate heat to other bodies and yet lose none of their weight or substance, reject the communication or admixture of the substance of another hot body.

5. On account of boiling water and air, and also on account of metals and other solids that receive heat but not to ignition or red heat, reject light or brightness.

6. On account of the rays of the moon and other

heavenly bodies, with the exception of the sun, also reject light and brightness.

7. By a comparison of ignited iron and the flame of spirit of wine (of which ignited iron has more heat and less brightness, while the flame of spirit of wine has more brightness and less heat), also reject light and brightness.

8. On account of ignited gold and other metals, which are of the greatest density as a whole, reject rarity.

9. On account of air, which is found for the most part cold and yet remains rare, also reject rarity.

10. On account of ignited iron, which does not swell in bulk, but keeps within the same visible dimensions, reject local or expansive motion of the body as a whole.

11. On account of the dilation of air in calendar glasses and the like, wherein the air evidently moves locally and expansively and yet acquires no manifest increase of heat, also reject local or expansive motion of the body as a whole.

12. On account of the ease with which all bodies are heated, without any destruction or observable alteration, reject a destructive nature, or the violent communication of any new nature.

13. On account of the agreement and conformity of the similar effects which are wrought by heat and cold, reject motion of the body as a whole, whether expansive or contractive.

14. On account of heat being kindled by the attrition of bodies, reject a principial nature. By principial nature I mean that which exists in the nature of things positively, and not as the effect of any antecedent nature.

There are other natures beside these; for these tables are not perfect, but meant only for examples.

All and each of the above mentioned natures do *not*

belong to the Form of Heat. And from all of them man is freed in his operations on Heat.

XIX.

In the process of Exclusion are laid the foundations of true Induction, which however is not completed till it arrives at an Affirmative. Nor is the Exclusive part itself at all complete, nor indeed can it possibly be so at first. For Exclusion is evidently the rejection of simple natures; and if we do not yet possess sound and true notions of simple natures, how can the process of Exclusion be made accurate? Now some of the above-mentioned notions (as that of the nature of the elements, of the nature of heavenly bodies, of rarity) are vague and ill-defined. I therefore, well knowing and nowise forgetting how great a work I am about (viz. that of rendering the human understanding a match for things and nature), do not rest satisfied with the precepts I have laid down; but proceed further to devise and supply more powerful aids for the use of the understanding; which I shall now subjoin. And assuredly in the Interpretation of Nature the mind should by all means be so prepared and disposed, that while it rests and finds footing in due stages and degrees of certainty, it may remember withal (especially at the beginning) that what it has before it depends in great measure upon what remains behind.

XX.

And yet since truth will sooner come out from error than from confusion, I think it expedient that the understanding should have permission, after the three Tables of First Presentation (such as I have exhibited) have been made and weighed, to make an essay of the Interpretation of Nature in the affirmative way; on the strength both of the instances given in the tables, and of any others it may meet with elsewhere. Which kind of essay I call the *Indulgence of the Understanding,* or the *Commencement of Interpretation,* or the *First Vintage.*

First Vintage concerning the Form of Heat.

It is to be observed that the Form of a thing is to be found (as plainly appears from what has been said) in each and all the instances, in which the thing itself is to be found; otherwise it would not be the Form. It follows therefore that there can be no contradictory instance. At the same time the Form is found much more conspicuous and evident in some instances than in others; namely in those wherein the nature of the Form is less restrained and obstructed and kept within bounds by other natures. Instances of this kind I call Shining or Striking Instances. Let us now therefore proceed to the First Vintage concerning the Form of Heat.

> From a survey of the instances, all and each, the nature of which Heat is a particular case appears to be Motion. This is displayed most conspicuously in flame, which is always in motion, and in boiling or simmering liquids, which also are in perpetual motion. It is also shown in the excitement or increase of heat caused by motion, as in bellows and blasts; on which see Tab. 3. Inst. 29.; and again in other kinds of motion, on which see Tab. 3. Inst. 28. and 31. Again it is shown in the extinction of fire and heat by any strong compression, which checks and stops the motion; on which see Tab. 3. Inst. 30. and 32. It is

shown also by this, that all bodies are destroyed, or at any rate notably altered, by all strong and vehement fire and heat; whence it is quite clear that heat causes a tumult and confusion and violent motion in the internal parts of a body, which perceptibly tends to its dissolution.

When I say of Motion that it is as the genus of which heat is a species, I would be understod to mean, not that heat generates motion or that motion generates heat (though both are true in certain cases), but that Heat itself, its essence and quiddity, is Motion and nothing else; limited however by the specific differences which I will presently subjoin, as soon as I have added a few cautions for the sake of avoiding ambiguity.

Sensible heat is a relative notion, and has relation to man, not to the universe; and is correctly defined as merely the effect of heat on the animal spirits. Moreover, in itself it is variable, since the same body, according as the senses are predisposed, induces a perception of cold as well as of heat. This is clear from Inst. 41. Tab. 3.

Nor again must the communication of Heat, or its transitive nature, by means of which a body becomes hot when a hot body is applied to it, be confounded with the Form of Heat. For heat is one thing, heating another. Heat is produced by the motion of attrition without any preceding heat, an instance which excludes heating from the Form of Heat. And even when heat is produced by the approach of a hot body, this does not proceed from the Form of Heat, but depends entirely on a higher and more general nature, viz. on the nature of assimilation or self-multiplication, a subject which requires a separate inquiry.

Again, our notion of fire is popular, and of no use;

being made up of the combination in any body of heat and brightness, as in common flame and bodies heated to redness.

Having thus removed all ambiguity, I come at length to the true specific differences which limit Motion and constitute it the Form of Heat.

> The first difference then is this. Heat is an expansive motion, whereby a body strives to dilate and stretch itself to a larger sphere or dimension than it had previously occupied. This difference is most observable in flame, where the smoke or thick vapour manifestly dilates and expands itself into flame.
>
> It is shown also in all boiling liquid, which manifestly swells, rises, and bubbles; and carries on the process of self-expansion, till it turns into a body far more extended and dilated than the liquid itself, namely, into vapour, smoke, or air.
>
> It appears likewise in all wood and combustibles, from which there generally arises exudation and always evaporation.
>
> It is shown also in the melting of metals, which, being of the compactest texture, do not readily swell and dilate; but yet their spirit being dilated in itself, and thereupon conceiving an appetite for further dilation, forces and agitates the grosser parts into a liquid state. And if the heat be greatly increased it dissolves and turns much of their substance to a volatile state.
>
> It is shown also in iron or stones, which, though not melted or dissolved, are yet softened. This is the case also with sticks, which when slightly heated in hot ashes become flexible.
>
> But this kind of motion is best seen in air, which

continuously and manifestly dilates with a slight heat, as appears in Inst. 38. Tab. 3.

It is shown also in the opposite nature of cold. For cold contracts all bodies and makes them shrink; insomuch that in intense frosts nails fall out from walls, brazen vessels crack, and heated glass on being suddenly placed in the cold cracks and breaks. In like manner air is contracted by a slight chill, as in Inst. 38. Tab. 3. But on these points I shall speak more at length in the inquiry concerning Cold.

Nor is it surprising that heat and cold should exhibit many actions in common (for which see Inst. 32. Tab. 2.), when we find two of the following specific differences (of which I shall speak presently) suiting either nature; though in this specific difference (of which I am now speaking) their actions are diametrically opposite. For heat gives an expansive and dilating, cold a contractive and condensing motion.

The second difference is a modification of the former; namely, that heat is a motion expansive or towards the circumference, but with this condition, that the body has at the same time a motion upwards. For there is no doubt that there are many mixed motions. For instance, an arrow or dart turns as it goes forward, and goes forward as it turns. And in like manner the motion of heat is at once a motion of expansion and a motion upwards. This difference is shown by putting a pair of tongs or a poker in the fire. If you put it in perpendicularly and hold it by the top, it soon burns your hand; if at the side or from below, not nearly so soon.

It is also observable in distillations *per descensorium;* which men use for delicate flowers, that soon lose their scent. For human industry has discovered the plan of placing the fire not below but above, that it may burn the less. For not only flame tends upwards, but also all heat.

But let trial be made of this in the opposite nature of cold; viz. whether cold does not contract a body downwards, as heat dilates a body upwards. Take therefore two iron rods, or two glass tubes, exactly alike; warm them a little, and place a sponge steeped in cold water or snow at the bottom of the one, and the same at the top of the other. For I think that the extremities of the rod which has the snow at the top will cool sooner than the extremities of the other which has the snow at the bottom; just as the opposite is the case with heat.

The third specific difference is this; that heat is a motion of expansion, not uniformly of the whole body together, but in the smaller parts of it; and at the same time checked, repelled, and beaten back, so that the body acquires a motion alternative, perpetually quivering, striving and struggling, and irritated by repercussion, whence springs the fury of fire and heat.

This specific difference is most displayed in flame and boiling liquids, which are perpetually quivering and swelling in small portions, and again subsiding.

It is also shown in those bodies which are so compact that when heated or ignited they do not swell or expand in bulk; as ignited iron, in which the heat is very sharp.

It is shown also in this, that a fire burns most briskly in the coldest weather.

Again, it is shown in this, that when the air is extended in a calendar glass without impediment or repulsion,—that is to say, uniformly and equably,—there is no perceptible heat. Also when wind escapes from confinement, although it burst forth with the greatest violence, there is no very great heat perceptible; because the motion is of the whole, without a motion alternating in the particles. And with a view to this, let trial be made whether flame does not burn more sharply towards the sides in the middle of the flame.

It is also shown in this, that all burning acts on minute pores of the body burnt; so that burning undermines, penetrates, pricks, and stings the body like the points of an infinite number of needles. It is also an effect of this, that all strong waters (if suited to the body on which they are acting) act as fire does, in consequence of their corroding and pungent nature.

And this specific difference (of which I am now speaking) is common also to the nature of cold; for in cold the contractive motion is checked by a resisting tendency to expand, just as in heat the expansive motion is checked by a resisting tendency to contract. Thus, whether the particles of a body work inward or outward, the mode of action is the same, though the degree of strength be very different; because we have not here on the surface of the earth anything that is intensely cold. See Inst. 27. Tab. 9.

The fourth specific difference is a modification of the last; it is, that the preceding motion of stimulation or penetration must be somewhat rapid and not sluggish, and must proceed by particles, minute indeed, yet not the finest of all, but a degree larger.

This difference is shown by a comparison of the effects of fire with the effects of time or age. Age or time dries, consumes, undermines and reduces to ashes, no less than fire; indeed with an action far more subtle; but because such motion is very sluggish, and acts on particles very small, the heat is not perceived.

It is also shown by comparing the dissolution of iron and gold. Gold is dissolved without any heat being excited, while the dissolution of iron is accompanied by a violent heat, though it takes place in about the same time. The reason is that in gold the separating acid enters gently and works with subtlety, and the parts of the gold yield easily; whereas in iron the entrance is rough and with conflict, and the parts of the iron have greater obstinacy.

It is shown also to some degree in some gangrenes and mortifications, which do not excite great heat or pain on account of the subtle nature of putrefaction.

Let this then be the First Vintage or Commencement of Interpretation concerning the Form of Heat, made by way of indulgence to the understanding.

Now from this our First Vintage it follows that the Form or true definition of heat (heat, that is, in relation to the universe, not simply in relation to man) is in few words as follows: *Heat is a motion, expansive, restrained, and acting in its strife upon the smaller particles of bodies.* But the expansion is thus modified; *while it expands all ways, it has at the same time an inclination upwards.* And the struggle in the particles is modified also; *it is not sluggish, but hurried and with violence.*

Viewed with reference to operation it is the same thing. For the direction is this: *If in any natural body you can excite a dilating or expanding motion, and can so repress this motion and turn it back upon itself, that the dilation shall not proceed equably, but have its way in one part and be counteracted in another, you will undoubtedly generate heat;* without taking into account whether the body be elementary (as it is called) or subject to celestial influence; whether it be luminous or opaque; rare or dense; locally expanded or confined within the bounds of its first dimension; verging to dissolution or remaining in its original state; animal, vegetable, or mineral, water, oil or air, or any other substance whatever susceptible of the above-mentioned motion. Sensible heat is the same thing; only it must be considered with reference to the sense. Let us now proceed to further aids.

XXI.

The Tables of First Presentation and the Rejection or process of Exclusion being completed, and also the First Vintage being made thereupon, we are to proceed to the other helps of the understanding in the Interpretation of Nature and true and perfect Induction. In propounding which, I mean, when Tables are necessary, to proceed upon the Instances of Heat and Cold; but when a small number of examples will suffice, I shall proceed at large; so that the inquiry may be kept clear, and yet more room be left for the exposition of the system.

I propose to treat then in the first place of *Prerogative Instances;* secondly, of the *Supports of Induction;*

thirdly, of the *Rectification of Induction;* fourthly, of *Varying the Investigation according to the nature of the Subject;* fifthly, of *Prerogative Natures* with respect to Investigation, or of what should be inquired first and what last; sixthly, of the *Limits of Investigation,* or a Synopsis of all Natures in the Universe; seventhly, of the *Application to Practice,* or of things in their relation to Man; eighthly, of *Preparations for Investigation;* and lastly, of the *Ascending and Descending Scale of Axioms.*

XXII.

Among Prerogative Instances I will place first *Solitary Instances.* Those are Solitary Instances which exhibit the nature under investigation in subjects which have nothing in common with other subjects except that nature; or, again, which do not exhibit the nature under investigation in subjects which resemble other subjects in every respect except in not having that nature. For it is clear that such instances make the way short, and accelerate and strengthen the process of exclusion; so that a few of them are as good as many.

For instance, if we are inquiring into the nature of Colour, prisms, crystals, which show colours not only in themselves but externally on a wall, dews, &c., are Solitary Instances. For they have nothing in common with the colours fixed in flowers, coloured stones, metals, woods, &c., except the colour. From which we easily gather that colour is nothing more than a modification of the image of light received upon the object, resulting in the former case from the different degrees of incidence, in the latter from the various textures and configurations of the body. These instances are Solitary in respect of resemblance.

Again, in the same investigation, the distinct veins

of white and black in marble, and the variegation of colour in flowers of the same species, are Solitary Instances. For the black and white streaks in marble, or the spots of pink and white in a pink, agree in everything almost except the colour. From which we easily gather that colour has little to do with the intrinsic nature of a body, but simply depends on the coarser and as it were mechanical arrangement of the parts. These instances are Solitary in respect of difference. Both kinds I call *Solitary Instances,* or *Ferine,* to borrow a term from astronomers.

XXIII.

Among Prerogative Instances I will next place *Migratory Instances.* They are those in which the nature in question is in the process of being produced when it did not previously exist, or on the other hand of disappearing when it existed before. And therefore, in either transition, such instances are always twofold, or rather it is one instance in motion or passage, continued till it reaches the opposite state. Such instances not only accelerate and strengthen the exclusive process, but also drive the affirmative or Form itself into a narrow compass. For the Form of a thing must necessarily be something which in the course of this migration is communicated, or on the other hand which in the course of this migration is removed and destroyed. And though every exclusion promotes the affirmative, yet this is done more decidedly when it occurs in the same than in different subjects. And the betrayal of the form in a single instance leads the way (as is evident from all that has been said) to the discovery of it in all. And the simpler the Migration, the more must the instance be valued. Besides Migratory Instances are of great use with a view to operation; because in exhibiting the form in connection with that which causes it to be or not to be, they supply a clear direction for practice in some cases; whence the passage is easy to the cases that lie next. There is however in these instances a danger which requires caution; viz. lest they lead us to connect the Form too much with the efficient, and so possess the understanding, or at least touch it, with a false opinion concerning the Form, drawn from a view of the efficient. But the efficient is always understood to be merely the vehicle that carries the Form. This is a danger however easily remedied by the process of exclusion legitimately conducted.

I must now give an example of a Migratory Instance. Let the nature to be investigated be Whiteness; an instance migrating to production or existence is glass whole and pounded. Again, simple water and water agitated into froth. For glass and water in their simple state are transparent, not white; whereas pounded glass and water in froth are white, not transparent. We must therefore inquire what has happened to the glass or water from this Migration. For it is obvious that the Form of Whiteness is communicated and conveyed by that pounding of the glass and that agitation of the water. We find, however, that nothing has been added except the breaking up of the glass and water into small parts, and the introduction of air. But we have made no slight advance to the discovery of the Form of Whiteness when we know that two bodies, both transparent but in a greater or less degree (viz. air and water, or air and glass), do when mingled in small portions together exhibit whiteness, through the unequal refraction of the rays of light.

But an example must at the same time be given of the danger and caution to which I alluded. For at this point it might readily suggest itself to an understanding led astray by efficient causes of this kind, that air is always required for the Form of Whiteness, or that Whiteness is generated by transparent bodies only; notions entirely false, and refuted by numerous exclusions. Whereas it will be found that (setting air and the like aside) bodies entirely even in the particles which affect vision are transparent, bodies simply uneven are white; bodies uneven and in a compound yet regular texture are all colours except black; while bodies uneven and in a compound, irregular, and confused texture are black. Here then I have given an example of an Instance Migrating to production or existence in the proposed nature of Whiteness. An Instance Migrating to destruction in the same nature of Whiteness, is froth or snow in dissolution. For the water puts off Whiteness and puts on transparency, on returning to its integral state without air.

Nor must I by any means omit to mention that under Migratory Instances are to be included not only those which are passing towards production and destruction, but also those which are passing towards increase and decrease; since these also help to discover the Form, as is clear from the above definition of Form and the Table of Degrees. Thus paper, which is white when dry, but when wetted (that is, when air is excluded and water introduced) is less white and approaches nearer to the transparent, is analogous to the above given Instances.

XXIV.

Among Prerogative Instances I will put in the third place *Striking Instances,* of which I have made mention in the First Vintage concerning Heat, and which

I also call *Shining Instances, or Instances Freed and Predominant.* They are those which exhibit the nature in question naked and standing by itself, and also in its exaltation or highest degree of power; as being disenthralled and freed from all impediments, or at any rate by virtue of its strength dominant over, suppressing and coercing them. For since every body contains in itself many forms of natures united together in a concrete state, the result is that they severally crush, depress, break, and enthrall one another, and thus the individual forms are obscured. But certain subjects are found wherein the required nature appears more in its vigour than in others, either through the absence of impediments or the predominance of its own virtue. And instances of this kind strikingly display the Form. At the same time in these instances also we must use caution, and check the hurry of the understanding. For whatever displays the Form too conspicuously, and seems to force it on the notice of the understanding, should be held suspect, and recourse be had to a rigid and careful exclusion.

To take an example; let the nature inquired into be Heat. A Striking Instance of the motion of expansion, which (as stated above) is the main element in the Form of Heat, is a calendar glass of air. For flame, though it manifestly exhibits expansion, still, as susceptible of momentary extinction, does not display the progress of expansion. Boiling water too, on account of the easy transition of water to vapour or air, does not so well exhibit the expansion of water in its own body. Again, ignited iron and like bodies are so far from displaying the progress of expansion, that in consequence of their spirit being crushed and broken by the coarse and compact particles which curb and subdue it, the expansion itself is not at all conspicuous to the senses. But a calendar glass strikingly displays expansion in air, at once conspicuous, progressive, permanent, and without transition.

To take another example; let the nature inquired into be Weight. A Striking Instance of weight is quicksilver. For it far surpasses in weight all substances but gold, and gold itself is not much heavier. But quicksilver is a better instance for indicating the Form of Weight than gold; because gold is solid and consistent, characteristics which seem related to density; whereas quicksilver is liquid and teeming with spirit, and yet is heavier by many degrees than the diamond and other bodies that are esteemed the most solid. From which it is obvious that the Form of Heaviness or Weight depends simply on quantity of matter and not on compactness of frame. . . .[1]

LII.

So much then for the Dignities or Prerogatives of Instances. It must be remembered however that in this Organum of mine I am handling logic, not philosophy. But since my logic aims to teach and instruct the understanding, not that it may with the slender tendrils of the mind snatch at and lay hold of abstract notions (as the common logic does), but that it may in very truth dissect nature, and discover the virtues and actions of bodies, with their laws as determined in matter; so that this science flows not merely from the nature of the mind, but also from the nature of things; no wonder that it is everywhere sprinkled and illustrated with speculations and experiments in nature, as examples of the art I teach. It appears then from what has been

[1] The next twenty-four instances are omitted as being of little significance for scientific method. *Editor.*

said that there are twenty-seven Prerogative Instances; namely, Solitary Instances; Migratory Instances; Striking Instances; Clandestine Instances; Constitutive Instances; Conformable Instances; Singular Instances; Deviating Instances; Bordering Instances; Instances of Power; Instances of Companionship and of Enmity; Subjunctive Instances; Instances of Alliance; Instances of the Fingerpost; Instances of Divorce; Instances of the Door; Summoning Instances; Instances of the Road; Instances Supplementary; Dissecting Instances; Instances of the Rod; Instances of the Course; Doses of Nature; Instances of Strife; Intimating Instances; Polychrest Instances; Magical Instances. Now the use of these instances, wherein they excel common instances, is found either in the Informative part or in the Operative, or in both. As regards the Informative, they assist either the senses or the understanding: the senses, as the five Instances of the Lamp: the understanding, either by hastening the Exclusion of the Form, as Solitary Instances;—or by narrowing and indicating more nearly the Affirmative of the Form, as Instances Migratory, Striking, of Companionship, and Subjunctive;—or by exalting the understanding and leading it to genera and common natures; either immediately, as Instances Clandestine, Singular, and of Alliance; or in the next degree, as Constitutive; or in the lowest, as Conformable; —or by setting the understanding right when led astray by habit, as Deviating Instances;—or by leading it to the Great Form or Fabric of the Universe, as Bordering Instances;—or by guarding it against false forms and causes, as Instances of the Fingerpost and of Divorce. In the Operative Part, they either point out, or measure, or facilitate practice. They point it out, by showing with what we should begin, that we may not go again over old ground, as Instances of Power; or to what we should aspire if means be given, as Intimating Instances. The four Mathematical Instances measure practice: Polychrest and Magical Instances facilitate it.

Again out of these twenty-seven instances there are some of which we must make a collection at once, as I said above, without waiting for the particular investigation of natures. Of this sort are Instances Conformable, Singular, Deviating, Bordering, of Power, of the Dose, Intimating, Polychrest, and Magical. For these either help and set right the understanding and senses, or furnish practice with her tools in a general way. The rest need not be inquired into till we come to make Tables of Presentation for the work of the Interpreter concerning some particular nature. For the instances marked and endowed with these Prerogatives are as a soul amid the common instances of Presentation, and as I said at first, a few of them do instead of many; and therefore in the formation of the Tables they must be investigated with all zeal, and set down therein. It was necessary to handle them beforehand because I shall have to speak of them in what follows. But now I must proceed to the supports and rectifications of Induction, and then to concretes, and Latent Processes, and Latent Configurations, and the rest, as set forth in order in the twenty-first Aphorism; that at length (like an honest and faithful guardian) I may hand over to men their fortunes, now their understanding is emancipated and come as it were of age; whence there cannot but follow an improvement in man's estate, and an enlargement of his power over nature. For man by the fall fell at the same time from his state of innocency and from his dominion over creation. Both of these losses however can even in this life be in some part repaired; the former by religion and faith, the latter by arts and sciences. For creation was not by the curse made altogether and for ever a rebel, but in virtue of that charter "In the sweat of thy face shalt thou eat bread," it is now by various labours (not certainly by disputations or idle magical ceremonies, but by various labours) at length and in some measure subdued to the supplying of man with bread; that is, to the uses of human life.

As will be seen from Aphorism XXI the projected program is far from completed. *Editor.*

POETRY

BROWNING: Poems and Plays
Edited by HEWETTE E. JOYCE, Assistant Professor of English, Dartmouth College

BROWNING: The Ring and the Book
Edited by FREDERICK MORGAN PADELFORD, Professor of English, University of Washington

TENNYSON: Poems
Edited by J. F. A. PYRE, Professor of English, University of Wisconsin

WHITMAN: Leaves of Grass
Edited by STUART P. SHERMAN, late Literary Editor of the New York *Herald Tribune*

WORDSWORTH: Poems
Edited by GEORGE M. HARPER, Professor of English, Princeton University

AMERICAN SONGS AND BALLADS
Edited by LOUISE POUND, Professor of English, University of Nebraska

ENGLISH POETS OF THE EIGHTEENTH CENTURY
Edited by ERNEST BERNBAUM, Professor of English, University of Illinois

MINOR VICTORIAN POETS
Edited by JOHN D. COOKE, Professor of English, University of Southern California

ROMANTIC POETRY OF THE EARLY NINETEENTH CENTURY
Edited by ARTHUR BEATTY, Professor of English, University of Wisconsin

ESSAYS AND MISCELLANEOUS PROSE

ADDISON AND STEELE: Selections
Edited by WILL D. HOWE, formerly head of the Department of English, Indiana University

ARNOLD: Prose and Poetry
Edited by ARCHIBALD L. BOUTON, Professor of English and Dean of the Graduate School, New York University

BACON: Essays
Edited by MARY AUGUSTA SCOTT, late Professor of the English Language and Literature, Smith College

BROWNELL: American Prose Masters
Edited by STUART P. SHERMAN, late Literary Editor of the New York *Herald Tribune*

BURKE: Selections
Edited by LESLIE NATHAN BROUGHTON, Assistant Professor of English, Cornell University

CARLYLE: Past and Present
Edited by EDWIN MIMS, Professor of English, Vanderbilt University

CARLYLE: Sartor Resartus
Edited by ASHLEY H. THORNDIKE, Professor of English, Columbia University

EMERSON: Essays and Poems
Edited by ARTHUR HOBSON QUINN, Professor of English, University of Pennsylvania

FRANKLIN AND EDWARDS: Selections
Edited by CARL VAN DOREN, Associate Professor of English, Columbia University

HAZLITT: Essays
Edited by PERCY V. D. SHELLY, Professor of English, University of Pennsylvania

ESSAYS AND MISCELLANEOUS PROSE

ADDISON AND STEELE: Selections
Edited by WILL D. HOWE, formerly head of the Department of English, Indiana University

ARNOLD: Prose and Poetry
Edited by ARCHIBALD L. BOUTON, Professor of English and Dean of the Graduate School, New York University

BACON: Essays
Edited by MARY AUGUSTA SCOTT, late Professor of the English Language and Literature, Smith College

BROWNELL: American Prose Masters
Edited by STUART P. SHERMAN, late Literary Editor of the New York *Herald Tribune*

BURKE: Selections
Edited by LESLIE NATHAN BROUGHTON, Assistant Professor of English, Cornell University

CARLYLE: Past and Present
Edited by EDWIN MIMS, Professor of English, Vanderbilt University

CARLYLE: Sartor Resartus
Edited by ASHLEY H. THORNDIKE, Professor of English, Columbia University

EMERSON: Essays and Poems
Edited by ARTHUR HOBSON QUINN, Professor of English, University of Pennsylvania

FRANKLIN AND EDWARDS: Selections
Edited by CARL VAN DOREN, Associate Professor of English, Columbia University

HAZLITT: Essays
Edited by PERCY V. D. SHELLY, Professor of English, University of Pennsylvania

LINCOLN: Selections
Edited by NATHANIEL WRIGHT STEPHENSON, author of "Lincoln: His Personal Life"

MACAULAY: Historical Essays
Edited by CHARLES DOWNER HAZEN, Professor of History, Columbia University

VOLUMES IN PREPARATION

ELIOT: Middlemarch
With an introduction by ARTHUR BEATTY, Professor of English, University of Wisconsin

MELVILLE: Moby Dick
With an introduction by CARL VAN DOREN, Associate Professor of English, Columbia University

NEWMAN: Selections
Edited by HENRY A. LAPPIN, Professor of English, D'Youville College

PHILOSOPHY SERIES

Editor, Ralph Barton Perry

Professor of Philosophy, Harvard University

ARISTOTLE: Selections
Edited by W. D. ROSS, Professor of Philosophy, Oriel College, University of Oxford

BACON: Selections
Edited by MATTHEW THOMPSON MCCLURE, Professor of Philosophy, University of Illinois

DESCARTES: Selections
Edited by RALPH M. EATON, Assistant Professor of Philosophy, Harvard University

HUME: Selections
Edited by CHARLES W. HENDEL, JR., Associate Professor of Philosophy, Princeton University

LOCKE: Selections
Edited by STERLING P. LAMPRECHT, Associate Professor of Philosophy, University of Illinois

PLATO: Selections
Edited by RAPHAEL DEMOS, Assistant Professor of Philosophy, Harvard University

Volumes in Preparation

BERKELEY: Selections
Edited by MARY W. CALKINS, Professor of Philosophy, Wellesley College

HEGEL: Selections
Edited by JACOB LOEWENBERG, Professor of Philosophy, University of California

KANT: Selections
Edited by THEODORE M. GREENE, Assistant Professor of Philosophy, Princeton University

PLATO: The Republic
With an introduction by C. M. BAKEWELL, Professor of Philosophy, Yale University

SCHOPENHAUER: Selections
Edited by DEWITT H. PARKER, Professor of Philosophy, University of Michigan

MEDIÆVAL PHILOSOPHY
By RICHARD MCKEON, Instructor in Philosophy, Columbia University